P9-DTJ-866

The (Other) American Traditions

810.99287
W253

The (Other) American Traditions

Nineteenth-Century Women Writers

EDITED BY
JOYCE W. WARREN

RUTGERS UNIVERSITY PRESS
New Brunswick, New Jersey

LIBRARY ST. MARY'S COLLEGE

Library of Congress Cataloging-in-Publication Data

The (Other) American traditions : nineteenth-century women writers /
edited by Joyce W. Warren.
p.   cm.
Includes bibliographical references and index.
ISBN 0-8135-1910-1 (cloth)—ISBN 0-8135-1911-X (pbk.)
1. Women and literature—United States—History—19th century.
2. American literature—Women authors—History and criticism.
3. American literature—19th century—History and criticism.
4. Women authors, American—19th century—Biography.   I. Warren,
Joyce W.
PS147.085   1993
810.9′9287′09034—dc20   92-10879
CIP

British Cataloging-in-Publication information available

Copyright © 1993 by Rutgers University Press
All rights reserved
Manufactured in the United States of America

❧ CONTENTS ❧

THE TRADITIONS

❧ PREFACE ❧

In 1857, a condescending review of a woman's book in the *New York Times* stated, "Courtship and marriage, . . . and children, these are the great objects of a woman's thoughts, and they necessarily form the staple topics of their writings and their conversation. We have no right to expect anything else from a woman's book." Fanny Fern, one of the most outspoken women writers of the period, responded sharply:

> Is it in feminine novels *only* that courtship, marriage, . . . and children are the staple? Is not this true of all novels?—of Dickens, of Thackeray, of Bulwer and a host of others? Is it peculiar to feminine pens, most astute and liberal of critics? Would a novel be a novel if it did not treat of courtship and marriage? and if it could be so recognized, would it find readers? When I see such a narrow, snarling criticism as the above, I always say to myself, the writer is some unhappy man. . . . I think I see him writing that paragraph in a fit of spleen—of *male* spleen—in his small boarding-house upper chamber, by the cheerful light of a solitary candle, . . . and all the wretched accompaniments of solitary, selfish male existence, not to speak of his own puckered, unkissable face.[1]

Whether or not the writer of the *Times* review had an "unkissable face," as the acerbic Fern concluded, his review clearly reflects an emphasis on the individual, and Fern was not wrong to call attention to the "solitary" characteristics of such a perspective. In the nineteenth century, and for much of the twentieth century as well, this pattern was the necessary component of "serious" fiction in American literature, and nineteenth-century American women writers, who focused on people and relationships, were denigrated or ignored.

As Fern's comment so graphically reminds us, however, the tradition that takes the male protagonist away from women and away from society is an aberration in world culture. World literature focuses on interrelationships among people, the subtleties involved in tribal courtship and marriage customs, and the problems and passions of women as well as of men. Although the *Times* critic would view the concerns of women novelists as aberrations from what "literature" should concern itself with, it is, in fact, the male American writers—the canonical writers—who are the aberration. The majority of the canonical male writers have been concerned primarily with the solitary male quest, the individual writ large. Yet, as Nina Baym pointed out in her pioneering study, *Woman's Fiction* (1978), it is not "purely" literary criteria that would identify a whaling ship as a better "symbol of the human community" than a sewing circle.[2]

In the mid-1980s I developed a course at Queens College in nineteenth-century American women writers, which I called "The (Other) American Tradition."[3] Since few texts were available at the time, I relied on photocopies of much of the material. The course was exciting and stimulating for me as well as for the students, and the success of this course confirmed my belief that these works can stand on their own. It also became apparent to me that the name of a work on a college syllabus helps to legitimize the work, and underscored what I already knew: if these works are to gain legitimacy, they must become a regular part of the curriculum. However, they need to be studied for themselves, not introduced tentatively as token women writers on a traditional male syllabus. After my successful experience in teaching this course for several semesters, I organized a panel on nineteenth-century American women writers at the Modern Language Association conference in Washington, D.C., in 1989. The response to the panel was overwhelming; it was clear that the work by these women writers was as interesting to scholars as it was to students.

Since the appearance of the first anthologies of nineteenth-century American women writers in 1985—*Hidden Hands*, edited by Lucy Freibert and Barbara A. White, and *Provisions*, edited by Judith Fetterley—scores of these writers have come into print. Some of the first twentieth-century reprints of these women's works include Elizabeth Stoddard, *The Morgesons*, edited by Lawrence Buell and Sandra Zagarell (1984); Elizabeth Stuart Phelps, *The Story of Avis*, edited by Carol Farley Kessler (1985); and Susan Warner's *The Wide, Wide World*, edited by Jane Tompkins (1987). Rutgers began publishing the American Women Writers series in 1986, and the Schomburg Library of Nineteenth-Century Black Women Writers appeared in 1988. With the work of so many nineteenth-century American women writers now in print, it is no longer difficult to teach their work in the classroom. There is need, then, for a book like this one, which will help those who teach and read these writers to understand some of the larger patterns underlying their work.

In the title of this book, I have put the word *other* in parentheses for several important and very specific reasons. First of all, I wish to point out that these writers represent traditions *other* than that of the solitary male quest, which for so long dominated the study of American literature. They also represent the traditions of "the other"—the individual who in nineteenth-century American society was regarded as "other" by the dominant culture. However, although they have been regarded as other by their society, the traditions of women's writing should be regarded not as subordinate to the tradition of male individualist fiction, but as existing parallel to it. Women and women's writing cannot simply be referred to as *other,* because the word *other* implies that they must be viewed in relation to something else, that they are other than the prescribed norm, and that they are somehow deviant from that norm. By itself, the word *other* suggests a hierarchical relationship. What I intend to indicate by the parentheses is that although these traditions and the women who wrote in them have been made to seem *other* by their society, we need to see them as primary and not simply as relational. In fact, in world literature, traditions like these, which focus on interpersonal relationships between men and women, relating the individual to society, are the major traditions. Looking at the work of nineteenth-century American women writers helps to bring American literature back into the mainstream of world literature, where it is the tradition of the insular male that is *other.*

Joyce W. Warren

NOTES

1. Fanny Fern, "Male Criticism on Ladies Books," *New York Ledger* (May 23, 1857).

2. Nina Baym, *Woman's Fiction: A Guide to Novels by and about Women in America, 1820–1870* (Ithaca: Cornell University Press, 1978), 14. See also Baym's "Melodramas of Beset Manhood: How Theories of American Fiction Exclude Women Authors," *American Quarterly* 33 (Summer 1981): 123–139.

3. For a description of this course and the results, see Joyce W. Warren, "Gender and Literature: Teaching 'The (Other) American Tradition,'" *Radical Teacher,* no. 37 (1989): 30–33.

❧ JOYCE W. WARREN ❧

Introduction:
Canons and Canon Fodder

AT A TIME WHEN an American book that sold five thousand copies was considered very successful, Fanny Fern's first work, *Fern Leaves from Fanny's Portfolio* (1853), sold seventy thousand copies in less than a year.[1] Although the reviews were generally favorable, an August 1853 article in the *United States Review* expressed an attitude that was shared by most critics:

> Where is American genius? Where are the original, the brilliant, the noble works, in whose publication we might take a lasting and national pride, from whose perusal we might derive delight, instruction, and elevation?
>
> Where are the men to write them? . . .
>
> American authors, be men and heroes! Make sacrifices, . . . but *publish* books . . . for the hope of the future and the honor of America. Do not leave its literature in the hands of a few industrious females.

The major criterion for being a "good" writer in America during most of the nineteenth century was that the writer must be a man. As Herman Melville commented in 1851 in his advice to the writer: "Let him write like a man, for then he will be sure to write like an American."[2] At the same time that this bias prevailed with respect to literature, however, much of the writing in the United States was being done by women—white women and minority women. Although some women writers were not well known in their day, many were widely read and some were highly acclaimed. In fact, all of the bestsellers in the mid-nineteenth century were by women. Yet

1

despite the numbers of American women who were writing at the time, in less than a century the names of all but one or two had virtually disappeared from the country's consciousness.[3]

Until very recently—at least until the 1970s and 1980s—nineteenth-century American women writers, even those who were acclaimed in their own day, were so thoroughly excluded from high school, college, and graduate school syllabi in the United States that most students were not even aware of their existence. It was possible for a student to graduate from college with a major in English or even American literature and not have read anything by a nineteenth-century American woman writer—except Emily Dickinson. The presence of Dickinson as the sole woman writer in the nineteenth-century American canon, compared to the numbers of women who were writing at the time, presents a distorted view of the facts. Although women dominated the literary scene in the United States in the mid-nineteenth century, the twentieth-century canon of nineteenth-century American literature has been predominantly white and male. Other works, if they were mentioned at all by the literary establishment, were discussed tangentially in a way that indicated that if they had any value it was to be found only in their usefulness to the authors included in the canon.[4] They were useful canon fodder, perhaps, but never candidates for the canon.[5]

Why were these works so systematically excluded? As recent scholarship has demonstrated, it is not sufficient to look at the quality of a work in order to determine why it has or has not been included in the canon.[6] It is also necessary to look at the context within which the work has been judged. As Michel Foucault makes clear in his study of language, external factors influence judgments that are ostensibly aesthetic.[7] The question "Is it good?" is inextricably bound up with other questions: "Good for whom?" "When?" and "Why?" Class, race, and gender biases influence literary judgments; specific historical periods provide different literary criteria; and ideological preconceptions determine what will be chosen.

In her discussion of literary canonization, Jane Tompkins writes in *Sensational Designs* (1985) that "a literary reputation could never be anything but a political matter"; "works that have attained the status of classic, and are therefore believed to embody universal values, are in fact embodying only the interests of whatever parties or factions are responsible for maintaining them in their preeminent position."[8] An analysis of the canon, then, cannot simply look at what has or has not been excluded; it must explore the reasons for the exclusion. The questions to ask are "What has been excluded?" and "Why?" As Paul Lauter notes in *Canons and Contexts* (1991), "What is at stake here is not simply a revisionist claim to prior occupation of valued turf. . . . The issue is, then, what of human knowledge a particular set of narratives, a canon, or an historical construct, encodes, makes accessible—or obscures."[9]

In order to understand the construct that is the American canon of nineteenth-century literature, we need to identify its historical base, that is, the context from which the canon was constructed. As I noted in my book *The American Narcissus* (1984), it is possible to identify one overarching assumption that has colored and influenced all other strands of thought in American life: the belief in individualism.[10] Involved in the growth of the new democracy and the needs of an expanding nation, nineteenth-century Americans developed the myth of American individualism, which has come to form the basis of American thought. As John Taylor indicated in his analysis of American government in 1814, "Individualism is the substratum of our policy."[11] And as the *Democratic Review* commented in 1839, Americans recognized the "individual man in himself as an independent end."[12] This belief, that the individual man was an end in himself, underlay nineteenth-century American thought and has been received as a given in the twentieth century. Reflecting this assumption of individualism, canonized American literature—that is, the literature that has come to form what has been regarded as the American tradition—has, for the most part, focused on the individual. And since nineteenth-century American individualism applied only to the white male, the individual that forms the center of American literature has been universalized as white and male.[13]

Much of the literature that has been excluded from the canon—almost from the American consciousness—is the literature that, either implicitly or explicitly, rejects this construction of American life: the assumption that the white male individual occupies center stage and that all "other" members of the cast are only supporting players—if they are even allowed on the stage. Most of the literature by nineteenth-century women writers focuses not on the male individualist but on the "other" members of the cast, moving them to center stage and questioning or rewriting the script. It is in this respect that the works by American women diverge from the ideological and sociological pattern of the canonized works.

Of course it would be simplistic to say that this reason alone is responsible for the exclusion of these works from the canon in the twentieth century. Other factors also come into play. The disillusionment following World War I, the scientific and technological revolution, the modernists' search for ambiguity: factors like these also helped to turn twentieth-century readers away from the moral earnestness and sentimentalism in some of the works by nineteenth-century women writers. It is my contention, however, that, more than any other single factor, it is their rejection of the hierarchies and exclusions of the dominant culture and their consequent focus upon and portrayal of the perspective of people that the dominant culture had defined as "other" that has kept these works out of the canon.

Not only did many of these works challenge the *gender* of American individualism, they challenged the concept of individualism itself. The women writers, explicitly and implicitly, critiqued a system that prided itself on providing opportunity for all but that in reality only provided opportunity for middle-class white males. In a society that liked to see itself as classless, the women writers called attention to the existence of classes and the relationship between class, race, and gender. Emerson, in his response to the claims of the women's suffrage movement in 1855, romantically declared that woman's best protection was to rely on a good man: "Woman should find in man her guardian."[14] Women writers who had struggled to support themselves recognized the fatuousness of ideas like Emerson's. For example, Fanny Fern, who worked as a seamstress after her husband died, pointed out in *Ruth Hall* (1855) and in her newspaper articles that not only did women have to work, but working women were the victims of class *and* gender discrimination. E.D.E.N. Southworth, in *The Hidden Hand* (1859), demonstrated that Capitola as a young girl could not find a job in New York City until she dressed as a boy. Louisa May Alcott, in "Behind a Mask" (1861), although she did not condone the machinations of Jean Muir, was sympathetic to the position that she was in: poor and friendless, she was treated with contempt by those who were more affluent than she. Harriet Wilson in *Our Nig* (1859) chronicled the non-success of Frado, her poor, racially mixed protagonist. By pointing out the different treatment that women receive when they do not have money, or when they are racially vulnerable, and by demonstrating that many women needed to work but that job opportunities were severely limited, these writers underscored the effects of gender, class, and racial differences—and thus called attention to the fallacies inherent in two important nineteenth-century American myths: the myth of individualism and its corollary, the myth of the male protection of "true womanhood."

The works by nineteenth-century American women writers—both white and black—are not written by and do not focus on the person that nineteenth-century American society conceptionalized as the American individualist: their central characters are female and sometimes non-white. Whereas there are numerous examples of works by nineteenth-century British and European male writers (for example, Flaubert, Ibsen, Tolstoy, Hardy) who were able to portray female characters as central to the action, there are very few by nineteenth-century American male writers.[15] The major exception is Hawthorne's *The Scarlet Letter*. For the most part, it was left to the nineteenth-century American women writers to portray women as central. Moreover, not only were these works by women and about women, they portrayed life from the perspective of women. Although women and non-whites appeared in the works by men, the story was not told from the perspective of these "others": Jim in *Huckleberry Finn,* Queequeg in *Moby-Dick,* Chingachgook in Cooper's Leatherstocking tales, like the female characters in these novels, are all seen from the point of view of the white male narrator.

In order to understand the ways in which nineteenth-century women's writing diverged from and critiqued the assumptions of American culture and specifically of American individualism—and consequently to understand better a principal reason why they have been excluded from the canon—let us look at the works of specific women writers in relation to the way in which their work differed from the dominant culture. I have divided the writers into five groups. Although there is some overlap, it will facilitate matters to look at each of these groups separately: (1) the early seduction novels, which raise questions about the circumscription of women's role in society; (2) the frontier novels, which give us another side to the issue of American expansionism and the treatment of the American Indians; (3) the domestic novels, which question the self-orientation of American individualism; (4) the domestic novels and the "local-color" novels, which emphasize the importance of community; and (5) the works of those authors whom I call "the questioners," who raise questions of class, race, and gender and pose a threat to the status of the male individualist himself.

Early examples of the view of woman as central in American literature are the seduction novels of the late eighteenth century. Susanna Rowson's *Charlotte Temple* (1794) and Hannah Foster's *The Coquette* (1797) each focus on the title character, a woman. The male characters in these novels are peripheral, just as the female characters are peripheral in the novels of the dominant tradition. The reader is able to see the action from the perspective of the principal female character. *The Coquette* particularly, thanks to the author's careful portrayal of Eliza Wharton's motivation and conflict, the dilemma of her circumscribed situation, and the poverty of her choices within American society, provides a provocative comment on the ideology of the dominant culture, which prescribes simply that the character should marry as soon as possible. She emerges as an individual at a time when her society did not grant her the privileges of individuality.[16]

Following these works are the early frontier novels *Hobomok* (1824) by Lydia Maria Child and *Hope Leslie* (1827) by Catharine Sedgwick, which differ from the frontier novels of Cooper, for example, primarily by giving a prominent role to the women characters. Moreover, in *Hope*

Leslie the heroine is a strong and competent individual, unlike the passive shadows of femininity in Cooper's novels. In addition, Sedgwick's white heroine, Hope Leslie, is balanced against the American Indian heroine, Magawisca, presenting a double picture of otherness. In both novels the theme of miscegnation (the recognition of which necessarily involves a recognition of otherness) contrasts with the careful separation between whites and American Indians maintained in the Cooper novels. Natty Bumppo and Chingachgook can be friends, but Uncas cannot marry a white woman. (In fact, Cooper is so careful to maintain a separation of races that he does not even permit the suggestion that Uncas might love a white woman; it turns out that Cora, the woman Uncas loves, is in fact of mixed blood, her mother being the descendant of a slave in the West Indies.) Although Child and Sedgwick do not encourage miscegenation, the fact that they not only portray it but portray it within marriage (in spite of virulent criticism from their culture) indicates that they were able to view "the other," in this case the American Indian, as a person. Clearly, the frontier novels by women present a different picture from the one portrayed in the dominant tradition: the male individualist does not take center stage; women are not only central, they can be competent instigators of the action; and the American Indians are seen as a real presence.

Another important work on the frontier by a woman writer is Caroline Kirkland's *A New Home—Who'll Follow?* (1839). Kirkland's perspective is explicitly different from that of the male authors of the period: she shows the frontier experience from the woman's perspective, and the graphic realism of her portrayal counters the more romantic and idealized picture apparent in the male portrayal of the experience as a glorious adventure. She also shows the pettiness and greed inherent in the masculine motivation: "In this newly-formed world," she says of the frontier, men look upon every new arrival simply as "somebody with whom to try the race of enterprize, i.e., money-making."[17] Kirkland's perspective is similar to that of other women writers who commented on frontier life. For example, Eliza Farnham in *Life in Prairie Land* (1846) and Margaret Fuller in *Summer on the Lakes* (1844) commented on the self-gratifying motivation of the male pioneers and the difference between the motivation of men and women.[18] The perspective of these writers is confirmed by the diaries kept by women who went West: in most cases, the women did not go West because they wanted to.[19] As one woman told Fuller, they went because it was "the man's notion."[20] The romance of the westward movement has been a part of American ideology and myth for so long that it has been difficult to recognize the ramifications of these voices of dissent, but one thing is clear: they did not fit into a canon that glorified expansionism and male prowess, and it should not be surprising that they have been so thoroughly excluded.

Other ways in which the noncanonized works diverge from the American literary tradition are apparent in the work of those nineteenth-century women writers who have been characterized as the domestic novelists. By this term I mean the nineteenth-century women writers who celebrated domesticity, centering their fiction in woman and the home.[21] Reacting to their society's diminishment of women by investing the domestic role of women with supreme importance, they accepted their society's image of woman as passive, dependent, and domestic but demonstrated that these very qualities gave woman significance. They focused on women's concerns, which the masculine tradition had excluded, and by that focus attempted to reveal the intrinsic value for women and for society of those aspects of life erroneously labled "trifles." The concerns of women are portrayed as positive and are redefined from a new perspective, where they are seen not as trifles at all but as important instances of human involvement and moral power.

In her 1917 story "A Jury of Her Peers," Susan Glaspell addressed herself to the conventional male attitude, and the story, which was originally written as a play under the title "Trifles," ironically demonstrates how men have undervalued women. What the men in the play regard as "trifles" are revealed to be the crux of the matter.[22] Glaspell's point is that men are foolish and shortsighted not to listen to women, and that men will lose if they continue to believe that women's opinions and observations do not count for anything. It is this aspect of otherness that is reflected in the work of the domestic novelists. In novels like Susan Warner's *The Wide, Wide World* (1850), Harriet Beecher Stowe's *Uncle Tom's Cabin* (1852), Maria Cummins's *The Lamplighter* (1854), and Augusta Evans Wilson's *St. Elmo* (1866), women and women's concerns are central. Although as a woman she lacks the political and economic power and influence of a man in society, in the domestic novel the principal female character wields a moral and religious influence that makes her ultimately superior to the men in the novel.

The first principle of the domestic novels is the necessity of selflessness and repression of the will. *The Wide, Wide World,* which was the first bestseller in the United States, focuses on the girlhood of Ellen Montgomery. Ellen, who learns religious devotion and personal sacrifice from her mother, struggles to repress her will until she has learned well the lesson that her mother taught her: "Though we *must* sorrow, we must not rebel."[23] A similar lesson is learned by Gertrude in *The Lamplighter*. Early in the novel she learns to subdue her will and gains "complete self-control," "submission," "the power of governing herself."[24]

Although the domestic novelists accepted their culture's definition of women as passive and selfless, and although they did not challenge the concept of male dominance, it is clear that they intended their definition of selflessness to apply to men as well as to women. In particular, they criticized the self-orientation of men in their relations with women. In *The Lamplighter,* for example, Maria Cummins comments on the selfishness of Gertrude's guardian:

> Mr. Graham was a liberal and highly respectable man; he had the rc utation, as the world goes, of being a remarkably high-minded and honorable man; and not without reason. . . . But, alas! he was a *selfish* man. . . . And yet, while he was ready to act the tyrant, he deceived himself with the idea that he was the best friend she had in the world. He was not capable of understanding that kind of regard which causes one to find gratification in whatever tends to the present or the future welfare of another, without reference to himself or his own interests.[25]

In addition to—and in conjunction with—this theme of selflessness, the domestic novelists also emphasized religious devotion. The books' religious earnestness is perhaps one of the most difficult hurdles for twentieth-century readers. Twentieth-century critics who have written religious criticism have focused on religion as an intellectual and symbolic exercise; earnestness has not been fashionable in religion (or in anything else) in twentieth-century literature.[26] The religious earnestness of the characters in the domestic novels, however, might be compared to the love felt by a character in a love story, a love that involves a love for and belief in the beloved that the reader might not share or understand. When we read *Romeo and Juliet,* for example, we do not question *why* the lovers love each other; that is a given, and the interest lies in the problems the characters face, and how they resolve them. Similarly, when we read the work of the domestic novelists, we need not question *why* the character believes so fervently in her religion; that is a given, and the interest lies in the problems that the character faces and how she resolves them.[27]

It is not only the earnestness of the characters' religion that creates a problem in the religious theme of the domestic novelists. Even more significant is the fact that the religious belief of the characters in the domestic novels is closely allied to the necessity to gain power over self. The characters' ability to gain power over the self is portrayed as a religious lesson. The selflessness taught by the domestic novelists coincided with the concept of femininity in the nineteenth century, and insofar as the novels intended religious selflessness to apply only to women, their theme created no conflict with the dominant culture. The domestic novelists made the woman-centered world dependent upon an acknowledgment of the moral superiority of women, however. Consequently, the male protagonist—even the most self-indulgent reprobate, St. Elmo Murray in Augusta Evans Wilson's novel *St. Elmo*—must learn selflessness from the female protagonist. Wilson asserts that women are "the custodians of national purity"; only they can "successfully arrest the tide of demoralization breaking over the land." Although Wilson is careful to portray a woman who in the end will be subordinate to her husband, and in this respect does not offend convention, Edna Earl will not marry St. Elmo until he has overcome all the pride of his "sinful, vindictive, satanic nature"—which includes totally giving up his selfishness to devote himself selflessly to Christ.[28]

It is this insistence upon selflessness for men as well as for women that helps to make the religious themes of the domestic novelists unpalatable to present-day American culture. The implications of such a philosophy are clearly in opposition to American individualism, which, while it insisted on female selflessness, was based upon an unquestioning belief in male self-assertion. One of the difficulties that twentieth-century critics have had with Harriet Beecher Stowe's *Uncle Tom's Cabin* is Stowe's insistence on religious selflessness for both men and women. Not only does Eva St. Clare incarnate the selflessness of Christian love, but Tom becomes a Christ figure whose last words, like the words of Christ on the cross, are to ask forgiveness for his murderers.[29] Twentieth-century Americans have criticized this portrayal of Tom so virulently that the term "Uncle Tom" has come to mean a black man who demeans himself to whites. It is significant, however, that this criticism of Tom derives from pride of gender as much as from pride of race; comments that criticize Tom's "submissiveness" because it "divests him of his sex" reflect the American emphasis on aggressive maleness.[30] Stowe's message is that all people—black and white, male and female—must learn the principles of love and charity. Americans have associated selflessness with the feminine, and even if that selflessness is more nearly a reflection of the teachings of Christ, it is not consistent with the construction of maleness—independent, assertive, self-reliant, powerful—that has dominated American culture.[31]

Implicit in the domestic novelists' female characters' religious and moral superiority is an assertion of the empowering nature of religious belief. As Jane Tompkins points out, in Susan Warner's *The Wide, Wide World* Ellen Montgomery and her mother before her, although they are portrayed as passive and subordinate to male rule, nevertheless, through their fervent subordination of self, become themselves gods and thus are empowered through their religious belief.[32] Even more significant is the example of *Uncle Tom's Cabin*. Stowe, when asked how she came to write such a powerful book, replied that *she* did not write it, "God did."[33] Writing in response to the Fugitive Slave Law of 1850, Stowe was empowered by her religious belief to attack slavery, which, at the time, was the law of the land. Her novel had a powerful political impact and worldwide circulation at the time of its publication; in the twentieth century, however, when its political raison d'être (slavery) was no longer a viable force, it was denigrated as "too religious." Yet the principal reason for the intensity of its impact at the time of its publication was its appeal to a higher authority. A woman, without legal or economic power, could, by appealing to a higher authority, directly attack and render defenseless the tenets of patriarchal authority. This appeal to a higher authority could give credence to and thus empower the powerless.

What is clear is that we need to take a closer look at the reasons for disparaging the religiosity in the work of the domestic novelists. It is easy to dismiss it as old-fashioned and accept that as the reason why their works have been ignored in the twentieth century. But this explanation is too simple. Religious earnestness, the insistence upon selflessness for men as well as for women, and the concept of an empowering force that could enable the powerless to challenge the power of the established order: clearly, the implications of the religious theme are an important reason for the omission of these works from the canon.

Another factor that has kept the domestic novelists' works out of the canon is apparent in the literary establishment's use of the term *sentimental*. Sentimentality, which did not always have the negative connotations that it has for Americans today, became a damning word in the twentieth century and is probably the most important weapon that has been used against the nineteenth-century American women writers—whether they wrote sentimentally or not. Like other words that were previously only descriptive (for example, *socialized* [medicine]; *liberal* [politician]), the word *sentimental* has been used so effectively to denigrate the work of the women writers that, until their recent resurrection, no one in this century with any pretensions of intellect would be caught dead reading their work. Moreover, the word *sentimental* in American criticism was made synonymous with "woman writer." Consequently, writers as diverse as satirist Fanny Fern and adventure writer E.D.E.N. Southworth were equally damned by the label *sentimental*, and generations of readers never took the trouble to read them to find out whether they were sentimental or not; the assumption was that if they were nineteenth-century American women writers, they were sentimental and consequently not worth reading.

In light of the dominant tradition in the United States, it is not accidental that sentimentality has been used to exclude women writers from the canon of American literature. Sentimentality requires an awareness of other people, a mental dialogue or displacement. The person who observes the sentiment-provoking situation must identify with or at least sympathize with the unfortunate person(s) whom he/she observes. The dominant American literary tradition, which reflects the individualism of American culture, focuses on the solitary male individualist. In a tradition that requires that the individual be insular and self-reliant, there is no room for such a dialogue. As Emerson said in his essay "Self-Reliance," "Friend, client, child, sickness, fear, want, charity, all knock at once at thy closet door and say,—'come out unto us.'" But, says Emerson, I will not come "into their confusion. . . . I cannot sell my liberty and power, to save their sensibility."[34]

Related to sentimentalism because of its recognition of other people is the emphasis upon connectedness of community that often forms the background of the works by nineteenth-century American women writers. Hawthorne rebelled against the insularity of the dominant tradition in his insistence upon the chain of humanity, but for most male writers the individual was preeminent. Melville portrayed the importance of interrelationships among people in such scenes as "The Squeeze of the Hand" chapter in *Moby-Dick,* and Twain portrayed the bonding between Huck and Jim, but they did not conceive of the community as central to the life of the individual. The dominant tradition in nineteenth-century American literature and culture was insular and self-asserting. Emerson expressed his society's priorities: "Society is compulsory and wasteful to the individual."[35]

Whereas the dominant tradition portrays the male individualist in flight from society, the women writers did not visualize a world without society. Thus, while the dominant masculine tradition focused on the insularity of the individual, the women writers portrayed characters who were enmeshed in a community of interpersonal relationships. They did not romanticize the concept of community; they portrayed the hurts and cruelties that associations with other people invariably bring. But they also acknowledged the bonds that can exist between people: between parents and children, between friends, even between strangers. Ellen in *The Wide, Wide World* is an orphan, but she must learn how to get along in the world, not how to escape it. Stowe's *Uncle Tom's Cabin* shows how the lives of all of the characters, black and white, are interrelated. Harriet Jacobs, in *Incidents in the Life of a Slave Girl,* portrays the courage and defiance of Linda Brent, but she acknowledges the bond between herself and the people who helped her: her grandmother, her brother, her uncle, the women who hid her, the young man who helped her, the Quakers, and the two Mrs. Willises.

Gertrude in *The Lamplighter* defies Mr. Graham so that she can go to help the family who needs her. Early realists like Caroline Kirkland and Alice Cary and late nineteenth-century writers such as Sarah Orne Jewett and Mary E. Wilkins Freeman focus on the community in which the characters live. Other people are important presences in the work of these women writers; they are not simply scenery. All societies, whether consciously or not, are, as Foucault pointed out, logophobic.[36] It is not surprising, then, that these other voices, which emphasized the importance of the "other," have been obscured and silenced.

Another aspect of the dissenting ideas of the women writers is their apparent questioning of the status of the male individualist and other sacrosanct concepts that underlay nineteenth-century American society. A significant group of women writers, whom we might call the questioners, criticized and questioned the assumptions of the dominant culture more than did the white male writers who were part of it. More explicit in some works than in others, this questioning took the form of negative character portrayal, thematic development, or explicit comment.

One important way in which women writers questioned their culture was in respect to the relationship between men and women. Instead of accepting the idealization of the position of women that was inculcated in them by nineteenth-century American culture, where the "cult of true womanhood" pretended that women were all regarded as ideal beings who would be treated accordingly, women writers showed the pettiness and selfishness in the male attitude toward women.[37] Rose Terry Cooke, in short stories like "Freedom Wheeler's Controversy with Providence," shows how women's lives have been destroyed by the twin patriarchal codes of Calvinism and male dominance. In Elizabeth Stoddard's *The Morgesons* (1862), Cassandra Morgeson comments that men "require the souls and bodies of women, without having the trouble of knowing the difference between the one and other."[38] Elizabeth Stuart Phelps, in *The Story of Avis* (1877), questions the conventions of society that would confine a woman, regardless of talent or inclination, to the home sphere. Rebecca Harding Davis, in "Life in the Iron Mills" (1861), focuses on class as an imprisoning factor for men in American society, thus denying the universal application of the myth of American individualism even for white men. In *Isa, A Pilgrimage* (1852), Caroline Chesebro' questions all of the restrictions of society, including marriage and religion: "If one would LIVE, one must have freedom."[39]

A similar kind of challenge is apparent in the work of nineteenth-century African-American women writers. Their work is particularly important to an understanding of the signficance of otherness in the formation of the canon because in American society they were doubly other. Although the slave narratives of male African Americans gained recognition (the most famous is the narrative of Frederick Douglass), the writings of nineteenth-century African-American women were almost unknown in the twentieth century until many were reprinted in the 1980s.[40] This reprinting coincided with the reprinting of works by nineteenth-century American women writers in general, and, like the writings of nineteenth-century white women, the writings of these African-American women challenged the premises of American culture. In Harriet Jacobs's autobiographical *Incidents in the Life of a Slave Girl* (1861), Linda Brent defies her white master, who attempts to force her to submit to his sexual advances. She hides for seven years in her grandmother's house; then she escapes to the North, where she earns her own living and educates her children. Assertive and independent, she epitomizes the qualities that women and slaves were not believed to possess. Moreover, in her contemptuous portrayal of Dr. Flint, in Linda's refusal to accept his authority as man or as master, and in her portrayal of Linda's independent pursuit of freedom and independence (which reflects Jacobs's own actions), Jacobs implicitly challenges the patriarchal authority of American society while explicitly criticizing the patriarchal institution of slavery.

Also important is Harriet Wilson's *Our Nig* (1859). Wilson, who was a free black woman living in the North, incorporated much of the material from her own life into her novel. Very different from the traditional slave narrative, *Our Nig* is not a success story. Negating all of the myths of American society, Wilson's novel, which portrays a woman who is born of a white mother and a black father, does not glorify motherhood or "true womanhood." Moreover, in portraying miscegenation within an apparently nonproblematic marriage, this novel, like the frontier novels of Catharine Sedgwick and Lydia Maria Child, tackles a subject that American society did not wish to consider. In addition, the theme of the novel represents an undercutting of the American belief in self-reliance: in *Our Nig* it is clear that the character's failure is due to society's faults, not her own. *Our Nig* was not a commercial success, and, in fact, was not reviewed or even mentioned in any literary periodicals when it was published.[41] Wilson's novel implicitly challenges all of the principal traditions of American society. It is not surprising that it has remained buried for so long.

Although *Our Nig* was little known at the time of its publication, when Frances Watkins Harper's novel *Iola Leroy* was published in 1893, it was generally favorably reviewed and was reprinted several times. In the early twentieth century, however, the novel disappeared from the country's literary consciousness. Part of the reason for its failure in the twentieth century was the same as for the novels by nineteenth-century white women: Harper's novel was criticized for its "sentiment and idealism," its "sincerity" and religiosity.[42] But other factors have made *Iola Leroy* incompatible with the dominant tradition. It is true that, unlike *Our Nig,* Harper's novel was a success story. The main character, however, was a woman, and, although the novel's primary theme is racial success, the individual success chronicled in the novel is primarily a woman's success. This is a novel not only of race but of gender. As Henry Louis Gates points out, even during the civil rights movement of the 1960s when earlier works by black men were being reprinted, there was no interest in this novel, or in many works by other nineteenth-century black women.[43] All women, Harper states in her novel, should be taught to be "useful and self-reliant,"[44] and in Iola she portrays a woman who is independent and self-supporting. Even after marriage Iola continues to do the world's work. She comments, "I think that every woman should have some skill or art which would insure her at least a comfortable support" (210). Even more important than material success, however, is the selfless devotion to others and specifically to the uplifting of the race. Harry devotes his life to the education of the less fortunate among his race rather than to material comfort. The world, says Harper, is more indebted to martyrs than to millionaires (219). On two counts, then, this novel is out of step with the dominant tradition of male individualism: its emphasis on female success and its advocacy of selflessness.

With respect to the independence of her heroine, Harper's novel is related to the work of the final category of women writers. The most explicit form of questioning of American society was engaged in by the women writers who challenged their society's definition of women as passive, dependent, and subordinate to men and portrayed women who were self-assertive, independent, and self-sufficient. The most outspoken of these writers was the journalist Fanny Fern (Sara Willis Parton), whose satirical columns undercut the hypocrisy and pompousness of male pretension. In her novel *Ruth Hall* (1855) Fern applied the concept of American individualism—which was regarded as a male phenomenon—to women.[45] This was the most threatening attack of all on the ideology of the dominant culture. Also important is E.D.E.N. Southworth, whose formidable heroine Capitola LeNoir, in *The Hidden Hand* (1859), is not passive or domestic. Nor is she sentimental; Southworth tells us that she never cries. In the course of the novel she captures a bandit, averts a rape, fights a duel, and engineers a jailbreak.[46] Louisa May Alcott, who is more widely known for her books for young girls, wrote anonymous fiction that portrayed the woman as an independent power seeker, a theme that was hardly consistent with the ideas of the dominant culture. Her 1866 novella, "Behind a Mask," portrays a woman who is as assertive, manipulative, and unsentimental as the most successful Wall Street entrepreneur.[47] In these works, the conception of the woman as not only central but also assertive, independent, and self-sufficient—in fact as much an individualist as the male individualist himself—was an open challenge to the premises of American society.

Although external forces have influenced the formation of the canon, literary works are not simply empty containers to be juggled by competing factions. If each work is to carry its own weight, we can only determine the significance of that weight by looking at the work for itself, not simply for its usefulness to other authors. As long as we continue to regard the works of nineteenth-century American women writers as valuable only in terms of their usefulness to the canonized male authors, we are regarding them in the same way that women themselves were regarded in nineteenth-century American society. But just as today we recognize that women have an independent existence, so too we must also acknowledge the independent existence of their writings. The works of these women writers are important for their inherent value; they cannot simply be regarded as "fodder" for the canon.

The works by nineteenth-century American women represent dissenting voices in American literature; they represent the perspective and concerns of persons who were defined as other by the dominant culture. Other, first of all, by virtue of their gender and sometimes also their race, the authors' position in the work force often gave them an affinity with working women as well. They focused on themes that diverged from and sometimes posed a threat to the ideas and traditions of the dominant culture. Not only is the white male individualist not the center of the books, but the theme of many of the books by nineteenth-century American women writers negates self-assertion and focuses on selflessness; the author values a sense of community and connectedness rather than the insular life that is portrayed in the novels of the solitary male quest. Many of the works by the nineteenth-century American women writers reflect a respect for the power of sentiment, which requires a respect for, even an identification with, "the other." And finally, the most threatening of these writers give to the central female character all of the self-assertiveness and self-dependence that the male writers portrayed in the male individualist. They also call attention to limitations, not only of gender but also of race and class. The mass exclusion of these "other" writers from the canon of American literature is not simply a matter of aesthetic taste; it is also a political act.

❧

These works by American women writers deserve to be read and studied. As reprints of their works have become available in the past few years, readers in increasing numbers have been reading them. Many of the books have become required reading in college courses throughout the country, and a new generation of students has been responding with enthusiasm to works that their parents and grandparents have never heard of. What has been lacking is a way of looking at the works by these writers, a way of talking about them that does not rely on methods of the past whose criteria precluded serious discussion of such works. This collection provides new ways of looking at such timeworn concepts as "local color" or "sentimentalism," for example, ways that avoid the negative stereotyping of the past. This book does not attempt to cover every nineteenth-century American woman writer and every tradition. There are many other writers that could have been included: Lydia Maria Child, Margaret Fuller, Susan Warner, for example. And there are other women's traditions that could have been included as well. The tradition of love between women, for example, although it figures in some of the discussions, is not the topic of a whole essay. But the purpose of this book is not to be all-encompassing. Rather, our intention is to provide representative essays that illustrate ways in which the work of women writers from this period can be approached.

While essays on some of these writers have occasionally appeared in academic journals, and while the essays introducing the reissued works of individual writers have outlined some useful ways of thinking about this material, this volume offers the first collection of critical essays on the subject. Most of the essays are published here for the first time; a few are reprinted from journals or books. We have organized the section on the writers chronologically, and the book begins with Jane Tompkins's essay on Susanna Rowson, the author of *Charlotte Temple* (1794): "Susanna Rowson, Father of the American Novel." Identifying Rowson as the first professional American author (rather than Charles Brockden Brown, who is usually given this title), Tompkins analyzes the assumptions about gender, social class, and economic status that have devalued popular works by women writers while privileging the commercially unsuccessful male writers. Her essay contains a timely warning, noting that these assumptions have become so ingrained in our culture that for many years readers and critics have made literary judgments on the basis of social and ideological ideas to which they no longer subscribe. The second essay is Carol Singley's "Catharine Maria Sedgwick's *Hope Leslie:* Radical Frontier Romance." Comparing Sedgwick's work with the work of male writers, principally Cooper, Singley demonstrates that in *Hope Leslie* (1827) Sedgwick provides an alternative literary history, one that exposes injustice against women, American Indians, and the land. In "Reinventing Lydia Sigourney," Nina Baym shows how the "social construction" of Sigourney as a "female author" is based on only a small portion of her work. A significant proportion of Sigourney's work was historical and political. Particularly important is her work on the American Indians, which denounces white injustice and the cruel treatment of the Indians and was clearly out of sync with the official policy of the early nineteenth century. Baym concludes, "That a writer with so obviously public a program should come down to us as the most private and domesticated of antebellum women authors suggests the need to look again at the scope of antebellum women's writing."

In "Domesticity and the Economics of Independence: Resistance and Revolution in the Work of Fanny Fern," I explore Fern's critique of the pretensions and abuses of male authority. Satirizing the idealization of marriage, Fern maintained that women would never be independent until they became economically independent—which was a revolutionary concept in mid-nineteenth-century America. Frances Smith Foster's essay, "Harriet Jacobs's *Incidents* and the 'Careless Daughters' [and Sons] Who Read It," focuses on the importance of class, race, and gender in readers' resistance to literary works. Noting that ever since *Incidents* first appeared in 1861, Jacobs's authenticity has been questioned, Foster analyzes the strategies Jacobs used to establish her authority, to revise her readers' attitudes, and also to agitate for social change. Judith Fetterley, in her essay, "Only a Story, Not a Romance: Harriet Beecher Stowe's *The Pearl of Orr's Island*," analyzes the novel Stowe had such difficulty in writing (published 1861–1862), revealing that Stowe's difficulty derived from her attempt to deal with issues that were counter to the prevailing culture. Rewriting theology as well as the conventions of the love story, Stowe subverts romance and critiques the tendency of men to see themselves as gods. The last essay in the "Writers" section, Karla F. C. Holloway's "Economies of Space: Markets and Marketability in *Our Nig* and *Iola Leroy*," examines the differences between Harriet Wilson's *Our Nig* (1859) and Frances Harper's *Iola Leroy* (1892). Wilson's economic motivation is reflected in a sparse narrative structure, which is limited in contextual space and in descriptive language, with metaphors that are governed by a spartan economy. Harper's political and inspirational motivation in *Iola Leroy*, however, is reflected in her expansive language and in her free manipulation of space and time. Yet, concludes Holloway, despite these differences in motivation and narrative style, the two works are linked by the common metaphor of the slave market, which provides a discomfiting reminder of the historic derivation of both texts.

The "Traditions" section begins with an essay by Sandra Zagarell, " 'America' as Community in Three Antebellum Village Sketches," which analyzes the view of community in works by Eliza Buckminster Lee,

Caroline Kirkland, and Lydia Sigourney. Zagarell finds that whereas the dominant tradition of village literature focuses on a static homogeneity, these writers portray heterogeneous, fairly open, dynamic communities. Their concept of community is polyphonic, including people of different backgrounds, beliefs, and positions and often focusing on people who are marginal or excluded from other literature. These women writers do not see their small villages as separate from America, but rather posit ideas and values that they foresee as valuable to the future course of the larger American community. In "The American Renaissance Reenvisioned," Joanne Dobson points out that in the twentieth century the literature of mid-nineteenth-century America was bisected: the romantic texts by male authors became the "seminal" texts, while women's texts were denigrated as frivolous or trivial. Asserting the need to reexamine the issues of classification and periodization, Dobson focuses on the limiting definition of the term "sentimental" and the exclusion of the works of early literary realism from the traditional canon.

In " 'Doers of the Word': Theorizing African–American Women Writers in the Antebellum North," Carla Peterson analyzes the work of northern antebellum African–American women writers for whom writing was a "form of doing." Her study includes genres and texts that modernist criteria have excluded from literary consideration: the work of evangelists, travel writers, and writers who used the conventions of domestic fiction. Looking at the texts in relation to the politics of publication and reception, Peterson analyzes the writers' self-marginalization as a method of legitimizing their actions and their use of writing as a strategy for racial uplift and community building. In the next essay, " 'What Methods Have Brought Blessing': Discourses of Reform in Philanthropic Literature," Deborah Carlin notes that although women were made aware of the ills of industrial society and were believed to be "uniquely suited" to ameliorate these ills, they were prevented by the restrictions of domesticity and "true womanhood" from attempting to effect any change in society. Consequently in the works that she studies, the women's response to the poverty that they saw was primarily philanthropic. They questioned the immutability of economic differences, yet, speaking from a position of powerlessness, these writers ultimately relied on individual agency and conscience rather than advocating any substantial change in the system.

Josephine Donovan's essay, "Breaking the Sentence: Local-Color Literature and Subjugated Knowledges," explores the way in which women writers of the local-color school recorded the clash between the dominant colonizing disciplines and a rural, deviant culture. The oppositional culture found in the women's local-color literature represents a counterhegemonic resistance to Calvinism, to the abstract exchange-values of modern industrial society, and to the normalizing disciplines that threatened women's life-worlds. Diane Lichtenstein's essay focuses on "The Tradition of American Jewish Women Writers." "Other" because they were women and also because they were Jewish in a predominantly Christian society, these women felt the need to negotiate among the complex fractions of selfhood: the true womanhood ideal of American middle-class Christian society, the expectations of Jewish womanhood, their identity as American, and their identity as Jewish. In her essay, " 'But is it any *good?*': Evaluating Nineteenth-Century American Women's Fiction," Susan K. Harris addresses the question of literary evaluation. Calling for new methodologies to construct evaluative critera for the work of nineteenth-century women writers, she posits a methodology that she calls "process analysis." Process, she says, focuses on structure and language, placing the text within the context of its own time, analyzing the ways in which the text may set up opposing modes of thought, and searching for traces of changing consciousness in succeeding texts. The final essay in the book is Paul Lauter's "Teaching Nineteenth-Century Women Writers," which is concerned with pedagogical method. Questioning the value of academic structures that have ignored works by women writers, Lauter outlines a method of teaching that focuses on difference. Pairing works by the marginalized women writers with works by male writers from the same period who were writing in the dominant tradition, he finds, provides a method that generates student response, evokes alternative ideas and genres for students to identify with, and forces students to reexamine assumptions about literary value.

We believe that this book will be valuable to students and teachers of works by nineteenth-century American women writers, as well as to general readers who are discovering these writers on their own. We have divided the book into two sections in order to indicate the general ways in which these writers can be looked at: each is valuable as an individual writer and also as part of a larger tradition.

NOTES

Parts of this essay appeared in *Annals of Scholarship* 7, no. 4 (1990): 419–439.

1. See John S. Hart, *The Female Prose Writers of America* (Philadelphia: E. H. Butler, 1857), 472. For a comparative analysis of sales figures, see Susan Geary, "The Domestic Novel as a Commercial Commodity: Making a Best Seller in the 1850s," *Papers of the Bibliographical Society* 60 (1976): 365–394. Between 1849 and 1858, for example, Ticknor and Fields published twenty-three novels; only two sold more than ten thousand copies (Geary, "The Domestic Novel," 368–370).

One spokesman for the publishing industry commented that a book was considered a success if it sold five thousand copies. See William Charvat, *The Profession of Authorship in America* (Columbus: Ohio State University Press, 1968), 241.

2. Herman Melville, "Hawthorne and His Mosses," reprinted in *Moby-Dick*, Norton Critical Edition, ed. Harrison Hayford and Herschel Parker (New York: Norton, 1967), 545–546. The term *American* has been appropriated by scholars in the United States to apply specifically to the history and culture of the United States, although, of course, the term could be applied to all of the countries in the Americas, not only to the United States. I use it in this paper in the generally accepted more limited sense partly for lack of another adjective and partly because of the ideological connotations of the term. The term "American" has come to represent the individualism of the dominant tradition in the United States, and the use of the term itself has been exclusionary; if the term is now used to apply to traditions other than the conventional one perhaps the exclusionary connotation will gradually change to one that more accurately reflects the diversity of voices. For a discussion of the use of this term see Sacvan Bercovitch, "America as Canon and Context: Literary History in a Time of Dissensus," *American Literature* 58 (March 1986): 99–107; Peter Cariofol, "The New Orthodoxy: Ideology and the Institution of American Literary History," *American Literature* 59 (December 1987): 626–638.

3. Feminist critics who have pointed out the obliteration of nineteenth-century American women's writing from the American tradition include Nina Baym, *Woman's Fiction: A Guide to Novels by and about Women in America, 1820–1870* (Ithaca: Cornell University Press, 1978); and Jane Tompkins, *Sensational Designs: The Cultural Work of American Fiction, 1790–1860* (New York: Oxford University Press, 1985). Within the past several years, texts have been made available that had been out of print for years. See particularly the American Women Writers Series of reprints of books by nineteenth-century American women writers published by Rutgers University Press; *The Norton Anthology of Literature by Women*, ed. Sandra M. Gilbert and Susan Gubar (New York: Norton, 1985); and *The Heath Anthology of American Literature*, 2 vols, ed. Paul Lauter et al. (Lexington, Mass.: D. C. Heath and Company, 1990). See also two anthologies of works by nineteenth-century American women writers, *Provisions: A Reader from 19th-Century American Women*, ed. Judith Fetterley (Bloomington: Indiana University Press, 1985); and *Hidden Hands: An Anthology of American Women Writers, 1790–1870*, ed. Lucy M. Freibert and Barbara A. White (New Brunswick, N.J.: Rutgers University Press, 1985). Other works that have helped to make a case for the reconsideration of nineteenth-century women writers include Sandra M. Gilbert and Susan Gubar, *The Madwoman in the Attic: The Woman Writer and the Nineteenth-Century Literary Imagination* (New Haven: Yale University Press, 1979); Elaine Showalter, *A Literature of Their Own: British Women Novelists from Brontë to Lessing* (Princeton: Princeton University Press, 1977); Susan K. Harris, *19th-Century American Women Writers: Interpretive Strategies* (New York: Oxford University Press, 1990).

In the 1980s feminist criticism in the United States was divided between disciples of the French theorists and the Anglo-American gynocritics. The theorists, who derived much of their theory from the deconstructionism of Jacques Derrida, the psychological criticism of Jacques Lacan, and French feminists like Hélène Cixous, Luce Irigaray, and Julia Kristeva, focused on the concept of "l'écriture feminine," or the idea that there is a peculiarly feminine mode of writing (which could be done by men or women), which is nonlinear and nonrational. Anglo-American critics like Nina Baym and Elaine Showalter, however, have focused on recovering the works of women writers of the past and on understanding why those works had been lost. Anglo-American critics have criticized French feminist theory on two counts: (1) that it was male dominated, that is, that it took much of its theory from male thinkers who are, in some cases, regarded as misogynists (e.g., Freud); (2) that in defining women's writing as nonlinear and nonrational, the French theorists placed women in the same position from which they have been fighting to emerge: the position of being categorized by the male establishment as hysterical and irrational. Both schools of feminist criticsm, however, have focused on and sought reasons for the silencing of women writers. See, for example, Hélène Cixous, "The Laugh of the Medusa," trans. Keith Cohen and Paula Cohen, *Signs* 1 (Summer 1976): 875–893; Luce Irigaray, *This Sex Which Is Not One,* trans. Catherine Porter (Ithaca: Cornell University Press, 1985); Elaine Showalter, "Women's Time, Women's Space: Writing the History of Feminist Criticsm," 30–44; and Nina Baym, "The Madwoman and Her Languages: Why I Don't Do Feminist Literary Theory," 45–61, both in *Feminist Issues in Literary Scholarship,* ed. Shari Benstock (Bloomington: Indiana University Press, 1987); and Elaine Showalter, *The Female Malady: Women, Madness, and English Culture, 1830–1980* (New York: Pantheon Books, 1985). See also Karen Ramsey Johnson, "Facing the Canon: Toward a Feminist Position," *Humanities in the South* 68 (Fall 1988): 6–9.

4. An example of this type of criticism is Van Wyck Brooks's comment on Rose Terry Cooke, whose work he values only as it foreshadows the work of other writers. See *New England: Indian Summer* (New York: Dutton, 1965), 86–88. That this tendency is still a part of literary scholarship is evident from David Reynolds's mammoth study, *Beneath the American Renaissance* (New York: Knopf, 1988), which provides important information about works that have been omitted from literary study, but which tends to view those works as valuable primarily for their relevance to the canonized texts; see also Ruth Perry and Martine Watson Brownley, eds., *Mothering the Mind* (New York: Holmes & Meier, 1984). An excellent study that counteracts this tendency in American scholarship is Cathy N. Davidson, *Revolution and the Word: The Rise of the Novel in America* (New York: Oxford University Press, 1986).

5. Lillian S. Robinson was the first to use this phrase in her essay, "Canon Fathers and Myth Universe," *New Literary History* 19 (Autumn 1987): 23. She does not, however, use it to describe the way in which women's works have been looked at, not for themselves, but with respect to their usefulness to male writers.

6. See, for example, Barbara Herrnstein Smith, "Contingencies of Value," *Critical Inquiry* 10 (September 1983): 1–35; Paul Lauter, "Race and Gender in the Shaping of the American Literary Canon: A Case Study from the Twenties," *Feminist Studies* 9 (1983): 435–463; Stanley Fish, *Is There a Text in This Class?: The Authority of Interpretive Communities 1980* (Cambridge, Mass.: Harvard University

Press, 1982); Frank Kermode, *Forms of Attention* (Chicago: University of Chicago Press, 1985). Other works that have contributed significantly to the discussion of the American canon include Annette Kolodny, "The Integrity of Memory: Creating a New Literary History of the United States," *American Literature* 57 (May 1985): 291–307; and the articles that followed in the "Extra" column of *American Literature* between 1985 and December 1988, e.g., Sacvan Bercovitch, "America as Canon and Context: Literary History in a Time of Dissensus"; Lawrence Buell, "Literary History without Sexism? Feminist Studies and Canonical Reconception," *American Literature* 59 (March 1987): 102–114. See also Lawrence Lipking, "Aristotle's Sister: A Poetics of Abandonment," in *Canons,* ed. Robert von Hallberg (Chicago: University of Chicago Press, 1984), 85–105; John Schilb, "Canonical Theories and Noncanonical Literature: Steps Toward a Pedagogy," *Reader* (Spring 1986): 3–23; Susan Sage Heinzelman, "Hard Cases, Easy Cases and Weird Cases: Canon Formation in Law and Literature," *Mosaic* 21 (Spring 1988): 59–72; Kathleen Diffley, "Reconstructing the American Canon: E Pluribus Unum?" *Journal of the Midwest Modern Language Association* 21 (Fall 1988): 1–15.

7. Michel Foucault writes: "In every society the production of discourse is at once controlled, selected, organised and redistributed according to a certain number of procedures, whose role is to avert its powers and its dangers." See Michel Foucault, *The Archaeology of Knowledge,* trans. A. M. Sheridan Smith (New York: Pantheon Books, 1972), 219, 234.

8. Tompkins, *Sensational Designs,* 4.

9. Paul Lauter, *Canons and Contexts* (New York: Oxford University Press, 1991), 57.

10. For a discussion of individualism in American thought, see Joyce W. Warren, *The American Narcissus: Individualism and Women in Nineteenth-Century American Fiction* (New Brunswick, N.J.: Rutgers University Press, 1984).

11. John Taylor, *An Inquiry into the Principles of the Government of the United States* (Fredericksburg, Va.: Green and Kady, 1814), 414–415.

12. "The Course of Civilization," *United States Democratic Review* 6 (1839): 213–214.

13. Richard Chase, for example, in his book *The American Novel and Its Tradition* (Garden City, N.Y.: Doubleday, 1957), which has for years been regarded as a classic analysis of the American novel, discusses the work of eleven novelists, all of them male. He defines the dominant tradition in the American novel as one that has a freedom from "verisimilitude, development, and continuity; a tendency towards melodrama and idyl; a more or less formal abstractness and, on the other hand, a tendency to plunge into the underside of consciousness; a willingness to abandon moral questions or to ignore the spectacle of man in society" (ix). In order to formulate this definition, Chase had to ignore the American women novelists of the nineteenth century and to derive his definition from a limited sample of male writers. The work of the nineteenth-century American women writers, in fact, reflects the opposite of all of the aspects of his definition. For a detailed analysis of the way the dominant tradition in nineteenth-century American literature has focused on the male individualist, see Warren, *The American Narcissus.* See also Judith

Fetterley, *The Resisting Reader: A Feminist Approach to American Fiction* (Blooming-ton: Indiana University Press, 1978); and Nina Baym, "Melodramas of Beset Manhood: How Theories of American Fiction Exclude Women Authors," *American Quarterly* 33 (Summer 1981); 123–139.

14. Ralph Waldo Emerson, *Complete Works,* Centenary Edition, ed. Edward W. Emerson, 12 vols. (Boston: Houghton Mifflin, 1903–1904), 11:403–426.

15. Nineteenth-century works in which a male author succeeds in portraying the female character as central include Tolstoy's *Anna Karenina,* Flaubert's *Madame Bovary,* Hardy's *The Return of the Native,* Ibsen's *A Doll's House.* The single major example in American literature is Hawthorne's *The Scarlet Letter.*

16. For a discussion of the novel's comment on society's limitations on Eliza Wharton, see Cathy N. Davidson, Introduction to *The Coquette* by Mrs. Hannah W. Foster (New York: Oxford University Press, 1986). xviii–xx.

17. Caroline Kirkland, *A New Home—Who'll Follow?* (New York: C. S. Fran-cis, 1839), 109.

18. See Margaret Fuller, *At Home and Abroad* (originally published 1856), ed. Arthur B. Fuller (Boston: Roberts Brothers, 1874), 46; and Eliza W. Farnham, *Life in Prairie Land* (New York: Harper, 1846), 36–38.

19. See John Mack Faragher, *Women and Men on the Overland Trail* (New Haven: Yale University Press, 1979). For a valuable analysis of this phenomenon see An-nette Kolodny, *The Land before Her: Fantasy and Experience of the American Frontiers, 1630–1860* (Chapel Hill: University of North Carolina Press, 1984).

20. Margaret Fuller, *Woman in the Nineteenth Century, and Kindred Essays,* ed. Arthur B. Fuller (New York: Jewett, 1855), 174.

21. Mary Kelley, *Private Woman, Public Stage: Literary Domesticity in Nineteenth-Century America* (New York: Oxford University Press, 1984), describes the nineteenth-century women writers that she discusses as "literary domestics," but she is referring to their private/public stance and includes other figures, for example, Fanny Fern and E.D.E.N. Southworth, whose fiction is not centered in the home.

22. For an early discussion of this concept, see Annette Kolodny, "A Map for Rereading: Or, Gender and the Interpretation of Literary Texts," *New Literary History* 11 (Spring 1980): 451–467.

23. Susan Warner, *The Wide, Wide World,* ed. Jane Tompkins (New York: The Feminist Press, 1987), 12.

24. Maria Cummins, *The Lamplighter* (Boston: Houghton Mifflin, 1902, origi-nally published 1854), 81, 121, 137.

25. Ibid., 165.

26. The New Critics in the 1930s to 1950s (e.g., T. S. Eliot, Allen Tate, John Crowe Ransom) prized ambiguity and intellectual complexity in religious writing. Moreover, since they did not value historical criticism, the works were read out-side their historical context. For an excellent analysis of twentieth-century critics' exclusion of works whose religious earnestness does not fit their definition of religion, see Jerome J. McGann, "The Religious Poetry of Christina Rossetti," *Canons,* ed. Robert von Hallberg (Chicago: University of Chicago Press, 1984), 261–278.

27. See Joyce Carol Oates, "Pleasure, Duty, Redemption Then and Now: Susan Warner's *Diana*," *American Literature* 59 (October 1987): 422–427: "I don't feel superior to these puzzling heroines of a bygone world. I simply feel different."

28. Augusta Evans Wilson, *St. Elmo* (New York: Cooperative Publication Society, 1866), 465–466, 537.

29. Harriet Beecher Stowe, *Uncle Tom's Cabin* (New York: AMS Press, Inc., 1967), 2:207, 212.

30. James Baldwin, "Everybody's Protest Novel," *Partisan Review* 16 (1949): 578–585. For a discussion of the response in the twentieth century to Stowe's portrayal of Uncle Tom, see Moira Reynolds, *Uncle Tom's Cabin and Mid-Nineteenth-Century United States* (Jefferson, N.C.: McFarland & Co., 1985), 162–163; and Thomas F. Gossett, *Uncle Tom's Cabin and American Culture* (Dallas: Southern Methodist University Press, 1985), 388–408. See also *New Essays on Uncle Tom's Cabin*, ed. Eric J. Sundquist (Cambridge and London: Cambridge University Press, 1986).

31. This association is evident, for example, in Ann Douglas's *The Feminization of American Culture* (New York: Knopf, 1977). Although Douglas's work is valuable for its contribution to the study of nineteenth-century American women's writings, it reflects the same contempt that American society has felt for the "feminine."

32. Tompkins, *Sensational Designs*, 163–165.

33. See, for example, Charles Edward Stowe, *Life of Harriet Beecher Stowe* (Boston: Houghton, Mifflin, 1890), 156; and *Life and Letters of Harriet Beecher Stowe*, ed. Annie Fields (Boston: Houghton, Mifflin, 1897), 163–165.

34. Emerson, *Works*, 2:72–74.

35. Ralph Waldo Emerson, *Journals and Miscellaneous Notebooks*, ed. William H. Gilman et al., 16 vols. (Cambridge, Mass: Harvard University Press, 1960–1982), 10:170.

36. Foucault, *Archaeology of Knowledge*, 229.

37. For a discussion of this phenomenon, see Barbara Welter, "The Cult of True Womanhood," *American Quarterly* 18 (Summer 1966): 151–162, 173–174. Welter defines "true womanhood" in nineteenth-century society as "piety, purity, submissiveness and domesticity."

38. Elizabeth Stoddard, *The Morgesons*, ed. Lawrence Buell and Sandra A. Zagarell (Philadelphia: University of Pennsylvania Press, 1984), 221.

39. Caroline Chesebro', *Isa, A Pilgrimage* (Clinton Hall, N.Y.: Redfield, 1852), 171.

40. See, for example, the Schomburg Library of Nineteenth-Century Black Women Writers published by Oxford University Press, 1988; Harriet Jacobs, *Incidents in the Life of a Slave Girl*, ed. Jean Fagan Yellin (Cambridge, Mass.: Harvard University Press, 1986); and Harriet Wilson, *Our Nig*, ed. Henry Louis Gates, Jr. (New York: Random House, 1983).

41. For a discussion of some of the reasons for the novel's failure, see Henry Louis Gates, Jr., Introduction to *Our Nig* by Harriet Wilson.

42. Frances Smith Foster, Introduction to *Iola Leroy, or Shadows Uplifted*, by Frances E. W. Harper (New York: Oxford University Press, 1988), xxxiv–xxxvii.

43. Henry Louis Gates, Jr., "Foreword: In Her Own Write," The Schomburg Library of Nineteenth-Century Black Women Writers (New York: Oxford University Press, 1988), xxv.

44. Frances E. W. Harper, *Iola Leroy, or Shadows Uplifted,* ed. Frances Smith Foster (New York: Oxford University Press, 1988), 253. Subsequent references will be to this edition and will be cited in the text.

45. Fanny Fern, *Ruth Hall and Other Writings,* ed. Joyce W. Warren (New Brunswick, N.J.: Rutgers University Press, 1986).

46. E.D.E.N. Southworth, *The Hidden Hand* (New Brunswick, N.J.: Rutgers University Press, 1988).

47. Louisa May Alcott, *Behind a Mask, The Unknown Thrillers of Louisa May Alcott,* ed. Madeleine Stern (New York: Quill, 1984).

The Writers

❧ JANE TOMPKINS ❧

Susanna Rowson,
Father of the American Novel

THE POINT I HAVE TO MAKE in this essay is so simple and obvious that I have trouble believing it myself. It is that by any normal, reasonable standard, the title "father of the American novel" or, alternately, "first American man of letters," should have gone not to Charles Brockden Brown, who has always held it (Brown is referred to variously as "father of the American novel,"[1] "the first of our novelists,"[2] "our first professional author,"[3] "the first of our writers to make a profession of literature,"[4] "the first professional man of letters in America,"[5] "the first American to make authorship his sole career,"[6] "the first American writer to devote himself wholly to a literary career"[7]) but to a person named Susanna Rowson, who wrote at the same time Brown did, whose literary production far exceeded his, whose influence on American culture was incomparably greater, and whose name was misspelled in the MLA program the year I gave the paper from which this essay derives.

If you have never heard of Rowson, do not feel bad. She is not someone you were supposed to have studied for your Ph.D. orals; nor have people who write for *Critical Inquiry* and *Representations* been dropping her name lately. She wasn't the father of the American novel; I am going to talk about why.

One reason is that the terminology of literary history is made for describing men, not women. One has never heard the phrase "mother of the American novel" (or the British novel or the Russian novel). Novels do not have mothers; nor do literary traditions of any sort, at least none that I know of. There is no mother of the Renaissance pastoral, or of the German theater, or of the Portuguese epic. We speak of masterpieces and

29

masterworks and "Masters of Modern Drama." And whether or not sex is specified overtly, the general terms we use to refer to people in the field of literature always designate men, not women. Words like "author," "artist," "creator," "poet," and "genius" automatically evoke a male image, even though women are commonly known to have been authors, artists, creators, poets, and, albeit rarely, geniuses (women do not as a rule get. that accolade). It follows then that if, when we say "author," we mean a man, literary genealogies will be patrilineal. Especially so in a country that has a political father (George Washington) and a spiritual father (the male Christian god), but no political or spiritual mothers. Such a country *must* have a father, not a mother, for its literature as well. I say this in order to assert that the sex of our literary progenitor was scripted from the start. No matter what the facts were.

Now let us look at the facts. If, taking into account the number, variety, and influence of their words, you compare the careers of Susanna Rowson and Charles Brockden Brown, there is no escaping the conclusion that Rowson is the more important and substantial figure by a considerable margin. Although she is known chiefly as the author of *Charlotte Temple*, one of the all-time bestsellers in our literature and by far the most popular novel of its period, Susanna Rowson published seven other novels, two sets of fictional sketches, seven theatrical works, two collections of poetry, six pedagogical works, many occasional pieces and song lyrics, and contributed to two periodicals. Her writing career spanned the thirty-six years betwen 1786 and 1822. Of the works she produced besides *Charlotte Temple*, several were very popular in her own day: the sequel to *Charlotte Temple, Charlotte's Daughter*, was published in over thirty editions; *The Fille de Chambre*, another of her novels, sold extremely well, as did *Reuben and Rachel; Trials of the Human Heart*, a four-volume novel, had a large number of socially prominent subscribers; *Slaves in Algiers* was popular as a theatrical stock piece; and the song "America, Commerce, and Freedom" was still recognized as popular in the 1820s.

On the other hand, with the exception of a few essays published in 1789, Charles Brockden Brown's literary production is confined to a three-year period, 1798 to 1801, during which he published a dialogue on the rights of women, and six novels. From then on he devoted himself to editing a magazine and wrote four political pamphlets. Whether or not we count the nonliterary productions of these authors, the contrast in their output is remarkable. Its nature can be gauged by some comments Evert and George Duyckinck make in their account of Brown in the *Cyclopedia of American Literature*.[8] The Duyckincks convey, with obvious relish, the image of a man, passionate, intense, introverted, and plagued by ill health

(Brown died of consumption). As part of this picture they mention several unpublished or uncompleted works he had embarked on at various times in his life: sketches for three epic poems on the model of Virgil and Homer, a geography (geography, they say, was Brown's great love), and a history of Rome under the Antonines. Brown had also written two acts of a tragedy, according to *The Cambridge History of American Literature,* but, told that the play wouldn't act, he burned the manuscript and kept the ashes in a snuffbox.⁹ When you turn to the entry for Susanna Rowson in the Duyckincks' encyclopedia, you find that she actually published translations of Virgil and Horace and wrote two geography textbooks, one history textbook, and seven works for the theater, all of which were performed and one of which became part of the period's standard repertory.¹⁰ The contrast here between the doer and the dreamer, money in the bank and ashes in the snuffbox, the published and the unpublished, the read and the unread only adds to the overall contrast between a woman who worked hard at writing over a period of more than three decades, stuck to her work through thick and thin, and exerted an extraordinary influence over the public imagination through one bestseller and several other very popular works, and a man who, in a burst of creativity, wrote six novels in a very short period, grew discouraged, and then turned his mind to other tasks. The question then is, if Rowson outproduces Brown, and outsells him, and has a much greater impact on American society, why don't we have a mother of the American novel instead of a father?

There are several ways of answering this question, one of which I touched on earlier, having to do with sexual attitudes. I will return to that in a moment, but first let me take up some more conservative suggestions for why Rowson didn't get the job. The first two reasons are technical. One is that although Rowson did write a great deal of imaginative literature, she did not devote herself solely to a literary career, and that is why the title went to Charles Brockden Brown. (Rowson began work as a governess to support herself and her parents, married, went on the stage with her husband, whose business had failed, and eventually founded a school for young ladies. She wrote throughout her adult life as a way of supplementing her income.) This would be a powerful argument were it not for the fact that Charles Brockden Brown started out studying for the law, edited a magazine, wrote his novels, went back to editing, and then from 1801 to 1806 became an active partner with his brothers in the mercantile firm of James Brown and Company; when the firm dissolved, he "continued until his death to conduct a small retail business alone, selling pots and pans by day and editorializing by night."¹¹ In view of these facts, it would be quite easy to argue, if one wanted to (although I do not), that Rowson had never actually engaged in business but had followed exclusively professional callings—teaching, acting, and writing—and that therefore hers was the better claim.

The second technical difficulty is that Rowson was not born in the United States. But this objection is, precisely, technical. Rowson is considered an American author by all of the literary historians who write about her; her Americanness, as far as I know, has never been in dispute. It becomes an issue only if you want to deny her importance on other grounds.

There are other grounds. Someone will say, why not cut through all this patriarchal-attitudes-and-cultural-influence stuff and admit what everybody knows: that *Charlotte Temple* is a sentimental tear-jerker, that Brown's first four novels are fascinating works of fiction, the beginning of an important tradition in American writing (in the nineteenth-century, Poe and Hawthorne, in the twentieth, Faulkner), and that all this talk about numbers of works written and length of career is just substituting quantity for quality. Brown was a truly interesting writer and Rowson was not and that is why he is the father of the American novel.

Why not admit all this? Because it isn't true. *Charlotte Temple* was interesting to tens, perhaps hundreds, of thousands of people for an extraordinarily long period of time. Between 1794 and 1860 it went through 160 *known* editions. It exercised such power over the minds of its readers that in 1905, more than a hundred years after its publication, people were still visiting the heroine's supposed tomb in Trinity churchyard in New York. On the other hand, if you count three French translations, Charles Brockden Brown's most successful novel, *Wieland,* went through thirteen editions before 1860. Yet the number of articles and reviews written on Brown in this period is greater than the number written on Rowson by a factor of almost thirteen to one. To say that *Charlotte Temple* is not interesting and that *Wieland* is is simply not to *count* the interest shown by a certain sector of the population. It is to define "interest" as that which attracts only a small group of literati. Moreover, to say that the value or quality of a work has nothing to do with considerations such as commercial success or the lack of it, or the size and character of its readership, is simply to ignore the data of literary history.

Facts about popularity, number of editions, and the inverse ratio of critical interest in a book to the book's popular success are not extrinsic to questions of literary merit, they are constitutive of it. They determine the way a text is identified, labeled, and transmitted to future generations; they determine whether an author will be seen as a literary ancestor or not. In the next few paragraphs I want to sketch in what I see as the determinants of the critical, as opposed to popular, success, in the cases of Susanna

Rowson and Charles Brockden Brown. I want to suggest that the answer to the question why, given her superior productivity and influence, Rowson did not become the first professional author in America, is that given the class structure, given the gender system, given the economic hierarchy, given the relationship of literature to all of these, and given a complex set of interrelated cultural attitudes, for the author of *Charlotte Temple* to have become an important literary figure was not simply an impossibility, it was literally unimaginable. "Why wasn't Susanna Rowson the mother of the American novel?" is a stupid question. Not because *Charlotte Temple* is a trashy book, but because, given the nature of American culture since the late eighteenth century, it could never have been seen as anything else by the people whose opinions counted.

These are the people who write literary histories, and in their portraits of Brown and Rowson you can see the entrenched habits of thought and standards of evaluation that produced the story of early American fiction we have now. The portrait of Brown that emerges from these histories reflects what we might call the "ashes-in-the-snuffbox" view of him that makes Brown out to be a sort of brilliant romantic failure. "Few have failed of 'greatness' by so narrow a margin," says the *Literary History of the United States,*[12] summing up a chorus of similar pronouncements made before and since. Although as editor first of *The Literary Magazine and American Register* and then of *The American Register, or General Repository of History, Politics, and Science,* he wrote quite a bit of literary criticism, lengthy historical surveys, and reports on recently published books at home and abroad, these solid accomplishments tend to be glossed over by the people who created the role of first professional man-of-letters. They like their Brown pale and distraught, the victim of "tortured nerves" and author of unfinished or unpublished works. They admire him for his passionate though brief dedication to imaginative literature at a time when no one else (allegedly) was writing fiction, and they like to picture him struggling to reach a disapproving, puritanical public. But Brown's commercial failure only adds luster to his reputation. The Duyckincks say, "We are not aware that the author ever derived any pecuniary advantage" from the novels, and William Peterfield Trent observes that despite their legendary status "new editions were not called for."[13] While it is true that in Brown's lifetime there were no new editions, by the time Trent wrote there had been almost a score.[14] His ignoring this is evidence of the general rule that commercial failure *is* success where literary distinction is concerned, for the subtext of such remarks is that only the discriminating few were able to appreciate Brown's peculiar genius. The fact that this genius was also failed, in the opinion of the critics, only enhances his attractiveness as a literary forebear. Here is a representative statement of the "flawed genius" position: "His novels are all structurally weak. The best of them, it must be admitted, are among the most seriously flawed."[15] But "overriding the major flaws are strong virtues which clearly reveal the undeniable genius of the author."[16] What is notable about these pronouncements is how clearly they show that Brown's "genius" exists not so much in spite of as because of its flaws. Accompanying this irresistible cliché is always an intimation that the present critic alone understands the special character of Brown's art. "Brown has been underestimated: he had powers that approached genius. . . . He had a creative imagination. . . . He had, more than this, the power to project his reader into the inner life of his characters; . . . he had poetic vision."[17] Literary portraits of Brown reflect an image of the artist as a tragic, sensitive, misunderstood "failure" so predictably and so often that one cannot help wondering why literary critics and their audiences needed this image so badly. Whatever other functions it serves, however, it clearly separates the sheep from the goats where taste and sensibility are concerned. Those who appreciate Brown appreciate passion, intellect, and genius; they look beyond the superficial faults that mislead others; they see the tortured nerves, the inner life, the poetic vision. And they are few and far between. The way this kind of portrait creates a special group of highly perceptive readers, a chosen few who alone understand genius, provides a clue as to why the author of *Charlotte Temple* could never have been taken seriously by the literary establishment.

If Charles Brockden Brown won critical success through commercial and artistic failure, Susanna Rowson, whose popular fame as a novelist was unequaled until Stowe wrote *Uncle Tom's Cabin,* won critical failure through popular success. Yet even to speak of her as a critical failure is to exaggerate her importance, because it implies that she had been at some point a *candidate* for critical success. It is quite clear that this was never the case. Although *Charlotte Temple* had gone through most of its 160 editions before the Duyckincks wrote, they were so little impressed with Rowson's fame that they didn't even bother to write an original entry for her in their *Cyclopedia* but reprinted an obituary from the *Boston Gazette* which they had found in the appendix to something called Moore's Historical Collections for 1824. In 1824, the year of Rowson's death, and over thirty years before the Duyckincks wrote, it appears that *Charlotte Temple*'s enormous sales garnered it small respect; the author of the obituary refers to it dismissively as "a popular little romance."[18] The ensuing description is worth attending to, because it expresses what became the general attitude toward this novel among literary people from that time forward.

Of the latter [*Charlotte Temple*] twenty-five thousand copies were sold in a few years. It is a tale of seduction, the story of a young girl brought over to America by a British officer and deserted, and being written in a melodramatic style has drawn tears from the public freely as any similar production on the stage. It is still a popular classic at the cheap book-stall and with travelling chapmen.[19]

This description, which seems neutral enough, combines all the ways in which *Charlotte Temple* has been devalued in American criticism. The apparently factual account, delivered offhand and deadpan, places the novel automatically beyond the pale of literature and writes it off without even trying. First of all, the novel's cheapness and general availability set it at a discount. Because it cost practically nothing, it is worth practically nothing, the equation of monetary value with literary value being unstated but assumed. Second, it is read by the wrong class of people—those who buy at cheap bookstalls and from traveling chapmen; hence, it is associated with readers who are at the bottom of the socioeconomic ladder, low social status and lack of literary taste being tacitly equated. (The tacit nature of these assumptions testifies to their strength; it is because they don't have to be argued that they can remain undeclared.) Third, its contents aren't nice. It is "a tale of seduction," and the moral degradation of the heroine lines up with the cheapness of the price and the socially undesirable character of the readers to reinforce an image of debased value, of something that has been cheapened by being made too accessible, too common. More than a hint of prostitution hangs about descriptions of this book—its easy availability becomes conflated with the heroine's easy virtue, the social status of its readers with the social status of unwed mothers, the low price with low behavior, so that the subject matter of the book and the object itself seem to merge and the book becomes a female thing that is passed from hand to hand for the purpose of illicit arousal.[20] Thus, the negative aesthetic judgment that arrives at the end is inevitable: inevitable and integrally related to the attitudes toward sex, social class, and economic status that subtend the preceding description. The terms of the judgment—tears and melodrama—are identifiable as an inferior, feminine form of response to literature, one that is implicitly contrasted to a superior male rationality and implicitly linked to the poorly controlled instincts of a proletarian readership. There is even a tiny hint of politically subversive behavior in the reference to the unruly feelings the novel provokes "freely as any similar production on the stage." The novel, in a word, is vulgar: loved by the *vulgus,* the crowd, and therefore bad.

The female-male, vulgar-genteel opposition established by the contrast between Rowson and Brown, as literary history has constituted them, perfectly illustrates Pierre Bourdieu's notion that art works function to define and maintain hierarchical social distinctions within a culture. Indeed, the oxymoronic term "popular classic" that the *Boston Gazette* uses to describe *Charlotte Temple* flags the work as something valued by the lower classes and therefore automatically excluded from consideration as a real classic. One might almost say that in order for Brown to be seen as the founder of our novelistic tradition, there had to be a Rowson to define his exclusiveness and distinction by contrast to her commonness, in both senses of the term. In fact William Peterfield Trent, in concluding his discussion of Rowson and the other "amiable ladies" who were her contemporaries, says, "Thus early did the American novel acquire the permanent background of neutral domestic fiction against which the notable figures stand out in contrast."[21] The "father of the American novel"— tragic, conflicted, failed, unappreciated except by a few—depends for his profile and his status upon his opposite number, the popular female novelist loved by the unwashed millions, whose vulgarity and debasement ratify and enable his preeminence.

The places assigned to discussions of Brown and Rowson in the literary histories tend to support this claim. These authors are assigned to separate spheres not only in the literary hierarchy but also in the volumes that "record" it; so complete is their segregation that although they were published at exactly the same time and shared at least one common element— seduction—they are never mentioned in the same paragraph, much less the same breath. This separation, which now we take for granted, goes with ways of thinking about gender, social class, and political and economic structures, all of which are inseparable from the way we think about literature. There is nothing natural or inevitable about any of these ways of thinking, but they are so ingrained and so intertwined that statements that challenge their authority—such as that Susanna Rowson should by rights be known as America's first professional author—seem not only counterintuitive, but absurd.

What is the upshot of all this? It is that, as members of the academy, we have for too long been the purveyors of a literary tradition to whose social and ideological bases we no longer subscribe. It means that when we teach early American fiction, it is time we stopped behaving as if Charles Brockden Brown were the only pebble on the beach. As Cathy Davidson demonstrates, the late eighteenth century produced an extremely varied and interesting array of novelists, many of them women, whose works performed a crucial role in shaping American culture.[22] The present genealogy of American novelists, which begins with Brown and proceeds to

Cooper, Irving, Hawthorne, Melville, Twain, James, and on down the line, must be revised, because it rests on a set of values that are not worth giving our lives for.

NOTES

This essay is based on a talk originally delivered at the Modern Language Association in December 1985.

1. Harry R. Warfel, *Charles Brockden Brown: American Gothic Novelist* (Gainesville: University of Florida Press, 1949), ix.

2. Evert A. Duyckinck and George L. Duyckinck, eds., *Cyclopedia of American Literature: Embracing Personal and Critical Notices of Authors and Selections from Their Writings from the Earliest Period to the Present Day* (New York: Charles Scribner, 1855), 1:586.

3. F. O. Matthiessen, *American Renaissance: Art and Expression in the Age of Emerson and Whitman* (London: Oxford University Press, 1941), 202.

4. Robert E. Spiller, Willard Thorp, Thomas H. Johnson, Henry Seidel Canby, eds., *Literary History of the United States* (New York: Macmillan, 1948), 1:181.

5. Fred Lewis Pattee, ed., *Century Readings for a Course in American Literature,* 3rd ed. (New York: Century, 1926), 168.

6. William Peterfield Trent, John Erskine, Stuart P. Sherman, Carl Van Doren, eds., *The Cambridge History of American Literature* (New York: G. P. Putnam's Sons, 1917), 1:287.

7. Darrel Abel, ed., *American Literature* (Great Neck, N.Y.: Barron's Educational Series, 1963), 1:294.

8. Duyckinck, *Cyclopedia,* 586–591.

9. Trent, et al. *Cambridge History,* 292.

10. Duyckinck, *Cyclopedia,* 502–504.

11. David Lee Clark, *Charles Brockden Brown: Pioneer Voice of America* (Durham, N.C.: Duke University Press, 1952), 216.

12. Spiller et al., *Literary History,* 181.

13. Duyckinck, *Cyclopedia,* 590; Trent, *Cambridge History,* 292.

14. Sydney J. Krause and Jane Nieset, "A Census of the Works of Charles Brockden Brown," *The Serif. Kent State University Library Quarterly* 3 (December 1966): 27–55.

15. Donald A. Ringe, *Charles Brockden Brown,* Twayne's United States Author Series, ed. Sylvia E. Bowman, no. 98 (New York: Twayne, 1966), 138.

16. Ibid., 140.

17. Charles Brockden Brown, *Wieland,* ed. Fred Lewis Pattee (New York, 1926), Introduction, xiv; quoted in Clark, *Charles Brockden Brown,* 316.

18. Duyckinck, *Cyclopedia,* 502.

19. Ibid.

20. See Susanna Haswell Rowson, *Charlotte Temple: A Tale of Truth,* ed. Francis W. Halsey (New York: Funk & Wagnalls, 1905), Introduction, xxxv–xxxvi.

21. Trent et al., *Cambridge History,* 285.

22. Cathy N. Davidson, ed., *Reading in America: Literature and Social History* (Baltimore: The Johns Hopkins University Press, 1989). Since this essay was written, Cathy Davidson's *Revolution and the Word* (New York: Oxford University Press, 1986) has reconstituted American literary history of the Revolutionary and post-Revolutionary period, giving Susanna Rowson and her contemporaries their proper place in the record.

✤ CAROL J. SINGLEY ✤

Catharine Maria Sedgwick's
Hope Leslie:
Radical Frontier Romance

HOPE LESLIE (1827), A HISTORICAL ROMANCE set in the early Colonial period, was Catharine Maria Sedgwick's third and most successful novel. It centers on the adventures of a spirited, independent young woman who resists traditional Puritan conventions yet ends in the most typical of ways, married to the young hero, Everell Fletcher. Like many American novels of its time, *Hope Leslie* has a convoluted, somewhat contrived plot, with many doubling structures, cliffhanging chapter endings, and narratorial intrusions. The novel primarily focuses on three issues: Hope's friendship with and eventual marriage to her foster brother, Everell; a rigid Puritan system intent on order and the suppression of women and American Indians; and the complex relationship of settlers, land, and American Indian culture, represented chiefly through Magawisca, the young Pequod woman who risks her life to save Everell's and who forms an indissoluble bond of friendship with Hope.

As historical romance, *Hope Leslie* combines historical fact, marriage plot, and frontier myth. Several events in the novel—the Pequod attack on the Fletcher family, Magawisca's rescue of Everell, Sir Philip Gardiner's Tory sympathizing and villainy—are documented facts culled from Sedgwick's reading.[1] The novel is primarily fiction, however, intended, as Sedgwick says in her preface, to "illustrate not the history, but the character of the times" (*HL,* 5). From the very beginning, *Hope Leslie* has been compared with the frontier romances of James Fenimore Cooper.[2] Sedgwick's contemporary Sarah Hale commented that no other American novel "except, perhaps, the early work of Cooper, ever met with such success." One reviewer found Sedgwick's "pictures of savage life more truthful than that of Cooper."[3] Another lamented that both she and Cooper "had fallen into the error" of "hav[ing] anything to do with Indians" (*HL*, x). Transcendentalist Margaret Fuller accorded Cooper measured praise and then complimented Sedgwick—the only American woman novelist she ever cited by name—for writing "with skill and feeling, scenes and personages from the revolutionary time." Sedgwick's fiction, Fuller wrote, "has permanent value."[4]

By the end of the nineteenth century, the historical romance, once thought to be *the* American literary form, had given way to the more imaginative, abstract romances of Cooper, Hawthorne, Melville, and other male writers—"melodramas of beset manhood," as Nina Baym has called them.[5] Men's narratives assumed the status of the universal while domestic novels became associated with the particularized, narrow interests of "scribbling women." Extraordinarily popular in her time, Sedgwick was practically unread in the twentieth century, excluded from anthologies that canonize Cooper and form the literary myths of Adam in the New World. In representative comments, Alexander Cowie notes that Sedgwick "modestly" and wisely did not try to compete with Cooper; Van Wyck Brooks writes that "no one could have supposed that her work would live."[6]

But live it has. Reprinted and accessible to a new generation of readers, *Hope Leslie* stands ready to take its place in the American literary tradition. I argue here that Sedgwick deserves as prominent a place in an American canon as Cooper, not only for the comparable literary value of her fiction—after all, the same "threadbare formulas" and assortment of escapes, rescues, and pursuits that Robert Spiller cites in Cooper's fiction are no less egregious in Sedgwick's novel, and, as Edward Foster points out, Sedgwick's prose is often cleaner and clearer in expression than Cooper's[7]—but for her alternative vision of the American woman, American culture, and the relationship to nature. While following romantic conventions, Sedgwick, in fact, undercuts many of the assumptions upon which romance is organized. Also, while apparently obeying the moral and literary dicta that literature teach by adhering to the facts of history, and by depicting authentic characters and events—Governor and Margaret Winthrop, the Reverend John Eliot, the Pequod chief Mononotto, for example—Sedgwick revises literary history, exposing injustice to women, American Indians, and the land. Finally, while Cooper's fiction is abstract, indulging the masculine fantasy of escape into some past golden age or into timelessness,[8] Sedgwick engages both the social and natural realms, suggesting a transcendental ideal achievable in society as well as nature.

Critics of American literature have persistently favored a mythology that David Levin describes as "a movement from the 'artificial' toward the 'natural.' "[9] This practice celebrates the individual white man—whether he be Natty Bumppo, Ishmael, Thoreau, or Huck Finn—either alone or in union with a same-sexed other.[10] For example, writing about Cooper's second Leatherstocking novel, *The Last of the Mohicans,* in which the hero supposedly "matures," D. H. Lawrence is exuberant: "In his immortal friendship of Chingachgook and Natty Bumppo, Cooper dreamed the nucleus of a new society. . . . A stark stripped human relationship of two men, deeper than the deeps of sex. Deeper than property, deeper than fatherhood, deeper than marriage, deeper than Love." With its "wish-fulfillment vision"[11] and yearning for escape, the male-defined mainstream American romance is constructed around impossibility. Sedgwick shows the resulting damage: nature and the very fabric of society are jeopardized. Order turns to confusion: America's promise is unfulfilled.

Because Sedgwick utilizes the conservative form of the romance—the so-called woman's novel—readers have by and large seen her fiction as reinforcing the conventional nineteenth-century notions that woman's fulfillment is found in the domestic and as validating the notion of the progress of history.[12] Only recently has attention been given to the deeply critical qualities of Sedgwick's novel. Sandra Zagarell, for example, reads Sedgwick's treatment of women and American Indians as two sides of the same repressive Puritan coin, noting not only Sedgwick's domesticity but her concern "with the foundations and organization of public life."[13] Contrary to critical consensus, *Hope Leslie* is not "an extraordinary conventional novel."[14] Nor is its comic marriage plot, as Northrop Frye explains, one "that brings hero and heroine together [and] causes a new society to crystallize around the hero."[15] Despite the conservative requirements of its genre, *Hope Leslie* exhibits signs of its own unraveling, as if to suggest the unworkability of romantic conventions. The novel replicates the chaos and contradiction inherent in the Puritan conception of its "errand in the wilderness," addressing problems that fall outside the accepted sphere of historical romance. It also posits a heroine who resists what Leslie Rabine calls the "totalizing structure" of romantic narrative and who struggles, valiantly and sometimes successfully, to sustain herself as an autonomous subject rather than become absorbed by the male quest for identity and mythic unity.[16]

On some levels, Catharine Maria Sedgwick and James Fenimore Cooper have much in common. Both choose fictional contexts to express concern over the rapid, careless encroachment of civilization on the wilderness and the extinction of the American Indians. And both depart from their privileged, Federalist backgrounds to advocate egalitarian notions of democracy. Important differences emerge, however, when comparing

Hope Leslie with a Leatherstocking novel published during the same period, when the Jackson Indian Removal Policy had effectively cleared the
eastern United States of American Indian presence. *The Last of the Mohicans* (1826), set in 1740 and depicting the French and Indian War, is only
tangentially Colonial. In contrast, *Hope Leslie* focuses specifically on a
nine-year Colonial period from 1636 to 1645, exploring, as Mary Kelley
notes in her introduction, "the roots of American moral character" (*HL,*
xiii). Cooper's characters seldom leave the forest or evince concern with
the political, economic, or social aspects of the law. Sedgwick's characters
directly confront Puritan social, religious, and legal systems, finding in
them the basis for discord and injustice. In Cooper's novels, the American
hero can thrive only outside the constraints of civilization. Sedgwick addresses questions of both culture *and* nature, criticizing the "Law" of the
Founding Fathers, which, by enforcing policies of actual repression, fosters patterns of imaginative escape.[17]

Hope's adventurous and generous nature contrasts with Puritan control
and self-absorpotion. Her many "doubles" in the novel—Faith, Magawisca, Esther, and Rosa—both challenge dichotomous views of womanhood and warn that the American psyche is so dangerously fragmented
that fusion of the individual, nature, and society is impossible.

The seeds of Sedgwick's discontent are evident in her biography as well
as publication history. Voicing disagreement with male authority, she
wrote to her brother Robert in 1814, "The country is condemned to the
ministration of inferior men."[18] In 1821, she left the more austere Calvinist
church to become a Unitarian. Her first novel, *A New England Tale* (1822),
is a blatant attack on Puritan hypocrisy: after a venture into a novel of
manners with *Redwood* (1824), she returned to a critique of Puritanism with
Hope Leslie, this time linking her era's concerns about American expansion
to the original project of the Puritan founders. Feeding the nation's appetite
for historical fiction, *Hope Leslie* became an instant success. But it is by no
means a book of reconciliation or progress. Below its seemingly accepting
surface are deep fissures that throw into question not only the American
project in the new land but also the romance literature that since Richard
Chase has been synonymous with the American project.

The novel opens in England with the thwarted romance of Alice,
Hope's mother, and William Fletcher, Hope's eventual guardian. Alice's
father prevents her from eloping to the New World with the liberal-
thinking Fletcher and pressures her to marry Charles Leslie instead. When
Leslie dies, Alice sets sail for the New World. She herself dies, leaving her
two daughters to the guardianship of her former lover, William Fletcher,
who has since married a "meek" and "godly maiden and dutiful helpmate"
(*HL,* 14), followed John Winthrop and John Eliot to America, and settled

on the western frontier near Springfield, Massachusetts. When Fletcher meets the two orphaned girls in Boston, he renames them Hope and Faith and sends Faith on ahead to Springfield. Pequods attack the Fletcher homestead, killing Mrs. Fletcher and her infant son. Faith and the Fletchers' older son, Everell, are captured, and two Indian children, Magawisca and Oneco, captives from a previous battle, are reunited with their tribe. Hope and William Fletcher, some distance away, are spared. The Pequod chief, Mononotto, intends to kill Everell, but Magawisca heroically saves his life and effects his escape; Faith, however, remains a captive, eventually converting to Catholicism and marrying Oneco.

As their names suggest, religious "Faith" of the Puritans is lost to the Indians, while the more secular "Hope" remains to confront the Puritan intolerance and repression spearheaded by Governor Winthrop and his docile, subservient wife. And although the younger William Fletcher embodies a more liberal Puritanism than his stern elders, he is by name indistinguishable from the authoritarian uncle he has left in England. With this naming, Sedgwick suggests that Old World repression is simply transferred to the New World, at least so far as American Indians and women are concerned. Themes of imprisonment, captivity, and family disruption, rather than the comic restoration of social order associated with romance, pervade the novel. And despite epigraphs from *A Midsummer Night's Dream* and *As You Like It,* there will be no return to a green world at the end of the story, as there is in Shakespearean romantic comedy. Society is not rejuvenated.

Sedgwick resumes the narrative nine years later after the Pequod attack and escape sequence. Everell is being educated in England; writing to him, Hope describes her own "education" in nature as well as an incident in which an Indian woman, Nelema, saves her tutor's life by curing a snakebite. The Boston authorities respond to news of Nelema's kindness by imprisoning her for witchcraft and removing Hope from Fletcher's custody so that she can profit from the more ordered training at the Winthrop residence. Here Hope shares a room with Winthrop's niece, Esther Downing, who is in love with Everell. Undaunted by Puritan restrictions, Hope manages to free not only Nelema but also Magawisca, who has been imprisoned as a result of a scheme by Sir Philip Gardiner to overthrow the Puritan government. The plot then follows a comedy-of-manners formula, with Hope escaping the seductions of Gardiner and his hired sailors and finally marrying Everell after predictable mistaken identities and confused affections. At the end of the novel, Esther returns to England and Magawisca to the forest.

Although Sedgwick bases the major elements of her narrative on documented history, it is her departure from rather than her adherence to facts that is so intriguing. Set in "an age of undisputed masculine supremacy" (*HL*, 16), Sedgwick's novel attempts an alternative history from a woman's perspective—a perspective also sympathetic to the plight of American Indians, who suffer a parallel oppression. This woman's history, which as Rabine tells us takes place outside "dominant frameworks," is deeply critical and seeks "to subvert romantic ideology."[19] For example, while the Springfield settlement is historically accurate, Sedgwick dramatizes with particular sensitivity the vulnerability of Margaret Fletcher and the children as they sit helpless and ignorant on their porch while the Pequods stealthily plan their attack. Women, the scene demonstrates, are powerless pawns in male battles. Whereas in the annals of history Philip Gardiner's mistress lives on to marry, Sedgwick has her die in a fiery explosion, graphically depicting society's intolerance of the sexually experienced, unmarried women. And while no exact historical figure exists for Esther, Sedgwick invents her as the submissive, dull counterpart to Hope, a model of passivity that only a patriarchal ideology like Winthrop's could endorse.

Sedgwick's rewriting of the Indian attack is most telling. The attack on the Fletcher homestead is preceded by Magawisca's narrative, in which it is clear that the Puritans—not the Indians—precipitated the violence by first attacking the sleeping, unsuspecting Pequod village. During this brutal raid, the Indian children Magawisca and Oneco are captured and their mother and brother killed. The structural symmetry of the two battles— in each a mother and son are killed and two children are taken captive— renders the acts of male violence morally indistinguishable and underlines the falseness of assigning blame to the Indians. The one inescapable difference, however, is that in the end the Puritans will prevail and the Indian tribes will be eradicated. Reinforcing this imbalance of power, Sedgwick depicts Magawisca raising and losing her arm to protect Everell from her father's axe, and noting later in the novel that the Indians cannot "grasp in friendship the hand raised to strike us" (*HL*, 292).

The parallel massacres by the Puritans and the Pequods—the first a "ghost chapter" in the novel—haunt the narrative, undermining dreams of harmony and unity that sent the Puritans to America. Kelley writes that the romance "is interwoven with the narrative of Indian displacement" (*HL*, xxi). In fact, the massacre threatens to displace the romance altogether, just as role inversions in the novel subvert the gender system in which the male provides and protects, and the female submits and obeys. The Indian attacks set into motion an alternative narrative of redemption, not through Calvinist devotion to doctrine, but through the wits and magnanimity of the female characters. Hope and Magawisca, more generous in spirit than their male counterparts, attempt to undo the wrongs of their male leaders, fundamentally challenging the precepts upon which the Puritan, male world is constructed. They do not offer a Cooperian escape or romantic/comic affirmation.

Like Natty Bumppo in *The Leatherstocking Tales,* Hope takes "counsel from her own heart" (*HL,* xxiv), but her independence is astonishing given nineteenth-century conventions governing female behavior. Hope's power extends beyond the domestic, or female, sphere. She exemplifies the selflessness associated with nineteenth-century femininity, but she also acts in a traditionally masculine, bold way to advance her own as well as others' interests. As Bell remarks, Hope "seems to specialize in freeing Indians":[20] she not only helps individuals escape unjust imprisonment, she also pursues a larger project of social justice. An "unfettered soul," Hope does not hesitate to commit "a plain transgression of a holy law" (*HL,* 280, 311) to further these goals.

If Hope stands for the white woman's resourcefulness and defiance of male law, Magawisca represents the integrity of the American Indian woman. But unlike Natty Bumppo's noble savages, who slay in order to achieve peace, Magawisca resists violence, whatever the personal risk. Foster and Bell speculate on Sedgwick's use of history for Magawisca's amputation, with Bell suggesting a source in the Captain John Smith–Pocahontas story.[21] But Sedgwick tells us in her preface that with respect to Magawisca, "we are confined not to the actual, but the possible" (6). Magawisca, her Indian double Nelema, and her white double Hope Leslie—all of whom save lives even when it means their own captivity—are Sedgwick's "hope" for a revised American history and new literary mythology. The magnitude of their heroism is Sedgwick's version of what Levin calls the movement from the "artificial" to the "natural." In Sedgwick's view, society must move away from the "artificial" imposition of violence and oppression and toward the "natural" coexistence of peace and mutuality.

Despite Hope's rebellions, the novel ends in the heroine's marriage to the young Puritan Everell Fletcher, seemingly validating Rabine's observation that women's protests and assertions occurring in the middle of romances are often negated by their endings. Marriage is an outcome Cooper assiduously avoids for his own heroes, but a more realistic Sedgwick reminds the reader that no matter how independent the heroine, marriage is not easily renegotiated.

Family is the mainstay of the woman's romance as well as the "familiar" domain appropriated by American male writers to provide contrast with the fears and unknowns of the American wilderness. And the family, Gossett and Bardes assert in their study of *Hope Leslie,* is the central "building block of the democratic republic."[22] Although Sedgwick's reputation rests on her domestic writing, and Kelley describes her as "a divinely appointed reformer within the confines of domesticity,"[23] in *Hope Leslie* no home is glorified. The Fletcher homestead is exposed and vulnerable, the Winthrop home is repressive, and Digby's parlor is the setting for mistaken identities and mismatched lovers. Families are repeatedly torn apart in this novel; women and children, rather than receiving men's protection, fall victim to their battles. Home, then, is not a comforting haven, with "good living under almost every roof," as de Crèvecoeur would have it,[24] but a precarious site of danger.

Ann Snitow notes that the "one socially acceptable moment of transcendence [for women] is romance,"[25] that is, conventional love between men and women leading to marriage. As her name implies, Hope Leslie is "hopelessly" committed to this bourgeois romantic ending. Yet Hope is also an individual—a "pathfinder" in her own right, to use Cooper's term, and through her, Sedgwick goes further than most previous American writers in exposing Puritan hypocrisy and affirming the value of American Indian and female culture. Hope breaks the boundaries of normal expectation for young women as she treks through nature, befriends Indians, frees political prisoners, and eludes drunken sailors. Her most inspiring and affecting experience is not marrying Everell but climbing a mountain with her tutor to survey an expanse of undeveloped land. "Gaz-[ing] on the beautiful summits of this mountain," Hope writes in a letter to Everell, who is receiving his education in England, not in nature, "I had an irrepressible desire to go to them" (*HL*, 99). Hope resists romantic seduction, political captivity, and traditional domesticity throughout the novel; she will not become a Mrs. Winthrop, who "like a horse easy on the bit . . . was guided by the slightest intimation from him who held the rein" (*HL*, 145).

Forever the adventurous youth, never the adult, Hope not only challenges conventional notions of what it means for a woman to grow up, she resists Puritan mandates to be "hardened for the cross-accidents and unkind events . . . the wholesome chastisements of life" (*HL*, 160). Hope, in fact, achieves a fantasy of indulgence *and* sacrifice, of selfishness *and* doing for others, proving as she moves undaunted through one escapade after another that, contrary to Calvinist doctrine, good deeds on earth *can* bring joy. Emerging from virtually every situation unscathed, Hope subverts Puritan ethics and behavior; and although she marries Everell at the end of the novel, the major events in her life revolve not around romance but around nature and the sense of fair play.

Neither is Everell Fletcher romantic or heroic in the traditional sense. Well-meaning but weak, he is an example of the dilution of the bloodline that so worried the Founding Fathers, a parallel to that most famous of feeble Puritan sons, Arthur Dimmesdale. Everell has more tolerance than his stern male forebears, but he lacks the vision and ability to put thought into action. His capture during the Pequod raid of the Fletcher farm inverts the traditional female captivity narrative: a white man, he must be saved by an Indian woman. Everell's significant instruction comes not from the Bible or from England, but from Magawisca's narrative about her own people's plight. When Magawisca is imprisoned because Puritan officials mistakenly believe her guilty of inciting an attack on Boston, Everell fails to free her because of his fears: the hapless young man struggles outside the jail with a ladder while Hope successfully accomplishes Magawisca's release. Passive and ineffectual, Everell is the hero because he marries the heroine.

The true bond—and the real romance—in this novel is between Hope and Magawisca. It is a same-sex bond that Fiedler has found essential to American romance. In constructing same-sex friendship between Magawisca and Hope, Sedgwick creates a parallel of the relationship between Natty Bumppo and Chingachgook in the *Leatherstocking Tales*—but with a difference. Doubles throughout the novel, Hope and Magawisca are drawn together by, and in spite of, the destructive acts of their fathers. Both have lost their mothers through war, both are torn between obedience to their fathers and the dictates of their own minds, and both oppose Puritan law, finding inspiration and guidance in nature or their own consciences. In prison the two learn the meaning of trust and betrayal, and in a secret meeting in a cemetery—symbol of death by male order—they stand at their mothers' graves and seal their bond: "Mysteriously have our destinies ⌐en interwoven. Our mothers brought from a far distance to rest here together—their children connected in indissoluble bonds" (*HL*, 192). Magawisca and Hope's union represents the waste caused by masculine violence as well as the need for feminine healing—a healing not between the Old World of England and the New World of America, as traditional American romances have it, but between the original culture of the Native Americans and the new, intrusive society of the Puritans. Unlike Natty and Chingachgook, Hope and Magawisca do not retreat into nature together, isolated but free. They participate in society, serving as its critics, mediators, and healers. When their relationship is sundered, Hope's marriage to Everell can be only a partial substitute.

Women, Sedgwick suggests, must play active and essential, not passive or secondary, roles in American society. In Cooper's fiction, in service to the American Adam mythology, women are rendered dichotomously. As Fiedler notes, Cooper establishes the "pattern of female Dark and Light that is to become the standard form" in American literature:[26] an innocent, passive woman juxtaposed with a vibrant, sexualized one, whether Alice and Cora in *The Last of the Mohicans,* Hetty and Judith in *The Deerslayer,* or Inez and Ellen in *The Prairie.* While women in nature figure as tokens of exchange in elaborate captivity sequences engineered by men in *The Leatherstocking Tales,* Cooper fundamentally endorses the standard nineteenth-century view of separate spheres for the sexes, with women "the repositories of the better principles of our nature."[27] This dichotomous view of women has its corollary in the masculine view of nature: a lone male figure either seeks a lover's alliance in nature as replacement for the relationship he fails to achieve with woman, or he views nature as a fearful object he must conquer or destroy in order to validate his own existence.

Sedgwick rejects these dichotomies for her female characters. Magawisca and Hope are as capable as their male counterparts of participating in nature and society. As sisters, Hope and Faith represent active and passive aspects of the female principle, but this distinction is never expressed in terms of sexual and spiritual purity or innocence. No female in *Hope Leslie* exhibits the "yearning felt by a presumably experienced woman to return to the pristine state of the innocent virgin" that Porte finds in Cooper,[28] a view that incidentally reads all female sexuality as a fall into sin requiring redemption or escape. Faith not only marries, she marries a "red-blooded" Indian; Hope, on the other hand, a virgin throughout the novel, romps from adventure to adventure unaffected by salacious sailors and villainous seducers. And Magawisca, who according to the Cooper paradigm must be "wild and dangerous" because Indian,[29] is, in fact, peaceable and socially oriented. Only Rosa, seduced and abandoned in the New World, appears as a stock character—a desperate reminder of romance's failure to accommodate women's sexuality. A prototype of Bertha Rochester, she takes vengeance on her oppressor, destroying herself in the process. Rosa gives angry expression to the female energy that her more socially integrated counterpart, Hope, channels into minor rebellions.

Hope Leslie forbids a reductionist view of women and romance. It rejects patriarchal concepts of female submissivess and purity, instead presenting women as complex models of democracy, adventure, mutuality, and sympathy. Sedgwick's characters have diverse destinies. Hope, Magawisca, and Esther all love Everell, but Magawisca and Esther give him up. Hope marries, but her union with her foster brother is more a friendship than a romance, modeled perhaps on Sedgwick's own relationship with her brothers.[30] Esther's single status endorses autonomous womanhood: "Marriage is not *essential* to the contentment, the dignity, or the happiness of woman," Sedgwick writes in defense of Esther's decision (*HL,* 350, original italics), and her own life is testimony that a single woman can find satisfaction as friend or sister.

The doublings become uneasy where American Indians are involved, however. By eschewing a retreat into nature that Natty Bumppo achieves with Chingachook, Sedgwick emphasizes a crucial historical reality: the decimation of the American Indian to make way for white expansion and greed. "We are commanded to do good to all" (*HL*, 312), Hope explains to her tutor as she works to free Magawisca. But she cannot prevent the inevitable. Esther, whose Puritan conscience keeps her from helping Magawisca escape from prison, gives herself up to the rigid law-of-the-father; and Magawisca, "first to none," returns to a nature that is blighted and a people "spoiled."[31] Dichotomies reemerge with Magawisca's declaration, "The Indian and the white man can no more mingle, and become one, than day and night" (*HL*, 330).

In *The Prairie*, published in 1827, the same year as *Hope Leslie*, Cooper uses a tree as a symbol to describe the natural cycles of growth, ripening, and death, comparing the monumentality of nature to the work of humans: "It is the fate of all things to ripen and then to decay. The tree blossoms and bears its fruits, which falls, rots, withers, and even the seed is lost! There does the noble tree fill its place in the forests. . . . It lies another hundred years."[32] Sedgwick also presents such a pantheistic notion of nature, giving Magawisca words that fuse the natural and the human: "'The Great Spirit is visible in the life-creating sun. I perceive Him in the gentle light of the moon that steals through the forest boughs. I feel Him here,' she continued, pressing her hand on her breast" (*HL*, 189). But this concept of nature has been destroyed by white encroachment. Sedgwick uses the familiar nineteenth-century symbol of the blasted tree, which to Mononotto represents his race at the hands of the white man, to signify not only the decimation of the American Indian but the assault against women and nature. Thus Magawisca's body, the right arm missing, is truncated like the blasted tree. Hawthorne uses the same symbol in "Roger Malvin's Burial" to convey Reuben's guilt over having failed to send a rescue party to his dying father-in-law. Hawthorne's message, anticipated by Sedgwick, is that the strong and able have responsibility to succor those in need.

Hope's sister Faith, another double, also goes off into the wilderness, married to chief Mononotto's son Oneco in one of the few cases of miscegenation in early American fiction—certainly one that Cooper disallows in *The Last of the Mohicans*. Faith and Oneco's relationship is mutually loving, gentle, and respectful. The bird imagery associated with the couple throughout the novel communicates a spirit of openness and freedom in nature. But just as Magawisca is mateless, Faith and Oneco's marriage has a sterile, frozen quality. Faith speaks no English, and the couple is without children.

Constrained by her own position in history, Sedgwick perhaps could not conceive of an ending that would both subvert *and* rewrite the white patriarchal plot. Even were she able to do so, the pressure to produce salable fiction most likely would have prevented its expression. Nonetheless, *Hope Leslie* strains against its conventions as surely as its female protagonist struggles against injustice.

Hope Leslie is discomfitting for literary critics and readers who prefer retreat into a fantasy world where one can ignore the injustices to nature by escaping further into the wilderness. In this novel, the frontier myth does not seem to be, as Annette Kolodny outlines it, a fantasy of the land as a domesticated garden.[33] It is, to some extent, what Leland Person suggests in his study of miscegenation: a successful intermarriage of races, an Eden where the white woman is included and the white man excluded.[34] The point is not that women ultimately prove superior—as they inevitably do, both in romance and in this novel—but that the pact with power engineered by men has jeopardized men, women, and nature. Cooper's paradisaical wilderness is a profound and evocative symbol in American literature, but Sedgwick, while valuing nature, forbids an egocentric or overly romantic view of it. She does not let us forget that we are usurpers and that there will be no regeneration through violence. Her view more closely resembles what David Mogen calls "a gothic tradition of frontier narrative," which expresses, among other meanings, "despair about our history and our future."[35]

The American literary hero feminizes the land, seeking in it a validation of his own creative principle. He wants to be the sole possessor of the virgin soil, which he penetrates with axe or gun and seeks to make pregnant with unresolved possibility.[36] Sedgwick tells us that this pregnancy is a false one and that woman/land will not be reduced to a medium for man's self-glorification. The white man will, like Everell, inevitably find himself a captive rather than a victor. A possessive relationship with nature only results in estrangement from it. Thus Edwin Fussell writes, "Cooper's heart was in his writing," but a "habitual need for recessive withdrawl . . . sprang from [his] fundamental alienation from his country"[37]

If the male fantasy is escapist, the female fantasy is integrationist, inclusive of the whole of woman's traits, religious, sexual, adventurous, heroic. Without this integration, there can be only fragmentation. Governor Winthrop's household "move[s] in a world of his own" (*HL,* 301), cut off from the very unity of nature, God, individual, and society that it seeks.

This transcendental vision of unity, suggested in Sedgwick's historical and romantic critique, is developed some years later—not in the individualistic transcendentalism of Ralph Waldo Emerson, but in the social transcendentalism of Margaret Fuller. Like Emerson, Fuller embraces the ideal of the individual in nature, but while valuing the abstract, she also advocates social awareness. Looking out at the land near the Great Lakes in the summer of 1843, Fuller seeks "by reverent faith to woo the mighty meaning of the scene, perhaps to foresee the law by which a new order, a new poetry, is to be evoked." Hope enjoys this same personal and transcendental relationship when she visits Mount Holioke [*sic*] with her tutor and Nelema. But Fuller's fantasy is modified by the "distaste I must experience at its mushroom growth": development "is scarce less wanton than that of warlike invasion," and the land bears "the rudeness of conquest." Emerson sought to unify technology and transcendental philosophy into a seamless fabric of hopeful expansion; Fuller, however, finds not transcendental insight but blindness: "Seeing the traces of the Indians . . . we feel as if they were the rightful lords of the beauty they forebore to deform. But most of these settlers do not see at all."[38]

The first writers, as Fussell notes, gave the West its mythology, finding in it their own dreams of possession and control. For women, identified with and through nature, the myth spells death and defeat. Sedgwick quietly but radically alters that mythology, transcending the limits of historical romance to express her own yearning for social and natural unity.

NOTES

An earlier version of this essay appeared in *Desert, Garden, Margin, Range: Literature on the American Frontier,* ed. Eric Heyne (Boston: Twayne, 1992).

1. For detailed discussions of Sedgwick's uses of historical sources, see Michael Davitt Bell, "History and Romance Convention in Catharine Maria Sedgwick's *Hope Leslie,*" *American Quarterly* 22 (1970): 216–218; Edward Halsey Foster, *Catharine Maria Sedgwick* (New York: Twayne, 1974), 73–80; and Catharine Maria Sedgwick, *Hope Leslie; Or, Early Times in the Massachusetts,* ed. Mary Kelley (1827; reprint, New Brunswick, N.J.: Rutgers University Press, 1987), xxi—xxxiii (hereafter cited as *HL*). Sedgwick also explains her fictional use of these materials in the preface to her novel (5–6).

2. Readers had difficulty distinguishing Sedgwick's and Cooper's fiction. Published anonymously in 1824, Sedgwick's *Redwood* was attributed to Cooper and actually appeared in France and Italy with Cooper's name on the title page. See Harold E. Mantz, *French Criticism of American Literature Before 1850* (New York: Columbia University Press, 1917), 43.

3. Quoted in Foster, *Sedgwick,* 95.

4. Bell Gale Chevigny, *The Woman and the Myth: Margaret Fuller's Life and Writings* (Old Westbury, N.Y.: Feminist Press, 1976), 190.

5. Nina Baym, "Melodramas of Beset Manhood: How Theories of American Fiction Exclude Women Authors," *American Quarterly* 33 (1981): 123–139.

6. Alexander Cowie, *The Rise of the American Novel* (New York: American Book, 1948), 204; Van Wyck Brooks, *The Flowering of New England* (New York: E. P. Dutton, 1936), 188.

7. Robert E. Spiller et al., *Literary History of the United States*, 3rd ed., rev. (New York: Macmillan, 1963), 1:256; Foster, *Sedgwick*, 94.

8. See, for example, Joel Porte, *The Romance in America: Studies in Cooper, Poe, Hawthorne, Melville, and James* (Middletown, Conn.: Wesleyan University Press, 1969): "Natty is the epic hero par excellence" (43), with *The Last of the Mohicans* and *The Pioneers* serving as Cooper's *Iliad* and *Odyssey* (39–52); and Georg Lukàcs, *The Historical Novel* (New York: Humanities Press, 1965), who finds "an almost epic-like magnificence" in Cooper's portrayals (64). Addressing Cooper's aesthetics, H. Daniel Peck, *A World by Itself: The Pastoral Moment in Cooper's Fiction* (New Haven: Yale University Press, 1927), finds in his landscapes not so much a frontier consciousness as a timeless, classic pastoral ideal. Robert E. Spiller, *Fenimore Cooper: Critic of His Times* (New York: Minton, Balch, 1931), John McWilliams, *Political Justice in a Republic: James Fenimore Cooper's America* (Berkeley: University of California Press, 1972), George Dekker, *The American Historical Romance* (New York: Cambridge University Press, 1987), and others have noted Cooper's social and political criticism, but these interests appear mainly in Cooper's middle and late novels, not his early fiction, which is more appropriately compared with *Hope Leslie*. As Yvor Winters writes in *In Defense of Reason* (Denver: University of Denver Press, 1947), "In the Leatherstocking Series . . . we have nothing whatever to do with social criticism, or at least nothing of importance" (185).

9. David Levin, *History as Romantic Art* (Stanford: Stanford University Press, 1959), ix.

10. See Leslie Fiedler, *Love and Death in the American Novel*, rev. ed. (New York: Stein and Day, 1975); and R. W. B. Lewis, *The American Adam: Innocence, Tragedy, and Tradition in the Nineteenth Century* (Chicago: University of Chicago Press, 1955).

11. D.H. Lawrence, *Studies in Classic American Literature* (1923; reprint, New York: Viking, 1964), 78, 73.

12. Suzanne Gossett and Barbara Ann Bardes, "Women and Political Power in the Republic: Two Early American Novels," *Legacy* 2 (Fall 1985): 13–30; Bell, "History and Romance," 216.

13. Sandra A. Zagarell, "Expanding 'America': Lydia Sigourney's *Sketch of Connecticut*, Catharine Sedgwick's *Hope Leslie*," *Tulsa Studies in Women's Literature*" 6 (Fall 1987): 225.

14. Bell, "History and Romance," 213–214.

15. Northrop Frye, *Anatomy of Criticism: Four Essays* (Princeton: Princeton University Press, 1957), 163.

16. Leslie Rabine, *Reading the Romantic Heroine: Text, History, Ideology* (Ann Arbor: University of Michigan Press, 1985), 7.

17. Philip Fisher, *Hard Facts: Setting and Form in the American Novel* (New York: Oxford University Press, 1988), argues that *The Last of the Mohicans* captures the spirit of the 1640s (39–40); but Cooper does not, like Sedgwick, take on the Puritan system of life in this novel. While one might argue that with its portrayal of the early stage of a hero's life, *The Deerslayer*, published in 1841, is a more appropriate companion text for *Hope Leslie*, this novel, even more than *The Last of*

the Mohicans, reflects a timelessness and abstract yearning for lost origins and freedoms. Wayne Franklin, *The New World of James Fenimore Cooper* (Chicago: University of Chicago Press, 1982), even while defending Cooper's involvement with history, admits "even in *The Deerslayer*, as far back as he could push Natty, [Cooper] . . . introduced Tom Hutter and Harry March. . . . This bit of realism upsets what otherwise might become pure dream" (107–108).

18. Catharine Maria Sedgwick, *Life and Letters of Catharine Maria Sedgwick*, ed. Mary E. Dewey (New York: Harper and Brothers, 1872), 101.

19. Rabine, *Reading the Romantic Heroine*, 107.

20. Bell, "History and Romance," 216.

21. Foster, *Sedgwick*, 77; Bell, "History and Romance," 216–217.

22. Gossett and Bardes, "Women and Political Power," 15.

23. Mary Kelley, "A Woman Alone: Catharine Maria Sedgwick's Spinsterhood in Nineteenth-Century America," *The New England Quarterly* 51 (June 1978): 209.

24. Michel-Guillaume Jean de Crèvecoeur, *Letters From an American Farmer* (1782; reprint, New York: Dutton, 1957), 64.

25. Ann Barr Snitow, "Mass Market Romance: Pornography for Women Is Different," *Radical History Review* 20 (Spring–Summer 1979): 150.

26. Fiedler, *Love and Death*, 21.

27. Quoted in Marvin Meyers, *The Jacksonian Persuasion: Politics and Belief.* (Stanford: Stanford University Press, 1957), 52.

28. Porte, *Romance in America*, 21.

29. Bell, "History and Romance," 218

30. Unmarried, Sedgwick apparently sublimated her erotic energies into an ethos of sibling love and comradeship: "The affection others have given to husbands and children I have given to brothers," she wrote. Cited in Kelley, "A Woman," 213.

31. Kelley, "A Woman," 224

32. James Fenimore Cooper, *The Prairie* (1827; reprint, New York: Signet, 1964), 250.

33. Annette Kolodny, *The Lay of the Land* (Chapel Hill: University of North Carolina Press, 1975.

34. Leland Person, "The American Eve: Miscegenation and a Feminist Frontier Fiction," *American Quarterly* 37 (Winter 1985): 668–685.

35. David Mogen, "Frontier Myth and American Gothic," *Genre* 14 (Fall 1981): 330–331.

36. See, for example, *Wyandote; or, The Hutted Knoll* (1843), where Cooper's langauge is explicitly sexual and generative: "There is a pleasure in diving into a virgin forest and commencing the labours of civilization. . . . [This diving] approaches nearer to the feeling of creating, and is far more pregnant with anticipation and hopes." Quoted in Edwin Fussell, *Frontier: American Literature and the American West* (Princeton: Princeton University Press, 1965), 28.

37. Fussell, *Frontier*, 28, 29.

38. Chevigny, *Woman and Myth*, 318, 322.

❧ NINA BAYM ❧

Reinventing Lydia Sigourney

IF LYDIA HOWARD HUNTLEY SIGOURNEY (1791–1865) had not existed, it would have been necessary to invent her. In fact, she *was* invented. As American women writers published in ever-larger numbers before the Civil War, one of them was bound to be construed as an epitome of the female author in her range of allowed achievements and required inadequacies. The prolific Sigourney was so well known from the late 1830s on that she would naturally become a candidate for this role.

She was, as it happened, a poor, virtuous, essentially self-educated woman whose writing had originally been sponsored by one of the leading families in Hartford, Connecticut, and patronized by many other New England aristocrats.[1] She published pious poetry on domestic subjects in the major magazines and wrote for the Sunday School League. Having made a good marriage (from the social point of view), she faithfully performed her duties as wife, mother, and hostess; she began to write for money only after financial reverses put the family under economic duress. She was, in short, a woman whose life could instruct all would-be literary women as to what they could do, what they should do, and also what they had better not do. Hers also was a life in which a modern success story of upward mobility through hard work and self-sacrifice led to an affirmation of traditional class structure. The social construction of Lydia Sigourney began, then, in her own lifetime. And, with Sigourney's canny participation, it continued throughout her lifetime as well.

For example, the prefatory "advertisement" to the 1815 *Moral Pieces in Prose and Verse,* which was written by Daniel Wadsworth, stresses the necessary haste with which she wrote: for the most part her compositions "arose from the impulse of the moment, at intervals of relaxation from such domestic employments, as the circumstances of the writer, and her parents, rendered indispensable." Thirty-two years later, Sigourney's preface to the fifth (1847) edition of her *Select Poems* iterates the implications of that early notice; most of the poems in the book "were suggested by passing occasions, and partake of the nature of extemporaneous productions; all reveal by their brevity, the short periods of time allotted to their construction."[2] The poet encourages readers to think that she wrote only short poems, and wrote them quickly; one would never guess from this preface that by 1847 she had also written (among other things) a four-thousand line historical epic in five cantos and two other historical poems each over five hundred lines long.[3] Haste, perhaps; extemporaneous brevity, no. But *Select Poems* culls from her work mainly "the more popular poems which had appeared during several years in various periodicals" (*Letters,* 337). That is, this book, designed to recirculate such work as had already proved itself in the public arena, was directed to the preferences of audience rather than author. (Or, the author preferences that it was directed toward were reputation-building and money-making.) The incremental popularity of collections of the already-popular (*Select Poems*—called simply *Poems* in its first edition of 1834—went through more than twenty-five editions during Sigourney's lifetime) further consolidated a representation of the author based on her best-loved, or most widely known, poetry. The reappearance of these poems in anthologies like Rufus Griswold's or Caroline May's added to the effect.

We conventionally lament the way in which careers of "major" nineteenth-century American authors were deformed by market pressures. "Dollars damn me," Herman Melville complained in a much quoted letter to Nathaniel Hawthorne. Dollars most certainly did *not* damn Sigourney; but the Lydia Sigourney who was so often, albeit so ambiguously and ambivalently, praised in her own lifetime, and has been so heartily calumniated subsequently, is a representation based on only some fraction of what she wrote and published. The Sigourney of the consolation elegy, the funerary poem, the Sigourney obsessed with dead children and dead mothers, has been constituted by a succession of critical audiences, each basing its commentary and opinion on an ever-smaller segment of the author's published writings. Even now, when writing by antebellum American women is more highly valued than it has been for a long time, the mere mention of Sigourney's name suffices to invoke a caricature: a mildly comical figure who exemplifies the worst aspects of domestic sentimentalism.[4]

There is no Sigourney bibliography; many of her published books are difficult to find, and much if not most of the uncollected periodical material is probably now unrecoverable. But the surviving work does not show Sigourney as primarily a poet of mortuary verse. This is not to say that

Sigourney did *not* write many poems about death, among which were poems about dead mothers and children. But such poems do not dominate even her poetic practice, and she also wrote significant quantities of prose. I count 16 elegies out of 114 pieces in her 1827 *Poems;* 50 out of 172 in the 1835 *Zinzendorff, and Other Poems;* 15 out of 115 in the 1841 *Pocahontas, and Other Poems;* and 32 out of 126 in the *Select Poems* already mentioned: overall, this works out to 32 percent.[5] Perhaps in recognition of the popularity of this segment of her writing, Sigourney herself frequently called attention to it, as for example in her preface to *Zinzendorff,* where she says that "should it be objected that too great a proportion of [the poems] are elegiac, the required apology would fain clothe itself in the language of the gifted Lord Bacon:—If we listen to David's harp, we shall find as many hearse-like harmonies, as carols; and the pencil of Inspiration hath more labored to describe the afflictions of Job, than the felicities of Solomon" (6).

The category of elegy, or consolation poetry, or funerary verse, more-over, is a broad one, and one may discern within the Sigourney elegiac corpus three poetic subtypes. There are reflective *memento mori* poems deriving from some general observation in nature or the world; there are what I would want to call generic or situational elegies whose subject is denoted as a member of a class, rather than as an individual; and then there are elegies for named persons—memorial or obituary poems. One need go no further afield than the table of contents of *Zinzendorff* for examples of each type. "Death among the Trees" would appear to be (and is) a general reflection on the inevitability of death, as is "Thoughts for Mourn-ers." "Death of the Wife of a Clergyman, during the Sickness of Her Husband," "Death of a Young Wife," "Burial of Two Young Sisters," "Death of a Young Lady at the Retreat for the Insane," "Farewell of a Missionary to Africa, at the Grave of his Wife and Child," and "Death of a Young Musician" are situational elegies. "Funeral of Dr. Mason F. Cogs-well," "Death of the Rev. Gordon Hall," "Death of Mrs. Harriet W. L. Winslow," "Death of a Son of the Late Honorable Fisher Ames," "Death of the Rev. Alfred Mitchell," and "Death of the Rev. W. C. Walton" are some of the specific memorials.

My distinctions here are not merely formal, or rather they are formal in Aristotle's sense of being configured with regard to an audience response. Each of the three kinds invokes a different type of occasion. (And, as the preceding titles show, the subjects are by no means exclusively women and/or children.) The *memento mori* poem, which Sigourney practiced the least, is an internal dialogue that dramatizes the persona's efforts to come to terms with death in general, with the death of a loved one, or with one's own inevitable death. Because it is reflective, it is distanced from the immediacy of death. Thus, it bespeaks an interval of leisure, privacy, and solitude for the persona as well as any reader whose mental processes it may seek to guide and mime.

The generic and specific consolation poetry that Sigourney most often wrote, in contrast, is designed for immediate intervention at the moment of death or funeral. A generic elegy, like a greeting card, is available to the large number of people whose circumstances it suits at the moment; the memorial for a named person is designed to palliate the grief of a unique set of mourners. This set extends beyond close family to friends, acquaintances, or those who knew the dead person by name only. So newspaper obituaries serve us today. Thus, both the situational elegy and the obituary poem bespeak a public arena and a practical goal. They do not have time to expatiate on religious uncertainty, to exhibit the depth and extent of one's own grief, or to manage a personal catharsis; they aim to make suffering people feel better—and make them feel better fast. "Her muse has been a comforter to the mourner," Sarah Hale observed, and one necessary aspect of this comforting function is that the elegies are never about the speaker, always about others.[6]

Invariably, these useful poems designed specifically for Christians plug in a strong affirmation of the life to come. From the converging perspectives of High Victorianism and High Modernism, Sigourney's unsympathetic biographer Gordon Haight derides the intellectual simplicity of her religiosity; but *In Memoriam,* to which he invidiously compares Sigourney's elegiac corpus, was certainly not supposed to comfort any mourner besides its author.[7] Perhaps this other-directedness of Sigourney's elegiac voice also explains her minimal position in the narcissistic woman's poetic tradition developed by Cheryl Walker's *Nightingale's Burden,* a tradition centered on the topic of how hard it is to be a woman poet.[8] The activist and interventionist element in this elegiac poetry—an element that by all accounts succeeded in its intentions—would also seem to tell against Ann Douglas Wood's construal of Sigourney's death poetry: its "heroine was herself, but emptied of conflict, sublimated, and desexualized . . . a small figure . . . seemingly submissive, submerged, half-hypnotized and half automaton," and also to qualify Richard Brodhead's recent Foucauldian suggestions that antebellum women readers were constructed isolated and passive consumers of mass-produced literary goods. Without denying that such reading practices might have existed, I would see them as only some in a range of practices; the memorial poem that forms part of the public occasion of the funeral and is then used, reused, and adapted by sucessive groups of mourners who find it pertinent implies a different kind of reading.[9]

In sum, even if we were to agree that Sigourney was a funerary poet and nothing but, literary history needs a less homogeneous and implicitly contemptuous representation of her elegiac project. But when we look at

her other poetry and her prose writings, we find materials for the construction of a very different Sigourney. I will call this figure a "republican
public mother," modifying the work on the ideology of republican
womanhood done by several historians of American women with a reference to the public sphere. For whereas the figure identified by these
historians—the woman who carries out her civic duties by training her
children in patriotism and republican values—performs her activities in
the home space, it is precisely the point of published writing that it enters
the public sphere. Too, Sigourney takes positions in her writing that have
a public resonance: she is by no means a "sentimental domestic," to use
Mary Kelley's phrase.[10]

Even where titles like *Letters to Young Ladies, Letters to Mothers,* and
Whispers to a Bride might seem to imply the Victorian female world of love
and ritual or the cult of true womanhood, the content reveals something
much more political and much less emotional.[11] In these books Sigourney's domestic ideology is inseparable from patriotic and republican politics. In the often reprinted *Letters to Young Ladies,* for example, she writes
that "the foundation of the unity and strength of all nations is laid in the
discipline of well-ordered families; and the consistency and beauty of a
well-balanced character may be resolved into the element of self-control";
that "to a republic, whose welfare depends on the intelligence, and virtue
of the people, the character and habits of every member of its family are of
value"; that "women possess an agency which the ancient republics never
discovered"; and, finally, that women, in return for all that America has
given them, owe it to their country to give their "hands to every cause of
peace and truth, encourage temperance and purity, oppose disorder and
vice, be gentle teachers of wisdom and charity."[12] The motherly persona
adopted by Sigourney in her advice book contains a significant Spartan
element in her makeup, and her advice authorizes women to move outside
the home when the cause is right.

Sigourney herself moved well beyond the halfway literature of domestic instruction (halfway, that is, between the private and public realms)
into a clearly public sphere in her many historical writings. Like many
women educators in the early years of the century—Sigourney taught
school for several years before her marriage in 1819—she saw history as
the core of a republican woman's education, so that in some sense the
domestic preceptress and the historian are facets of the same female construction. In *Letters to Young Ladies* she wrote, quite conventionally, that
fiction should be eschewed and history embraced: "History has ever been
warmly commended to the attention of the young. It imparts knowledge
of human nature and supplies lofty subjects for contemplation" (65). Her
memoirs recalled her pleasure in unfolding with students "the broad an-

nals of History. Seated in a circle, like a band of sisters, we traced in the afternoon, by the guidance of Rollin, the progress of ancient times, or the fall of buried empires" (*Letters*, 203). But as a writer rather than a teacher of history to girls, Sigourney is more directly part of the polity, for historical writings construct a view of the public sphere that extends well beyond women, and aggressively comment on it.

It would appear, in fact, that well over half of what she published in both prose *and* poetry was historical in content; and it was also political—in a fairly conventional sense of the term—in implication. Through the learning, teaching, and writing of history, Sigourney, like a number of other literary women between 1790 and the Civil War, enacted womanly behavior that in many ways nullified the distinction between public and private that operated so crucially in other contexts. [13]

The subject matter of Sigourney's historical writing falls into four categories: ancient and biblical history; the local history of the region around Hartford, Norwich, and New London, Connecticut from settlement through Revolution; [14] the American Revolution; and the history of the American Indians after the European arrival on the continent. Although she wrote numerous biographical sketches of exemplary women, she did not attempt to construct a separate history of women; indeed her progressive Christian view suggested that women had only very recently emerged as a force in history. There is history in Sigourney's short poems and long poems, in sketches of varying length, in free-standing and embedded fictional narratives, and in a variety of nonfictional modes, including biography, narrative history, and children's textbooks designed for school or home use. [15]

The only work from this sizable segment of Sigourney's output previously excavated and analyzed is the 1824 *Sketch of Connecticut, Forty Years Since* (Hartford: Oliver D. Cooke). An important essay by Sandra A. Zagarell claims that the *Sketch* is "quite directly concerned with the foundations and organization of public life," with a vision that "deliberately extended official definitions of the nation to imagine an America grounded in inclusiveness and communitarianism." [16] Since the sketch features real events from the past, I take it as a work of history that indeed has public intentions. But rather than psychologize those intentions, as Zagarell does, I would prefer to historicize them. When historicized, Sigourney's politics emerge as a self-conscious advocacy of the tenets of "classical" (that is, conservative) republicanism in an age of increasing liberalism; as an urging of the merits of nonsectarian evangelical Christianity on an increasingly disputatious and fragmented religious scene; and as an effort to reconcile the civic with the spiritual realms in an amalgam of Christianity and republicanism. [17]

The *Sketch* is designed to celebrate the benevolent aristocratic widow Madam L——, whose charities and liberalities sustain a hierarchical republican community in productive harmony. Almost certainly it would have been recognized as a political counterstatement to the Scotswoman Anne Grant's intensely Tory and anti–New England *Memoirs of an American Lady: with Sketches of Manners and Scenery in America, as they existed previous to the Revolution,* a work similarly configured around a benefactress recalled from childhood, which had its American publication in Boston in 1809. The real-life model for Sigourney's *Sketch* was Jerusha Talcot Lathrop, widow of Daniel Lathrop, a prosperous druggist of Norwich. Until Madam Lathrop died in 1806, Sigourney's father, Ezekial Huntley, was gardener and general handyman on her estate. After her death the family of a nephew, Daniel Wadsworth, took an interest in the Huntleys, and in Lydia particularly (see note 1). Sigourney's own life story, then, would confirm to her the efficacy of a moral republicanism wherein the fortunate supported the virtuous poor by giving them opportunities to support themselves.

This conservative republican theme is sounded at the very start of the sketch with its evocation of the town of N—— [Norwich] as site of "the singular example of an aristocracy, less intent upon family aggrandizement, than upon becoming illustrious in virtue" (4). Unlike other sections of the country in the years immediately following the Revolution, there was no "agitation" in Connecticut, because "the body of the people trusted in the wisdom of those heroes and sages of whom they had furnished their proportion. They believed that the hands, which had been strengthened to lay the foundation of their liberty, amid the tempests of war, would be enabled to complete the fabric, beneath the smiles of peace" (16). Madam L——'s contribution to the fabric, as a woman of social prominence and fortune, is to disburse appropriate charity and thereby maintain harmonious relations among the social classes. She gives out money, food, clothing, jobs, and advice to the deserving poor around her in return for their loyalty and subordination.

Madam L——'s beneficence usually succeeds in producing a peaceful and cohesive community and is especially effective with marginalized women. As one impoverished woman is made to say, "What a blessed thing it is, when the hearts of the rich are turned to give work to the poor, and assist them to get the necessaries of life, for themselves and families" (73). But with the Indians the story is different. And nine of the eighteen chapters of the *Sketch*—fully half the book—are about the remnant of the Mohegan tribe. In chapters 12 and 13, two tribal leaders—the tribe's chief and its Christian minister—inform her that most members of the tribe have decided to leave Norwich and move to the interior, where they will

unite with another tribe. This decision shows that Madam L——'s charities are insufficient and beside the point where Indians are concerned.
Individualistic Indians cannot accept a position at the bottom of a class
hierarchy, which is where the community of N—— places them. Their
distaste for settled agriculture makes it impossible for them to survive on
their reservation, which "would have been more than adequate to their
wants, had they been assiduous in its cultivation" (31). Most of all, they
believe—they *know*—that the whites are determined to exterminate them
(always excepting Madame L—— herself), and after experiencing a century and a half of violence, they have given up all thought of resisting.
Their move is only a stopgap. "Ere long, white men will cease to crush us,
for we will cease to be" (160). Occum, the minister, insists that Christianity holds promise for Indians, but Robert Ashbow, the chief, counters that
"Christianity is for white men" (161). As they depart, one young warrior
asks despairingly, "Whither shall we go, and not hear the speech of the
white man?" (173).

In fact, of the four historical subjects that most concerned Sigourney,
the American Indians were foremost. The history of her own region and
Indian history were in some sense identical: the Pequod War had been
waged there, the Mohegans had fought with English settlers against first
the Pequods and then the Naragansetts, and the Mohegan chief Uncas was
supposed to have given the land around Norwich to the English in exchange for protection from King Philip and other enemies. This meant
that the establishment of the Christian American community that Sigourney extolled in the *Sketch of Connecticut* and elsewhere depended directly
on white access to Indian land.

Sigourney drew from this history the conclusion that the Anglo-
American national character was defined by how whites acquired the land
they needed and what happened to the Indians afterward. In writing about
the Indians she confronted the insoluble narrative problem that while three
of her subjects were representable as comedies (the pagan world gave way
to the Christian; the American Revolution was won by the right side; the
Connecticut Valley fostered the most moral society ever known on earth),
the fourth was an unmitigated tragedy. Sigourney also faced the insoluble
political and *moral* problem that the triumphs of Christianity and republicanism in America were achieved at the cost of their own basic tenets. In
destroying the Indians rather than domesticating them, republicanism ignored its commitments to civic virtue and to the amelioration of the lot of
the needy by the fortunate; Christianity neglected its imperatives of charity
and of taking all souls as equals before God. Her historical writings are
internally fractured because their attempt to affirm the progress of history is
continually frustrated by the evident failure of Christian-republican ethics

to meet the single most important test of the moral caliber of the American nation—the obligation to preserve the continent's "aborigines" by Christianizing them and integrating them into American society.

The *Sketch of Connecticut* concludes, for example, with three fantasy chapters given over to the story of Oriana, a beautiful white woman whose life has been saved in war by a Mohegan warrior who adopts her to replace his own dead daughter. In this allegory the historically documented Indian behavior of welcoming, feeding, and protecting the original white colonists, wherever they set foot on American soil, is reciprocated by Oriana's willingness to become their daughter and help Christianize them. The representation entails a radical Christianity that leaves republican ideology, even as practiced by the exemplary Madam L——, completely out of the picture. Sigourney saw enough potential in this segment of the *Sketch* to extract it and republish it as "Oriana" in her twice-reprinted collection *Sketches* (Philadelphia: Key and Biddle, 1834).

In contrast to Oriana's example, the core story of American Indian history after the European arrival is one where Indian generosity is answered by European brutality. The narrative is epitomized in a short poem called "The Indian's Welcome to the Pilgrim Fathers," which appeared in *Zinzendorff* and reads in part:

> When sudden from the forest wide,
>   A red-brow'd chieftain came,
> With towering form, and haughty stride,
>   And eye like kindling flame:
> No wrath he breath'd, no conflict sought,
>   To no dark ambush drew,
> But simply *to the Old World brought,*
>   *The welcome of the New.*
>
> That *welcome* was a blast and ban
>   Upon thy race unborn.
> Was there no seer, thou fated Man!
>   Thy lavish zeal to warn?
> Thou in thy fearless faith didst hail
>   A weak, invading band,
> But who shall heed thy children's wail,
>   Swept from their native land?
>
> (47–48)

Sigourney's narratives of the Indian disaster lead to the culminating plea that her countrymen should return to the essence of republican and Christian doctrine and stop destroying the Indians by murder and relocation.

But this plea undermines the affirmative dynamic of her other historical representations by substituting an implicit declension model of American and Christian history; and it does this without mitigating in the least the unrepublican and unchristian carnage that has already taken place. From her historical perspective, the cessation of Indian destruction in the future—although it is much to be hoped for and although her writings are designed in part to further that goal—could not justify the erasure of past massacre. Whatever happened in future, that is, it was necessary to remember what had happened in the past. Unwilling to adopt a tragic or ironic stance toward history (though she could not always avoid doing so), Sigourney could not accept the palliating conviction found in so many writings of the time that the destruction of the Indians was merely inevitable. And convinced that a Christian must see the Indians as human kin, however, "other" they may be, she cannot write a history in which their obliteration could be frankly presented as a sign of historical progress.

There is no honest way to resolve her dilemma, so Sigourney's Indian narratives typically end with a forthright contradiction. "We are struck with the prominence and discordance of some of the features in the character of our ancestors," she writes in a prose sketch called "The Fall of the Pequod." Boldness, cruelty, and "the piety to which they turned for sanction, even when the deed and motive seemed at variance," make a strange combination.

> The unresting vigilance with which they blotted out the very name of Pequod . . . was not less arbitrary than the dismemberment of Poland, and savored more of the policy of heathen Rome than of Christ. Mason, in common with the historians of that age, bitterly blamed the Indians for stratagems in war, but chose to adopt the creed he had denounced, and to prove himself an adept in the theory that he condemned. . . . The once-powerful aboriginal tribe . . . perished without a hand to write its epitaph: an emblem of the fate of that vanishing race to whom the brotherhood of the white man hath hitherto been as the kiss of Judas.[18]

No doubt, some might see prose like this as intellectually confused. But it could be equally described as intellectually honest in a political setting where blunt hypocrisy and debonair obfuscation were the order of the day.

"Traits of the Aborigines of America," which preceded the *Sketch of Connecticut* by two years, was Sigourney's first work about American Indians. Despite its bland title and its anonymous publication, this five-canto work of four thousand blank verse lines, with extensive scholarly annotation, is her longest and most ambitious poem, packed with classical references and historical allusion and dense with information about Indian tribes.[19] While it ought to be considered a belated entry in the competition for "the" American epic, it is uniquely structured from the Indian point of view and its narrative extends beyond the territorial United States to include the story of the continent from the Arctic circle to South America. This story, regardless of where it transpires, is always the same: the Indians welcome the newcomers and are exterminated.

Canto 1 begins with the Indians in undisturbed possession of the continent and then introduces a chronicle of incursion: "First, to their northern coast/Wander'd the Scandinavian" (1.253–254); after a while Columbus comes—the Indians thought he and his men were Gods, "nor dream'd their secret aim/Was theft and cruelty, to snatch the gold/That sparkled in their streams, and bid their blood/Stain those pure waters (1.44–47); Portuguese, French, Irish, English—everybody comes. Christians come too, bringing the potential benefit of their religion to the Indians. But that benefit does not develop, because the Christians do not behave like Christians.

In Canto 2, incursions become more extensive and frequent: "Almost it seemed/As if old Europe, weary of her load,/Pour'd on a younger world her thousand sons/In ceaseless deluge" (2.8–11). The bulk of the canto narrates the life of John Smith, allowing the poet to provide a geography and history of most of the world through a chronicle of his travels. Pocahontas's rescue of him is compared to Pharoah's daughter rescuing Moses—and with the same disastrous effect on her people: "Little thought/The Indian Monarch, that his child's weak arm/Fostered that colony, whose rising light/Should quench his own forever" (2.1093–1096). Sigourney vacillates between comic and tragic interpretations of the narrative and simultaneously avoids and intensifies both readings by focusing on the conversion and early death of Pocahontas herself. There is some unspecified and contradictory connection between the conversion and the death—on the one hand it seems that Christianity itself is what kills Pocahontas, on the other that, thanks to her conversion, she dies regenerate. The canto ends with brief attention to the founding of Pennsylvania, Delaware, and Florida, always from the vantage point of those who are forced out by European settlement. "Pressing west/O'er the vain barrier, and retreating tide/Of Mississippi, spread our ancestors,/Taking a goodly portion, with the sword,/And with their bow" (2.1186–1190).

Canto 3 positions itself with the now outcast and understandably hostile Indians in their various forest refuges, describes many instances of savage warfare, and contains a ringing attack on whites for their instigatory barbarism as well as their hypocrisy in faulting the Indians. "Who are these,/Red from the bloody wine-press, with its stains/Dark'ning their raiment? Yet I dare not ask/Their clime and lineage, lest the accusing blasts,/Waking the angry echoes, should reply/'Thy Countrymen!'" (3.905–910).

Canto 4, the shortest in the poem, begins by praising the few missionaries—Eliot, Heckewelder—who went among the Indians to preach Christianity, but gives most of its lines to Tuscarora, who mocks those of his tribe who want to convert:

> Behold! what glorious gifts
> Ye owe to white men. What good-will and peace
> They shed upon you! Exile and the sword!
> Poisons and rifled sepulchres! and see!
> They fain would fill the measure of their guilt
> With the dark cheat of that accursed faith
> Whose precepts justify *their* nameless crimes,
> *Your* countless woes.
>
> (4.348–354)

The point that Sigourney is after here is that the whites have created not only justifiable Indian hostility to them as a group, but hostility as well to the Christianity that they claim to represent. The necessary task of joining with the Indians in brotherly love has been made infinitely more difficult by the white people's betrayal of their own religion.

Canto 5 then departs from the historical record to urge on Christian Americans the true obligations of their Christianity. "Make these foes your friends" (5.546–547). The narrator acknowledges that most living Indians are already demoralized and degraded and sees the possibility— albeit at some horrendous bloody cost to themselves—of the whites completely exterminating the Indians. But it argues vehemently that "our God hath made/All of one blood, who dwell upon the earth" (5.406–407); the only important difference between red and white people is that whites are (supposedly) Christian. Their very religion requires whites to Christianize the Indians. And when the Indians also become Christians, their justified desire for revenge will be set aside; they will then become an integral part of the American republic, and that republic, though no longer purely white, will be purely Christian.

Not the least interesting aspect of "Traits" is its continual recourse to references from what would have been called "Universal History" simultaneously to heroicize the Indians and deheroicize the Europeans. At various points in the poem the Indians are likened to, for example, "stern Regulus" (1.60); "the warlike Earl, stern Steward" (1.208); "the Scythian tribes" (1.224–225); "sublime Demosthenes" (2.143); "the impetuous Hannibal" (3.535); "the stern, Spartan lords" (3.656). Sometimes Sigourney accompanies these comparisons with the lament that the Indians—equally valiant, noble, eloquent as these historical figures—are doomed to extinction *without a history,* and hence to oblivion rather than remembrance. On the other hand, she interrupts the Indian narrative for long accounts of historical carnage that far exceed anything the Indians have perpetrated: "O'er the tow'rs/Of lofty Ilion, wreck'd by Grecian wiles,/Why does the dazzled eye prolong its gaze/In breathless interest, yet averts its glance/ Disgusted, and indignant, at the scenes of Indian stratagem?" (3.721–726).

Sigourney's obvious missionary perspective works from an idea of the Indians' likeness to whites rather than of their dignity in difference; it assumes that Indian culture is inferior and must give way to Christian culture. Even so, "Traits of the Aborigines" made public demands that at the time were thoroughly utopian. In the memoir written some forty years later, Sigourney dryly observes that the poem "was singularly unpopular, there existing in the community no reciprocity with the subject." But her own views had not changed in the intervening years; "our injustice and hard-hearted policy with regard to the original owners of the soil has ever seemed to me one of our greatest national sins" (*Letters,* 327).

The poem that gives the *Zinzendorff* volume of 1835 its title is another work about Indians. The 584-line annotated poem in blank verse centers on the 1742 mission of Count Zinzendorff, founder of the radical Christian Moravian sect, to the Indians of the Wyoming Valley in Pennsylvania. It praises Zinzendorff for going among Indians whose experience with whites makes them deeply suspicious of him. "Sought he to grasp their lands?/To search for gold? to found a mystic throne/Of dangerous power?" (100–102). Zinzendorff's peaceful persistence and his appeal to the women, children, and old people of the tribe, as well as the evidence of his remarkable escapes from plots against his life, persuade the Indian rulers to take his message seriously.

Sigourney begins this poem with a brief mention of a much-written-about incident of the Revolution, the Wyoming Valley massacre of 1778, when an alliance of Pennsylvania Tories and Indians slaughtered emigrant settlers from Connecticut. She explains that white appropriation of Indian land in the decades before the massacre has created Indian hostility and thus was the actual historical cause of the massacre. Zinzendorff, in contrast, had gone among the Indians with only Christian motives. When, toward the end of the poem, the Indians are made to lament Zinzendorff's return to Europe, their grief is interpreted by the poet as prophetic of their future at the hands of people who will settle with self-aggrandizing rather than self-effacing intentions (495–505). In brief, Zinzendorff's was the road not taken. The poem closes with an appeal to Christians to desist from sectarian controversy and unite in peaceful missionary activities among the Indians. There may still be time, the poem says, to reverse history's direction and bring Indians into the nation.

Sigourney wrote another piece about the Wyoming massacre, the "Legend of Pennsylvania," collected in *Myrtis*. She begins with the history that led to carnage. "The Connecticut colonists evinced their national courage and tenacity in defence of their homes, and what they deemed their legal possessions. The Pennsylvanians were equally inflexible in what they considered their antecedent rights. The Aborigines contended for their favorite dominion with a lion-like despair" (179). One disaster after another is represented in the destruction of families and registered in the responses of surviving women. At the story's end, the last member of a once-thriving family of Connecticut pioneers in the valley joins the Moravians at Nazareth, living out the rest of her life as a teacher in the girls' school there. (The Moravians had an interest in women's education and founded some of the earliest boarding schools for young women in the country.) Here again Sigourney typically invokes the pacific and womanly alternative to carnage.

The mood of "Pocahontas," published in the 1841 volume *Pocahontas, and Other Poems,* is not hopeful. The 504-line poem, in fifty-six modified Spenserian stanzas, recounts the life of Pocahontas as a memorial to the Indian princess. Although by 1841 American literature was full of tributes to her, Sigourney puts a recognizable stamp on the story material. She begins as she had begun "Traits of the Aborigines," from an assumed Indian perspective in the New World before the Europeans arrive. Apostrophizing the "clime of the West," she asks whether it was not "sweet, in cradled rest to lie,/And 'scape the ills that older regions know?" An entrance into history, long deferred, begins when the "roving hordes of savage men" look up to "behold a sail! another, and another!" She sounds her motif of Christian brotherhood: "What were thy secret thoughts, oh red-brow'd brother,/As toward the shore those white-wing'd wanderers press'd?" And when Powhatan, moved by his daughter's intercession, spares John Smith's life, Sigourney notes the ironic outcome of that event with the same comparison to Pharaoh's daughter that she made in *Traits* (stanza 20).

"Thou wert the saviour of the Saxon vine,/And for this deed alone our praise and love are thine" (stanza 21), Sigourney says, once again stressing the self-destructive, ironically Christian tendency of the Indians to nurture and protect white intruders. Then, moving forward in time to the era of Indian surprise attacks on white settlements, she challenges the historians' accounts: "Ye, who hold of history's scroll the pen,/Blame not too much those erring, red-brow'd men,/Though nursed in wiles. Fear is the white-lipp'd sire/Of subterfuge and treachery. 'Twere in vain/To bid the soul be true, that writhes beneath his chain" (stanza 24). The whites, answering Indian generosity with oppression and dislocation, created the vengeful Indians whose behavior they now slander and use as a pretext for further incursions against them.

The poem then chronicles Pocahontas's capture, conversion, marriage, journey to England, and early death; but it refers beyond this personal narrative to another, larger narrative—especially when it returns at the end to the long view with which it began and addresses the Indians en masse:

> I would ye were not, from your fathers' soil
>   Track'd like the dun wolf, ever in your breast
> The coal of vengeance and the curse of toil;
>   I would we had not to your mad lip prest
> The fiery poison-cup, nor on ye turn'd
>   The blood-tooth'd ban-dog, foaming, as he burn'd
> To tear your flesh; but thrown in kindness bless'd
>   The brother's arm around ye, as ye trod,
> And led ye, sad of heart, to the bless'd Lamb of God
>   (stanza 54)

I wish we hadn't, but we have—this is undoubtedly a weak, sentimental, acknowledgment of national crime; but at least it is an acknowledgment. Sigourney's conventional memorializing of Pocahontas, savior and servant of the whites, leads to an invocation of those nameless Indian dead who heroically *resisted* white incursion—"King, stately chief, and warrior-host are dead,/Nor remnant nor memorial left behind" (stanza 56). Sigourney's poem memorializes them as well as Pocahontas.

All history writing, in Sigourney's literary approach to it, is a memorial to the past—not the past made to live again, not even a representation of the past, but a memorial of it. (And this point allows us to think of her elegiac verse as another, individualized, form of history writing.) Her writing about Indians can be seen as an attempt to influence the present moment in three ways. First, it argues for a sense of white responsibility toward the surviving remnants of Indian tribes; second, it tries to ensure that the Indian story became a part of American history no matter how badly the story reflected on the white conquerors; third, it insists that the Indians were Americans. Here, her schooling in ancient history, with its chronicle of aggressor empires culminating in the mighty, yet decadent Rome, served as a storehouse of parallels for interpreting and representing more recent history. The conventional classical references through which the Founders historicized their vision of a nation became, when Sigourney treated the Indians, references to empire rather than to republic.

In the 1850s Sigourney turned her attention to the West and the New England pioneers who were settling it. A long poem from this decade, about a pioneer family from Connecticut settling in Ohio, features a stalwart Indian woman whose medicinal skills save the life of one of the settler children, and the quasi-fictional quasi-autobiographical *Lucy Howard's Journal* conjoins Lucy Howard, the New England heroine, with both a black and an Indian woman in an image of triracial (although inegalitarian) harmony.[20] The historical strain in her writing continues to the end of her life, when *Letters of Life* returns to the Norwich of her girlhood, the beloved Madam L——, and the memories of early republican Connecticut that had animated the *Sketch* of 1822. Whether Sigourney was a "good" writer or not, she was obviously an important one in her own time; and we will understand that time much better if we abandon a social construction of her based on extremely limited awareness of her work. In particular, that a writer with so obviously public a program should come down to us as the most private and domesticated of antebellum women authors suggests the need to look again at the scope of antebellum women's writing.

NOTES

An earlier version of this essay was published in *American Literature* 62 (1990): 385–404.

1. Sigourney's first book was *Moral Pieces, in Prose and Verse* (Hartford: Sheldon & Goodwin, 1815). Publication was arranged by Daniel Wadsworth of Hartford. The 721 subscribers listed at the back of *Moral Pieces* are a virtual roll call of conservative first families from Hartford, Farmington, New Haven, New London, Norwich, Middletown, Fairfield, Litchfield, Boston, Salem, Cambridge, Charlestown, Marblehead, and other Connecticut and Massachusetts towns.

2. Lydia Sigourney, *Select Poems* (Philadelphia: E. B. and J. Biddle, 1847), vii.

3. Sigourney's memoir lists fifty-six different books published in her lifetime, a few of these edited by her; the posthumous memoir itself becomes the fifty-seventh. She asserted that uncollected material published in almost three hundred different periodicals would easily amount to several additional volumes, a claim accepted by Gordon Haight, her only biographer. See her memoir, *Letters of Life* (New York: D. Appleton, 1866), 366 (hereafter cited parenthetically as *Letters*). See also Gordon Haight, *Mrs. Sigourney: The Sweet Singer of Hartford* (New York: Yale University Press, 1930), 173.

4. For example, Jane Tompkins, in "The Other American Renaissance," *Sensational Designs: The Cultural Work of American Fiction, 1790–1860* (New York: Oxford University Press, 1985), alludes to "Mrs. Sigourney—who epitomizes the sentimental tradition for modern critics" (160). In *Notable American Women*—whose purpose, one thought, was to overturn stereotypes—Gordon Haight says that "death was always her favorite theme—the death of infants, of consumptive children, of missionaries in Burma and Liberia, of poets and lunatics, of artists and

sailors, of college students and deaf-dumb-and-blind girls. Her rhyming of pious truisms made a wide appeal and established a trade that newspaper poets have carried on prosperously" (*Notable American Women* [Cambridge; Harvard University Press, 1971], 3:289).

5. Sigourney, *Poems* (Boston: S. G. Goodrich, 1827); *Zinzendorff, and Other Poems* (New York: Leavitt, Lord, 1835); *Pocahontas, and Other Poems* (New York: Harper, 1841).

6. Sarah Hale, *Woman's Record*, 2nd ed. (New York: Harper, 1855), 783.

7. "There were plenty of strong souls in the Victorian age whose 'piping took a troubled sound' when they chose to struggle with their doubts rather than drown them out with the cymbals of conformity" (Haight, *Mrs. Sigourney*, 160). What Griswold did to Poe is, for students of American literature, a national calamity; what biographers have done to women still passes for urbanity and even (heaven help us) gallantry.

8. Cheryl Walker, *The Nightingale's Burden: Women Poets and American Culture Before 1900* (Bloomington: Indiana University Press, 1982). Walker briefly cites three Sigourney poems—two elegies and a poem praising Felicia Hemans—but centers the antebellum women's poetic tradition on Frances Osgood and Elizabeth Oakes-Smith.

9. Ann Douglas Wood, "Mrs. Sigourney and the Sensibility of the Inner Space," *New England Quarterly* 45 (1972): 163–187; the cited passage is on pages 170–171. Douglas has since modified the severe judgment of sentimental writing expressed in this essay and also in her influential *Feminization of American Culture* (New York: Knopf, 1977). Richard Brodhead, "Sparing the Rod: Discipline and Fiction in Antebellum America," *Representations* 21 (1988): 67–96, and "Veiled Ladies: Toward a History of Antebellum Entertainment," *American Literary History* 1 (1989): 273–294. Emily Stipes Watts thinks that Sigourney's obituary verse responds to, rather than acquiesces in, women's increasing isolation as antebellum industrialization separated the worlds of men and women; see *The Poetry of American Women from 1632 to 1945* (Austin: University of Texas Press, 1977), 83–97.

10. For example, Linda Kerber, *Women of the Republic: Intellect and Ideology in Revolutionary America* (Chapel Hill: University of North Carolina Press, 1980); Mary Beth Norton, *Liberty's Daughters: The Revolutionary Experience of American Women* (Boston: Little, Brown, 1980). See also Mary Kelley, *Private Woman, Public Stage: Literary Domesticity in Nineteenth-Century America* (New York: Oxford University Press, 1984).

11. I allude to two well-known essays: Carroll Smith-Rosenberg's "The Female World of Love and Ritual: Relations between Women in Nineteenth-Century America," *Signs* 1 (1975): 1–29, and Barbara Welter's 1966 "Cult of True Womanhood, 1800–1860," reprinted in her collection, *Dimity Convictions: The American Woman in the Nineteenth Century* (Athens: Ohio University Press, 1976).

12. Sigourney, *Letters to Young Ladies* (Hartford: P. Canfield, 1833), 125, 143, 144–145. I base the discussion to follow on a reading of eighteen of Sigourney's books and on her descriptive catalog of all her books in *Letters*, 324–365.

13. Linda Kerber's "Separate Spheres, Female Worlds, Woman's Place: The

Rhetoric of Women's History," *Journal of American History* 75 (1988): 9–39, treats the "separate spheres" as a discursive construct rather than an empirical fact and discusses its use and limitations as a tool of cultural analysis. Little work has been done on American women's historical writing; for more findings from an excavatory project of which this essay is also part, see my "Onward, Christian Women: Sarah J. Hale's History of the World," *New England Quarterly* 73 (1990): 249–270; "Mercy Otis Warren's Gendered Melodrama of Revolution," *South Atlantic Quarterly* 90 (1991): 531–554; "Women and the Republic: Emma Willard's Rhetoric of History," *American Quarterly* 43 (1991): 1–23; and "The Ann Sisters: Elizabeth Peabody's Millenial Historicism," *American Literary History* 3 (1991): 27–45. See also my *Feminism and American Literary History* (New Brunswick, N.J.: Rutgers University Press, 1992).

14. One of Sigourney's first pupils, and a lifelong friend, Frances Manwaring Caulkins (whose name has disappeared completely from literary history), wrote two massive local histories of Norwich and New London and became the first (and for a long time the only) woman member of the Massachusetts Historical Society; her work was in part inspired by Sigourney's tutelage.

15. For examples of lesson books, see Sigourney, *Evening Readings in History: Comprising Portions of the History of Assyria, Egypt, Tyre, Syria, Persia, and the Sacred Scriptures; with Questions, Arranged for the Use of the Young, and of Family Circles* (Springfield, Mass.: G. & C. Merriam, 1833)—"written with a desire of aiding a laudable custom, established by some of my particular friends, of devoting an hour in the evening to a course of reading with the younger members of their families, and examinations into their proficiency on the general departments of Education."), v; and Sigourney, *History of Marcus Aurelius, Emperor of Rome* (Hartford: Belknap & Hamersley, 1835)—"This book was commenced as an assistant to parents in domestic education. Its highest ambition is to be in the hand of the mother, who seeks to aid in that most delightful of all departments, the instruction of her little ones" (iii). Haight's bibliography mistakenly attributes Lydia Child's 1837 *History of the Condition of Women* to Sigourney.

16. Sandra A. Zagarell, "Expanding 'America': Lydia Sigourney's *Sketch of Connecticut,* Catharine Sedgwick's *Hope Leslie,*" *Tulsa Studies in Women's Literature* 6 (1987): 225–246. In "Narrative of Community: The Identification of a Genre," *Signs* 13 (1988): 498–527, Zagarell situates the *Sketch of Connecticut* in a specifically female genre conformable to the psychological model developed by Nancy Chodorow in *The Reproduction of Mothering: Psychoanalysis and the Sociology of Gender* (Berkeley: University of California Press, 1978) and Carol Gilligan in *In a Different Voice: Psychological Theory and Women's Development* (Cambridge: Harvard University Press, 1982).

17. For succinct descriptions of republican ideologies see Linda Kerber, "The Republican Ideology of the Revolutionary Generation," *American Quarterly* 37 (1985): 474–495; and Joyce Appleby, "Republicanism in Old and New Contexts," *William and Mary Quarterly* 43 (1986): 20–43. On the religiocentric strain in antebellum New England writing, see Lawrence Buell, *New England Literary Culture: From Revolution Through Renaissance* (New York: Cambridge University Press, 1986).

18. Sigourney, *Myrtis, with Other Etchings and Sketchings* (New York: Harper, 1846), pp. 137–138.

19. Sigourney, "Traits of the Aborigines of America. A Poem" (Cambridge, Mass.: "from the University Press," 1822). Sigourney says that the poem was written two years before her marriage in 1819 (that is, in 1817) but that its publication was delayed. Even the 1822 date makes this one of the earlier noncaptivity publications on the Indian topic. Haight declares that it was Charles Sigourney's idea to annotate the poem, and that he wrote the notes as well (*Sweet Singer,* 25; *Notable American Women,* 3:289); Sigourney says only that her husband helped her revise the notes (*Letters,* 327).

20. Sigourney, "The Western Home," in *The Western Home, and Other Poems* (Philadelphia: Parry & McMillan, 1854); *Lucy Howard's Journal* (New York: Harper, 1858).

JOYCE W. WARREN

Domesticity and the Economics of Independence: Resistance and Revolution in the Work of Fanny Fern

I believe that when one woman is pushed to the wall, all her sex are injured by it. And though she may box my ears for saying it, it only shows what moral and mental rasping the poor thing has experienced that she cannot see a friend in Fanny Fern.[1]

THROUGHOUT HER TWENTY-ONE-YEAR CAREER as a newspaper columnist, Fanny Fern (Sara Willis Parton, 1811–1872) wrote on many subjects: literature, prison reform, prostitution, venereal disease, family planning, divorce, education, child rearing, and rights for women. If, however, one were to ask what ideas emerge as the most important in Fern's work—the most important to her and also the most important for the readers of today—one would point to Fern's critique of the domestic scene in mid-nineteenth-century America and her call for economic independence for women. Fern was not unique in expressing these ideas; other women writers who addressed one or both of these issues at the time included Margaret Fuller, Lydia Maria Child, and other women's rights advocates, abolitionist feminists, and utopian philosophers. The principal difference was that, unlike many of these other writers, although Fern's ideas were controversial, she did not write for a limited audience. In fact, she was one of the most popular writers of her day—and the most highly paid newspaper writer of her time.[2]

Fern's writing was not only polemical; it was also satirical, and it was

her pungent satire that sold newspapers and books. It is this combination
of popularity and unpopular ideas that makes a study of Fern's work
essential to an understanding of nineteenth-century American literature
and culture. Earlier interpretations have assumed that in mid-nineteenth-
century American society the naysayers—usually male—were unpopular
while the popular writers—usually female—were acquiescent.[3] That the
outspoken Fanny Fern was so popular among people of all classes and
backgrounds clearly shows that this image of American literature and
culture needs to be looked at with new eyes. A principal significance of
Fern's work, then, is that it indicates that popular women writers in
nineteenth-century America were not uniformly supportive of convention, or even just subtly subversive.[4] Fanny Fern's work says "No," if not
"in thunder," then in chain lightning; and in some respects it is revolutionary. In the following essay, I will analyze Fern's writings, first with respect
to her critique of domesticity, and second with respect to her call for
economic independence for women.

"The Tear of a Wife"

In Mary E. Wilkins Freeman's 1891 short story "The Revolt of 'Mother',"
Sarah Penn says to her daughter:

> You ain't found out yet we're women-folks, Nanny Penn. . . . One
> of these days you'll find it out, an' then you'll know that we know
> only what men-folks think we do, so far as any use of it goes, an'
> how we'd ought to reckon men-folks in with Providence, an' not
> complain of what they do any more than we do of the weather.[5]

Despite individual differences among nineteenth-century women writers regarding the ideology of domesticity, this advice, handed down from
mother to daughter, can be said to represent the one tenet of a woman's
domestic life—and since her life at the time was primarily domestic, of her
life in general—the one tenet that remained a given in the lives of
nineteenth-century American women of all classes and backgrounds.[6]
One woman who did question male authority, however, without qualifica-
tion and without apology, both in her private life and in her public voice,
was Fanny Fern. Her main theme was that women should be treated as
individuals, not treated as voiceless, unthinking adjuncts to their husbands, fathers, or brothers. Attacking the nineteenth-century construct of
domestic life, Fern used pungent satire and down-to-earth prose to ham-
mer home her criticism of the conventional view. A formidable critic, she
wrote as, a century later, Hélène Cixous would advise women to write: in
her own woman's voice, and, like the Medusa, she laughed.[7] Before we

examine her ideas, let us look briefly at two articles published early in her career which exemplify her attitude.

In "The Tear of a Wife," published in 1852, Fern began with a quotation from a contemporary newspaper: "The tear of a loving girl is like a dew-drop on a rose; but on the cheek of a wife, is a drop of poison to her husband." In response to this comment, Fern wrote:

It is "an ill wind that blows *nobody* any good." Papas will be happy to hear that twenty-five dollar pocket-handkerchiefs can be dispensed with *now*, in the bridal *trousseau*. Their "occupation's gone"! Matrimonial tears "are poison." There is no knowing what you will do, girls, with that escape-valve shut off; but that is no more to the point, than—whether you have anything to smile at or not; one thing is settled—*you mustn't cry!* Never mind back aches, and side aches, and head aches, and dropsical complaints, and smoky chimneys, and old coats, and young babies! *Smile! It flatters your husband.* He wants to be *considered* the source of your happiness, whether he was baptized *Nero* or *Moses!* Your mind *never* being supposed to be occupied with any other subject than himself, of course a tear is a tacit reproach. Besides, you miserable whimperer, what have you to cry for? A-i-n-t y-o-u m-a-r-r-i-e-d? Isn't that the *summum bonum*—the height of feminine ambition? You *can't* get beyond *that!* It's the *jumping-off* place! You've arriv!—got to the end of your journey! Stage puts up *there!* You've nothing to do but retire on your laurels, and spend the rest of your life endeavoring to be thankful that you are Mrs. John Smith! "*Smile!*" you simpleton![8]

The second article, "Awe-ful Thoughts," was published in 1856 in response to a quotation that stated, "*Awe* . . . is the most delicious feeling a wife can have toward her husband." Fern wrote:

"AWE!"—awe of a man whose whiskers you have trimmed, whose hair you have cut, whose cravats you have tied, whose shirts you have "put into the wash," whose boots and shoes you have kicked into the closet, whose dressing-gown you have worn while combing your hair; . . . who has hooked your dresses, unlaced your boots, fastened your bracelets, and tied on your bonnet; who has stood before your looking-glass, with thumb and finger on his proboscis, scraping his chin; whom you have buttered, and sugared, and toasted, and tea-ed; whom you have seen asleep with his mouth wide open! Ri---diculous! (NYL, November 1, 1856)

These two articles give us an idea of Fern's perspective. Laughing at and consequently undercutting the hallowed image of husbands and marriage,

Fern wrote from the perspective that marriage is *not* the romantic institution it was believed to be and that husbands are *not* gods.

In her critique of the domestic scene, Fern developed her argument around certain major assertions. Her first assertion was that the current concept of marriage was not just; it gave men all of the advantages. Fern said that she would like to make a bonfire of all the books of advice to women (OB, February 14, 1852). "There is not one sensible or *just* book of advice for women," she said; they are all "selfish" and one-sided" and would make a woman "reflect *his* thoughts, *his* opinions, narrow as they often are, as if God had endowed her with no individuality, no brain to think, or heart to feel" (NYL, March 17, 1860). Women are told by pulpit and press to hide their own irritations and put on an angelic smile for their husbands, Fern said; at the same time they are told that they must expect harsh words from their husbands. "Away with such one-sided moralizing," she wrote in 1857; "I have no patience with those who would reduce woman to a mere machine" (NYL, October 24, 1857). And she added in 1861, "We believe in laying down no rule of conduct for the wife which will not apply equally to the husband" (NYL, June 18, 1861).

Fern's second assertion was that marriage had been falsely romanticized. In "A Whisper to Romantic Young Ladies," published in 1852, Fern pulled the rug out from under the romantic notion of marriage. Responding to a quotation idealizing marriage, she wrote:

> Girls! *that's a humbug!* The very *thought* of it makes me groan. It's all moonshine. In fact, men and moonshine in my dictionary are synonymous. . . . When . . . your wedding dress is put away in a trunk for the benefit of posterity, if you can get your husband to *smile* on anything short of a "sirloin" or a roast turkey, you are a lucky woman. . . . Lovers have a trick of getting disenchanted, too, when they see their Aramintas with dresses pinned up round the waist, hair powdered with sweeping, faces scowled up over the wash-tub, and soap-suds dripping from red elbows.
>
> We know these little accidents never happen in novels—where the heroine is always "dressed in white, with a rose-bud in her hair," and lives on blossoms and May dew! There are no wash-tubs or gridirons in *her* cottage; *her* children are born cherubim, with a seraphic contempt for dirt pies and molasses. *She* remains "a beauty" to the end of the chapter, and "steps out" just in time to anticipate her first gray hair, her husband drawing his last breath at the same time, as a dutiful husband *should;* and not falling into the unromantic error of outliving his grief, and marrying a second time!

> But this humdrum life, girls, is another affair, with its washing and ironing and cleaning days, when children expect boxed ears, and visitors picked-up dinners. All the "romance" there is in it, you can put under a three-cent piece.[9]

Not only did Fern insist that marriage was not idyllic, she also pointed out that it was often destructive to women. One of her most moving articles is the short piece "Owls Kill Humming-birds," published in 1852, which depicts the tragedy for a woman of marriage to a Casaubon:

> If you have the bump of mirthfulness developed, don't marry a tombstone. . . . You go plodding through life with him to the dead-march of his own leaden thoughts. *You* revel in the sunbeams; *he* likes the shadows. You are on the hill-tops; he is in the plains. . . .
> No—no—make no such shipwreck of yourself. Marry a man who is not too ascetic to enjoy a good, merry laugh. *Owls kill humming-birds!* (TF, December 11, 1852)

In this article Fern's use of the word "kill" can be interpreted figuratively to mean the wearing down of a woman's spirit. However, in other articles she makes clear that she also believed that marriage could literally kill. Women, she said, were worn down by neglect and cruelty, and worked to death by too much housework and too many children. As Fern wrote in 1861, "Life for most women is a horrid grind. They are placed in a treadmill and then taunted for being narrowed down to its peck-measure limit" (NYL, March 23, 1861). Men would hang themselves, she said, if they had to do the repetitive, grinding work that women do 365 days a year (NYL, June 8, 1861). Fern also used strong words about the women and children who were destroyed by the venereal disease that their husbands brought home. It was all of these abuses of male authority that caused Fern to conclude that some marriages were "legal murders." She wrote in 1870:

> What do I mean by "legal murders"? Well, if a woman is knocked on the head with a flat-iron by her husband and killed, or if arsenic is mixed with her food, or if a bullet is sent through her brain, the law takes cognizance of it. But what of the cruel words that just as surely kill, by constant repetition? What of the neglect? What of the diseased children of a pure, healthy mother? What of the ten or twelve, even healthy children, "who come," one after another, into the weary arms of a really good woman, who yet never knows the meaning of the word *rest* till the coffin-lid shuts her in from all earthly care and

pain? . . . I could write flaming words about "the inscrutable Providence which has seen fit to remove our dear sister in her youth from the bosom of her young family," as the funeral prayer phrases it.

Providence did nothing of the sort. Poor Providence! It is astonishing how busy people are making up bundles to lay on *His* shoulders! I imagine Providence meant that women, as well as men, should have a right to their own lives. (NYL, March 12, 1870)

In this article and elsewhere, Fern makes clear that it is not *Providence* that causes the premature deaths of women; the deaths of many women, she says, are caused by the selfish attitude of husbands who have absolute authority over their wives and are permitted by culture and the law to mistreat, use, or neglect their wives with impunity.

As Fern realized, the problem was not only that society protected and countenanced the concept of male authority, but that for the most part women themselves did not question it. Consequently, the third aspect of Fern's argument was that women needed to assert themselves and put a stop to their enslavement and victimization. Although they might love their families, she said, they should not sacrifice themselves for anyone. She wrote in 1869, "Nobody will thank you for turning yourself into a machine. When you drop in your tracks, they will just shovel the earth over you, and get Jerusha Ann Sombody to step into your shoes. . . . So you just take a little comfort yourself as you go along, and look after 'No. 1'" (NYL, September 4, 1869). In a society that believed the ideal woman to be totally selfless and acquiescent, Fern's assertion that a woman must look out for "No. 1" was startling. But, she said, the insane asylums and cemeteries were full of women who had been denied their individuality by husbands who treated them like machines. Broken in body and spirit, they went insane or died of overwork (NYL, September 20, 1862).

Given this assessment of marriage, the fourth aspect of Fern's argument was to urge women to develop themselves intellectually and financially so that they could be independent of marriage as a means of fulfillment and/ or support. Women, she said, need to take time to cultivate themselves by reading and writing, either to find employment outside the home or simply to save themselves from "dying," literally or figuratively. "Be clean but not too clean," she wrote in 1872. "Stop and take a breath and while you stop . . . to rest, read. So shall the cobwebs be brushed from your neglected brain, and you shall learn that something else besides cleanliness is necessary to make home *really* home" (NYL, April 6, 1872). She also advised women to write—for publication, if they had the talent, but also just for themselves. Surprisingly modern in her realization of the therapeutic value of writing, Fern insisted that a woman who was unhappy and depressed could find comfort in expressing her thoughts on paper (NYL, August 10, 1867).

Finally, Fern's solution to the dilemma in which women found them-selves was not simply for women to assert their independence, either by independent action within the home or by pursuing financially rewarding occupations outside the home; she also urged men to take an active part in the domestic scene. Men need to become partners in the domestic scene, helping with child care and housework, she said, and in general making the home a pleasant place to be; they should not be simply the selfish recipients of female service. Writing of the "*mutual* obligations" of the married couple (NYL, June 18, 1861), Fern urged men and women to "pull evenly in the matrimonial harness" (NYL, October 4, 1856). This meant that a man should do his best to make his home bright and cheerful, not expect his wife to do all the soothing while he remained surly and irritable (NYL, October 4, 1856; June 18, 1861; July 9, 1870). In addition, she urged the husband to help with the housework if necessary. And, most important she said, a father should help with the children: "Don't be too dignified or manly (?) to tend your own flesh-and-blood baby, when your wife has little or no assistance" (NYL, March 6, 1858; November 18, 1865).

Maintaining that it was ridiculous to assume that just because a woman was a woman she should enjoy housework (NYL, October 7, 1871), Fern wrote in an article entitled "An Honest Growl": "I am sick, in an age which produced a Brontë and a Browning, of the prate of men who assert that *every* woman should be a perfect housekeeper, and *fail to add,* that every man should be a perfect carpenter" (NYL, November 17, 1860). A husband should recognize when his wife has too much to do, Fern said, and should help her. In an 1866 article called "Our Real Need," she wrote, "[A weary wife] needs some kind voice to say . . . : 'Come—leave all your cares just *now—this minute*—and if you can't leave without I take your place, I'll take it, and it will be a gain to both of us' " (NYL, May 26, 1866).

Fanny Fern believed in the family state, but as she wrote early in her career. "If you are romantic, dig clams, but don't get married" (OB, August 14, 1852). Moreover, although she was fond of children, she did not idealize motherhood. She insisted that mothers *and* fathers should share in child rearing. Fern was not a theorist; she dealt with life as it was lived. Her articles portray real-life situations with which she had become familiar through experience or observation. She satirized the pretensions and abuses of male authority and criticized injustice wherever she found it. If she did not portray marriage and domestic life as all sunshine and flowers, it was because she did not see them that way. As she said in 1852,

"I have seen too much of life to be merry at a wedding" (OB, May 1, 1852).

The Economics of Independence

The most revolutionary aspect of Fern's assessment of the domestic scene was her conclusion that women would never be free of male domination until they were financially independent. Fern realized that even when a woman was wealthy because of her husband's or father's status, as long as she was dependent upon a man—husband, father, brother—for financial security, she could have no autonomy as a human being. The woman's opinions were not listened to; her conversation was regarded as trivial. She had no more autonomy in society than a child. Fern herself said that she resented the "fence that was put up around women to keep them from seeing anything but feathers and bracelets." When women are interested in other matters, she said, they are "patronizingly soothed like some amiable lunatic or else majestically snubbed" (NYL, December 28, 1861). Having the vote would help, Fern said, and other rights were important. But if women were to be taken seriously, she concluded, they would have to be able to earn and possess money independently of the men in their life.

In expressing these sentiments Fern was far in advance of her time. Her contemporaries—male and female—were highly critical of a woman who was assertive enough to compete with men and defy the restrictions placed on women's activities by the "cult of the lady."[10] In an 1857 article Fern advised women to follow her example, despite criticism and accusations of being unfeminine. Women should not be intimidated by the criticism of "conservative old ladies of both sexes," she asserted. As she said of Harriet Hosmer, the sculptor, she was glad that she "had the courage to assert herself—to be what nature intended her to be—a genius—even at the risk of being called unfeminine, eccentric, and unwomanly" (NYL, December 19, 1857).

Moreover, Fern commented, once a woman becomes successful, she need not worry about her critics: "*Take* your rights, my sisters; don't beg for them! Never mind what objectors say or think. Success will soon stop their mouths. Nothing like that to conquer prejudice and narrowness and ill-will" (NYL, July 16, 1870). And, as she said in an 1866 article supporting women lecturers against the criticism they received: "They can stand the spiteful criticism with a good house over their independent heads, secured and paid for by their honest industry, . . . with greenbacks and Treasury notes stowed away against a rainy day" (NYL, December 8, 1866).

Not only would success silence the critics or soften their sting, but women would receive better treatment once they were independent. They would not be vulnerable to insult or "rough usage"; even people who were naturally rude would be self-seeking enough to modify their behavior around an independent—and consequently powerful—woman. "She won't *have* rough usage. She will be in a position to receive good treatment from *motives of policy,* from those natures which are incapable of better, and higher. She will, in short, stand on her own blessed independent feet as far as 'getting a living' is concerned, as I do to-day" (NYL, September 16, 1869).

Fern's main argument in favor of economic independence for women derived from her own experience in being coerced into marriage as a means of support.[11] Marriage, she insisted over and over, should not be viewed as a way of "getting a living." No way of getting a living, she said, was harder. Moreover, the independent woman would not need to be driven to marry someone she did not love and respect just to keep the wolf from the door. In response to a newspaper writer who had criticized female physicians, Fern wrote in the *Ledger* on July 16, 1870: "Why shouldn't women work *for pay?* Does anybody object when women *marry for pay?*—without love, without respect, nay with even aversion? . . . How much more to be honored is she who, hewing out her own path, through prejudice and narrowness and even insult, earns honorably and honestly her own independence."

Not only should a woman be financially independent so that she would not be driven to marry for support, she should also be independent so that she could extricate herself from a brutalizing marriage. In a courageous article in the *Ledger* in 1857, Fern wrote that a woman had the right to leave her husband, and even her children if necessary (since the law at the time would not give her custody), rather than remain in a brutalizing marriage. "Don't shrink from the toil of self-support," Fern advised (NYL, October 24, 1857).

Fern advocated that all avenues of employment be open to women as they were to men and that women receive equal pay for equal work. In 1857, after seeing women working in the Philadelphia mint, she commented, "I was glad, as I always am, in a fitting establishment, to see *women* employed in various offices . . . and more glad still, to learn that they had respectable wages" (NYL, July 18, 1857). Fern's position on this matter grew out of her own experience of poverty after her husband died. Trying to support herself and her two children by working as a seamstress, she gained a sympathy for poor working women that caused her to say that it was not surprising that desperate young women were driven into prostitution, because they could not earn a living wage in the few employments open to them (e.g., TF, January 29, 1853).

Fern also urged economic independence for women because she believed that too many women lived purposeless lives and that economic endeavors would give them purpose. The average middle-class woman's life was trivialized and meaningless, a round of fashions and social calls. The woman who is constantly going to the doctor, Fern said, may not even be sick: "Half the time nothing in the world ails [her] but the want of some absorbing occupation or interest" (NYL, October 10, 1868). In an article about women's art, Fern commented that she was always glad to see women do a meritorious thing: "Every such step helps lift them from the torpid aimlessness which is the bane of so many women's lives" (NYL, June 3, 1865). In 1868 she commended the "self-supporting women" who put "to shame the useless lives of the idle ladies who remorselessly wear out the souls of men in vain struggle for fashionable supremacy" (NYL, December 5, 1868).

Finally, Fern wanted to see women active outside the home because, as she wrote with respect to women lecturers, every woman has a right to use her "God-given talents": "If the lady had a gift for something else than 'darning stockings' all her life, she had a right, and did well to exercise it" (NYL, May 23, 1863).

What had happened to bring Fanny Fern to a position so different from that of most of her contemporaries? During the time that she was living in poverty, and as she portrays so graphically in *Ruth Hall*, she found that her friends and relatives wanted to have nothing to do with her. Friends she had entertained at her home when she was in comfortable circumstances were embarrassed to know her in poverty. Once she became famous, however, people who had cut her on the street were anxious to know her; her relatives and friends all sought to be remembered by the famous writer. This experience caused Fern to recognize with bitterness the gap between society's ostensible values and the reality of the effect of poverty. Although it was an accepted fact in American capitalistic society that in a man "money talks," nineteenth-century Americans regarded the fluid social structure as a male phenomenon. Women were outside the money economy; they were simply expected to reflect the status of their male protectors. Nineteenth-century American middle- and upper-class white women were conditioned to believe that their value as women was intrinsic, that they needed only to be good wives and mothers and religiously devout and they would be respected and esteemed for their "womanly" qualities. [12]

Fern's descent into poverty showed her the hypocrisy behind the facade of society's values; she concluded that in American society, "worth"—with respect to women as well as men—was in actuality measured in dollars. In effect, she was radicalized by her widowhood and the ensuing circumstances. As long as she was dependent upon her male relatives, she was powerless to determine her own fate or the fate of her children.

Two factors in Fern's private life are particularly significant in assessing her independent stance: her second marriage, which was a marriage of convenience that she had entered into under pressure from her father, but which her daughter later characterized as a "terrible mistake"; and the terms of her father-in-law's will, which withheld money from her children unless she agreed to give them up.[13] These two experiences helped drive Fern into her position on the financial independence of women. Forced into a brutalizing marriage and threatened with the loss of her children by her father-in-law's will, she recognized the vulnerability of the woman who was economically dependent. It was only after she acquired money of her own that she gained the power of self-determination. And even after she married a third time, she refused to give up the independence she had struggled so hard to win.[14] Fern's strong position on these issues was at a great personal cost to herself: her husband's family refused to accept her; her contemporaries spread malicious gossip about her; and "respectable" people refused to meet her.[15]

In order to come to this position of independence, Fern not only defied tradition, she also diverged from the religious teachings of her society. Although she was criticized for her defiance, she refused to accept the religious view that woman was dependent by nature and divine law. Responding directly to theologians such as Horace Bushnell and John Todd, who, writing against women's rights, warned of the dangers of women "unsexing" themselves by pursuing "masculine" activities, Fern cited examples of specific women working in the eighteenth and early nineteenth centuries. Such women, she said sarcastically, "did not ask leave of Doctors Bushnell or Todd to step out of [their] 'God-appointed woman's sphere'" (NYL, November 6, 1869). Moreover, unlike many of the women writers of her period who portrayed religion as an aid in women's "practice of submission,"[16] Fern saw religion as a spur to female achievement. In Susan Warner's *The Wide, Wide World* (1851) and Maria Cummins's *The Lamplighter* (1854), for example, religion helps the heroine gain a victory over self and assists her in her struggle to put down her feelings of rebellion. The protagonist of Fern's novel *Ruth Hall* (1855), however, finds in religion the encouragement she needs to continue her struggle for independence in defiance of society and of her male relatives. After her brother has refused to help her, her father has connived with her in-laws to take one of her children away from her, and she has tramped the streets unsuccessfully for days in the attempt to sell an article to one of the newspapers, Ruth, weary and filled with despair, takes her little daughter into a church. Inspired by prayer and the religious injunction not to be afraid, she gains the courage to renew her struggle; where she had entered the church with a "broken wing," she goes out "soaring," and ready to do battle with those who would restrain her.[17]

In this respect Fern's autobiographical novel *Ruth Hall* is closer to the slave narrative of Harriet Jacobs, *Incidents in the Life of a Slave Girl* (1861), than to the novels written by middle-class white women of the period. Both Jacobs and Fern were critical of the church as an institution when it diverged from the Christian principles of love and charity.[18] And both rejected the attempts of others to use religion to force submission: Fern rejected the patriarchal preaching that would make a woman passive in the name of "femininity"; Jacobs rejected the teachings of slavery, the "patriarchal institution" that claimed that slavery was the ordinance of God.[19] Jacobs, who had hidden for seven years in a tiny space in her grandmother's house rather than surrender to her white master, gained encouragement from religion to defy her master and the society that would enslave her. When Linda Brent is about to run away from her master, for example, she stops to pray in the cemetery at her parents' graves; she seems to hear her father's voice coming from the demolished church urging her to seek her freedom, and she goes away with "renovated hopes."[20] After seven years in hiding, when she is about to leave for the North, she prays with her grandmother and her young son and feels inspired to go on.[21] Both Fern and Jacobs rejected the patriarchal religion that would crush them; instead their spiritual beliefs helped provide them with the strength to rebel.

Susan Warner's heroine in *The Wide, Wide World* is taught submissiveness by her mother, who counsels passive acceptance in the face of her father's tyranny.[22] Fern and Jacobs, however, differentiate between acts of Providence and man-made cruelty. As Jacobs writes in *Incidents in the Life of a Slave Girl*, "When separations come by the hand of death, the pious soul can bow in resignation, and say, 'Not my will, but thine be done, O Lord!' But when the ruthless hand of man strikes the blow, regardless of the misery he causes, it is hard to be submissive."[23]

This similarity between the ideas of Fern and Jacobs is not only coincidence—they knew each other quite well.[24] There are other important parallels, also. Jacobs was driven to her desperate action by the same two motives that drove Fanny Fern. First, they shared a desire to preserve their sexual integrity. In Fern's *Rose Clark*, Gertrude Dean, whose story was based on the second marriage of Fern herself, shudders at the footsteps of the husband she does not love, whose financial power gives him the right to use her sexually even while she despises him; she can see her "bill of sale" on all of his possessions.[25] In desperation, Fanny Fern left her husband, just as

Harriet Jacobs fled rather than submit sexually to the master she despised. Obviously, the situation of the slave woman is not comparable to that of the free woman, who has rights and privileges and the respect of society, all of which are denied the slave. There are similarities, however, in the lack of power and the sexual vulnerability of both women.

The other parallel between Fern and Jacobs is the motivating factor of their children. Fern, as we have seen, was driven to seek her independence by the terms of her father-in-law's will, which would have taken her children away from her. Similarly, Jacobs was driven to run away in order to save her children. Her grandmother urged her to stay, but she saw her masters' plan to put her children "into their power in order to give them a stronger hold" on her. She realized that the only way she could save her children was to leave: "Nothing less than the freedom of my children would have induced me" to run away.[26] Jacobs, of course, sought more than independence; she sought freedom also. But a comparison of the two writers provides a significant comment on the position of women in nineteenth-century America: slave or free, women were dependent upon and answerable to men; without autonomy in society or in the home, their bodies and their children were not their own.

What was most unusual about Fern's concept of the independent woman was that not only did most people of the time not believe women should be independent, but those who did think women should have the right to earn a living generally were speaking of single women. Fern, however, did not view career and marriage as an either-or choice. Nor did she view a woman's professional career as only a stopgap measure to fill in the period between childhood and marriage. She believed the independent woman should remain independent after marriage. She recognized the difficulties, but she did not see the two as mutually incompatible. She wrote in the *Ledger* on September 18, 1869:

> Woman, be she married or single, being able to earn her own living independent of marriage—that often harder and most non-paying and most thankless road to it—will no longer have to face the alternative of serfdom or starvation, but will marry, when she does marry, for love and companionship, and for cooperation in all high and noble aims and purposes, not for bread and meat and clothes.

And in a July 9, 1870, article called "Self-Supporting Wives," in response to a newspaper writer who had worked himself "into a foam" at the idea of such wives, Fern wrote that women need not spend their lives suppressing their own worries to soothe irritable husbands; if they have the will and the ability to do so, they can go out into the world and support themselves.

Combining marriage and a career was not easy, Fern admitted. And in some cases—the right kind of man not being available—it might not be possible. She found it difficult to conceive of a woman doctor simultaneously carrying on the vocation of wife and mother, for example, and she noted that few men of her day would be unselfish enough to be a good husband to an artist wife (NYL, October 17, 1857; December 19, 1857; December 31, 1859). However, she believed that independence in marriage, such as she herself had attained, was possible and preferable. Near the end of her life she wrote, "A literary life is a tread-mill grind; and it is always that to a *married* literary woman, even if she be successful; because, to the ordinary labor and cares of all other wives and mothers, she superadds that of her profession. [But if] you pilot your steps safely, all the better for you; for sweet is the bread of independence" (NYL, July 8, 1871).

Ruth Hall was unlike most other American novels of the period: whereas most nineteenth-century American writers portrayed the female protagonist as submissive to male authority and ultimately content with the domestic sphere, Fern portrayed a protagonist who was bold, defiant, and a formidable economic competitor. It was this final point, Fern believed, that made the concept of financial independence for women so unpalatable to nineteenth-century American men. On September 21, 1872, a month before she died, Fern wrote of a conversation she had heard regarding a widow who had taken over her husband's construction business and managed it brilliantly. Fern was appalled to hear not one word of praise for this admirable woman. Even men from whom she would have expected sympathy could only ask, "Where was the baby?" or other sniping questions. Fern found that although there was no fault in the woman's character, she was universally criticized. Why? Fern asked herself: "At last I hit upon it. . . . She was *not* 'the clinging vine!'" This was what men objected to: she was able to function independently of and in a position superior to men, not only keeping the books, but superintending work on the building site and paying the men's salaries. It was this image of the woman having power over men that was so threatening. As Fern had concluded about men's opposition to women's voting: "This would place in our hands a weapon of power which they are very unwilling we should wield" (NYL, May 29, 1858).

A financial competitor wields a certain amount of power—power that Fern did not believe men were ready to see in women. She was not humble—that is, not "feminine"—in her recognition of her own power. When she was criticized by another woman writer for being "egotistical" because she referred to herself as famous, she replied that she did not believe in false modesty (NYL, December 10, 1864). Fanny Fern proudly asserted that she had attained her success on her own; she did not, like many women writers of the period, humbly ascribe her success to a husband or father or brother, or even to God.[27] On July 19, 1856, after she had bought a house with her own money, she wrote an apostrophe to her inkstand, "My Old Ink-Stand and I," in which she gloried in how "they," she and her inkstand, had done it all by themselves: bought a brand-new house (with title deed and insurance to prove it), fine furniture for the house, and food, clothes, and toys for her children.

This kind of self-assertion in a woman was shocking and somewhat unnerving to men. When Fern was criticized by an editor for not doing her own washing, she replied: "As long as Mr. Bonner pays me enough to buy out the editor's office, I will do just what the editor would do—turn from the washtub to the inkstand" (NYL, September 18, 1869). The suggestion that she had the power to buy and sell the editor who had criticized her was discomfiting to the editor—as she obviously intended it to be. Fanny Fern's challenge to men was loud and clear: "I believe in the woman *that is to be*. . . . She has as yet had to struggle with both hands tied, and then had her ears boxed for not doing more execution . . . Cut the string gentlemen. . . . Pooh! you are afraid" (NYL, June 18, 1870).

In 1852, one year after Fanny Fern began her career, she wrote on the Fourth of July that it was ironic to see *women* celebrating their independence, "dragging around with their fetters at their heels." "They'll know better when I get up that Fern Insurrection!" she said (OB, July 10, 1852). The revolution that Fern referred to here might have been interpreted as a political one, or her words could simply have been interpreted as a joke. In retrospect, however, and after examining her writings over the twenty-one years of her career, one can see that she did indeed preach revolution. It was not a political revolution, however; it was a gender-related economic revolution. "I want all women to render themselves independent of marriage as a mere means of support," she wrote in the *New York Ledger* on June 26, 1869. This was the "Fern Insurrection."

NOTES

Material used in this essay appeared in my biography of Fern, *Fanny Fern: An Independent Woman* (New Brunswick, N.J.: Rutgers University Press, 1992).

1. Fanny Fern, *New York Ledger*, September 12, 1868. Subsequent references to the *Ledger* will be cited in the text as NYL.

2. In 1855 Fern was paid one hundred dollars a column to write for the *New York Ledger*. Information about Fern's life derives primarily from her papers in the Sophia Smith Collection at Smith College; her husband James Parton's papers at the Houghton Library, Harvard University; and her newspaper articles. Recent studies of Fern that gives useful biographical information include Joyce W. Warren,

Fanny Fern: An Independent Woman (New Brunswick, N.J.: Rutgers University Press, 1992); Warren, Introduction to *Ruth Hall and Other Writings* (New Brunswick, N.J.: Rutgers University Press, 1986); Mary Kelley, *Private Woman, Public Stage: Literary Domesticity in Nineteenth-Century America* (New York: Oxford University Press, 1984); Ann Douglas Wood, "The Scribbling Women and Fanny Fern: Why Women Wrote," *American Quarterly* 23 (September 1971): 3–14.

3. This assumption is behind the thinking of writers like Fred Lewis Pattee, for example, *The Feminine Fifties* (New York: D. Appleton-Century, 1940). Twentieth-century scholars have been fond of quoting Melville, who lamented his inability to write works that would sell, and Hawthorne, who criticized the "damned mob of scribbling women" because their works sold better than his own.

4. Writers who have sought to prove that the popular nineteenth-century American women writers were not as acquiescent as they are usually perceived have tended to look for subversive elements. The most obvious example of this tendency is Helen Papashvily, *All the Happy Endings* (New York: Harper & Brothers, 1956).

5. Mary E. Wilkins Freeman, "The Revolt of Mother," in *A New England Nun and Other Stories* (New York: Harper & Brothers, 1891), 451–452.

6. For a discussion of the definition of womanhood in nineteenth-century America see Barbara Welter, "The Cult of True Womanhood," *American Quarterly* 18 (Summer 1966): 151–162, 173–174. Welter writes: "The attributes of True Womanhood, by which a woman judged herself and was judged by her husband, her neighbors, and society could be divided into four cardinal virtues—piety, purity, submissiveness and domesticity. . . . Without them, no matter whether there was fame, achievement or wealth, all was ashes." Although the issue is more complex than this prescription might imply, the idea that woman's most important role was her role as wife and mother was a dominant feature of nineteenth-century thought. It was the opinion, for example, of Catharine Beecher, the principal and founder of the Hartford Female Seminary, which Fern attended. Beecher was herself an independent woman and a pioneer in the education of woman, yet she held the conventional view of women as passive and subordinate to men in all areas; she opposed political equality for women; and her main purpose in educating women, besides training them as teachers, was to train them for their domestic role. See, for example, Beecher's *Suggestions on Education; The Elements of Mental and Moral Philosophy, Founded upon Experience, Reason, and the Bible* (Hartford, Conn.: Peter B. Gleason & Co., 1831); *An Essay on Slavery and Abolitionism, with Reference to the Duty of American Females* (Philadelphia: Henry Perkins, 1837); and *A Treatise on Domestic Economy, for the Use of Young Ladies at Home, and at School* (Boston: Marsh, Capen, Lyon, and Webb, 1841). Of course, one cannot assume that all men and women shared these beliefs. Feminist-abolitionists in the mid-nineteenth century, for example, although they accepted the virtues of piety, purity, and domesticity, argued women's right to pursue activities other than the domestic, and they rejected the concept of submissiveness. See, for example, Blanche Glassman Hersh, *The Slavery of Sex: Feminist-Abolitionists in America* (Urbana: University of Illinois Press, 1978), 189–190, 208–209. Recent studies of

male-female relationships in the mid-nineteenth century, however, indicate that although "the mid-nineteenth century exalted the idea of a loving, companionate, egalitarian marriage, . . . in reality, the wife remained subordinate." See Ellen K. Rothman, *Hands and Hearts: A History of Courtship in America* (New York: Basic Books, 1984), 145. See also William Leach, *True Love and Perfect Union: The Feminist Reform of Sex and Society* (New York: Basic Books, 1980); and Karen Lystra, *Searching the Heart: Women, Men and Romantic Love in Nineteenth-Century America* (New York: Oxford University Press, 1989). Lystra writes that although patriarchal control in a household had come into question in the nineteenth century, "hierarchical gender distinctions nonetheless remained powerful" (230, 236). A particularly useful study of women's roles in the nineteenth century is Carroll Smith-Rosenberg, *Disorderly Conduct: Visions of Gender in Victorian America* (New York: Alfred A. Knopf, 1985). In her study of the causes of hysteria, for example, she analyzes the effects of the narrow socialization of women: "Nineteenth-century American society provided but one socially respectable, nondeviant role for women—that of loving wife and mother. Thus women . . . had to find adjustment in one prescribed social role, one that demanded continual self-abnegation and a desire to please others" (213).

7. Hélène Cixous, "The Laugh of the Medusa, *Signs* 1 (Summer 1976): 875–893. Cixous writes: "Woman must write her self: must write about women and bring women to writing. . . . You only have to look at the Medusa straight on to see her. And she's not deadly. She's beautiful and she's laughing."

8. Fern, *Olive Branch,* August 28, 1852. Subsequent references to the *Olive Branch* will be cited in the text as OB.

9. Fern, *True Flag,* June 12, 1852. Subsequent references to the *True Flag* will be cited in the text as TF.

10. For an analysis of the problems faced by twelve women in mid-nineteenth-century America who attempted to combine a successful writing career with the period's limited definition of womanhood, see Kelley, *Private Woman, Public Stage.*

11. After Fern's first husband died in 1846, her relatives, particularly her father, pressured her to remarry in order to support herself and her two children. In January 1849, frankly asserting that she did not love him but under pressure from her father, Fern married Samuel Farrington, a widower with two children. In January 1851 she left Farrington. See, for example, Ethel Parton, "Fanny Fern, An Informal Biography," manuscript, Sophia Smith Collection, Smith College.

12. In an article entitled "The True Woman" in the *Ladies' Repository* in August 1853, the Reverend Jesse T. Peck expressed the general opinion of his age: "The true woman," he said, was "timid, shrinking, and retiring"; whereas man is suited to the "rude antagonisms and fierce collisions" of a public and professional life, woman is "meant for kindlier labor, where delicate sentiment, deep felt sympathy, devout affection, and subduing tenderness, can soften the asperities of life" (337)

13. For information about Fern's second marriage see The Farrington Papers in her papers in the Sophia Smith Collection, Smith College. A copy of Hezekiah Eldredge's will, dated July 16, 1851, is in the Register of Probate Court, Boston, Massachusetts.

14. Before Fern married James Parton in January 1856, after she was already famous as Fanny Fern, she had Parton sign a prenuptial agreement, stating that any money that she had already earned or would thenceforth earn would belong solely to her and to her children. This agreement, dated January 5, 1856, is in the Houghton Library, Harvard University.

15. That James Parton's family, particularly his sister, did not accept Fern into the family is apparent from the diary of Thomas Butler Gunn, 1856–1859, in the Missouri Historical Society, St. Louis. Gunn himself refused to be introduced to Fern before she married Parton because he regarded her as an immoral woman. Gossip circulated by her second husband and by William Moulton, an editor whom she had satirized in *Ruth Hall*, portrayed Fern as sexually promiscuous. This gossip was without foundation but was readily accepted by those who assumed that an "independent" woman must also be an immoral one. See, for example, the anonymous *Life and Beauties of Fanny Fern* (New York: H. Long, and Brother, 1855).

16. In *Sensational Designs: The Cultural Work of American Fiction, 1790–1860* (New York: Oxford University Press, 1985), Jane Tompkins points out that the use of religion in most nineteenth-century women's fiction is to aid the heroine in submission, not to man, but to God (162–163). However, the result in this world was the same: women could not rebel against the injustice of men. Tompkins points out the powerlessness of nineteenth-century American women and notes that rebellion was impossible because "they lacked the material means of escape or opposition" (161). The domestic novelists, Tompkins asserts, portrayed the way in which women forced themselves to submit to what appeared to be a necessity, and made it a source of power. Fanny Fern sought another way out: she advised women to gain "the material means" that would make rebellion possible.

17. Fern, *Ruth Hall* (New York: Mason Brothers, 1855), 123.

18. See, for example, Harriet Jacobs, *Incidents in the Life of a Slave Girl*, ed. Jean Fagan Yellin (Cambridge: Harvard University Press, 1987), 70–72, 74; Fanny Fern, NYL, February 10, 1872.

19. See, for example, Jacobs, *Incidents*, 18, 70–71, 74.

20. Ibid., 91.

21. Ibid., 155.

22. Susan Warner, *The Wide, Wide World*, ed. Jane Tompkins (New York: The Feminist Press, 1967), 12.

23. Jacobs, *Incidents*, 37.

24. For several years I had used *Ruth Hall* and *Incidents in the Life of a Slave Girl* as pivotal texts in a course on nineteenth-century American women writers, noting the similarities between them. Jean Fagan Yellin also notes the relationship between the two works in the notes to her edition of *Incidents* (254). It was not until my discovery of the diary of Thomas Butler Gunn in the Missouri Historical Society in March of 1987 that I knew for a certainty that Jacobs and Fern knew each other, and that they knew each other well. When Gunn visited the home of Fern and Parton in 1856 he noted that a young woman named Louisa Jacobs was living in their home and reported that Fern told him that the young woman's mother,

"Hattie," had been a slave in the South and had hidden for seven years in a small place in her grandmother's house. On March 16, 1856, Gunn wrote that Fern told him that she felt a special obligation to Louisa's mother, who was one of the few people who had stuck by her when she (Fern) was reduced to poverty and shunned by her family and friends.

25. Fern, *Rose Clark* (New York: Mason Brothers, 1856), 235–238.

26. See Jacobs, *Incidents*, 95–96.

27. Women writers often modestly ascribed their success to others. Harriet Beecher Stowe claimed that she did not write *Uncle Tom's Cabin;* God did, she said. See, for example, Charles Edward Stowe, *Life of Harriet Beecher Stowe* (Boston: Houghton, Mifflin, 1890), 156; and *Life and Letters of Harriet Beecher Stowe,* ed. Annie Fields (Boston: Houghton, Mifflin, 1897), 163–165. Sarah Josepha Hale took pleasure in the fact that her husband's name bore the celebrity for any praise she might receive. See Hale, *Women's Record, or Sketches of All Distinguished Women from The Creation to A.D. 1854* (New York: Harper & Brothers, 1855; originally published 1852), 686–687.

FRANCES SMITH FOSTER

Harriet Jacobs's Incidents *and the "Careless Daughters" (and Sons) Who Read It*

ALTHOUGH IT IS INCLUDED among the more than fifty rediscovered texts published as the Schomburg Library of Nineteenth-Century Black Women Writers, *Linda; Or, Incidents in the Life of a Slave Girl* is one of the few that had not been "lost" before the intrepid Henry Louis Gates, Jr., marshaled that magnificent search-and-rescue mission.[1] For years, *Incidents* has been cited in most bibliographies of African-American autobiography, and, since the early sixties, reprint editions have been easily obtainable. Although it was readily available and is one of a very few extant female slave narratives, until recently, scholarly interest has been minimal. At first glance, one might think its cover dissuaded serious attention, for the most ubiquitous edition was published by Harcourt Brace Jovanovich as a paperback with a fire-red cover depicting a hunched female figure surrounded by a mob of males who watched intently as three of their number flogged her bared back. It was not the lurid cover that put scholars off, however. It was the content that made them uncomfortable.

As a personal account of life in bondage and the struggle to escape it, *Incidents* clearly fits within the definition of a slave narrative. But the majority of slave narratives were written by men who endured physical brutality and emotional deprivation until they could make their flights North to freedom. In *Incidents,* the oppression was more psychological than physical, the protagonist chose to hide close to her family rather than run off and begin a new life alone, and the persecution did not end with her arrival in the North. While scholars knew that *Incidents* existed, they did not know what to do with it. They could not fit the text into the established paradigm for slave narratives, but instead of reconsidering their expectations as readers, they judged the author or the text to be unreliable. Many agreed with John Blassingame that the narrative was "too orderly" and "too melodramatic" to be credible. Some declared that Linda Brent was a pseudonym for an actual person but dismissed the text as a heavily edited and highly fictionalized account of an unknown and relatively unimportant ex-slave woman. Others opined that L. Maria Child was not, as the title page declared, the editor but that she was in fact the author of what they believed to be a sentimental novel masquerading as an autobiography.[2]

In 1981, when Jean Fagan Yellin published "Written By Herself: Harriet Jacobs' Slave Narrative," this changed. The evidence assembled by Professor Yellin proved that Harriet Jacobs wrote the book and that Child's role was limited to the "condensations and orderly arrangement" claimed in the book's introduction. In 1987 Yellin augmented her earlier article by publishing a new edition of *Incidents* that included evidence that verified the reported incidents. Then Jacobs's narrative began to attract more serious attention, and it appeared that this text could take its rightful place in literary history. Today, *Incidents* is generally accepted as a "classic slave narrative" and "one of the major nineteenth-century autobiographies in the Afro-American tradition."[3] Yellin's text with its sepia-colored grandmotherly image of Harriet Jacobs had become the standard edition.[4]

However, the controversy over the authenticity of *Incidents* and the authority of its writer waned only briefly before waxing once more in a slightly different position. Since Jacobs's narrative had been authenticated again,[5] modern-day readers have conceded some basic points. No longer is it acceptable to profess one's inability to believe that such a person lived or that such a person might experience such melodramatic moments or that such a person could actually write her own life. Now that the slave girl has been identified and the incidents verified, the "Written by Herself" has begun to encounter close skepticism of a different kind. Recent studies are questioning the power and the resolve of the writer to testify to her experience in her own way and on her own terms. They are questioning the reliability of Harriet Jacobs's stated intentions and her ability to resist the private and cultural interests that would constrain her aspirations and her depictions.

The interesting thing here is not that such concerns are voiced, but that the circumstances under which they are articulated, the assumption that these concerns are central to textual analysis or interpretation, and the kinds of extratextual evidence that are peculiarly privileged seem to emanate less from academic or literary concerns than from political and

personal ones. There is, for example, nothing intrinsically wrong with
Alice Deck's desire to examine the ways in which the collaboration between Harriet Jacobs and L. Maria Child influenced the text.[6] The nature
of editorial relationships and their influences upon published texts interest
many scholars, including me. Indeed, her discussion of the "two narrative
voices" that produce a "dialogue of authorial and editorial voices in *Incidents* that resembles a debate between a subjective (insider's) and an objective (outsider's) representation of one black woman's life" (40) has merit.
But Deck's characterization of the relationship between Jacobs and Child
as a situation wherein a socially prominent "scribe" assisted a lower-class
"subject" slights the extratextual evidence about the circumstances that led
Jacobs to write her narrative as well as the evidence that Deck herself
presents concerning Jacobs's personality and the procedures to which
Child adhered. Deck writes that Jacobs was "proud and possessive of her
manuscript" (40), that Child consistently sought Jacobs's opinions on
editorial concerns, and that "Child's inserted digressions are . . . glaring"
(39). Since the editor regularly consulted with the possessive author and
since their "debate" was limited to a relatively small portion of the book,
and since the two voices are clearly marked, Deck's conclusion that Jacobs
"did not sacrifice completely her 'self' and 'life' in her story in the name of
a cause" (40), is problematic. Rejecting the authority that her own discussion demonstrates, Deck represents Harriet Jacobs's achievement as a limited sacrifice. She characterizes the relationship between editor and author
as Jacobs versus Child and her conclusion implies that in this contest
between "subjective" insider and "objective" outsider or "subject" and
"scribe," we should assume that Child's influence was greater than Child's
testimony, Jacobs's assertions, and the evidence of the text document.

Deck's characterization of the editorial/authorial relationship as oppositional is strikingly similar to those in other recent discussions and is logical
only if one shares the unstated and unexamined cultural assumptions upon
which it and the others appear to be based. For example, John Sekora's
concern with "the presumption that the essential questions concerning the
[slave] narrative as literary form have been satisfactorily answered" (484)
is quite valid, if such a presumption does exist.[7] It does not follow, however, that "because nearly thirty white antislavery societies *played some part*
in the publication of narratives after 1830, *the signal question is, what did
abolitionists believe* they were doing when they sponsored slave narratives?
[emphasis mine]" (495). And even if the intentions of the publishers were
paramount to our understanding of these texts, Sekora's conclusion that at
best the former slaves were able to deliver black messages in white envelopes requires additional support. Why, for example, should we assume
that slave narrators readily acquiesced to abolitionists' desires? These were

individuals who had already withstood the physical and psychological force of a centuries-old system designed to eliminate all vestiges of self-esteem and self-determination. If and when they were faced with attempts to control their discourse, could they not have more creative responses than simple capitulation? Might not the messages and their envelopes be gray? Or, why wouldn't readers apply the same designation to the products of literary intercourse that they did to other results of racial consorting: Why wouldn't one drop of black heritage make the entire text a black thing?

Probably the most intriguing instance of resisting authorial prerogative is that manifested by Elizabeth Fox-Genovese in her epilogue to *Within the Plantation Household: Black and White Women of the Old South.*[8] Fox-Genovese accepts "Linda Brent" as Harriet Jacobs's nom de plume and as the participant/observer narrator whose role exceeds that of a mere reporter. However, despite Jacobs's repeated assertions that she is not writing fiction, Fox-Genovese urges us to read *Incidents* as "story." And, when the author's words or the narrator's explanations conflict with her own version of reality, Fox-Genovese privileges her own interpretations. Using the plural and thereby aligning herself with unnamed others, Fox-Genovese claims "our skepticism permissible" because "probably [Jacobs] and her witnesses, in accordance with the literary conventions of the day, embellished an account that was true in its essentials" (392). Even such "essentials" as Jacobs's depiction of the struggle between master and slave as being a struggle over the slave's view of herself and her intrinsic relationship to this world were, in Fox-Genovese's estimation, not above embellishments. She recognizes situations wherein Jacobs "depicts Linda Brent as if she were, in essential respects, her master's social and racial equal" (381), and Fox-Genovese correctly interprets Linda's confinement as the manifestation of her "deepest purpose of setting her will against that of her master" (392). Yet Fox-Genovese concludes that the "pivotal authentication of self probably rested upon a great factual life, for it stretches the limits of all credulity that Linda Brent actually eluded her master's sexual advances. The point of the narrative lies not in her 'virtue,' which was fabricated for the benefit of her northern readers, but in her resistance of domination, which the preservation of virtue imperfectly captures" (392). Despite Jacobs's statements to the contrary and her careful account of how and why she was able to elude Dr. Flint's sexual advances, Fox-Genovese finds it too hard to believe that a black female slave could summon such power. Virtue might be the foundation upon which Jacobs chose to rest her self-image, but, having decided that Harriet Jacobs could not have prevailed over her master, Fox-Genovese terms this a "fabrication," then dismisses it as "no matter" because she has determined that "Jacobs's book should be read as a crafted representation—as a fiction or as a cautionary tale—not a factual account. Its purpose, after all, was to authenticate her self, not this or that detail" (392). In this example, a reader will grant that a woman could live six years and eleven months in virtual solitary confinement, but cannot grant that such a strong-willed individual could fend off an old lecher even if she did have the help and protection of her family, her community, and a U.S. congressman. Having calmly claimed the ultimate authority to privilege her limited credulity and putative "literary conventions of the day" over the stated intentions of the author, the testimony of her witnesses, and the research that has corroborated their account, Fox-Genovese essentially rewrites the text to fit her version of reality.

If the questions of authority and authenticity that encumber Harriet Jacobs's *Incidents* were isolated phenomena, perhaps it really is "no matter" whether the text embellished reality. But this is not an isolated case. The obsession with authorship, with editorial relationships, and with the right way to read a text continues a reader-response pattern that can be seen from the publication, in 1773, of the first volume by an African-American, Phillis Wheatley's *Poems on Various Subjects, Religious and Moral;* it is a pattern that especially plagued nineteenth-century African-American women writers. Their readers' extreme reluctance to grant the usual assumptions of authority and authenticity to them and their texts may well stem from the unspoken, perhaps unconscious, recognition that particular writers and their writings challenge existing dogma in ways that these readers are unable to grant as legitimate or desirable. As my rehearsal of its history implies, the situation with *Incidents in the Life of a Slave Girl* is a salient example of a competition between writer and readers that seems never-ending. And I am arguing that the problem may rest more with overly resisting readers than with unreliable authors or texts.

Although this discussion focuses on Jacobs and her text, I intend it to apply in general to the work of other writers, particularly the work of nineteenth-century African-American women. Therefore, I want to be clear about some of my underlying assumptions. First of all, I do not mean to imply that consideration of questions of authority and authenticity is inappropriate or unimportant in the study of literature or that when faced with direct statements of intention, readers should squelch any inclination to contest the validity or the relevance of those declarations. But it is important to recognize that such inclinations seem to arise more often when readers are invited into communicative contexts with writers of a race, gender, or class that the readers assume to be inferior to their own. Then questions about authority and authenticity tend to take on an intensity and texture that obscure other aspects of the discourse. Readers generally begin to compete with the writers, to rearrange the writers' words, details, and intentions to make them more compatible with the readers' own experiences and expectations. African-American women writers, particularly those who were or had been slaves, almost without exception provoke such challenges. Gender and class conventions of reading lead to assumptions that such writers have less right to public discourse, thereby granting them fewer subjects about which they may claim knowledge. In effect, these conventions of reading seek to limit the terms by which African-American women may command their readers' attention.

I find it reasonable to assume that African-American women who wrote for publication in the eighteenth and nineteenth centuries knew as well as other writers that successful communication required appropriate attention to content and context. I am assuming that these writers knew that some readers would be unable or unwilling to concede that they legitimately could or would act, think, and write in ways contrary to the ideas with which the readers approach that text. And I am suggesting that being unable to trust their readers to respond to their texts as peers, many of these writers developed literary strategies to compensate. Harriet Jacobs, for example, probably understood that a large segment of her readers would resist or would find it difficult to accept her authority and the authenticity of her statements. She knew that she needed a narrative mode and rhetorical strategies to ameliorate that situation. When Harriet Jacobs decided to join the effort "to convince the people of the Free States what Slavery really is," she knew that the strategies of persuasion developed by male slave narrators and by white women writers were inadequate for her purposes and that she needed to create different applications for their techniques and to invent some methods of her own. Jacobs may well have underestimated the strength of her readers' resistance, but she did in fact create narrative strategies that were relatively successful at the time and that continue to be examples of literary efforts to allow writers like her maximum freedom to testify in their own ways and to their own ends.

Briefly summarized, *Incidents* is Harriet Jacobs's account of portions of her life as a slave and her attempts to become free. Jacobs recounts these experiences in the first person but changes names and obscures locations. She was, in many ways, a privileged slave. Until her escape to the North, Harriet Jacobs enjoyed the emotional support of a strong network of family and friends. Her father was a skilled artisan who hired himself out and created a home for his wife and children wherein they were insulated from most of the physical indignities of slavery. Jacobs says she was six years old before she even knew that she was a slave. Her grandmother was a free woman of property who purchased those relatives that she could and who used influence and money to provide for and to protect those she could not free. During her enslavement, Harriet Jacobs was assigned domestic duties. She was not sent to work in the fields, not whipped, not chained. Nor, as she specifically says, was she raped, although she was, for years, persecuted by a licentious master and his jealous wife. Finally, when she felt that she and her protectors in the black community could not continue to defend her virtue, Jacobs sought the protection of a leader in the white community. His protection was not without its price. He became her lover, the father of her two children, and eventually her betrayer: though he purchased the children, he did not free them as promised. While serving in Congress, he married a white woman, and when they returned from Washington, D.C., he made his slave child the nursemaid to her half sister.

When even the influence of her prominent lover seemed too limited, Harriet Jacobs decided to enter the place that she called "The Loophole of Retreat." Although her master believed that she had fled to the free states, actually Jacobs hid for six years and eleven months only a few doors from his office in an attic crawl space three feet high, nine feet long, and seven feet wide. When Jacobs finally escaped to the North, she was reunited with her children, but they did not live happily ever after. She was a single black woman with two children to support. Her hiding had left her crippled. Her fugitive status made it difficult to obtain employment and dangerous to remain in one place for any length of time. Nonetheless, she managed to secure a position as maid for the Nathaniel Willis family in New York and eventually—despite Jacobs's strong protests that she was not an object to be bought or sold—Mrs. Willis purchased her and made Harriet Jacobs a legally free woman.

In many ways, this was the stuff of which melodrama is made, a story of pursuit and evasion, one full of heroes and villains of bright young men seeking their fortunes and desperate maidens trying to preserve their virtue, of mothers trying to protect their children and of the hardworking poor trying to survive the greed and exploitation of the powerful and wealthy. And yet Jacobs was narrating a real life, involving real people, real events, and real issues that were complicated and conflicted. As she wrote to her friend Amy Post, Jacobs chose "to come before the world as I have been an uneducated oppressed Slave"; she chose to write just as she lived, and of what she witnessed. "You shall have truth, but not talent" (236), she promised.

Jacobs depicts her persona, Linda Brent, as her letters show that she was herself: intelligent, strong, resourceful, and loving, but also proud, rebellious, and vengeful. Linda was only fifteen when Dr. Flint began to make sexual advances toward her, but she was quite his equal in psychological manipulation, and the text makes it quite clear that theirs was less a sexual struggle than a duel for power. She chose Sands as her lover not only because he could protect her from Flint but also, she says, because there were "other feelings mixed with those I have described. Revenge, and calculations of interest, were added to flattered vanity and sincere gratitude for kindness. I knew that nothing would enrage Dr. Flint so much as to know that I favored another, and it was something to triumph over my tyrant even in that small way"" (55). Moreover, an affair with Sands promised increased freedom. If physical and legal freedom were impossible, there still remained the freedom of having chosen the circumstances under which she would surrender her virginity: "To be an object of interest to a man who is not married, and who is not her master, [was more] agreeable to [her] pride and feelings. . . . It seems less degrading to give one's self, than to submit to compulsion. There is something akin to freedom in having a love who has no control over you, except that which he gains by kindness and attachment" (54–55), she explains. But Brent firmly believed that a liaison with Sands would be her path to legal freedom as well. She expected Sands to purchase her, and since she judged him to be "a man of more generosity and feeling" than Flint, she believed she could convince Sands to free her. "I knew what I did, and I did it with deliberate calculation" (54), Linda says.

Harriet Jacobs wrote *Incidents in the Life of a Slave Girl* as the account of her struggle to retain her self-control in defiance of her master's assertions that she was his "property" and "must be subject to his will in all things" (27). She also wrote it as an abolitionist text, as her own assault upon the institution of slavery and upon the various individuals who were products of that institution, individuals who in divers ways attempted to dispossess her of her inalienable rights to life, liberty, and the pursuit of happiness. Yet she knew that in writing *Incidents* she was waging another battle in a continuing war to keep herself her own property. In this case, her antagonists were the middle-class white women of the North whom she intended to enlist as allies in the great struggle against slavery.

Harriet Jacobs knew it was risky to write her life history. She was well acquainted with many of the attitudes and assumptions of the Anglo-American literary establishment, for not only did she read widely, she lived in the household of Nathaniel Willis, the editor and writer whose home was a New York literati rendezvous. She knew also the conventions of abolitionist and African-American literature. Jacobs had worked for a year in her brother's Rochester antislavery reading room. Since it was located over the offices of Frederick Douglass, she may have heard the history of the resistance that Douglass had encountered, especially from his most ardent abolitionist friends, when he decided to tell his story his way. When she wrote in the preface, "I want to add my testimony to that of abler pens to convince the people of the Free States what Slavery really is," the words "convince" and "really" were undoubtedly chosen with care. In short, it is clear to me that Harriet Jacobs had ample reason to know the perils that African-American writers, especially women, faced and that it would be very strange indeed if she had not carefully considered the rhetorical and narrative strategies that they had used as she outlined her own story. Although she had no perfect literary model and she knew that she could not trust her readers to understand or accept what she would relate, Jacobs chose nonetheless to record her history as she had lived it, to confront her readers with an alternative truth, and to demand that they not only acknowledge it but act upon it. To that end, Harriet Jacobs created a new literary form, one that challenged her audiences' social and aesthetic assumptions even as it delighted and reaffirmed them.

I believe that Harriet Jacobs's strategy is based upon a speech act regularly used by blacks in conversation with whites. Her strategy has much in common with what Robert B. Stepto calls a "discourse of distrust." In such a situation, Stepto tells us, "distrust is not so much a subject as a basis for specific narrative plottings and rhetorical strategies. . . . [T]he texts are fully 'about' the communicative prospects of Afro-Americans writing for American readers, black and white, given the race rituals which color reading and/or listening."9 Such writers often try to initiate "creative communication" by getting readers "told" or "told off" in such a way that they do not stop reading but do begin to "hear" the writer. In Jacobs's text the telling off begins with the title page and the author's preface. That aspect of "authority," with its implicit claims to accuracy and reliability, is then supplemented by the characterizations and the reconstructed relations among the characters.

Although the spine of the book carries the primary title *Linda*, the title page carries only the subtitle, *Incidents in the Life of a Slave Girl, Written by Herself*.10 Without the proper name, the subtitle emphasizes the generic and general over the personal and individual. The subtitle also reverses the usual hierarchy of race, class, and gender. Since it is her life of which she writes, the author's authority is invested in her participant/observer status and supersedes that of the readers. The subtitle establishes this as a black woman's text, and *her* authority is not easily disputed since it is *her* life of which she writes. It also states that hers is not the mere reporting of her life history, but a narrative of incidents in that life. The unnamed author writes as a mediator, a participant/observer now more experienced but still sympathetic, who looks back upon her girlhood and selects those experiences that she deems most appropriate for her audience and her literary intentions. Reading the words "Written by Herself" that follow the subtitle and the words "Published for the author" that come at the bottom of that page, a reader confronts not only the exercise of literary prerogative, of claiming authorial responsibility for the text's selection and arrangement, but also an assumption of self-worth, of meaning and interest in her personal experiences that exceed the specific or personal.

The author's preface follows the title page. As is expected in the discourse of distrust, Jacobs's first words "tell off" the reader in ways that she or he must "hear." "Reader, be assured this narrative is no fiction." This statement is neither apology nor request. It is a polite command, soothingly stated but nonetheless an imperative. The next sentence neither explains nor defends. "I am aware that some of my adventures may seem incredible; but they are, nevertheless, strictly true." Instead of elaborating upon her claim to authenticity in the preface, Jacobs requires an even higher level of trust, for she advises her readers that she has not told all she knows. "I have not exaggerated the wrongs inflicted by Slavery; on the contrary, my descriptions fall far short of the facts," she writes. With these words, the author claims superior knowledge and plainly privileges her own interpretation over any contrary ideas that the reader may have about the text's authenticity.

Another important element in Jacobs's strategy was her appropriation of what Karlyn Kohrs Campbell has termed "'feminine' rhetoric." Although several scholars have described the characteristics of literature by women in the mid-nineteenth century, Campbell's description is representative. Such writing, she says, is

> usually grounded in personal experience. In most instances, personal experience is tested against the pronouncements of male authorities (who can be used for making accusations and indictments that would be impermissible from a woman). . . . [It] may appeal to biblical authority. . . . The tone tends to be personal and somewhat tentative, rather than objective or authoritative . . . tends to plead, to appeal to the sentiments of the audience, to "court" the audience by being "seductive." . . . [to invite] female audiences to act, to draw their own conclusions and make their own decisions, in contrast to a traditionally "Masculine" style that approaches the audience as inferiors to be told what is right or to be led.[11]

What Campbell terms "feminine rhetoric" is comparable to "the discourse of distrust." It too strives to thwart the resisting reader's urge to compete with the author for authority and to enlist the reader instead as a corroborator. Not all the strategies of "feminine rhetoric" would work for Jacobs's purposes. Although she was a woman writing primarily to other women, she was also a black woman writing to white women. Racism exacerbates distrust. Racial stereotypes would make certain conventions, such as the seductive speaker, the tentative tone, and laissez-faire lecturer, work against her. But the use of quoted authority to state the more accusatory or unflattering conclusions had great potential. And those "feminine" literary conventions that Jacobs does adopt are adapted to project images more in line with her purposes as a writer and her status as a black woman.

Consider, for example, the ways in which she employs verification, the process of using quotations from others to state the more accusatory or unflattering conclusions. As Campbell notes, women writers frequently used references from scripture to validate their claims and they often cited the words of others, especially the pronouncements of men, to state directly the accusations or indictments that the women writers were implying. Jacobs has two quotations on her title page. The first declares, "Northerners know nothing at all about Slavery. . . . They have no conception of the depth of *degradation* involved . . . if they had, they would never cease their efforts until so horrible a system was overthrown." This quotation is unmistakably patronizing if not actually accusatory or indicting. However, Harriet Jacobs does not attribute these words to a man, but cites, instead, an anonymous "woman of North Carolina." Given the assumed inferiority of blacks to whites, this modification would be acceptable to most of her readers. They would assume that a black woman's appeal to authority by citing a white woman was comparable to a white woman's seeking verification from a white man, and given the racism of that time, they would undoubtedly assume that the anonymous woman was in fact white.

But this quote may be more subtly manipulative, for, the woman's race is not stated, and while there are at least two southern white women in *Incidents* who surreptitiously work against slavery, none is as outspokenly antislavery as the black women in Jacobs's narrative or the northern white women who wrote the authenticating statements that frame Jacobs's narrative. The only women from North Carolina in Harriet Jacobs's text who exhibit the spirit and audacity of the woman quoted on her title page are black. Since Harriet Jacobs was a "woman of North Carolina" and her book is designed to effect the kind of awareness and action referred to in the quotation, it is quite likely that Jacobs is quoting herself to validate her own words.

Jacobs's second quotation is biblical. It, too, functions as verification, to increase her authority. The words are those of Isaiah 32:6: "Rise up, ye women that are at ease! Hear my voice, ye careless daughters! Give ear unto my speech." The relation between this statement and the theme of *Incidents* is fairly obvious. But the quotation does more than refer to a precedent for women becoming politically active. This quotation comes from the section of Isaiah that warns directly against alliances with Egypt, a word synonymous in the antebellum United States with "slavery." And in this chapter, Isaiah's prophecy is actually a warning. The women "that are at ease," the "careless daughters" who fail to rise up and support the rights of the poor and the oppressed will find themselves enslaved. Again, Jacobs has revised the "feminine" rhetorical convention, for this citation is more instructive and didactic than it is seductive or suggestive.

The instructive and didactic tone that Harriet Jacobs employs to subdue her resisting readers does not stop with abolitionist matters. When one considers the context within which Harriet Jacobs was writing, particularly the contemporary conversation about women and their roles, and when one considers Jacobs's female characters within this context, there is evidence that she was offering her critique of the two major and contrasting ideals of womanhood then vying for popular acceptance. One, by now almost a cliché, was the ideal of True Womanhood, a concept that privileged the "pale, delicate, invalid maiden" and promulgated the four female principles as domesticity, piety, submissiveness, and purity. This is an ideal found in much of the women's literature of that time (including some by women of color) and an ideal that Jacobs does not support. In "Adding Color and Contour to Early American Self-Portraitures," I examined some of the inherent problems that this definition of womanhood held for black women in general and for slave women specifically.[12] Suffice it to say that though Harriet Jacobs's complexion may have been pale enough and her manner sufficiently refined and elegant, the facts that her two children were from a white man, not her husband, that she survived imprisonment in an attic, and that she had managed to support herself and her children by working as a domestic servant eliminated any serious claim to True Womanhood.

Another, competing ideology of that era, however, is one that Frances Cogan has termed "the ideal of Real Womanhood."[13] Real Womanhood was not, Cogan explains, simply an opposition to True Womanhood. (That place was claimed by radicals such as Elizabeth Cady Stanton and Amelia Bloomer, women the publicist who wrote the summary on the back cover of Cogan's book slightingly terms "alienated, steely protofeminists who rule their worlds with a rigid back.") Rather, Real Womanhood was a moderate approach, one that assumed, for example, that women did have a separate sphere, but a sphere that was in a far different relationship to the male domain than the advocates of true womanhood or androgyny would concede. "The Real Womanhood ideal" says Cogan, "offered American women a vision of themselves as biologically equal (rationally as well as emotionally) and in many cases markedly superior in intellect to what passed for male business sense, scholarship, and theological understanding. . . . [It] demanded that the woman's duty to herself and her loved ones was not . . . to die, but rather to live, not to sacrifice herself, but to survive" (5).

The ideal of the Real Woman was a concept more appropriate to Jacobs's authorial needs and one that informs her female characterizations. Obviously, her persona, Linda Brent, was a Real Woman. But Jacobs does not offer only one black woman as a Real Woman—she populates her text with an entire community of them. Aunt Martha, Linda's grandmother, is one example. Aunt Martha was so skilled in the domestic sciences that she baked both her and her son's way out of slavery and into her own home. She understood the economics of her acquisition, for she frequently used her home equity to supplement the good will of her white neighbors and friends. As a "real woman" Aunt Martha was both self-sufficient and maternal. In her house, she nurtured and sheltered her children, grandchildren, friends, and relatives. And her house was not the mean abode of the working poor, but a real home with books and silver spoons and linens and cupboards of jams and jellies.

Like Real Women, Aunt Martha possessed real emotions. Jacobs writes, "She was usually very quiet in her demeanor; but if her indignation was once roused, it was not very easily quelled"; she had in fact "once chased a white gentleman with a loaded pistol, because he insulted one of her daughters" (29). In conflict with the major antagonist, Dr. Flint, Aunt Martha was not submissive, and she was certainly his intellectual and moral superior. Although she preferred that Linda remain with her children, she did not believe that Linda should sacrifice her life for theirs.

Not only does Jacobs present her positive women characters as Real Women, but Jacobs's negative female characters generally assume the trappings of True Women to hide their hypocrisy and moral weaknesses. For example, Jacobs says:

> Mrs. Flint, like many southern women, was totally deficient in energy. She had not strength to superintend her household affairs; but her nerves were so strong, that she could sit in her easy chair and see a woman whipped, till the blood trickled from every stroke of the lash. She was a member of the church; but partaking of the Lord's supper did not seem to put her in a Christian frame of mind. If dinner was not served at the exact time on that particular Sunday, . . . [after it was dished] she would . . . spit in all the kettles and pans . . . to prevent the cook and her children from eking out their meager fare with the remains of the gravy and other scrapings (12).

In presenting Aunt Martha (and Linda; Linda's daughter, Ellen; Linda's aunt, Nancy; Linda's friend, Fannie; and other black women) as models of Real Women and in exposing the facade that masked some who were considered True Women, Jacobs continues to get her readers "told." Not only is her knowledge of slavery superior to theirs, but she too belongs to a sisterhood of Real Women who despite the tremendous forces that would sweep away all vestiges of culture and gentility maintain the essence of those virtues. Her text not only privileges this version of womanhood, it provides her readers with the knowledge that they need to join.

The "discourse of distrust" was but one of the many elements that Jacobs employed in order to so firmly establish her authority and authenticity that her readers would not revise their attitudes but would agitate for social change. Her strategies include an innovative melding of literary elements generally associated with politics (antislavery novels) and with domesticity (novels of seduction) into the service of autobiography (especially the slave narrative genre). They include her use of dialect and folk characters, as well as deepening and complicating of characterizations commonly found in popular literature of the mid-nineteenth century. Particularly interesting are the ways in which she revises some of Harriet Beecher Stowe's trademarks, especially in relation to the mulatto stereotypes.

In these and other ways, Harriet Jacobs reveals herself to be an individual of interest, a social critic of perspective, and a writer of daring and skill. As a slave, Harriet Jacobs was dispossessed of some very real privileges and rights. To some extent, whether she embellished the details of her text, even whether she had sexual intercourse with her master, are "no matter." But if the question is raised, unless we have clear evidence to the contrary, it might be wiser to accept the word of the writer and her witnesses. Many women, regardless of race or class, were sexually abused during the nineteenth century, and sexual violence toward slave women and slave men was common. It does not follow, however, that every slave woman was raped. Nor is it inevitable or even probable that the testosterone level in every slavemaster was so high that he couldn't realize that not every attraction, or obsession, he might feel for his beautiful bondswoman could be satisfied by raping her. It does matter that Jacobs chose to create her entire narrative around her successful defense of physical and psychological integrity. It may strain the limits of credulity for some readers, including a few very eminent scholars, to believe that Harriet Jacobs was telling the truth, that she was capable of exciting passions beyond the physical, or that she could exercise some control over her own body and over her alleged superiors. It does require an adjustment of attitude to consider that former slaves, even those who were female or fugitives, could prevail against the personal preferences of northern white editors or publishers as they had against the assaults of southern white slaveholders and sympathizers. "Hard to believe" is not the same as "untrue" or "fictitious." In bondage and in freedom, as an individual and as a writer, Harriet Jacobs struggled to maintain her right to be and to think and to narrate as her imagination and experience determined. She was without many desired facilities—she didn't have a room of her own in which to write, nor did she believe she could sign her own name to that which she had written. But she possessed what nineteenth-century African-American women writers and others have continued to possess—a story to tell and the ability to tell it. In the paradigm of subject, writer, and reader, it is sometimes the last who has to rise to the occasion. Despite all efforts to silence her or to contest her statements, Jacobs has created strategies that enable her readers to do just that.

NOTES

1. Harriet Jacobs, *Linda: Or, Incidents in the Life of a Slave Girl* (Boston: Published for the Author, 1861). A second edition was published the next year (*The Deeper Wrong: Or, Incidents in the Life of a Slave Girl* (London: W. Tweedie, 1862). With the exception of the title change, the second edition appears to be identical with the first. Since the early 1970s, the following scholars are among those who have written introductions for or edited versions of Jacobs's *Incidents:* Walter Teller (New York: Harcourt Brace Jovanovich, 1973); Jean Fagan Yellin (Cambridge: Harvard University Press, 1987); Valerie Smith (New York: Oxford University Press, 1988); Henry Louis Gates, Jr. (New York: New American Library, 1990). The modern edition that has been available longest and the one that sported the cover described in the text is the one by Teller. Quotation from *Incidents* that appear in this article are from the edition by Jean Fagan Yellin.

2. John W. Blassingame, *The Slave Community: Plantation Life in the Ante-Bellum South* (New York: Oxford University Press, 1972), 234. So completely does he resist Jacobs as author that Blassingame's index does not include entries for either "Harriet Jacobs" or "Linda Brent." The index reference for his dismissal of *Incidents* is under "Lydia Maria Child." In his 1979 "revised and enlarged edition," there are index notations for Jacobs and for Child, both of which indicate page 373, where the text of the first edition remains unchanged. Three particularly important literary texts that resist Jacobs's authorship are *Negro Caravan*, ed. Sterling A. Brown, Arthur P. Davis, and Ulysses Lee (New York: Citadel Press, 1941), 695; *Great Slave Narratives*, ed. Arna Bontemps (Boston: Beacon, 1969); and Blyden Jackson, *A History of Afro-American Literature: The Long Beginning* (Baton Rouge; Louisiana University Press, 1989), 155–156.

3. These quotations are representative of the attitudes now endorsed by most scholars, but they are the exact words of Henry Louis Gates, Jr., "Introduction," *The Classic Slave Narratives* (New York: New American Library, 1987), xvi.

4. Harcourt Brace Jovanovich has replaced the sensational red-and-black cover with a subdued combination of red, black, and green, but its new picture of a dark-skinned female traveler resting near a pine tree has no more relation to Jacobs's narrative than the earlier picture had.

5. Its original appearance as an anonymous work occasioned some speculation about the author and the publication of additional testimonials. In a short time,

Harriet Jacobs was not only publicly identified as the author, but in her subsequent publications she adopted the sobriquet, "Linda."

6. Alice A. Deck, "Whose Book Is This?: Authorial Versus Editorial Control of Harriet Brent Jacobs' *Incidents in the Life of a Slave Girl: Written by Herself,*" *Woman's Studies International Forum* 10 (1987): 33–40.

7. John Sekora, "Black Message/White Envelope: Genre, Authenticity, and Authority in the Antebellum Slave Narrative," *Callaloo* 10 (1987): 482–515.

8. (Chapel Hill: University of North Carolina Press, 1988).

9. Robert B. Steptoe, "Distrust of the Reader in Afro-American Narratives," in *Reconstructing American Literary History,* ed. Sacvan Bercovitch (Cambridge: Harvard University Press, 1986), 305.

10. Here I am assuming that if the presentation of the book was not orchestrated by Jacobs, it certainly met her approval. Although it is possible that the cover and the title page were her publisher's or her editor's design, Jean Fagan Yellin's documentation of the relationship between Jacobs and Child suggests that Jacobs was actively concerned with every aspect of the production of her text. Moreover, since the original publisher went bankrupt and Jacobs purchased the plates, she had the opportunity to change the design if it were contrary to her intentions.

11. Karlyn Kohrs Campbell, "Style and Content in the Rhetoric of Early Afro-American Feminists," *Quarterly Journal of Speech* 72 (1986): 434–445.

12. Frances Smith Foster, "Adding Color and Contour to Early American Self Portraitures: Autobiographical Writings of Afro-American Women" in *Conjuring: Black Women, Fiction, and Literary Tradition,* ed. Marjorie Pryse and Hortense Spillers (Bloomington: Indiana University Press, 1985), 25–38.

13. Frances B. Cogan, *All-American Girl: The Ideal of Real Womanhood in Mid-Nineteenth-Century America* (Athens: University of Georgia Press, 1989).

❧ JUDITH FETTERLEY ❧

Only a Story, Not a Romance: Harriet Beecher Stowe's The Pearl of Orr's Island

TO OUR READERS

In commencing again "The Pearl of Orr's Island," the author meets the serious embarrassment of trying to revive for the second time an unexpected pleasure.

That a story so rustic, so woodland, so pale and colorless, so destitute of all that is ordinarily expected in a work of fiction, should be advertised in the columns of *The Independent* as this was last week, as "Mrs. So-and-so's *great* romance," or with words to that effect, produces an impression both appalling and ludicrous. . . .

We beg our readers to know that no great romance is coming,—only a story pale and colorless as real life, and sad as truth.

WITH THESE WORDS Stowe prefaces the first installment of the second half of *The Pearl of Orr's Island* and signals the completion of a fictional project whose composition had required nearly a decade. E. Bruce Kirkham's detailed account of the writing of *The Pearl of Orr's Island* establishes a history of interruption, of which the break in serial publication was merely the last, from the novel's beginnings in 1852, shortly after the completion of *Uncle Tom's Cabin*, to its conclusion in 1862. Stowe returned from Europe in the summer of 1860 on the same ship as James and Annie Fields, whom she had first met in Florence that winter. Upon her return, she contracted to publish *Agnes of Sorrento*, a fiction she had begun while still in Europe, in the *Atlantic Monthly*, whose editorship James Fields would assume within the year. At the same time, and no doubt under considerable pressure given her family connections to the paper, she agreed to furnish *The Pearl of Orr's Island* as a serial for the New York *Independent*, a Congregational newspaper to which her brother, Henry Ward Beecher, contributed weekly sermons and to which she herself had been a special contributor since July of 1852. The first half of *The Pearl of Orr's Island* appeared in weekly installments from January 3, 1861, until April 4, 1861. In the April 4 issue there appeared a note from Stowe explaining that "with this number ends Part First of the 'Pearl of Orr's Island.' Part Second will be ready to appear in the Autumn, and will extend through the year." The story, however, did not resume until December 5; the last installment appeared on April 24, 1862.

Why did Stowe find *The Pearl of Orr's Island* so difficult to write? Yet why did she commit herself to its serial publication from which, while there might be a reprieve, there could be no final escape? What ambivalence of desire to both write and not write this text led her to contract for simultaneous publication of *Agnes of Sorrento* and *The Pearl of Orr's Island* and thus to create a situation that mirrored her ambivalence by at once foregrounding her difficulties with composing *Pearl*—as witness her letters of the period to both Fields and Theodore Tilton, managing editor of the *Independent*—and forcing her to complete it? Stowe returned from Europe intending to write *Agnes*, but she backed into writing *Pearl*. For *Agnes*, the favored twin, she arranged publication in the *Atlantic Monthly*; she gave *Pearl* to the *Independent*, a religious newspaper making its first venture with fiction. She would finish it but not showcase it. Why?

To readers familiar with *The Pearl of Orr's Island* there are many possible answers to these questions. In this essay I wish to explore but one, and I take my cue from a misreading in the "apology" Stowe published to reintroduce her readers to her text. Since I recognize, however, that not all my readers are familiar with this text, I offer a brief summary by way of introduction.

The Pearl of Orr's Island tells the story of Mara Lincoln and Moses Pennel, girl and boy, "brother" and "sister," growing up together on an island off the coast of Maine. Mara, orphaned at birth, is raised by her grandmother and grandfather. Her mother has watched her husband's ship sink moments before entering the harbor; the shock precipitates Mara's premature birth, and the double strain of death and birth kills her mother. Moses comes to Orr's Island when Mara is four, himself orphaned by shipwreck and washed ashore in the arms of his dead mother. Mara's grandparents adopt Moses as well and thus he becomes her "brother." The first half of *The Pearl of Orr's Island* describes the childhood of Mara and Moses as "true girl" and "true boy," tracing the implications of their different natures, particularly for their relationship with each other, and detailing the differential education accorded girls and boys in "democratic" New England. The second half explores the consequences of these differences in nature and nurture for the relationship of Mara and Moses as young adults positioned to transform the relationship of brother and sister into that of lovers. The book does not, however, end with their marriage, for Mara dies of consumption shortly after their engagement. Years later Moses and Sally Kittridge, Mara's best friend and confidante, come together in a marriage enabled and sanctioned, much like Stowe's own, by the love they both bear for the dead Mara, Moses' "first wife."

In her remarks prefatory to recommencing *The Pearl of Orr's Island* Stowe desires to disabuse her readers of their expectations for a romance—"we beg our readers to know that no great romance is coming"—and she attributes the raising of those expectations in part to the nature of fiction ("all that is ordinarily expected in a work of fiction"), but most particularly to the advertising strategy of the *Independent* in announcing the resumption of "Mrs. So-and-so's *great* romance." Yet the notice actually published in the *Independent* referred to *The Pearl of Orr's Island,* albeit in commanding capitals, as "MRS. STOWE'S GREAT STORY," and one might argue that the writer of this notice understood quite well that Stowe's fame as a writer did not derive from romance. In her first significant publication, "A New England Sketch" (1834), Stowe had clearly subordinated the interest of romantic love, the heterosexual plot of courtship culminating in marriage, to the interests of portraying the New England regional character, Uncle Lot, after whom the piece would eventually be named, and to telling the story of Christian conversion. Similarly *Uncle Tom's Cabin* managed to rivet the attention of the nation without recourse to romance. Those characters in the book who might possibly be seen as conventional lovers—George and Eliza Harris—are already married before the story begins, and whatever heterosexual love interest the book generates can best be described as the wish to see marriage culminate in the establishment of family life. So why would Stowe, even as she recognizes it as a misreading ("or words to that effect") read "romance" for "story"? And to what extent can we see in this misreading an anxiety that might explain her ambivalence toward her text and her difficulties with its composition?

To contextualize this question, it might be helpful to consider an event that may have precipitated for Stowe a renewed interest in her half-finished text and led her to commit herself to finishing it. During her trip to Europe of 1859–1860, Stowe had a last meeting with the elderly and ill Lady Byron, whose decision to entrust her with the secret of Byron's incest had so moved Stowe four years before and would lead her at the end of the decade to risk her own reputation in order to vindicate Lady Byron's. Stowe viewed Lord Byron as the most romantic man of his generation and read the relationship between Lord Byron and Lady Byron, for her his long-suffering, innocent, and still-loving wife, as a tragedy of romance. While Lady Byron's death in May of 1860 technically released Stowe from the obligation of her earlier decision not to tell the story while Lady Byron was still alive, writing the story of Mara and Moses might have seemed a way to both keep and break silence, a way to tell a general truth that was still a version of this specific history and thus to indirectly vindicate her dead friend. At the beginning of the second half of *The Pearl of Orr's Island,* Stowe reintroduces Mara to her readers through the sign of "a suppressed sigh" that only a "close observer," a good reader like Stowe herself, might notice: "What was in that sigh? It was the sigh of a long, deep inner history, unwritten and untold—such as are transpiring daily by thousands, and of which we take no heed."[1] In *The Pearl of Orr's Island* Stowe, casting herself as the "voice of the voiceless,"[2] a role she had earlier assumed in *Uncle Tom's Cabin* and would later assume in writing directly of Lady Byron, writes out the long, deep inner history of the sigh of a woman like Mara or Lady Byron and traces its origins to her relationship with a man like Moses or Lord Byron.

Although Stowe was still several years away from the furor produced by her effort to tell "The True Story of Lady Byron's Life" (1869), she might well have suspected that telling such truths, even in the form of fiction, could infuriate her readers. On January 16, 1861, two weeks after *The Pearl of Orr's Island* began appearing in the *Independent,* Stowe sent James Fields the delayed first installment of *Agnes of Sorrento* (it would begin with the May 1861 issue of the *Atlantic*) and, perhaps to allay his anxieties as to which project would take precedence for her, wrote: "I write my Maine story with a shiver, and come back to this as to a flowery home where I love to rest."[3] In her introduction to the book version of *Agnes of Sorrento,* Stowe disclaims any "responsibility for historical accuracy," defining her text as "mere dreamland." Did Stowe find it easy to write *Agnes* and did she privilege this twin precisely because she constructed it as exempt from the requirements of truth? The game reader willing to make her or his way through *Agnes* may be struck, as I was, by the similarities between the two texts written concurrently, and struck as well by the signal difference in their conclusions. In *Agnes* are all the elements of *Pearl*—the spiritual heroine; the Byronic hero; the prospect of romance between them as a form of damnation for both. But in the final chapter, without warning or preparation (indeed as I came to the end of the volume in hand I concluded, despite appearances to the contrary, that there must be a second half and that in this second half we would discover that Agnes and her hero were brother and sister), all difficulties vanish, the text collapses into marriage, and ends. Romance, however belatedly invoked, evidently gave Stowe the structure she needed to finish her story and without a "shiver."

In *The Pearl of Orr's Island* Stowe saw herself as telling the "truth" about "real life," and that truth had to do with her perception of the danger to both women and men of romance. Aware that she herself had been somewhat complicit in leading her readers to expect a romance from her, Stowe may have felt a particular need to warn her readers against her book. She had, after all, concluded the first half of *Pearl* with the following comment: "Here for a season we leave both our child friends, and when ten years have passed over their heads,—when Moses shall be twenty, and Mara seventeen,—we will return again to tell their story, for then there will be one to tell" (189). Yet I would argue that Stowe's anxiety on the subject of romance, an anxiety sufficient to turn her from a close observer into a misreader, had less to do with her concern for violating her reader's expectations, whether she was complicit in raising them or not, and more to do with what she intended to substitute in place of the expected romance. For in *Pearl* she was neither subordinating romance to other interests as she had done in "A New England Sketch" nor ignoring it entirely as she had in *Uncle Tom's Cabin;* nor was she even fulfilling it belatedly as she had done in *Agnes* and to greater effect in *The Minister's Wooing* (1857). Rather she was subverting it, subjecting the conventions of romance to a critique that eventuated in a story that not only violated her readers' expectations but called those very expectations into question and aimed to expose and displace them.

Toward the end of *The Pearl of Orr's Island* Aunt Roxy Toothacre, a woman of "faculty" who serves the community of Orr's Island as nurse, seamstress, and expert on child rearing, and who articulates her author's most radical thought because Stowe keeps her safely distanced as a regional "character," attacks her sister Ruey for her "silly" obsession with romance and for having a head "always full of weddin's, weddin's, weddin's— nothin' else—from mornin' till night, and night till mornin'" (377). Like Emily Sewell, sister to the minister of the Protestant community of Orr's Island, who "regarded Mara as her godchild, and was intent on finishing her up into a romance in real life, of which a handsome young man, who had been washed ashore in a shipwreck, should be the hero," Ruey represents the reader who interprets everything through the grid of romance (260). Against the foolishness of this totalizing script, Roxy sets the observation that "there's other things have got to be thought of in this world besides weddin' clothes, and it would be well, if people would think more o' gettin' their weddin' garments ready for the kingdom of heaven" (377). Stowe realizes that both fiction and culture conspire to make it difficult for women and men to think of other things: "Sally was getting romantic. Had she been reading novels? Novels! What can a pretty woman find in a novel equal to the romance that is all the while weaving and unweaving about her, and of which no human foresight can tell her the catastrophe? . . . Is there not an eternal novel, with all these false, cheating views, written in the breast of every beautiful and attractive girl whose witcheries make every man that comes near her talk like a fool? Like a sovereign princess, she never hears the truth, unless it be from the one manly man in a thousand, who understands both himself and her" (334).

Halfway through the second part of *The Pearl of Orr's Island,* Stowe inserts a love story that defines what is wrong with romance, giving particularity to her general indictment of its "false and cheating views." Stowe here identifies the romance, although conventionally considered a woman's genre, as a story written by one man to another, for the Reverend Mr. Sewell writes the narrative of "poor Dolores" to Moses Pennel as a way of telling Moses his origins. When Sewell was a young man, just graduated from Harvard, he served as tutor in the house of a wealthy man of Spanish heritage recently emigrated from the West Indies to Saint Augustine, Florida. Don Jose had one daughter by a former marriage who was among the pupils Sewell had been engaged to tutor. In her father's household Dolores, although presumably loved by her father, occupied, in Sewell's analysis, a position no different from that of his slaves; she was "to be disposed of for life according to his pleasure" (272). During the time of Sewell's engagement as tutor, Don Jose arranged a marriage for Dolores with Don Guzman, a man as rich and dissolute as himself. Terrorized by the prospect of this marriage and already in love with her tutor, Dolores turned to Sewell to escape her father. Their plan to elope was discovered, Sewell fled for his life, Dolores married Don Guzman and moved to Cuba. Sewell did not see her again until her dead body washed up on the shore of Orr's Island, holding the still-living child, Moses. He confirmed her identity by the bracelet she wore always, a gift from the mother who had died when Dolores was still a child.

Sewell tells Moses this story with the intent of persuading him of his good fortune in having been saved from so corrupt and corrupting an inheritance. He explicitly contrasts the chaos and violence of Don Jose's Spanish, Catholic, and slave-owning household with the purity and simplicity of Protestant, free, democratic New England, thus affirming the moral superiority of the North and Moses' luck in having been raised in Maine rather than Cuba. His narrative, however, has precisely the opposite effect. It leaves Moses feeling "like a leaf torn from a romance," his pride and ambition "stirred" to reclaim the inheritance he believes to be "rightfully" his (287). Sewell's narrative reinforces the very values he presumes to critique; for Stowe love stories do not persuade men of their good fortune in being dispossessed but rather stimulate men to desire power. The implications of such power become clear when, shortly after finishing Sewell's narrative, Moses encounters Mara and concludes his list of all the things he might buy if he just had money with "a wife, of course" (290). Moreover, Sewell's story leaves intact the deep structure of female dependency, for Dolores's idea of escape extends no further than to turn to one man to rescue her from another. And while his story records his failure to accomplish the rescue, this failure does not alter the fact that his story casts him in the role of rescuer. In Stowe's analysis, then, the romance, the love story, encourages women to see themselves as powerless and men to see themselves as powerful.

Stowe believed in the pedagogical power of fiction. If novels provided the model for and conspired in the production of that "eternal novel with all these false and cheating views," might not a story "so destitute of all that is ordinarily expected in a work of fiction" provide a framework for reading that would free women of the dependencies of romance and persuade men to relinquish the power romance gives them over women? In contrast to "the story of Dolores," *The Pearl of Orr's Island* seeks to counter the tendency of such fiction to eroticize male power and female powerlessness by making difference the ground of romance and by presenting romance as the single most compelling story to be lived and told. (Sewell, after all, has never married and finds no other story worth telling).

Yet such pedagogy might well have made Stowe anxious, for at its heart lay a scene of discipline and an act of dispossession. In Stowe's story, boy does not get girl, and by this lesson he is taught the falsity of his view of self and others and forced to recognize the limits of his power. Above all else, Moses intends never to be "brought down" or "brought under" (118, 181); yet Stowe's story does precisely that, for while Dolores, creature of romance, has only the fetish of a hair bracelet, gift of her dead mother, to protect her, Mara has access to the living God from whom she receives "that invisible measuring rod, which she was laying to the foundations of all actions and thoughts" (177–178). Through Mara, who, possessed of a ground outside the structures of romance from which to evaluate and judge all things, prefers death to marriage, Stowe most particularly lays the rod on Moses, "the saucy boy" who will yet one day "learn to tremble at the golden measuring-rod, held in the hand of a woman" (178). Since Moses figures in her text as the reader of romance, he represents as well Stowe's own presumptive reader whose expectations she intends not merely to frustrate but to expose. The prospect of making her hero and her reader "tremble" may well have caused Stowe herself to "shiver."

One might argue that the moment Stowe introduces Moses into her text, she leads her readers to expect a love story. One might also argue that she further encourages those expectations by presenting Moses as a "true boy" and by identifying Mara as quintessentially feminine. Given a serviceable dress and stout shoes for playing on the beach, Mara, ordinarily tractable, refuses, saying, "Mara don't want—Mara want pitty boo des—and *pitty shoes*" (54). For the conventions of romance assume that the more masculine the boy and the more feminine the girl the greater will be the erotic potential of the text. Yet it is precisely such assumptions that Stowe seeks to challenge, for as she develops her story, we discover that her emphasis lies on neither the erotic energy generated by difference nor its potential to bring difference together, but rather on the irreconcilability of such difference and on the moral dubiousness of the attempt to bring difference together. Her text proves the problematic nature of romantic love as the agency designed to bridge such differences and questions the assumptions behind such a cultural construct.

From the moment of his arrival on Orr's Island, Moses appears to be "a perfect little miniature of proud manliness" (86). And Stowe immediately begins to explore the nature of the relationship "proud manliness" establishes with "the little Mara." Having taken the measure of the requirements of child care from her previous experience with Mara, Aunt Ruey is deep into her reading of the "prophecies" when a loud scream from the barn brings her to witness "pitty" Mara covered with hay and broken eggs. Moses has enticed her into the hay loft and she has fallen through a hole, landing on and smashing the nest of "a very domestic sitting-hen" (88). When Mara astonishingly takes Moses' side against her efforts to reprimand him, Ruey announces her belief that Moses has "bewitched" her. She offers the children cake in an attempt at appeasement but Moses refuses to eat until Mara, "with much chippering and many little feminine manoeuvres, at last succeeded in making him taste it" (90).

Her pretty dress a mess, domestic life disrupted, Mara angry at Ruey and concerned only that Moses should eat—proud manliness appears rather dangerous to the little Mara. A subsequent incident intensifies this note and suggests the possibility that the danger lies in Mara's being eaten herself. Although Moses will not learn the "romance" of his origins until later, he already knows the script for a romantic adventure. Discovering one day an abandoned canoe on the shore, he imitates what he "had seen men do" (114). Getting Mara into the boat, he pushes it out to sea, where he glories in the triumph of having gotten her all to himself. As sharks threaten to upset the boat, Sewell arrives to break the "spell" and save the children. But Moses' script, fashioned on the lives of men, as yet contains no lines for recognizing himself as dangerous or in danger, and so this time he defies Aunt Roxy with "the spirit of Sir Francis Drake and of Christopher Columbus . . . swelling in his little body" (118).

Stowe establishes the link between the danger posed to Mara by this "adventure," the danger of herself being the food Moses needs to sustain his view of himself, and the consumption that finally kills her in a long section that treats of Moses' first voyage. Here Stowe indicates that differences in nurture sustain and reinforce differences in nature and make such differences still more dangerous. Although Stowe calls her New England "democratic" and shares Sewell's position that Moses' luck lies in having been cast ashore in the moral North, she clearly records the differential opportunities for education and development afforded to New England boys and girls. Moses at the age of ten accompanies Captain Pennel on a fishing voyage of several months; Sally Kittridge meanwhile has learned to turn a sheet, the discipline considered most appropriate for raising young girls and one that Stowe labels "a perfect torture" (35). Although Mara's more indulgent grandmother does not force her to turn sheets or learn any of the domestic arts that Sally must master, she has nothing to offer in its place, and in consequence Mara is left essentially to her own devices, an example of the woman "self-raised." After completing the education of the voyage, Moses will learn Latin from Sewell and then, should he take the hook thus baited (Stowe's metaphor suggests the natural progression in male education from the physical to the mental), he can continue his development in college. Mara meanwhile will be offered lessons in mortuary art from Miss Emily and a season at Miss Plucher's in Portland where she can learn more of the same. Sewell, perceiving in Mara the physical delicacy associated with the consumption that he himself has traveled to escape, realizes that she too could use a good voyage. " 'But she's a woman,' he said, with a sigh, 'and they are all alike. We can't do much for them, but let them come up as they will and make the best of it' " (167).

Because he can go to sea and Mara can't, Moses returns home more contemptuous of girls than ever, and in this homecoming, shaped as it is by Moses' continual disparagement of her "girlhood," Mara experiences "a shivering sense of disappointment" (160). The word "shivering" here might well alert us to the significance of this textual moment. Though Mara can not or will not speak to Moses of her pain, Stowe can alert her readers to the implications of Mara's disappointment: "But if ever two children, or two grown people, thus organized, are thrown into intimate relations, it follows, from the very laws of their being, that one must hurt the other, simply by being itself; one must always hunger for what the other has not to give" (161–162). Stowe returns throughout her text to the theme of Mara's wound, increasing with each reiteration the intensity of her language, until at last we are told that "there are griefs which grow with years, which have no marked beginnings,—no especial dates; they are not events, but slow perceptions of disappointment, which bear down on the heart with a constant and equable pressure like the weight of the atmosphere, and these things are never named or counted in words among life's sorrows; yet through them, as through an unsuspected inward wound, life, energy, and vigor, slowly bleed away" (298).

Although Stowe does not explicitly blame Moses for Mara's wound, she sees the "law" of difference, exaggerated and reinforced by an educational system that values the masculine over the feminine, as fatal to Mara. Yet there is danger in difference for Moses as well, for the criticism Stowe never allows herself to voice directly emerges indirectly, and Moses, subjected to the judgments of that "invisible" rod, is visibly found wanting. Believing himself to be "god," and supported in this belief by nurture as well as nature, Moses faces the danger of missing God completely. The law of difference and the love to which it leads bring both Mara and Moses dangerously close to the sin of idolatry. Stowe recognizes the existence of a class of women like Mara's grandmother, "to whom self-sacrifice is constitutionally so much a nature, that self-denial *for her* must have consisted in standing up for her own rights, or having her own way when it crossed the will and pleasure of any one around her. All she wanted of a child, or in fact of any human creature, was something to love and serve" (109). And she concludes her analysis of this class by asserting that "the chief comfort of such women in religion is that it gives them at last an object for love without criticism, and for whom the utmost degree of self-abandonment is not idolatry but worship" (109). When Stowe tells us that Mara "has no dreams for herself—they are all for Moses" and that he is her "cherished idol," we realize how close they both have come to the sin of idolatry (133, 162). What saves them from this danger, however, is the criticism that even a woman like Mrs. Pennel can feel toward the "object" of her love because it results from the very structure of difference that is at issue. Man is not God, and to the degree that difference leads him to believe he is, to that degree it carries within it the contradiction that is its own undoing.

Mara's "criticism" of Moses begins in childhood and derives from their differing values. When Mara voices the wish that she too were going on the fishing voyage, Moses replies, "You're a girl—and what can girls do at sea? you never like to catch fish—it always makes you cry to see 'em flop" (136). Mara does not consciously question Moses' values here, but in her perplexity at having to choose between her sympathy for the fish and her desire for Moses' glory, we find the origins of the moral dilemma Stowe associates with romantic love. A later incident elaborates this point. On a picnic to Eagle Island, Moses spies an eagle's nest at the top of a tree, climbs the tree, and comes back with the eggs in his pocket. Mara, hearing the eagles scream above her (we remember here the earlier "clamors" of

the disrupted hen), expresses concern for the "poor birds" and wonders
how they must be feeling. Against Mara's gentle challenge to the morality
of his act, Moses defends himself by occupying the familiar ground of
"you are a girl,—I'm a man"; and besides, he adds, "I am older than you,
and when I tell you a thing's right, you ought to believe it" (177). But
Mara doesn't just believe it, for "Reader," says Stowe, "there is no independence and pertinacity of opinion like that of these seemingly soft, quiet
creatures, whom it is so easy to silence, and so difficult to convince" (177).
If loving Moses means Mara must subordinate her judgment to his, and if
she measures him and finds his judgment faulty, how is she to love him
and remain moral? And without her judgment how is he to learn that he is
not in fact God?

When Sewell offers to teach him Latin, Moses feels "elevated some
inches in the world" and assumes he will master declensions just as he has
mastered boats, fish, and birds (180). His difficulties, figured here through
his inability to remember the endings of *penna,* a word that literally means
"feather" and, by extension, "soaring ambition" and that reminds us that
Moses Pennel's idea of mastery is to spoil the nests of birds and send their
feathers flying, provide an additional framework for formulating the
moral dilemma of the romance of true boy and true girl. At one lesson,
Moses gives the wrong ending and Mara "involuntarily" calls out the
right one. When Sewell discovers that in helping Moses study Mara has
learned more than he, he decides to give her the wish she expressed earlier,
that she too "had been invited to share this glorious race," and let her
study Latin with Moses (181). As a consequence Moses begins to respect
Mara, for when the ground shifts from the physical to the mental, his
"natural" superiority does not seem so apparent. In this textual moment
Stowe has established the truth of Sewell's assertion that in the nineteenth
century the way to greatness "lies through books," for now "there is more
done with pens than swords" (166). Mara's success with the "pen" (for
penna is also of course the root of the English word "pen") has raised
questions for Moses about his superiority relative to her.

Moses keeps his respect "secret," but Stowe makes no secret of the
questions this experience poses for the relations of men and women. Mara
enters the race by accident and is allowed to continue only because Sewell
is willing to engage in a limited and contained experiment. Without such
accidents Moses' sense of superiority would receive no check. But if men's
sense of superiority derives on the one hand from physical strength, primarily expressed in acts of mastery over others that cause pain, and on the
other hand from intellectual strength based on keeping women out of the
race, how can the woman who understands this believe that men are really
superior? How can she avoid the conclusion that a sense of superiority so

based is really inferior? And what is such a woman to do when faced with the seduction of romance, the universal solvent of "I love you" that has "conclusive force as argument, apology, promise,—covering, like charity, a multitude of sins" (346), and that leads to a marriage in which her own values will inevitably be subordinated to his? For Moses, at the moment of telling Mara "I love you," admits that "I would not wish to be second in your heart even to God himself" and secretly believes that someday "she will worship me" (348); and Mara, dying, affirms that had they married she would have lost her influence over him, and while he might not have led her to idolatry, she would not have led him to God. Since romantic love functions to bring about such a dangerous conclusion and to obscure its very danger, may not romantic love itself be morally suspect?

When Moses and Mara meet after a separation of some years, Moses assumes that romance, courtship, and marriage will form the "natural" extension of their relationship. Since Moses' relation to Mara as a lover does not differ from his earlier relation to her as a despised girl, we can assume that for Stowe romantic love, despite any conventions to the contrary, has no conversionary power and can not transform difference into something other than danger. Although as a girl Mara has not been inclined to assert the claims of "womanhood" as Moses has of "manhood," upon Moses' return she sets the "power of womanhood" not *for*, as one might expect, but *against* romance, resisting his script as an instinctive act of self-defense: "Something swelled and trembled in her when she felt the confident pressure of that bold arm around her waist,—like the instinct of a wild bird to fly. Something in the deep, manly voice, the determined, self-confident air, aroused a vague feeling of defiance and resistance in her which she could scarcely explain to herself" (243). Mara's resistance provides the structure for the second half of *The Pearl of Orr's Island,* and while it might appear that her resistance is simply a version of the difficulties with which authors traditionally beset fictional lovers in order to intensify the pleasure readers take in their ultimate union, Stowe's deferrals have a different design.

Stowe provides an explicit critique of courtship and the view of romance that fuels it in the first event that defers the anticipated courtship between Moses and Mara. Although Moses returns home ready to court Mara, he quickly turns his attention to the flirtatious Sally, who seeks to test the power of her womanhood to attract a lover. In Stowe's view Moses and Sally are well matched because both of them recognize courtship as a struggle for power, a kind of war, and as such an amusement that will gratify the ego of the winner. Sally, initially convinced that Mara does not love Moses and sharing Mara's resistance to Moses' arrogant assumption of masculine power, determines to bring him to declare himself in love with her, at which point, speaking for herself and Mara and indeed for "women," she will have the exquisite pleasure of deflating his ego by rejecting him. Moses, on his part, seeks at once to punish Mara for what he perceives to be her indifference to him and to have the fun of beating Sally at her own game. For Stowe, the definitive feature of romance lies in its falseness. It places men and women in a false relation to each other, with frequently disastrous consequences. Indeed, when Moses and Sally finally reach the point toward which their game has been tending, Sally draws back in horror, for she recognizes that if she were to continue to play the game and to answer yes to his question, "you love me, do you not?" she would be committing them both to a lifetime of falsehood. Sally summarizes their courtship by declaring it a period in which neither of them has "spoken a word of truth or sense to each other" (340).

In a different story, the clarification between Sally and Moses, by removing the obstacles in the path of true love, would precipitate a second clarification between Moses and Mara in which all would be understood and forgiven. In a different story, we would expect, as do Moses and Sally, that the rest of the text would be devoted to the courtship of Mara and Moses and its successful conclusion. But Stowe frustrates these expectations because she makes no distinction between true and false courtship. In her text it is courtship itself that is false, and both "true" and "false" courtship end in separation. Thus the moment when Moses and Mara finally come together signals the beginning of their ultimate separation. Although his conversation with Sally has led Moses to realize he has spent his summer trifling with her, and has led him to wonder whether his love for Mara has not also been a form of trifling, what truly catches his attention in their exchange is Sally's revelation that Mara does indeed love him, for this knowledge gives him a power previously lacking in his relationship with Mara. Armed with this knowledge, he returns home, prepared to invoke the love he has moments before considered to be trifling as the apology for his behavior. Since Moses has undergone no transformation, his courtship of Mara will prove no different in essence from his courtship of Sally.

Mara accepts Moses' declaration that, despite his behavior during the summer, he actually loves Mara and not Sally, but her response is quite different from what Moses expects. When Moses reveals that he loves her, Mara reveals that she loves God and loves Moses because God has given him to her as a sacred charge. Her revelation that "God has always been to me not so much like a father as like a dear and tender mother," not Moses' revelation that he loves her, constitutes the emotional climax for Mara of this scene of clarification (348). Yet since Moses has just moments before averred that he would not wish to be second to God himself in her affection, what this "clarification" clarifies is the distance between these "lovers." Although now technically engaged to Moses, Mara has in fact begun the process of disengagement, and Stowe's displacement of engagement by disengagement signals her differing analysis of the conclusion to which the law of difference leads.

Shortly after their engagement Moses leaves on the voyage that he believes will make his fortune, and Mara begins to die. Her death constitutes the final displacement and critique of romance, for Mara dies to escape the loss of self and God that marriage to Moses would entail for both him and her. Stowe gives her readers something else to think about as wedding preparations give place to Mara's preparation for her reunion with God and as the story of her death and its transformative effect on those around her displaces Moses' romantic script of Mara waiting patiently for him to return, possessed at last of his inheritance. When Moses finally does return, enraged at the displacement of his script and convinced that either the reports of Mara's impending death have been exaggerated or that her illness has been induced by his absence and thus can be cured by his return, he too is made subject to the lesson of Mara's death. And in his subjugation we see, perhaps most clearly, how *The Pearl of Orr's Island,* in resisting, denying, and deconstructing the love story, might have made its author anxious, for through Mara's death the "saucy" boy is finally made to "tremble" as here boy most emphatically does not get girl. Mara's death confronts Moses with a fact utterly against his will and utterly beyond his power to control. Her death, so cheerful, so desired, brings him down, substituting the humiliating recognition of his own limitations for the empowering script of romantic possession, his belief in his power to revitalize her and take God's place in her heart.

Yet Stowe offers this humiliation as essential for accomplishing the sea change that will transform Moses into both manliness and godliness and make it possible for him to enter into a mutually enhancing relationship with another human being. In Stowe's pedagogy, then, bringing men down is the only way of bringing them up, and in dispossessing men of their inheritance she teaches them the fortune of their fall.

Stowe begins her text with an event that establishes the theological context for the motif of dispossession: the wreck of a homeward-bound ship at the moment of entering the harbor. This story so resonates with significance that it "is yet told in many a family on this coast" (4). For Stowe the event reflects the contingency of human life and the limits on humans' ability to shape and control their fate. At the moment of greatest success, the moment when humans are most likely to believe in their ability to master and control—a successful voyage successfully completed—they are brought up against the greater power of God to dispose of their lives, and those who from the shore watch the ship go down find in the scene a powerful reminder of the need to be always ready to meet God. Yet this scene is not without gender. As we have seen, the opportunity to make a voyage serves to separate boy from girl and provides men with a basis for their sense of superiority by offering them and denying women access to life-giving physical development and experiences associated with mastery. Stowe further connects the prerogative of voyaging with the opportunity for imaginative development through the figure of Captain Kittridge, whose tales of life at and under the sea strike his wife as pure fable. Yet she can never successfully challenge him because as she puts it, "You've been where we haven't" (68).

In a world in which voyaging is used to establish masculine superiority over women and to confirm in men their ability to master their natural environment and hence by extension to master women, Stowe's choice of opening serves to remind her reader that men in their turn are subject to God, who can master them. Shipwreck serves to contextualize men's sense of superiority and their definition of power. As his name suggests, Moses represents at once mankind, burdened with the original sin of Adam, and gendered man, embodying characteristics associated with masculinity, and from the start Stowe constructs Moses' masculine identity as problematic at once for his relation to God and his relation to women. Stowe's opening scene implies that men need to become more like women to the extent that they define "women" as those humans who have learned humility and submission. For the particular tragedy of this event lies in the fact that the men on board the ship are within sight of home and of the women who wait for them. Men may sail to and fro over the face of the earth, figuring themselves as masters and heroes, but voyages can not last forever and eventually they must come home—to women, to God— and if they can not reach home they are truly wrecked. So men require a "sea change" to recognize these facts, and shipwreck, which sends fathers to the bottom of the ocean, provides both the literal and figurative conditions for such a change.

Stowe does not weaken the effect of her opening scene by repeating it with a description of the shipwreck that casts Moses on the shores of Orr's Island, but she draws on that opening scene to underscore the significance of the event that takes place off stage. As we later learn, this shipwreck drowns Moses' father and dispossesses him at once of father and patrimony. Yet Moses' dispossession goes deeper than the loss of estates and slaves in Cuba. He survives the wreck by God's grace and his mother's love, his rebirth recapitulating the original dependencies of birth, for although his arrival on Orr's Island may be said to begin the action of the novel, this world precedes Moses. In a stunning reversal of the Old Testament story of creation, Stowe describes the Eden of Orr's Island as originally inhabited by Mara, whose own prior birth out of a shipwreck that kills both father and mother casts her as the original unparented creation. Moreover, it is Mara's longing for "something," a playmate to complete her existence, that brings Moses into being. Mara dreams of Moses before he is "born," dreams of a woman in white leading a little boy by the hand, putting the boy's hand in hers, and saying, "Take him, Mara, he is a playmate for you" (53). In Mara's dream Stowe rewrites the theology of the New Testament as well, for here God, the mother, gives mankind into the keeping of her daughter. As New Englanders "read Moses with the amendments of Christ" (131), so Stowe reads the story of God the father and Christ the son with the amendments of her own time, appropriating the revisionary potential of the nineteenth-century identification of feminine values with Christian values to rewrite God as the mother who creates "man" in her own image and later offers her own daughter as the instrument through whose death man can be saved. Throughout the text the relationship of mother and daughter, Mara's longing for her mother and her mother's longing for her, constitutes the almost visible link between this world and that other world from which we come and to which we return.

In dispossessing Moses of the texts that would establish his primacy, Stowe creates the necessary conditions for the fortune of his fall, his eventual recognition of the value of his dispossession, and his attendant transformation. Through the figure of Captain Pennel, who in the opening scene watches from the shore with his daughter Naomi as the ship goes down, powerless to avert what he knows to be a fatal change of course, Stowe indicates that men are capable of such transformation, that men too can be home. Long ago, when Naomi was five, Captain Pennel sold his ship and settled down to farming, convinced that in his child at home he has found the pearl that those who voyage continually seek. After Mara's death the Captain has a dream in which, as he looks everywhere for his lost pearl, Christ comes walking down the beach and finds the pearl and places it in his forehead. From this dream the Captain awakes happy and calm, and Stowe gives her readers an image of the rewards of undergoing sea change.

In shipwreck Moses undergoes a form of sea change, and this fact, in conjunction with his surviving such a wreck, suggests that he too is capable of change. Although it requires Mara's death, Moses does experience a spiritual transformation. Sharing with her the last days of her life, Moses finally attends to Mara, entering her world of flowers and books and even of God, and finding there beauty and peace. So transformed,

Moses can later reap the rewards of this change in marriage to Sally Kittridge, realizing a love that begins not with their earlier courtship but with their mutual devotion to Mara and one based on the equality of similarity rather than on the inequality of difference. Mara's life and death have done the work of educating both Sally and Moses, and thus educated they become the models for a new Adam and Eve. In its own way *The Pearl of Orr's Island* has a happy ending.

Ironically, Stowe found her way through to an end for her story during the first year of the American Civil War, an event that both in itself and in its consequences had an effect precisely opposite to the intent of her text, for it valorized and made it possible to romanticize the power of the sword. In the folklore according to which *Uncle Tom's Cabin* caused the Civil War, a hypothesis that implicitly values the pen as it leads to the sword, we might ourselves find a key to *Uncle Tom's Cabin,* one source for the relative ease with which Stowe wrote her first novel as compared to her "second." For despite its overt commitment to maternal values,[4] at the heart of *Uncle Tom's Cabin* is rage, the vision of an avenging sword retaliating violence for violence. The *Dies Irae* to which Saint Clare alludes finds textual embodiment in the figures of the two Georges, one black and the other white, whose most heroic moments occur when they resort to violence. George Harris raises his hand to heaven, "as if appealing from man to the justice of God," and moments later shoots the slave trader Loker, authorized by Stowe to be the executor of God's justice. George Shelby strikes Simon Legree to the ground and emerges as the "true" George, "blazing with wrath and defiance," capable of slaying the dragon of slavery, a vow he makes on the grave of Uncle Tom. Both scenes release the rage the book has accumulated and both foreshadow the release of rage in the violence of war a scant decade later.

Of course there is rage in *The Pearl of Orr's Island.* And of course the plot to bring Moses down, to dispossess him of his masculine perogatives and his sense of superiority, the desire to make the "saucy" boy tremble before the rod of the judging women, are ways of acting out anger. Yet in *The Pearl of Orr's Island* Stowe resolves her anger within the text. Moses is brought down, but then he is brought up, and in the final analysis Stowe identifies herself as author with God the "dear and tender mother," not God the avenging father. In the vision of Moses transformed we might read a message more radical and more anxious than that contained in the image of Moses trembling before the rod. But if Stowe resolves the contradictions in her treatment of Moses—God is a dear and tender mother but Moses must be dispossessed, humiliated, and punished—through the working out of the pedagogy of bringing down as the way of bringing up, we may feel her to be less successful in her treatment of Mara. For has she not in fact committed the very crime Aunt Roxy identifies as central to the conventions of her culture? When informed that the Pennels "are e'en a'most tickled to pieces" at the engagement of Moses and Mara " 'cause they think it'll jist be the salvation of him to get Mara," Roxy replies, "I a'n't one of the sort that wants to be a-usin' up girls for the salvation of fellers" (352). Yet hasn't Stowe used up Mara for the salvation of "fellers"? In the issues Stowe faced with her heroine and the question of "what can a heroine do?"[5] we might find an equally powerful source for her shiver and her difficulty in completing her text. But that is another story.

NOTES

1. Harriet Beecher Stowe, *The Pearl of Orr's Island* (Hartford, Conn.: Stowe-Day Foundation, 1979), 200. All subsequent quotations are from this edition and will be cited parenthetically in the text.

2. Susan Wolstenholme, "Voice of the Voiceless: Harriet Beecher Stowe and the Byron Controversy," *American Literary Realism* 19 (1987): 48–65.

3. Quoted in E. Bruce Kirkham, "The Writing of Harriet Beecher Stowe's *The Pearl of Orr's Island*," *Colby Library Quarterly* 16 (1980): 158–165.

4. See Elizabeth Ammons, "Stowe's Dream of the Mother-Savior: *Uncle Tom's Cabin* and American Women Writers Before the 1920s," *New Essays on* Uncle Tom's Cabin, ed. Eric J. Sundquist (New York: Cambridge University Press, 1986).

5. See Joanna Russ, "What Can a Heroine Do? Or Why Women Can't Write," *Images of Women in Fiction: Feminist Perspectives,* ed. Susan Koppelman Cornillon (Bowling Green, Ohio: Bowling Green University Press, 1976).

❧ KARLA F. C. HOLLOWAY ❧

Economies of Space: Markets and Marketability in Our Nig *and* Iola Leroy

I am forced to some experiment which shall aid me in maintaining myself and child without extinguishing this feeble life. I would not from these motives even palliate slavery at the South, by disclosures of its appurtenances North. My mistress was wholly imbued with *southern* principles. I do not pretend to divulge every transaction in my own life, which the unprejudiced would declare unfavorable in comparison with treatment of legal bondmen; I have purposely omitted what would most provoke shame in our good anti-slavery friends at home.

"Preface," *Our Nig*, Harriet E. Wilson

I have woven a story whose mission will not be in vain if it awaken in the hearts of our countrymen a stronger sense of justice and a more Christlike humanity . . . if it inspire the children of those upon whose brows God has poured the chrism of that new era to determine that they will embrace every opportunity, develop every faculty, and use every power God has given them . . . to grasp the pen and wield it as a power for good, and to erect above the ruined auction-block and slave-pen institutions of learning.

—Closing "Note," *Iola Leroy*, Frances E. W. Harper

THE ELEMENTS of Harriet Wilson's *Our Nig; or Sketches from the Life of a Free Black* (1859) are outlined in her preface to the autobiographical novel.[1] A quotation from that preface is my first epigraph, and its focus on the poverty and illness that make her "experiment" necessary foreshadows the

126

slim structures of her textual language and the limited places of her story's enactment. Here, the imagery and language of her text are *pre*viewed, and the readers' engagement with the text is clearly directed toward the narrow and meager literary environments that will frame her story.

My second quotation, from a closing "Note" to Frances Harper's 1892 novel, *Iola Leroy*, calls attention to its relationship to the text that has, in this case, preceded it.[2] As a closing comment it reflects rather than anticipates the story. Harper's final words *re*view the goals of her novel, and their ornate composition accurately mirrors the embellished and elaborate narrative whose telling has just been accomplished.

I've selected these passages because they call attention to a critical difference between these two novels—Harriet Wilson's, the first written by an African-American woman, and Frances Harper's, among the last published in the century. The difference is one wherein both textual space and language are negotiated through a dialectic of economic materialism and sociopolitical aspiration.

In "Writing 'Race' and the Difference It Makes," Henry Louis Gates, Jr., draws our attention to the correlations between writing, race, and "economic and political alienation" in Anglo-African and African-American discourse.[3] The act of writing, a "response to allegations of its absence," was to constitute a "voice of deliverance from the deafening discursive silence which an enlightened Europe cited to prove the absence of the African's humanity" (11). Using the evidence from "scores of reviews" of Phillis Wheatley's 1773 book of poems that "argued that the publication of her poems meant that the African was indeed a human being and should not be enslaved," Gates explains that "writing, for the slave, was not an activity of mind; rather it was a commodity which they were forced to trade for their humanity."[4] *Our Nig* and *Iola Leroy* illustrate the historic evolution between these oppositional enterprises. Further, when the provocation for Wilson's novel and the avocation of Harper's are juxtaposed, we can see how the earlier novel's provocative initiation is structured within the narrative as an expressive enactment of writing as a "*commodity* which [she was] forced to trade for [her] humanity." The avocation that led to the later novel's publication also has textual and structural parallels. Its "activity of mind" is reflected in what Harper intended as the ethical appeal of her argument.

Wilson's and Harper's novels occupy opposing poles—one economic and physical, the other political and spiritual. Shifts in linguistic structures parallel these strategies. Wilson's largely monologic work subordinates the textual structure, the characters' voices, and the narrative to its economic intent, effectively making the economies of narrative spaces a primary metaphor in the novel. In contrast, the dialogic form of Harper's novel allows its voices to echo the expanse of physical spaces the novel covers and encourages the variety of voices that she allows into these spaces.

The constructions of these works are either anticipated by or reflected within the context and place of the notes that I use as an epigraph to this essay and that either precede or follow each author's text. Their physical position in the text is a structural decision that reveals the tactical plan of the authors. Wilson writes in order to claim some means of productive economy, and Harper writes in order to create and fulfill spiritual substance. My argument is that their choices affect the construction of contextual "spaces" within their works and the linguistic structures of their narrative. The spare and meager means of Wilson's world, acknowledged in her "Preface," intrude into the linguistic and substantive dimensions of her narrative spaces. In contrast, the expansive and creative goals of Harper's sociopolitical agenda, annotated in her closing note, are reflected in the elaborate language and sweeping contexts of her novel. This narrative architecture emphasizes how the issue of space is an intimate reminder of the idea of liberation—the constant metaphor in both these works.

> For women to undertake tactical strikes, to keep themselves apart from men long enough to learn to defend their desire, especially through speech, to discover the love of other women while sheltered from men's imperious choices that put them in the position of *rival commodities* . . . to earn their living in order to escape from the condition of prostitute . . . are certainly indispensible stages in their escape from their proletarization on the *exchange market* [emphasis added].
> —Luce Irigaray, *This Sex Which Is Not One*[5]

Irigaray's references to "rival commodities" and the "exchange market" are useful to this discussion as points of reference to the economies of textual production within Harriet Wilson's *Our Nig*. In contrast to the "epilogic" space of Harper's afterword, Wilson places the textual economy up front. Her preface initiates and structurally controls the appended text.

Wilson's decision to foreground the economic parameters of her own situation was a tactical maneuver that extended itself into the narrative boundaries of the text. If we shift Irigaray's references so that they might include these productive metaphors, the particular form of Wilson's "defense of desire through speech" can be seen as her effort to negate and exercise some control over the restrictive economic parameters of her obviously "proletarian" status. In this interpretive schema, Wilson's decision to sell her labor in exchange for her livelihood would trap her into a version of Irigaray's "prostitution" because her creative talents were (artificially) manufactured and sold.

Although Wilson's motives were an effort to deconstruct the economic restrictions of her life, she was writing in 1859, and only by living in New England, did she (logistically) escape slavery. Claudia Tate draws our attention to Wilson's obvious understanding of this predicament of place and suggests that the story's full title (*Our Nig; or, Sketches from the Life of a Free Black, in a Two-Story White House, North—Showing that Slavery's Shadows Fall Even There*) indicates how the "authorial posture, narrative tone and perspective, vacillate between representing direct social criticism and self-reflexive irony . . . by revising the idyllic plantation romance and by evoking an incomplete analogy between Our Nig's place of residence— 'white house, North'—and its absent referent—the idealized plantation mansion, South."[6] Wilson's strategy assures that this irony is not lost on her reader. Her prefatory disclaimer, "I would not from these motives even palliate slavery at the South, by disclosures of its appurtenances North," is clearly set aside in the text. Instead, the persistent parallels between Frado's own pitiable experiences and the actual situations of a slave are constantly inscribed in the narrative. Despite her promise not to "disclose [the] appurtenances" of slavery's appearance in the North, the sorry circumstances of her indenture in the Bellmont household are rendered in a way that makes clear their relationship to the miserable conditions of slavery. Given her promise to avoid this type of comparison, we must look closely at the intention of this preface and give Wilson credit for its design and execution. The craft within the intentionally framed irony of the claim that "[m]y mistress was wholly imbued with *southern* principles" parallels the structures of this preface and the metaphors of the text wherein her value is constantly measured by the standards of slavery. Her labors and her worth are clearly a matter of her productivity. "Just think how much profit she was to us last summer"—her mistress argues—"she did the work of two girls . . . I'll beat the money out of her, if I can't get her worth any other way" (90).

Wilson's own description labels *Our Nig* an "experiment" designed to "maintain" her life and her child's because the physical effort required by some alternative industry might "extinguish [her] feeble life." For Wilson then, a viable product, not only in terms of market value but in terms of its successful production, would be an enterprise that would not demand an exertion that her weakened health could not allow her to sustain. The concluding chapters' reference to Frado/Harriet as "still an invalid" supports her prefatory claim and frames the narrative with the reader's knowledge of her physical disability.

Both the effort and the essence of Wilson's novel are a version of "social-ization into capitalism." Susan Willis points to this process, noting that it allows us to "substitute alienation and commodities for human relation-ships." Wilson's project reifies Karl Marx's nineteenth-century challenge to the working class "to recognize and seize the buried human relationships in labor and in the products of labor which have been abstracted and alien-ated."[7] However, the economic agenda has a diffuse presence that makes the relationship between the author, the productive enterprise, and the product especially intimate. As a consequence of this intimacy, there is a metaphorical reenactment of the tentative, restricted, and unstable econ-omy of Wilson's "experimental" enterprise—exactly the kinds of linguistic structures and literary contexts that compose the text. Wilson has no access to the power that Marx's working class could lay claim to because she is not only economically disenfranchised, she is black and woman. Instead of the creative and inspirational objectives of Harper's work that allow us to read *Iola Leroy* as the product of a leisurely and (economically) optional enter-prise characterized by health and physical stamina, an oppositional frame constructs our reading of *Our Nig*. The "social status that compels recogni-tion" that Irigaray describes is inscribed as a monologic materialism in this work. Once language and writing become exchangeable commodities, Wilson's text barters away the creative essence that Harper's retains. The value of her commodity is contingent not only upon the economic needs that generate it, but upon the market she anticipates would be her salvation. Herein lies the trope of the market metaphor. It juxtaposes the economic market she would gain access to against the slave market that she has barely escaped. The difference is that she effectively exchanges the value of her body (ironically rendered frail and "worthless" by her labour and forced indenture in the Bellmont household) for her mental/creative self.

Wilson's "experiment" in writing implies a kind of freedom that her race, gender, and economic situation belie. The juxtaposition of the effort to experiment and her socioeconomic and political situations are essen-tially contradictory. Because her experimental enterprise is controlled by limiting socioeconomic factors, the productive object of the experiment, the text, is subordinate to the enterprise. In consequence, the novel's failure to rescue her from her condition is due at least in part to her effort to replicate the "phallocratism" (the phrase is Irigaray's) of economic models that her class, race, and gender clearly exclude from her control.[8]

The intentional desire of Wilson's project places her work in direct contrast to Harper's novel, where the "defen[se] of desire through speech" is centered on spiritual values—a position that liberates the text from the nexus of economy and product. Wilson's loss of creative freedom is mir-rored in the creative restraint within the text. A tightly controlled narrative, meager in its language and its forms and spare in description and narration, constantly offers reminders of its economic motive. Consider the opening page. Much like the McGuffy readers of the day it builds syntactic density.[9] Beginning with a simple declarative "Lonely Mag Smith!" it moves toward the more demanding imperative "See her as she walks with downcast eyes and heavy heart" (5). The persistence of these fairly straightforward and syntactically uncomplicated forms throughout the story contribute to its simple (some might argue unsophisticated) and direct tone. Even when dialogue is a part of the narrative, it too takes on the spare tone of declaration and reinforces the economic metaphor of the text. "Lonely" Mag Smith, the (white) mother of Harriet/Frado, is victimized mostly by the economics of her situation. Although an orphaned background and a moral fall (an illegitimate child excludes her from membership in the community) set the stage for her isolation, Wilson takes little time with these early travails and moves quickly to Mag's liaison with Jim, a black man whose attentions to some degree relieve her from "drudgery" and a melancholy that increased as "her means diminished" (9). Jim's first recorded words to her reflect his concern with her means ("How much you earn dis week, Mag?"), and their conversation is frequently marked with references to her material condition. The idea of marriage is referred to as a "sudden expedient," and Mag is a "prize" who is "down low enough" to be "take[n] care of" by Jim. She agrees to their relationship only because she "can do but two things . . . beg my living or get it from you" (13). Jim asks her to "take me [because] I can give you a better home than this." Although the narrator cautions the reader that improprieties can be attributed to this relationship (because Mag is white), the concluding narrative declaration of this opening chapter is that "*want* is a more powerful philosopher and preacher. *Poor* Mag" (13, emphasis added). The structural repetition of the novel's opening sentence ("Lonely Mag. . . . See her as she walks") is also an emphasis of tone. But the image of Mag as "poor" seems at this point in *Our Nig* to focus our specific attention on Mag's economic poverty—a status Jim attempts to ameliorate. However, even after this marriage is accomplished, Wilson does not abandon the economic metaphors. The birth of Frado and her brother is described as the "levy" of "an additional charge," and, as a "white wife," Mag is Jim's "treasure."

In contrast to the ideas and images of spartan economies that govern the metaphors in Wilson's text, Harper's novel freely indulges in literary excess. Harper's claim in her "Afterword" that inspiration and moral uplift were the motives (literally) behind her work allows her to avoid Wilson's somewhat materialistic textual ethics. Harper's creative effort, to "awaken" and "inspire" her readers, indicates a version of a laissez-faire doctrine as the operative ethic of her choice. Because of her economic stability, the leisure of language ("papers" delivered in plush sitting rooms, speeches made before comfortable and well-situated audiences) was hers to manipulate.

An example of the stylistic differences in the novels can be clearly seen in the descriptive language of these texts. Description in *Iola Leroy* is lush and effusive—engaging without restriction in the linguistic excess that characterizes the sentimental novel. Compare the following passages that refer to an impending journey in both novels. The first passage, from *Iola,* encourages reverie and calm:

> The air was soft and balmy. The fields and hedges were redolent with flowers. Not a single cloud obscured the brightness of the moon or the splendor of the stars. The ancient trees were festooned with moss, which hung like graceful draperies. Ever and anon a startled hare glided over the path, and whip-or-wills and crickets broke the restful silence of the night. . . . Iola rode along, conversing with Aunt Linda, amused and interested at the quaintness of her speech and the shrewdness of her intellect. To her the ride was delightful. (175)

The rich and descriptive language is stylistically paralleled with the "quaint" speech of Aunt Linda's dialect, whose conversation "amuses and interests" Iola. Linda's language is a textual digression; it's critical neither to the plot nor to the development of character. But Harper has space for this latitude and digression because her language has the freedom to be decorative and imaginative—the spare economy of restriction and constraint does not impede the flexibility of the text. It is instead a "delightful" accompaniment to a journey occurring on a "lovely evening."

A comparative passage from *Our Nig* also precedes the description of a journey. And although the situations that compel the trips are quite different, that contextual difference is not sufficient explanation for the extreme differences in structure and tone between these extracts:

> The morning for departure dawned. Frado egaged to work for a family a mile distant. Mrs. Bellmont dismissed her with the assurance that she would soon wish herself back again, and a present of a silver half dollar.
>
> Her wardrobe consisted of one decent dress, without any superfluous accompaniments. (117)

The entire narrative eschews "superfluous accompaniments" and obeys the stoic economic directive. It is almost as if superfluousness or excess would betray the intent and leak a distracting flexibility into the static structure.

Certainly one could argue that the difference in language between these two novels was a difference of class between the two writers. Frances Harper published her first collection of verse and prose fourteen years before the publication of *Our Nig*. Harper was an accomplished and financially secure poet, essayist, and public speaker. The number and extent of her lectures and writing expose an economic stability that could support that kind of enterprise. In contrast, although little detail is known about the situation of Harriet Wilson, it is clear that her economic status was so bleak that she was "separated from her son, whom she had been forced to foster to another family" because of her desperate financial condition.[10] These conditions notwithstanding, more evidence is called for to explain the intimate association between the textual language and the economic situations of the writers. I suggest that it is not only the personal education or financial situation of the writer that explains these parallels in narrative structures, but the mission of the text itself as a commodity of exchange or as a vessel of promise and inspiration.

All of Harper's narrative, not just her use of language, is expansive. The opening chapter, the "Mystery of Market Speech and Prayer-Meeting," predicts this narrative freedom. The market that threatens a proletarian dissolve for Irigaray is a grim (but indirect) reminder of the auction block. This shadow of one of the most horrific places of slavery is a discrete but necessary dimension of the novel's linguistic configuration. As a "mystery," the dialect that characterizes the language in this chapter is divested of its humor and its stereotypical status as an innocuous reminder of black folks' cognitive disabilities. Harper makes certain that it can no longer be construed as a trustworthy and known element of black folks' lives. The reader is warned that this mysterious language is likely to be subversive and connected to a spiritual hope of deliverance (and its "prayer-meeting" metaphors for flight and freedom) rather than the physical shackles of slavery (the threatening place of the slave "market"). Harper reveals how "they contrived to meet by stealth and hold gatherings where they could mingle their prayers and tears and lay plans for escaping" (13). Their language was a shape-changing dialect, the province of "shrewd" slaves who, "coming in contact with their masters and overhearing their conversations, *invented a phraseology* to convey in the most unsuspected manner news to each other" (9, emphasis added). Even literacy was not a barrier to subterfuge—"I can't read de newspapers, but ole Missus' face is newspaper nuff for me" (9). The white man's access to literacy afforded him no necessary protection because "slavery had cast such a glamour over the Nation, and so warped the consciences of men, *that they failed to read aright the legible transcript of Divine retribution* which was written upon the shuddering earth" (14, emphasis added). In this opening chapter on the mystery of language, a nexus between language and place is established—the prayer-meeting and market are metaphorically engaged as heterological enactments of the textual ideology—"to erect above the ruined auction-block and slave-pen [the architecture within the marketplace] institutions of learning."

One of the accomplishments of *Iola Leroy* lies in its revision of the traditional use and interpretation of words—an enterprise that Harper accomplishes by destabilizing our perceptions about language in that initial chapter on the "Mystery of Market Speech." In addition to the shifts of language, however, there is a parallel "shiftiness" of place. The settings of this work move about with a freedom that contradicts the context of slavery in this story. There are scenes from armed encampments in the woods, battlefield hospitals, "pleasant and spacious" northern sitting rooms, and "large and lonely" southern parlors. The novel foregrounds this consciousness of its shifting scenery. At one point, one of the mulatto freedmen remarks:

> When I sat in those well-lighted, beautifully furnished rooms, I was thinking of the meetings we used to have in by-gone days. How we used to go by stealth into lonely woods and gloomy swamps, to tell of our hopes and fears, sorrows and trials. (260–261)

Although the argument and the text remain the same, the scenes radically change. These often lovely and austere places belie the story line that persistently instantiates the threat of slavery, or the memory of slavery, or its consequences. This oppositional structure has a complex presence that makes *Iola Leroy* more substantive and dense than the spare and diminished *Our Nig*.

In contrast, neither the argument nor the scenes change in *Our Nig*. Instead, the linguistically uncomplicated structures of Wilson's novel complement its spare geography. In some instances, the specificity of place is dispersed within the dialogue and narration. The narrative action occurs in a nebulous kind of limbo where a collocation of unstable events allows the text to support, by imitation, the frail and insubstantial condition of its protagonist. Perhaps it is because "[t]he world seemed full of hateful deceivers and crushing arrogance" (6) that we have only a minimal sense of the physical places in this story. Wilson's exercise of prefatory control requires this ambiguity. In this way, if we choose to grant the vision within the subtext, only the narrative assurance that we are still in that "two-story white house, North" keeps us away from the subtextual vista of the plantation fields of the South that are distanced from this work only by the shadowy and insubstantial focus of metaphor:

In the summer I was walking near the barn, and as I stood I heard sobs. . . . "why was I made? why can't I die? Oh, what Have I to live for? No one cares for me only to get my work. And I feel sick; who cares for that? Work as long as I can stand, and then fall down and lay there till I can get up. No mother, father brother or sister to care for me, and then it is, You lazy nigger, lazy nigger—all because I am black! . . . but we must go work in the field." (74, 75)

It is likely that Wilson's loyalty to the subtext is the reason that "a new home" for Mag in this story that is "soon contaminated by the publicity of Mag's fall" has no physical locus and no description. A similar "village" is only specified so that it might direct the reader toward Mag's alienation from it. Her "hovel" is merely that; we are told no more than it was an "untenanted" place that "she had often passed in better days." Beyond these few references, we have no visual sense of the place where Frado's story begins. Because of our lack of vision, the intrusive but nevertheless veiled subtext maintains enough control over the story to argue that Frado's conditions were too close to slavery for her "good anti-slavery friends at home" to tolerate. That they would come to her (economic) rescue was the objective of her thinly veiled allusions to the parallels between her life and the experience of a southern slave.

Frado's first residence in the Bellmont home is more thoroughly de-scribed than her mother's "hovel." The slim description offered here serves the narrative purpose just as the lack of description in the novel's opening pages underscores the emptiness and alienation that characterized Mag's experience. The dismal language, carefully meted out, allows the reader a visual connection to the dreariness of Frado's life at the Bell-monts. The "L chamber" that will be her room seems as much a torture place as the Gothic-inspired name intimates. After she has been abandoned by her mother, the Bellmonts lead her to the garret where she will stay "until she outgrows the house."

[T]hey ascended the stairs without any light, passing through nicely furnished rooms. . . . He opened the door which connected with her room by a dark, unfinished passage-way. . . . [H]er apartment [was] an unfinished chamber over the kitchen, the roof slanting nearly to the floor, so that the bed could stand only in the middle of the room. A small half window furnished light and air. (27)[11]

The substance of this Attic-style narrative reflects the setting of this story beyond that spare and lean garret space, the kitchen, and the "nicely furnished" rooms of the Bellmont home. Much of the activity of the story happens offstage, or is reported by letters to the home, or by visiting relatives. The narrative concerns itself mostly with engendering our sympathy for poor Frado whose sickness, incarceration, beatings, and spiritual neglect—most of which occur in these meagerly described spaces—inscribe the pitiable state that has called forth this narrative and disclose, either in spite of or because of the prefatory intent, how near Frado is, in spirit and body, to her enslaved sisters of the South.

> I sincerely appeal to my colored brethren universally for patronage, hoping they will not condemn this attempt of their sister to be erudite, but rally around me a faithful band of supporters and defenders.
> —"Preface," *Our Nig*

> The race has not had very long to straighten its hands from the hoe, to grasp the pen and wield it as a power for good, and to erect above the ruined auction-block and slave-pen institutions of learning.
> —Closing "Note," *Iola Leroy*

Although thirty-three years and the climactic events of the Civil War and Emancipation separate the publication of these works, it is somewhat ironic that this span of time is nearly diffused by the persistence of a single metaphorical space. Marketability is as much a formative principle for *Our Nig* as the varieties of speech that move within and without "market" places are in *Iola Leroy*.

Wilson nudges her text into an economic arena—a literary marketplace—where she has the most hope for its sale. However, the plea she makes to her "colored brethren" to "rally around me" visually reconstructs the scene of the slave market—not a space where she would be likely to negotiate her own situation successfully. Certainly this reconstruction is unintentional; however, it is my sense that Wilson is trapped by the structural echoes of this metaphor precisely because of her effort to enter a market that, in 1859, is essentially unavailable to her.

In a reference to the appendix of letters that follows Wilson's story (they are putatively written by whites who testify to the reliability of her narrative), William Andrews also notes remnants of the slave's discourse in the structures of the story. His speculation about these intrusive images of slavery leads to his suggestion that "when Wilson . . . solicits such authentication to buttress the status of her voice, one might wonder if she is not still writing a kind of *enslaved* narrative, in which the privilege of authority is implicitly yielded to the natural discourse of white literary overseers" (emphasis added; 27).[12] It is my sense that as long as her white audience is still an "overseer," the space she wants to diminish between them that would allow her to benefit from their empathy and financial expressions of support will not be bridged. They too are trapped by the logistics of the market metaphor that place them into positions of dominance and ownership rather than patronage and support.

Perhaps more wary then Harriet Wilson of the need to negotiate a narrative or fictive space in which both the author and the reader can co-exist, Frances Harper strives mightily to cast aside the negative shadows of race and gender that could restrain *Iola Leroy*'s effort. Much is made of her protagonist's white looks—"My! but she's putty. Beautiful long hair comes way down her back; putty blue eyes, an' jis' ez white ez anybody's in dis place" (38). Barbara Christian argues that Iola's appearance is white enough to allow wealthy and privileged white women readers to identify with her.[13] Hazel Carby suggests that mulattos like Iola were acceptable mediators for a white readership because they could more easily negotiate "the division between mental and manual labor."[14] Carby and Christian capture important and essentially complementary aspects of this figure.[15] Harper's story must have a marketplace that will accept it, and therefore the idea of a sympathetic (and comfortable) readership is crucial. In addition, it must have a textual environment that allows a black woman to have access to some aspect of the world that white women inhabit. Unlike the dismal poverty of *Our Nig,* the generally more healthy economic spheres of *Iola Leroy* are shared between whites and blacks. This negotiation of space becomes a critical feature of Iola's responsibility. Financial stability—that which constantly eluded both Harriet Wilson and her protagonist Frado—is the common and acceptable element that enables the successful negotiation of *Iola Leroy.* Although Frances Harper had published successfully during the same year that *Our Nig* was published, Harper's situation was never yoked by the poverty that initiated and brought to closure Wilson's effort. The combined pejorative effects of class, race, and gender restrain the "marketability" of Wilson's 1859 text rather than liberate its author. Although Wilson's hope is that a literary marketplace would behave differently from the one she and her "colored brethren" escape only by benefit of the geographical space offered by a few New England states, her effort is a failed one. Tate reminds us that its "appeal for patronage failed and immediately after publication it fell into obscurity for more than a century" (108).[16]

In contrast to *Our Nig, Iola Leroy* does not beg too much indulgence or tug too relentlessly at her readership's (guilty) memories or complicity in the slave market. Instead, Harper's text gives testimony, both in form and substance, to the rewards of labor. The story quickly rescues Iola from slavery and shifts toward a narrative that is less discomfiting than the reminders of "southern principles" of slavery that are persistent in *Our Nig.* Although promising not to overly "disclose" appurtenances of slavery in

the North, Harriet Wilson does exactly that. Her story is an unrelenting
exposé and Harriet/Frado is a constant victim that neither Christian virtue
nor hard labor can rescue. There is no relief from the unrelenting poverty
and hardship in *Our Nig.* The persistence of these images diminishes the
necessary mediation that Harper shrewdly positions in her narrative. Iola is
surrounded by an intellectually elite black community who give evidence
of life beyond the "auction-blocks" and "slave-pens" of the market place.
Further, the novel valorizes the themes of motherhood and loyalty. Iola's
work underscores socially acceptable roles for women. Her comforting
ministrations as a Civil War nurse, her lecturing on the "Education of
Mothers," her plans to "teach in the Sunday-school, help in the church,
[and to] hold mothers' meetings to help these boys and girls to grow up to
be good men and women" (276) were viewed as appropriate enterprises for
women and were familiar roles to her reading audience. Within the domestic spheres she chose to articulate her experience and to inscribe her place, it
was relatively easy and nonthreatening for an audience of white women to
lend this narrative their empathetic support.

At the center of these works rests the metaphor of the slave market—
the intrusive spectacle that mirrors the authors' worlds. Either its "shackles and pens" urge the work toward the elaborate language of liberation or
they "rally round" in a perverse act of textual restraint—acquiescence to
the nearness of the threats of slavery and poverty. The syntactic echoes
within this configuration bridge the dimensions of time and place that
would separate them. The metaphor of the market—its economy and its
spatial constraint—insists upon an association between Frado's dismal
world and Iola's (finally) pastoral one. The force of the metaphor instantiates in both works a discomfiting and persistent vision of the historic
space in America that is their common referent.

NOTES

1. Harriet E. Wilson, *Our Nig; or, Sketches from the Life of a Free Black* (1859;
reprint, New York: Vintage Books, 1983). Page references to this edition will be
given parenthetically in the text.

2. Frances E. W. Harper, *Iola Leroy* (1892; reprint, Boston: Beacon Press,
1987). Page references to this edition will be given parenthetically in the text.

3. *"Race," Writing and Difference,* ed. Henry Louis Gates, Jr. (Chicago: University of Chicago Press, 1986), 9. Subsequent references will be cited parenthetically
in the text.

4. An interesting parallel exists between the major emphasis of Gates's
argument—that writing was proof of humanity—and my thesis of economy. If the
act of writing was not evidence *enough* of the African's humanity, then the economic incentive that could accrue from the productive act of writing was an

economic trade-off—a purchase that constituted an escape, of sorts, from the slavery of the European's ignorance.

5. Irigaray's discussion makes a critical distinction between proximity (*nearness*) and property (ownership) that is particularly useful for my argument that black women's essential dilemma was their own *nearness* to a physical self that their spiritual selves constantly sought to reclaim. As a consequence of slavery—the paradigmatic structure of ownership and property—the decision to "market" the product that was *nearly* ourselves (through fictive autobiographies like *Our Nig* and *Iola Leroy*) is a tropological revision of the identity-quest narratives. Black women were in search of a physical self that slavery removed from their control. See Luce Irigaray, *This Sex Which Is Not One*, trans. Catherine Porter with Carolyn Burke (Ithaca, N.Y.: Cornell University Press, 1985), esp. 31–33.

6. Claudia Tate, "Allegories of Black Female Desire; or, Rereading Nineteenth-Century Sentimental Narratives of Black Female Authority," in *Changing Our Own Words: Essays on Criticism, Theory, and Writing by Black Women*, ed. Cheryl A. Wall (New Brunswick, N.J.: Rutgers University Press, 1989), 98–126.

7. Willis writes that "[a]s Marx defined it, the commodity negates the process and the social relations of production"(403). However, because production in this instance *forms* the human (see note 4) rather than merely articulating a social relationship, the entire process of the capitalist market is rendered suspect. See Susan Willis, "Gender as Commodity," *South Atlantic Quarterly* 86, no. 4 (Fall 1987): 403–423.

8. In the Introduction to the Vintage edition, Henry Gates reviews the details of Wilson's life ("Frado's story . . . as well") and acknowledges "autobiographical consistencies" between the poverty of Wilson's life and Frado's (xi–lv).

9. The *McGuffy Eclectic Readers* were the basal reader of the public schools in the middle and late 1800s. They taught reading as an ordered progression through syntactically more complex sentences.

10. See Wilson, *Our Nig*, note 7, page xvii.

11. This garret space is re-created in Harriet Jacobs's *Incidents in the Life of a Slave Girl* (1861). The protagonist of this work, Linda Brent, conceals herself for seven years in a succession of cramped spaces in an attic and in closets. These spaces—narrow, tiny, and close—reflect the narrow and diminished options that both she and Frado/Harriet experience as black women.

12. William L. Andrews, "The Novelization of Voice in Early African American Narrative," *PMLA* 105, no. 1 (January 1990): 23–34.

13. In an essay on *Iola Leroy* in *Black Feminist Criticism* (New York: Pergamon Press, 1985), 165–170, Barbara Christian extends the discussion of this novel from *Black Women Novelists: The Development of a Tradition* (Westport, Conn.: Greenwood Press, 1980). In both discussions, Christian emphasizes the ease with which Harper's white female readership could identify with and respond to the nearly white Iola. This familiarity was critical to the reception of the novel and the potential success of its ideology.

14. In the Introduction to the Beacon Press edition of *Iola Leroy*, Hazel Carby argues that the mulatto was a "mediating device" who "enabled an exploration of the social . . . and an expression of the sexual relations between the races" (xxii).

15. Carby suggests some tension between her view and Christian's. She questions the "underlying assumption" that "the prime motivation for writing was to counter negative images [and that] social conventions determine the use of literary conventions" (xxi). Although Carby makes this effort to distinguish her reading from Christian's, they are essentially complementary. The public space of the novel's appearance (Christian's focus) cannot easily be abstracted from the private spheres that it attempted to influence.

16. Tate, "Allegories," 108.

The Traditions

SANDRA A. ZAGARELL

"America" as Community in Three Antebellum Village Sketches

GARRISON KEILLOR'S LAKE WOBEGON, "the little town that time forgot," where all the women are strong, all the men are good-looking, and all the children above average, strikes a note that has been familiar to Americans for centuries. Lake Wobegon is the ironic-affectionate avatar of a tradition whose roots are practically identical with those of English settlement of this continent: the equation of a village or small-town community with quintessential "America." This equation was given important expression by John Winthrop on the ship *Arabella* in 1630, when he assured others en route to the "new world" that the settlement they were about to found would be "as a citty [sic] upon a hill" to which all nations would look for guidance. Wending its way through three and a half centuries of American poetry and prose, the image of America as a community was popularized in the 1820s and 1830s in the village sketch,[1] a new kind of fictional narrative that proliferated in the magazines, annuals, and gift books of the era and took the form of book-length works like Lydia Sigourney's *Sketch of Connecticut, Forty Years Since* (1824). By the 1830s, the village sketch had acquired a repertoire of motifs so resonant that they still inform American self-representation, enjoying prominence not only in the fiction of writers like Keillor but also in films, including Frank Capra's classic *It's a Wonderful Life* and David Byrne's *True Stories*.

Few scholars have studied antebellum village-sketch literature seriously,[2] but it merits our close attention. It is more than the source of a group of quaint, enduring cultural motifs; it constitutes one important site of an ongoing debate about the composition and character of America—a dispute about the place of difference and diversity in this nation. This dispute divides village sketch literature into two strains—one in which "America" is tantamount to a homogeneous village community, another that proclaims the Americanism of diversity and features communities with diverse populations. The existing characterizations of village-sketch literature, however, do not identify two strains, and in general take only the first into account. One, Laurence Buell's "The Village as Icon" (a chapter in his recent study, *New England Literary Culture*), provides a valuable abstract of this first strain's representation of village life. "The village," Buell explains, "is a self-contained unit, sheltered from the outside world and organically interdependent. . . . It is ethnically homogeneous and institutionally stable: the population stays the same, the houses stay the same color; nobody leaves, nobody even dies. The social structure is simple (headed by the minister . . . just as sabbath keeping is one of the main cultural activities mentioned and most of the characters are given scriptural names)."[3] Descriptions of the meetinghouse and school, of their presiding dignitaries, and evocations of such community rituals as the observation of Thanksgiving or Election Day also figure in the roster of motifs Buell establishes.

The cultural work of this literature is not Buell's main subject; still, his description reveals the nativist ethos that informs much village-sketch literature. At a time when non-Protestant immigrants were a source of distress to many native-born Americans and when the predominance of Anglo-Saxon New England seemed challenged by many changes, including increased immigration and the diffusion of the nation beyond the Appalachians, a literature that conflated American community life with "the" (generic) New England village and featured practices like the celebration of the Sabbath and Thanksgiving asserted such customs as genuinely American. It also implicitly cast both Catholicism and the areligiosity that seemed to some to threaten the expanding nation as non- or anti-American. Buell observes that regardless of the length of a sketch, "the traits . . . of smallness, isolation, cohesiveness, innocence, and unchangingness are central."[4] He thus registers the way literature in which community is homogeneous actively repudiates changes afoot in the nation. From Stowe's New England sketches of the 1830s and 1840s to George Lunt's full-length narrative *Eastford* (1855), the predominant strain of village-sketch literature, Buell's typography suggests, expressed a version of "the" American community that consistently, although with varying degrees of intention, sought to preserve the image of America from forces that, in the decades before the Civil War, were actually altering the nation in many ways.

Buell's paradigm accounts elegantly for sketches in which the village is fixed and uniform. Yet grounded as it is in this literature, it casts little light on the other strain of village-sketch literature—the strain that conceives of villages as heterogeneous and fairly open communities. It is my purpose here to make this second strain visible: to ask how this literature constructs community and to illuminate the cultural work to which it is dedicated. Although I outline key characteristics of sketches in which the village is an open community, I do not develop a single explanatory model for this literature. To do so would entail forcing it into a distorting mold, for the narratives in this group are not simply about diversity, they themselves are diverse. Central to each are an understanding that the community represented is in some ways distinct and a commitment to representing that uniqueness as well as to reflecting how the community resembles other American communities. In the three narratives on which I concentrate— Eliza Buckminster Lee's *Sketches of a New-England Village, in the Last Century* (1838), Caroline Kirkland's *A New Home—Who'll Follow?* (1839), and Sigourney's *Sketch of Connecticut*—the diversity of the community takes quite different forms,[5] and I will discuss each text separately. Still, they do have many commonalities. All, for instance, assume a link between "America" and "small community." All conceive of community as a form of group life whose membership is diverse. The narrative structure of each highlights the inclusiveness of the community. Most strikingly—and arguably of key importance for these and other shared characteristics—the authors of all of these works were women.[6] It is to this crucial circumstance that I first turn.

Lee, Kirkland, and Sigourney, as well as writers like Alice Cary, Fanny Forrester, and Charlotte Jerauld, were apparently inspired by and wrote within the confines of their positions as northern antebellum white women of the middle class. This position was constructed by that combination of economic, cultural, and ideological limitations associated with women's sphere and by the rich nexus of values, rituals, and activities historians call "women's culture." These women's physical mobility was curtailed. The scope of their subject matter was generally restricted to local life about which they had firsthand experience (although, as Nina Baym's recent work on women historians shows, women writers were not uniformly circumscribed in this way).[7] Confined as it was in some ways, however, these women's writing was also enriched by the limitations of operative cultural norms in others, as it was also enriched by the value system of women's culture, which Carroll Smith-Rosenberg and Nancy Cott elaborate as having been relational, inclusive, and generally empathic. It profited, moreover, from what educational psychologist Carol Gilligan, speaking in a different context and often unfortunately seeming to presume the existence of one essential woman's moral perspective, has called women's ability "to attend to voices other than their own and to include in their judgment other points of view."[8] Concentrating on actual communities, these writers portray the realities of community life with considerable nuance and literary inventiveness. Making relatively little use of established motifs of the kind Buell describes, they focus imaginatively on the details, and in some cases the microdynamics, of village life. In particular, they excel at accentuating the kind of diversity that existed increasingly in actual American communities. In their work, "community" tends to include people with divergent histories, positions, expectations, and beliefs—although it also encompasses shared values and interests. In fact, all of these writers acknowledge differences in community members' vantage points and circumstances, although they do so in diverse ways and with varying degrees of intensity. All stress difference within gender (particularly among women) and a few depict cultural and other kinds of difference. To varying degrees, "community" in their narratives is dynamic: it must be negotiated and renegotiated across its members' differences.

No two narratives in this group are alike, but they exhibit features (not all necessarily present in each work) consistent with a view of every community as unique, internally heterogeneous, and dynamic. Very likely building on the format that Mary Russell Mitford originated in *Our Village,* most of the narrators work their way through the village, tracing its physical boundaries and portraying various residents. The understanding of community as a form of group life that must be achieved within the circumstances of a specific place is enhanced by an empirical, almost ethnographic, approach to character. "Character" tends to be cultural rather than individualized or psychologized, as it usually is in the literary realism with which we are most familiar. Many of the featured "characters" cannot readily be discussed using concepts on which readers of ninteenth-century fiction have tended to rely—"round" or "flat," psychologically or morally conceived, major, minor, or stereotypic.[9] Sigourney's *Sketch* and Lee's *Sketches* do contain recognizable character types of the sort generally found in the predominant mode of village-sketch literature—village clergymen, stalwart farmers, nubile maidens—but these are usually either given depth or relegated to background positions. And these narratives give places to people who exist in ethnographic studies or memoirs but have little place in the era's conventionally plotted fiction and are excluded or marginalized by sketches about homogeneous village life. These include white women not defined in relation to men; frontier farmers; African-Americans pursuing their domestic lives; American Indians seeking to come to terms with the consequences of deracination.

Narratives such as *A New Home* are also in some measure polyphonic.

They highlight the diversity of a village's population by bringing many voices in the populace into conjunction. Probably influenced by the attentiveness of antebellum women's culture to separate voices, perhaps inspired by Mitford's featuring of the stories of numerous inhabitants of her village, most call attention to the voices and stories that exist simultaneously in the community. Sometimes the narrator appears to reproduce the teller's words, in which case, like Kirkland's persona, Mary Clavers, she may proffer what appears to be "an impartial record of every-day forms of speech (taken down in many cases from the lips of the speaker)."[10] Sometimes the stories are recast in the narrator's own voice (Lee's *Sketches,* Forrester's *Alderbrook*). Some works, like Sigourney's *Sketch,* mix approaches. Their polyphony is channeled through participant/observer narrators, all women, who mediate between the voices of community members and the language of a readership living elsewhere.[11] Although in transmitting community voices these narrators translate them into the discourse of their readers, the narrators also show respect for the integrity of the experiences embedded in each community member's story.

In overall design, as well, these narratives reflect the diversity of community members and point to the various juxtapositions and intersections among them that constitute village life. In highlighting individuals' separate stories yet conjoining them, the narratives suggest the process of negotiation among perspectives and experiences in which "community" is grounded for these writers. Further, reflecting an inclusive concept of community, these narratives are loose and open-ended. Linear organization and plotted resolutions sometimes shape individuals' stories, but such sequencing is subsumed within a large-scale structure in which sustained development and definitive conclusion have little place: the books are collections of personal histories and voices that capitalize on the capacity of the sketch, a relatively new form, to accommodate synchronicity and resist closure. All the community members, all the voices, seem to exist simultaneously, and individuals' lives often appear to continue beyond the stories the narratives relay. Often, moreover, the macronarrative stops rather than concluding, suggesting both that life in the community continues and that more voices, different people, other experiences, could also be included.

Despite the inclusiveness of these works and their highlighting of diversity, however, they also exhibit more restrictive values and objectives commensurate with those of most of the era's literary culture. As historians like Linda Kerber remind us, the women's culture whose ethos they express was neither spatially nor ideologically separate from the dominant culture. Limited mainly to women who were white and middle class, women's culture functioned in part to distinguish them from working-class white women and from women of color.[12] Works by Sigourney and her cohort contain contradictions that are strikingly similar to those of women's culture itself: they express a relational and inclusive ethos, but they also inscribe the superior class and racial position of white women. Thus, for example, their compassionate recognition of the interests of diverse groups coexists with an assumption that community should be hierarchical, taking shape under the aegis of members of their own class and race. This contradiction shows up in the construction of the participant/observer narrators. Like the authors for whom they stand in, these narrators embrace the community, but they also almost always occupy a higher social class than most community members. As listener/transmitters, moreover, they possess an unexamined authority. The ear that listens compassionately to stories of individual lives or the history of a race or social group, or catches the shadings of the vernacular, may be empathic and open, but it always retains final textual authority; indeed the narrator alone appears to decide what is relayed to the reader. Similarly, while the narrator's walks and encounters with people extend the community into many corners, it is her movements, her choices, that give the text, and the community, their shape. Although the narrator often seems so transparent as to have little or no textual presence, the texts alway bear the mark of the decisive control she exercises. And that control, far from being merely personal, affirms the preeminent position of white women of the middle or gentry class even while it sanctions a vision of heterogeneous community. I take Sigourney's *Sketch* as my example because it is the most liberal of the works I am considering. *Sketch* pointedly extends the community of N—— (Norwich, Connecticut) to members of all groups, although the American nation of 1784, when *Sketch* takes place, was highly restrictive. Like the nation, however, the community is Toryesque. N—— is governed by a benevolent but firm aristocratic matriarch, Madam L——. And while *Sketch* takes unusual pains to represent the perspectives and histories of marginalized people, it also reproduces the kind of racist and nativist ideology that permeates more conservative literature. It empathically seeks to present the history of the Mohegan Indians of Connecticut as they themselves experienced it, yet at the same time it includes numerous images in which the "red man" roaming in "his" forest embodies a primitive stage of human life "naturally" replaced by the more advanced white civilization.[13] Historically speaking, of course, such stereotypes helped validate the dispossession, deracination, and genocide that American Indians experienced at the hands of white Americans—the very circumstances against which *Sketch*'s Indians testify with extraordinary eloquence.

Like other works by antebellum white women, then, these village

tuates both the flexibility of true community bonds and a woman's capacity for self-support. Miriam is marked by her differences from other villagers—she and the younger brother with whom she lives are orphaned, he is epileptic, she unusually beautiful. She falls victim to the "witchcraft delusion" that served some antebellum writers, Hawthorne among them, as a trope for coercive conformity, that dark side of American community life. Accused of witchcraft, Miriam refuses to save herself through false confession; although the authorities sentence her to death, other villagers "work out her deliverance" in the spirit of genuine community (97). Lee also includes a young girl, "half idiot, half insane," with an illegitimate son. In sketches about uniform villages, illicit sexual relations necessitate a young woman's explusion from the community (invariably, she dies); often, as in Nathaniel Dodge's "Cary Aram," other women family members also die—of shame. Sketches, however, emphasizes the status of both the girl and her mother as full community members. It concentrates on the way the mother, in the course of supporting the entire family by gathering and bartering berries and trading the flax she spins, participates in the exchange of goods and charity that constitutes W——'s material—and emotional—economy.

Complementing and amplifying the portraits of these three women are two that suggest even more strongly that a community like W——offers women a place even when they are without the security and status normally conferred by the patriarchal family. The story of Alice, the other woman in the triangle involving Grace, begins as a commentary on the ruthless individualism that romantic love, which leads women into marriage and family, fosters in women. Alice lies in order to separate her beloved cousin, Henry, from Grace, but she thereby loses her own sense of identity and almost dies. She learns, however, to replace destructive love with communal commitments, and ultimately establishes an identity that is communal, not narrowly familial. Able to live with herself only after she confesses her treachery, she thenceforth devotes herself to caring for the grandmother and mother whom Grace and Henry abandon in dying. Finally, the extended sketch of the narrator's family servant, Hannah, shows that community encompasses women whose peculiarities might isolate them under other circumstances. Hannah is opinionated and brusque, loyal to the Church of England, a strong Tory—but she is also deeply devoted to the narrator and her family. She had been the nurse of the narrator's mother, accompanying her to W——upon her marriage "purely from affection" (24), and remaining after the mother's death to nurture, and bully, the minister's family and the community at large. Her history, like Alice's, points both to the threat to community that women's surrender to heterosexual romance and the patriarchal family can entail (often, in Lee's eyes, because of men's preference for money over community ties) and to the broader, more enduring nature of communal bonds. After the minister dies and his family breaks up, Hannah marries a man who, the narrator explains, wanted only the money she had saved. Although Hannah thenceforth lives in extreme poverty, community ties sustain her: the narrator reports that "the little that I could do for her alone saved her from want and misery" (28). At her death Hannah proves the reciprocal and persisting nature of such generosity: she bequeaths to the narrator "the few articles she possessed that had belonged to my mother. Despite all her poverty and distress, she could never be induced to part with one of them" (29).

Sketches indicates that the American community of which W——is emblematic has been eroded by indigenous changes, not by the influx of foreigners or the geographic diffusion to which many other village sketches point. The narrator consistently singles out as the destroyers of the "earlier world" she portrays the substitution of a commodity economy for one based on communal self-sufficiency and the transformation of human relations from reciprocal exchange to the kind of instrumental, money-based individualism that motivates Hannah's husband. Lee's critique generally takes the form of a sustained, low-key contrast between everyday practices in the village community and the "extravagant ostentation" (1) of nineteenth-century America. It is elaborated most fully with regard to books and literature. In the nineteenth century, books have become a plentiful commodity with little value. The narrator's edition of Shakespeare, in contrast, symbolizes the interdependent economy of W——. The circumstances of this edition's purchase lay the groundwork for a rich train of associations through which Shakespeare's writing, the narrator's family history, and life in W——merge. She and her sister buy the Shakespeare with money their father gives them in appreciation of "two complete undersuits of lamb's wool" (50) they knit for him. For the narrator, these books always bring "back, with the forest of Ardennes, the still more secluded woods of W." (sic), along with many other family and community associations, and she "can never read Shakespeare in any other edition. The words seem not the same" (51). Lee also attempts to bring an era when books were inseparable from personal and group life into a century during which they have become mere commodities. Although the narrator imagines books being "heaped upon each other, till our library tables groan with the weight" in the present of 1838 (21), her effort to make her associations with her own edition of Shakespeare come alive includes making these books seem actually to materialize before her readers. The "old, black, worn, and disfigured" volumes, she says, "are now before me" (50). Sketches itself similarly constitutes an attempt to restore for its readers the kind of organic, communitarian life the narrator attributes to W——. The epistolary mode gives it a depth and immediacy that seem calculated to elicit a response as deep as the narrator's to her Shakespeare. Every reader is potentially the letter's recipient. Each, then, may feel personally addressed by the writer's evocations of a communitarian way of life—and each may feel moved to reform a nation in which relations between people are instrumental, and books are piled on a table, not written on the heart.

While community is harmonious in Lee's W——, in Caroline Kirkland's *A New Home* it is dynamic and vexed. Kirkland features the arduous process through which a kind of group life hitherto unimagined in America is achieved between two very different kinds of people who had settled in frontier Michigan by the late 1830s: the enterprising but rough farmers and woodsmen who formed the backbone of Jacksonian democracy and the middle-class and better-educated settlers who arrived later and tended to hold on to their ties to a genteel, East Coast–based culture.[16] A major obstacle to the creation of this new kind of American community is genteel elitism, and *A New Home* exposes the consequences of that mentality to its addressees, East Coasters who share it. The narrative thereby fosters the kind of cultural tolerance it shows to be necessary for the creation of community within new national circumstances—although Kirkland never abandons her belief in the superiority of her readers' culture, and often openly makes common cause with it.

A New Home is organized around the gradual development of the village of Montacute—its physical construction, the emergence of such local institutions as a school, a women's sewing circle, a system of justice. Its greatest interest, however, is the process through which a new community culture is created: the often ambivalent negotiations between the two groups of settlers across cultural and class differences and the slow emergence of a new, hybrid community culture. Kirkland's construction of the narrator, Mary Clavers, is indispensable to her dynamic representation of cultural formation. Clavers combines auto-ethnographer with participant/observer. She plays an active but only half-willing role in the creation of the community and continues to identify with her East Coast readers. Because Clavers is highly self-reflexive, often exposing the biases in her attitudes toward her "Wolverine" neighbors, the drama of Montacute's formation takes place within her as well as around her. And, in an unusual version of the ability of these texts' narrators to listen to "voices other than [their] own," she is always zestfully alert to the different languages of the Montacutians as well as to their stories. From the beginning, in fact, both groups of settlers have bona fide cultures, and their languages form the main arena in which cultural clashes and negotiations occur.

An examination of the narrative at midpoint (chapter 20) reveals Kirkland's characteristic dramatization of cultural differences and tensions by focusing on language. Mary Clavers remains profoundly ambivalent about the developing community, and her snobbery is subjected to even greater satiric exposure than her neighbor's indubitable roughness. Centering on Clavers's efforts at gardening and the skepticism with which her "Wolverine" neighbors meet her enthusiasm, the chapter concentrates on easterners' penchant for evisioning themselves as cultivated and westerners as boorish by ironizing Clavers' attitudes. In a typical passage, Clavers plays the linguistic registers of her neighbors off against the language she and her readers share in mockery of what she sees as the indigenous westerners' pigheaded practicality:

> The ordinary name with us for a rose is "a rosy-flower"; our vase of flowers, usually a broken-nosed pitcher, is a "posy-pot"; and "yaller lilies" are among the most dearly-prized of all the gifts of Flora. . . . A neighbour . . . coolly broke off a spike of my finest hyacinths, and after putting it to his undiscriminating nose, threw it on the ground with a "pah!" as contemptuous as Hamlet's. But I revenged myself when I set him sniffing at a crown imperial—so we are at quits now (79–80).

Clavers's insularity is satirized here more than the older settlers' crudeness, for her neighbors' versatility comes into focus immediately after this disparaging of their narrowness. Local floral interest is not, the narrative shows, limited to "yaller lilies," for Clavers soon concedes that both gardener and florist can be found within three miles of Montacute. More dramatically, when she is momentarily able to abandon her rigid categorizing and take note of the diversity of the local culture, her language transforms into a marvelous polyglot appropriate to the multiplicity of Montacutians' many talents and practical expertise. In a proto-Whitmanesque catalogue of occupations, she celebrates the local blacksmith, cooper, milliner, the " 'hen-tailor' for your little boy's pantaloons," and finally the versatility of her neighbor, Mr. Jenkins: "Is one of your guests dependent upon a barber? Mr. Jenkins can shave. Does your husband. . . . demolish his boot upon a *grub?* Mr. Jenkins is great at a *rifacciamento.* Does Billy lose his cap in the pond? Mr. Jenkins makes caps *comme il y en a peu.* Does your bellows get the asthma? Mr. Jenkins is a famous Francis Flute" (80).

Clavers's appreciation of difference is at this point only momentary, and when she abandons it for her more habitual elitism, she returns to the style of the first passage I quoted, surrounding and containing the vernacular with the more restricted code of proper English much as she would like to control her plain-speaking neighbors. She tartly labels her rhapsody mere "wandering," and the chapter closes with her snide appropriation of her neighbors' vernacular: "I hope my reader will not be disposed to reply in that terse and forceful style . . . cultivated at Montacute, and . . . more than once . . . employed in answer to my enthusiastic lectures on [gardening]. 'Taters grows in the field, and 'taters is good enough for me' " (82). *A New Home* accentuates here the cultural clashes that hamper community development by exposing the bias in Clavers's snobbish browbeating of her neighbors for their taste in flora. Although she cannot see the implications of the "'taters" remark, its placement at the end of the chapter gives those neighbors the last word. It stands as their resentful parody of her condescending image of them and reasserts the value, and the tones, of *their* culture.

As the two groups achieve greater tolerance and acceptance, Clavers's deepening capacity to appreciate her neighbors' standpoints becomes emblematic of the formation of a genuinely Montacutian local culture. The closing chapter attests to the eventual, although still unstable, achievement of community on the frontier and dramatizes Clavers's achievement of a newly inclusive mentality and language. She now calls Montacute "our secluded little village" (187) and, in a structural echo of the closing chapter of *Our Village,* surveys the present circumstances and the prospects of various residents and of the village as a whole. Her blending of linguistic registers exemplifies the cultural mix appropriate to Montacute's developing community. Whereas she earlier pitted genteel English against the vernacular, as in "vase" versus "posy-pot," she now delights in melding sentimental jargon with pithy localese to describe the villagers' lives, referring, for instance, to a "nascent *tendresse* between Mrs. Nippers and Mr. Phlatt, a young lawyer, whose resplendent "tin" [sign] graces . . . the sidepost of [his landlord's] door" (188). Her satire is now openly directed at eastern readers' snobbery. Parodying these readers' judgments, Clavers compares herself to an awkward "rustic damsel" imposing too long on a city acquaintance, and her narrative to a country dance, a "Scotch reel, which [has] no ending, save the fatigue of those engaged" (189). She ends with "an unceremonious adieu to the kind and courteous reader," but her identification of her narrative as a "simple and sauntering story" that has no natural ending testifies that community formation of the sort that occurs in Montacute is ongoing. Suggesting that community will continue to take shape through the vital, often difficult, always absorbing process of cultural interchange and re-formation, *A New Home* also passes on to its readers the burden of participating in this process with a new self-awareness. Still, this move, although educational, also represents a reconfiguration of the narrative's alliance with these readers: it instructs them in how to prevail. *A New Home* thereby closes with a final assertion that the values of Clavers's, and

Kirkland's, own class and region should predominate in the new kind of community and culture that it depicts with such freshness.

The community in Lydia Sigourney's *Sketch of Connecticut, Forty Years Since* is apparently the most heterogeneous in antebellum village-sketch literature.[17] N——contains not only intragender differences but also differences of religion (religions include Congregationalism, Methodism, Episcopalianism, and Catholicism), ethnicity (ethnic groups include "Yankees," the Irish, and the British), and race (characters are Caucasian, African-American, and Mohegan Indian). *Sketch*'s narrative structure highlights the particular characteristics and histories of diverse groups. It calls attention to cultural and structural conflicts among them yet affirms *all* as legitimate participants in the community of N——.

Sigourney constructs N——as an open community, a Christian civil order that contrasts with the American nation as it officially existed in 1784. Such community is made possible by the wisdom of a local aristocracy whose virtues its primary representative, seventy-year-old Madam L——("the Lady"), embodies. Her home forms the spiritual and economic center of N——. It also forms the structural hub of *Sketch*, for the narrative alternative between Madam L——'s parlor and the quarters of various groups in N——, using what Elizabeth Ammons, in a different context, has called a "radial structure."[18] This structure affirms N——as comprehensive but hierarchical. It constantly reasserts the Lady's centrality, for many of *Sketch*'s chapters are situated in her parlor, where members of various groups in N——seek aid and advice, and articulate their viewpoints and histories. Yet the alternation also quite literally inscribes the community as inclusive of everyone who happens to live in N——.[19] In addition, this structure expresses marked respect for the distinct identity of each kind of person. Every "radial line" consists of a discrete chapter or cluster of chapters formed around the history of a member of one group. Going further than Lee and Kirkland in her attentiveness to multiple voices, Sigourney thus appears to reproduce the experiences of each group in its own terms.

Generally, N——'s residents recount their group's distinctive history by telling representative personal stories. The story of Primus, a former slave, for instance, encapsulates the history of Africans in the northern United States.[20] It begins with his separation from his family and enslavement in Western Africa, includes a powerful description of the Middle Passage, and concludes with his life as the slave of a fairly enlightened Connecticut man, his conversion to Christianity, his manumission on the death of his owner, and his subsequent life as a free black in the north. Even the life of Yankee farmer Larkin, who belongs to the class that forms the center and unquestioned norm of most village-sketch literature, is shown to be inseparable from a specific group history. Larkin's description of his domestic arrangements and family life reflects his membership in a group whose prosperity results from its having been accorded a form of citizenship even under English rule.

In *Sketch,* intragroup difference, confined to gender in Lee's narrative, characterizes all of N——'s member groups, complicating considerably the antebellum tendency to represent minority groups by one or two reified types.[21] African-Americans do include Madam L——'s stereotypically manipulative servant Cuffee, but also Primus and his daughter, Flora, a complicated woman who dislikes people but lavishes affection on her garden and cats. Presenting even greater diversity among the Mohegans, *Sketch* deploys a range of narrative techniques rare in antebellum representations of American Indians, which tend to assimilate them to a few stereotypes. One chapter is constructed around thumbnail sketches of five men who balance Mohegan and Christian Euro-American values and practices in different ways. Another presents the Mohegans' political history by reading recorded Anglo-American histories against the grain, exposing the bad-faith treaties and land sales the colonists imposed on the Indians as the sources of the Mohegans' present-day deculturation and consequent degradation. This chapter also includes representation of Mohegan women (who make little appearance in recorded history), taking an ethnographic tack that contrasts sharply with the historians' moralism. The narrator closely observes the women's clothing, the child care they perform, their economic role, their commercial activities (weaving and pottery making), as well as their cooking and their status as "the physicians of their tribe" (35–36). Yet another chapter features a debate between two Mohegan leaders—the Christian minister, the assimilationist Reverend Mr. Occam, and the tribe's more culturally nationalistic chief, Robert Ashbow. In this debate the direct speech of each man grants full weight to his viewpoint while conveying the irreconcilable differences between the two.[22] *Sketch* also dramatizes the domestic arrangements and marital/familial love among Mohegans by including the story of Oriana, the young widow of a British soldier who has been adopted by an elderly Mohegan couple, Arrowhamet and Martha.

Because *Sketch* grants distinct chapters to the experiences and viewpoints of separate groups without subordinating the history of any to a predominant narrative line, it never suggests that divergent standpoints can blend readily into harmonious group life. On the contrary, it invites recognition of the frequent incommensurability of the histories and needs of N——'s inhabitants. Thus the stirring recountings, by veterans of the Revolutionary War, of the Battle of Bunker Hill and the deeds of the American officer Champe express a perspective very different from that in the next narrative block, which centers on an English couple and includes sympathetic descriptions of the husband's activities as a British soldier. Similarly, whereas the Mohegans are shown to have endured progressive loss of land, the Yankee farmer Larkin's "father had been, for many years, tenant of the same estate," and when a younger brother who succeeds to the farm dies, Larkin resumes "with delight the culture of those fields, where he had 'driv-team when a leetle boy'" (107). *Sketch* also actively promotes the view that true community must inhere in the negotiation of these perspectives no matter how much they conflict. In alternating among these groups without privileging any, and according the same narrative unit—the chapter—to each, the text makes it impossible to dismiss or diminish any group *even as* it draws attention to their incompatibilities.[23]

Rooted in history, *Sketch* cannot work out the actual negotiation of these interests, since they were not in fact negotiated. Most of the groups making up the community of N——were formally excluded from the polity when the United States was established as a nation. Rather, the narrative recasts the equation village sketches tended to make between the local community and the true "America" by positing heterogeneous, woman-governed N——as a counterweight to the nation that actually came into being. In early 1784, when *Sketch* begins, ratification of the peace treaty with Great Britain has just made the country's independence official. The narrative equates the nation's birth with a grim precariousness—"The British Colonies of America were numbered among the nations. The first tumults of joy subsiding, discovered a government not organized, and resting upon insecure foundations" (15). It remains conspicuously silent about the political and juridical activities that would, three years later, establish the former "British Colonies" as a full-fledged nation in which most of N——'s residents, including Madam L——, were denied full citizenship. The text shifts, instead, to N——, where "the agitation, which pervaded the general council of the nation, was unknown" because it has long been governed by its own "heroes and sages" (16), chief among them Madam L——. Presenting "the Lady" as a combined Christ and Washington figure, *Sketch* rebukes the nation that actually developed by implying that only a woman, and one of Madam L——'s qualities, could head a Christian, and communitarian, civil order.[24]

In many ways these three village sketches anticipate some of the literature of community that emerged after the Civil War, a literature that was often self-consciously regional. In the stories of Mary E. Wilkins [Freeman] and Rose Terry [Cooke], New England villages, having been pushed to the nation's sidelines, are shown to have turned in on themselves. Such later writers not only represent increasing diversity within each gender but also pay keen attention to the sharpening struggles between men and women, struggles occasioned by broad changes in the cultural constructions of gender and by deepening New England provincialism. Often, they explore the nature and consequences of male dominance, unconscious in Freeman's "The Revolt of 'Mother'," malignant in Cooke's "Mrs. Flint's Married Experience." Women-centered communities such as Lee's W—— also become more fully elaborated in the work of writers like Harriet Beecher Stowe and Alice Brown. Their representation culminates in the village of Dunnet Landing in Sarah Orne Jewett's *Country of the Pointed Firs* (1896). This community welcomes highly nuanced individual differences and survives by negotiations that are extremely intricate—although it also inscribes, however delicately, a cultural and ethnic exclusiveness reminiscent of the homogeneous communities of the nativist strain of village-sketch literature.

In postbellum literature, moreover, "community" sometimes becomes separate not just from "America," but from "village" or small town, as an awareness of regional and ethnic cultures, and of the predominance of urban centers, helped place into question the belief that there was, or could be, a single national culture. Stephen Crane's *Whilhomeville Stories* (1899–1900), for example, offers a sustained critique of the narrowness and noncommunal character of small-town life. Alice Dunbar-Nelson's *The Goodness of St. Rocque* (1899) illuminates the institutionalization of polarizing differences in American society. It also posits as a counterbalance the creation of a cross-racial community in urban New Orleans.

Reading *Sketch of Connecticut* and *A New Home* thus does far more than expand our understanding of antebellum literature. It calls attention to the diversity—and the creativity—with which, since the 1820s, Americans have been envisioning community. Our most familiar cultural images of community may still be as uniform as Lake Wobegon, yet for over a century and a half, our literature has actually told far more complicated stories about the possibilities for community in America.

NOTES

Material in this essay appeared in my Introduction to Caroline Kirkland's *A New Home—Who'll Follow?* (New Brunswick, N.J.: Rutgers University Press, 1990); and "Expanding 'America': Lydia Sigourney's *Sketch of America*, Catharine Sedgwick's *Hope Leslie*," *Tulsa Studies in Women's Literature* 6, no. 2 (Fall 1987): 225–247. An NEH Summer Stipend supported some of the research for this article.

1. The village sketch was inspired in the United States partly by indigenous poetic celebrations of the Americanness of thriving village life like Philip Freneau's "The American Village" (1772), partly by Irving's *Sketch-Book* (1819–1821) and Mary Russell Mitford's *Our Village* (1824–1832), which, together, established the

fictional sketch as a mode of representing everyday, ordinary life. The poetic and pre-village-sketch prose tradition also includes Timothy Dwight's poetic narrative "Greenwood Hill" (1794) and his four-volume *Travels in New England and New York* (1820). See Perry Westbrook, *The New-England Town in Fact and Fiction* (Rutherford, N.J.: Fairleigh Dickinson University Press, 1982), and Lawrence Buell, *New England Literary Culture* (Cambridge: Cambridge University Press, 1986),.for discussions of the development of village-sketch literature and its connections to earlier representations of American village life. Irma Honacker Herron, *The Small Town in American Literature* (Durham, N.C.: Duke University Press, 1939), is an invaluable earlier study.

2. The popularity of village-sketch literature, its generally formulaic character, and the near-obscurity of most of its writers probably account for this relative neglect. Among writers familiar today, Stowe, Hawthorne, and Sedgwick worked with the genre, but it was frequently produced by writers who remain virtually unknown, including Judge George Carver, Esq. (Nathaniel Shatswell Dodge), or those considered inferior until very recently, like Lydia Sigourney. Nina Baym's outstanding "Reinventing Lydia Sigourney," reprinted in this volume, positions Sigourney as an important historical writer.

3. Buell, *New England Literary Culture,* 306. Far from seeing this strain as monolithic, Buell identifies in it two distinct attitudes, one celebratory, the other a critical one in which the village is seen as a backwater; he also points to the considerable interplay between these two attitudes in the literary constructions of the New England village on which he focuses.

4. Ibid. The General Association of Congregational Churches commissioned Timothy Dwight and several other clergymen, including Lyman Beecher, to write *An address to the emigrants from Connecticut, and from New England generally, in the New Settlements of the United States* (1817) to help civilize the West. In that work, the authors invoke their "common origin" with the emigrants to urge the latter to live as they had in New England. Barbara Solomon notes that the perceived need to preserve common origins and culture also explicitly formed the basis for Dwight's preaching of the necessity to establish New England institutions on the frontier. (See Timothy Dwight, *Travels in New England and New York,* ed. Barbara Miller Solomon with the assistance of Patricia M. King [Cambridge, Mass.: Belknap Press, 1969], "Introduction," 1:xxxiii). Among other discussions of the New England elite's efforts to retain political and cultural primacy during this period are Wesley Frank Cronin, *The Legend of the Founding Fathers* (New York: New York University Press, 1956), and Robert H. Wiebe, *The Opening of American Society. From the Adoption of the Constitution to the Eve of Disunion* (New York: Alfred A. Knopf, 1984).

5. This strain also includes Alice Cary's *Clovernook* (1852); *Alderbrook* (1847), by Fanny Forrester (Emily Chubbuck Judson); and Charlotte Jerauld's *Hazelhurst* (1850).

6. One aspect of the homogeneous communities constructed by the predominant strain of village-sketch literature is that they were governed by male authorities, usually the village minister. Although most of the authors of this literature

were men, some were women—women who, like Stowe in her early sketches and Sarah Josepha Hale in *Northwood* (1827), seem to have accepted male authority. I develop this idea at greater length in my forthcoming study, *The Narrative of Community.*

7. They lived at a time when restrictions on women's autonomy and mobility were so strong that whereas literary men often moved to the cities that formed the centers for the production of a new national literature, literary women—even such enterprising ones as Ann Stephens, editor of the Portland *Gazette,* originator of the dime novel, and writer of popular woman's fiction—often stayed behind in the provinces. Most of the writers under discussion here literally remained in, or near, and often wrote about, the communities in which they grew up. Alice Cary moved to New York as an adult, but she wrote about "Clovernook," the Ohio village in which she matured. Caroline Kirkland did leave her home in the East, but she did so in the company of her husband and she tended to write about experiences she had as a woman who stayed in one place—the village that she and her husband founded in Michigan. Nina Baym's "Reinventing Lydia Sigourney," as well as her "Women and the Republic: Emma Willard's Rhetoric of History" (*American Quarterly* 43, no. 1 (March 1991): 1–21) and "Between Enlightment and Victorian: Toward a Narrative of American Women Writers Writing History" (*Critical Inquiry* 18, no. 1 (Autumn 1991): 22–41), show that many women engaged in historical writing, an enterprise that situated their work well beyond the domestic sphere. These essays are part of a full-scale study-in-progress of American women writers from the period just following the Revolution to the Civil War that analyzes their entry into the public realm via the writing of history. This work substantively alters the assumption that has long prevailed in feminist reconstructive work that the domestic and private realms formed virtually the sole locus of American women's writing before the Civil War. From a different perspective, Barbara Bardes and Suzanne Gossett, *Declarations of Independence; Women and Political Power in Nineteenth Century American Fiction* (New Brunswick, N.J.: Rutgers University Press, 1990), show that, beginning in the 1830s, fiction by Americans, both women and men, reflected on women's entry into the public sphere.

8. The classic works on "women's culture" are Carroll Smith-Rosenberg, "The Female World of Love and Ritual," *Signs: Journal of Women in Culture and Society* 1, no. 1 (Autumn 1975): 1–29, and Nancy Cott, *The Bonds of Womanhood: "Woman's Sphere" In New England, 1780–1835* (New Haven, Conn.: Yale University Press, 1977). On women's voices see Carol Gilligan, *In a Different Voice: Psychological Theory and Women's Development* (Cambridge, Mass.: Harvard University Press, 1982); the passage I quote is on page 16. Although Gilligan does not historicize her findings, the values she ascribes to twentieth-century women were prominent in nineteenth-century women's culture and probably originated there. They have remained part of the discourse of many of her white and middle-class subjects, although not necessarily part of their practice (it is also questionable that they fully shaped the practice of middle-class white women even in the nineteenth century); moreover, as much commentary on her study suggests, they are not subscribed to equally by women of all groups.

9. This discussion of character is indebted to my earlier essay, "Expanding 'America': Lydia Sigourney's *Sketch of Connecticut,* Catharine Sedgwick's *Hope Leslie.*" I would like to thank *Tulsa Studies in Women's Literature* and the University of Tulsa for permission to use both this material and some comments on *Sketch of Connecticut* that also appeared in "Expanding 'America.'"

10. From *A New Home—Who'll Follow? or Glimpses of Western Life* by Caroline M. Kirkland, ed. Sandra A. Zagarell (New Brunswick, N.J.: Rutgers University Press, 1990), 3. Copyright © by Rutgers, The State University. Reprinted with permission of Rutgers University Press. All further references are to this edition and are cited in the text.

11. Occasionally, as in Sigourney's *Sketch,* the narrator is barely embodied or individuated at all and has little presence in the narrative. In *Sketch,* however, an intricate narrative voice and structure, complemented by frequent cross-referencing between the town of N——in 1784 and the America of Sigourney's 1824 readership, perform the kind of mediations that the narrators of other works perform.

12. Linda Kerber, "Separate Spheres," *Journal of American History* 75, no. 1 (June 1988): 9–39. Hazel Carby, *Reconstructing Womanhood: The Emergence of the Afro-American Woman Novelist* (New York: Oxford University Press, 1987), discusses ways in which predominant nineteenth-century constructs of white femininity were grounded in establishing white womanhood as the polar opposite of black womanhood.

13. See Richard Slotkin, *Regeneration Through Violence: The Mythology of the American Frontier, 1600–1800* (Middletown, Conn.: Wesleyan University Press, 1973), for a discussion of such representations. William Cullen Bryant's "The Prairies" is one of the best-known poetic variations on this theme.

14. I use the first edition, [Eliza Buckminster Lee] *Sketches of a New-England Village, in the Last Century* (Boston: James Munroe, 1838). All citations are in the text.

15. On the position of the local minister in American villages as mediator between translocal structures and small localities in the eighteenth and early nineteenth centuries, see Thomas Bender, *Community and Social Change in America* (New Brunswick, N.J.: Rutgers University Press, 1978), 77–78, and Cathy Davidson, *Revolution and the Word: The Rise of the Novel in America* (New York and Oxford: Oxford University Press, 1986), 42.

16. A sophisticated cultural critique, *A New Home* is innovative in its focus on the cultural clashes of life in the West and in its canny satire of popular genres within which contemporary writers evoked the West. See my "Introduction" to *A New Home* for a fuller discussion of the generic mix in *A New Home* and a more extended discussion of its representation of the cultural negotiations by means of which the community of Montacute takes shape. The present discussion is adapted from that essay.

17. I refer throughout to [Lydia Huntley Sigourney] *Sketch of Connecticut, Forty Years Since* (Hartford: Oliver D. Cooke & Sons, 1824). All references are cited in the text.

18. See Elizabeth Ammons, "Going in Circles: The Female Geography of Jew-

ett's *Country of the Pointed Firs,"* *Studies in the Literary Imagination* 16, no. 2 (Fall 1983): 83–92.

19. The hierarchical ideal of community that informs *Sketch* is affirmed in other ways as well. For instance, Madam L——'s reign and her dominion are framed strikingly by an initial description of her garden, which at once establishes her commitment to promoting a heterogeneous community and endorses her predominance. The garden is laid out in "quadrangles, triangles and parallelograms" much like the different neighborhoods of N——; like N——, they have a "centre" ruled by a "queen" (the peony). Because it is so orderly the garden can retain its structure while accommodating a seemingly endless variety of flowers, from perennials to "personified" flowers that prefigure some of N——'s residents: "gaudy soldiers in green—the tawdry ragged lady—the variegated bachelor—the sad mourning bride—and the monk in his sombre hood" (6). While she nurtures the garden's variety, Madam L——also exercises her authority freely. "[L]ike our first mother," she often "amused herself by removing whatever marred [the garden's] beauty, and cherish[ed] all that heightened its excellence" (7).

20. It is supposedly told in his own words, although, as the narrator points out, it is "divested of its vernacular" (84)—quite possibly because many white writers exploited African-American language as the object of mockery, and white readers regarded it as an expression of stupidity.

21. *Sketch* is outspoken about its subscription to a "realistic" conception of character. Commenting on readers' possible boredom with an extensive description of Madam L——'s attention to the education of N——'s children, its narrator defends her comprehensiveness by noting that "it [is] deemed of some importance, in pourtraying [sic] a character which really existed, to represent things as they were" (103).

22. Nina Baym, "Reinventing Lydia Sigourney," calls attention to ways in which Sigourney expresses moral and historical dilemmas rather than containing or repressing them through formal resolutions. She observes that "Sigourney's Indian narratives typically end with a forthright contradiction" (63).

23. Madam L—— herself exemplifies this commitment to engaging with incommensurate standpoints: not only does she extend her concern and charity to everyone, she actively solicits their very different stories. Never smoothing over differences, she listens sympathetically and fully to the position of each.

24. See "Expanding 'America,'" 228–229, for a slightly different, and fuller, discussion of Madame L——as a model for the kind of leadership the new nation needed—a woman who assimilates aspects of Christ and George Washington.

❧ JOANNE DOBSON ❧

The American Renaissance
Reenvisioned

WITH THE ALMOST SIMULTANEOUS PUBLICATION fifty years ago of two literary studies, Fred Lewis Pattee's *The Feminine Fifties* (1940) and F. O. Matthiessen's *American Renaissance* (1941), the turf of nineteenth-century American literature was bisected by gender. Both studies took as their subject the watershed decade of the 1850s. Both defined this decade, and rightly so, as an era of unprecedented achivement by a newly self-aware body of American writers. Here, however, is where the similarities end. Matthiessen's subject, as emblemized by the frontispiece daguerreotype of sturdy New England shipbuilder Donald McKay, was the 1850s as a coming-of-age period for a literary achievement inherently masculine by definition, a literature of "the common man in his heroic stature."[1] Pattee's was the 1850s as a decade characterized by what he calls " 'f' words": "*fervid, fevered, furious, fatuous, fertile, feeling, florid, furbelowed, fighting, funny*" (italics in original). The paradigmatic category, he states, designated by all these alliterative adjectives, is a word that is "a veritable world in itself." That word/world—silly and separate—is, of course, "feminine."[2]

The division of an energetic and pluralistic literature into masculine/serious and feminine/frivolous cannot, of course, be laid solely at the door of these two scholars; the assumptions and prejudices of that division are ancient and endemic, and have long permeated literary evaluation. These two concurrent studies, however, represent a significant definitional moment in the study of American literature: a moment of inclusion and of exclusion. The effect upon the study of American literature has been pernicious. By trivializing and misrepresenting women's literature, the radical bisection of the decade that produced our most important national setting-out texts has robbed us of an understanding of the true vitality and variety of our literary heritage: the romantic texts of a selected few male writers have been included in American literary history as "seminal," constructing for generations of literary students and scholars a definition in masculine terms of what is important, indeed valid, in our national literature; women's texts from the era, patronized and ridiculed with dismissive contempt, have been excluded. By eliminating "unmasculine" sentiments, cross-gender dialogue, and what was seen as contamination by the popular, this exclusion, significantly at the moment of the initial institution of American literature as a major field of study, has simplified our literary history; it has also distorted it.

The American Renaissance is the era commonly considered to represent the birth of a distinctively American imagination and literary voice. In the arbitrary and tightly restricted construct of American literature that has been passed down to us, the mid-nineteenth century is not an era that even the classic writers would recognize. In actuality the 1850s saw a variegated literary arena in which realism contended with romanticism, popular sentimentalism influenced private thinking and public policy at least as much as did high-minded cultural analysis, and the writing of women achieved a visibility equal to that of the writing of men. The current movement toward inclusion of women's literature in our literary history and recognition of the cultural and aesthetic questions such inclusion raises will help set the record straight. Not only will such a movement restore woman's voice to the American record, it will provide American readers, students, and scholars with the fullness of their tradition—a vivid and compelling past. In addition, it will allow access to the dialectic of American literature across gender boundaries, thus encouraging new and more complete understanding of classic texts.

Until very recently, it has been convenient, not to say comfortable, for scholars of American literature, educated in the conventions of a particular definitional moment and socialized in pervasive gender biases, to share a coherent set of priorities upon which to base judgments about literary value. This has freed Americanists from the necessity of dealing with issues as complex as the evaluation of modes of literature dependent upon literary and cultural dynamics—sentimentality, for instance—foreign to the dominant critical ideology, dynamics that put off academics educated in a modernist, new-critical aesthetic, and make them uneasy.

A truly revisionary literary history of nineteenth-century America will work toward dismantling hierarchical assumptions that privilege masculine experience over feminine, elite literature over popular, and the culturally dissenting over the culturally embedded.[3] In order to reenvision with insight and clarity, scholars will need to address fundamental issues raised by the inclusion of women's literature, issues of genre, of periodization, of evaluation. It will be difficult, for instance, to evaluate the scope and significance of women's literature in general, and of individual texts in particular, until we grapple more extensively with the question of sentimentalism, investigating as thoroughly as possible its actual nature and appeal. Further, any relatively accurate envisioning of the literary era must take into account the presence and impact of early women's realism. The problematizing of masculinist critical constructs and the recovery of feminine texts have been necessary first steps in the reconstruction of the American literary past; further evaluation is dependent upon a further clearing of the conceptual ground.

In chapter two of *Forest Life* (1842), one of her lively studies of her experiences in frontier Michigan, Caroline Kirkland directly addresses the issue of seeing what actually exists in opposition to seeing through the lenses of tradition and expectation. Kirkland presents her narrator, Mary Clavers, as setting out to the West in an old lumber wagon with a notebook and a pair of magic glasses lent to her by a politician. When she puts on these "glorification spectacles," "a prismatic halo" appears around the edges of her notebook, and she begins to record golden-thatched cottages veiled with satin-leaved ivy and inhabited by "bewitchingly beautiful" mothers and children. At the request of one mother she entrusts her magic glasses to "the dimpled fingers of an infant cherub," who shatters them to fragments and Clavers's beatific literary vision with them. For a moment she is appalled. There is nothing left to *write* about. "Why should I describe the dingy locks,—the check-apron,—the shoeless feet. . . . Why picture anew a tumble-down log-house, with its appropriate perfumes of milk-emptins, bread, and fried onions?" Chastened, however, the narrator resigns herself to "seeing with my own eyes."[4]

To some degree, the canonical construct of nineteenth-century American literature has operated on a principle similar to that of Kirkland's "glorification spectacles." Rather than mere glorification, however, our evaluative lenses have offered a double distortion: at one and the same time they have glorified *and* eliminated. What has been visible in American literary history, for instance, has not been "the dingy locks,—the check-apron,—the shoeless feet" of early women's literary realism, or the orphaned children of the sentimental imagination, but rather the black cat, the scarlet letter, the white whale of men's romanticism—these symbols construed as manifestations of a suprahistorical literary consciousness unconstrained by, or struggling against, the conditions of its cultural generation.

A feminist, reconstructionist approach to literary history cannot be said to operate free of ideological preconceptions; we work on the assumption that women's experience *counts*. In the lenses we wear the focus manifestly is sharpened to heighten the visibility of women's texts, women's imaginative priorities, and women's concerns. We aim for a kind of x-ray vision, allowing us to see what has been masked by previous constructs of the literary past, but did, in historical actuality, exist. To many scholars it has become clear that women's writing from mid-century offers a number of interesting and significant texts, texts that, as Jane Tompkins says, are "complex . . . in ways *other than* those that characterize the established masterpieces."[5] An approach to texts that focuses on the interconnections of literature and culture, of literary evaluation and power, provides an optimal methodology for accessing the significance of women's texts. Where until very recently most Americanists have been trained to value what they have seen as "transcendent" literary qualities (which Nina Baym calls "consensus criticism of the consensus"[6]), such an approach asks us instead to consider imaginative engagement with pressing social and political issues, a representative range of racial, ethnic, and gender experience, accurate representation of ordinary life, skillful employment of a range of cultural discourses,[7] a compelling embodiment of female subjective experience, and, let us not forget, simple storytelling expertise. For the first time a body of reliable scholarship on the women writers, of accurate biography, of gender-conscious social history, and of available texts is being put into place, and new theoretical approaches enable us to widen our vision as we engage with our literary heritage.[8] Like Kirkland, we see afresh. And, as for Kirkland, certain problems of recognition immediately become apparent: problems of classification, of evaluation, of periodization, of subject matter, of style.

The period from 1820 to 1870 constitutes an era in the development of American women's fiction and poetry characterized by certain distinctive intellectual, imaginative, and political preoccupations,[9] which, for the most part, scholars only now are prepared to recognize as being components of a valid literary vision. These include the primacy and power of human affections and affiliations, within a generally Christian framework, and the value of ordinary life.[10] Connection, commitment, community: out of these priorities spring both domestic sentimentalism and a realist/ regionalist aesthetic. In some cases the feminine imaginative predilections combine with an empowering Christian imperative for social justice to create important social activist texts. In addition, a preoccupation with codified gender roles, a central aspect of sentimentalism, produces at one and the same time impassioned domestic novels and sharp-tongued social satire, focusing to a considerable degree upon gender roles. Thus American literary realism, humor, and social activism owe a generally unacknowledged debt to women's writing of the early and mid-century. It is not some failure on the part of women authors to engage significant issues in compelling bodies of discourse that has caused the long obscurity of women's writing from mid-century America. Rather, the problem rests with modes of definition and evaluation developed exclusively within the framework of a critical valorization of romantic, individualistic, culturally dissenting, self-consciously artistic aspects of the classic masculine texts. In an era defined primarily as characterized by romantic individualism, for instance, it has been all too easy to overlook the emerging realist aesthetic of much women's writing, and to despise and misconstrue the immediately apparent sentimentalism.

A serious investigation of the significance of women's literature necessitates fundamental alterations in certain basic assumptions about the nature and development of the American literary tradition. These alterations will require a number of conceptual, institutional, and material readjustments in order to correct deeply ingrained distortions in our representation of the literary past. From a reconstruction of the literary milieu, to reconsideration of the nature of valid evaluative criteria, through the preparation of accurate and useful pedagogical material, much work needs to be done. In this essay I want to look specifically at the issue of literary classification as it affects sentimental texts, and the issue of conventional periodization as it relates to early women's realism. Although it will certainly not solve all the problems raised by the reinclusion of women's literature, redressing the distortions surrounding these two issues will provide essential reconstructive clarification.

In our current critical lexicon the word *sentimentalism* has no clear denotation—such as exists for *realism* and for *romanticism*—especially when it comes to nineteenth-century American literature. Critics, according to their literary politics, have variously defined antebellum sentimentalism as being characterized, on the one hand, by degraded language and spurious feeling, or, on the other, by cultural power.[11] As Jane Tompkins tells us, "the very grounds on which sentimental fiction has been dismissed . . . [are] grounds which have come to seem universal standards of aesthetic judgment. . . . [C]ritics have taught generations of students to equate popularity with debasement, emotionality with ineffectiveness, religiosity with fakery, domesticity with triviality, and all of these, implicitly, with womanly inferiority."[12] Tompkins and other cultural critics decode the complexity and skill with which certain sentimental writers, especially Harriet Beecher Stowe in *Uncle Tom's Cabin*, embodied powerful cultural discourses in texts brilliantly designed to alter a reader's comprehension of the world and influence his or her actions. Yet neither the traditional dismissive treatment nor the recent cultural analysis attempts to define in any comprehensive manner the fundamental nature of the sentimental imagination as it generated in nineteenth-century America a significant and influential literary movement with its own integrity. Indeed, in the second half of the 1980s the new feminist/cultural criticism was in danger of canonizing a newly restricted body of texts—a sentimental canon consisting almost exclusively of *Uncle Tom's Cabin* and *The Wide, Wide World*. A truly comprehensive investigation will include the full range of imaginative texts (including poems and sketches along with novels) and encompass issues of subject matter, philosophical and psychological preoccupations, genre, and aesthetics. [13] When we discuss realism or romanticism we share common definitions: we are speaking of imaginative modes characterized by certain social and philosophical concerns, characterization and narrative conventions, and distinctive uses of language. Thus we are able to make an initial identification in a more or less judgment-neutral manner of the mode in which the text defines itself. Evaluation of individual texts proceeds from there. Only when we cease inevitably addressing sentimentalism first in an evaluative mode ("Is it good? Does it work to some good end?"), or when an implicit evaluation ("trivial," "ludicrous") is no longer built into the word, [14] can we begin truly to reconstitute the sentimental literary experience. Only then can we clear the ground for evaluation of individual texts unbiased by either prejudice or defensiveness. Indeed, the biases are so entrenched that it may take years before this is possible.

Sentimental is perhaps the most overworked, imprecise, misapplied, emotionally loaded, inadequately understood term in American literary classification. Yet in actuality it denotes a major imaginative mode of nineteenth-century American literary expression. Not exclusively a woman's expressive mode, in American literature in particular it has been so defined. [15] As Judith Fetterley says about conventional critical thinking, "One might well ask whether 'sentimental' is not in fact a code word for female subject and woman's point of view and particularly for the expression of women's feelings." [16] If this is indeed so, and I think it clearly is, then the consistently pejorative treatment of the word in conventional critical usage indicates a reaction linked to what Susan Harris defines as a fundamental "revulsion from the feminine" in modern criticism. [17] A bias toward masculine experience, as Nina Baym has so convincingly documented, has served to structure our literary priorities and preferences. [18] In addition, a gendered anxiety equating "emotional" with "feminine" and nervously rejecting both has also operated as a primary shaping factor in the construction of the American literary canon.

The articulation of an accurate definition of literary sentimentalism is central to the reconstructive project, one aspect of which involves a reenvisioning of an American literature that contains, rather than segregates or suppresses, women's literature. The issue of sentimentalism is a vexed one. It's not simply that we're dealing with *feeling* here, but that we're dealing with feeling of a particular kind and with a particular function. "The issue . . . is not tears but whose tears," Fetterley notes.[19] I would like to add that the issue seems also to be one of what the crier is crying *about*. Sentimental concerns by their very nature have been suspect. However, as Jane Tompkins suggests, if we dismiss sentimental literature from consideration a priori we will never understand the basis of its appeal, "unless we choose to believe that a generation of readers was unaccountably moved to tears by matters that are intrinsically silly and trivial."[20] In order to recover the full range of mid-nineteenth-century American literature we must clear our thinking of decades of critical bias and examine with a renewed interest the concerns of the predominating women's imaginative mode. It may well be the particular nature of sentimental interests that has repulsed (and perhaps even frightened) traditionalist literary critics over the years.

What *do* we mean when we talk about sentimentalism? Central to what has been designated as the sentimental imagination is an orientation toward feeling, and nineteenth-century women writers did use the term *sentimental* in that sense. Yet "feeling" is a vast category, encompassing a multitude of experiences, both emotional and physical, many of which are not usually associated with the term *sentimentalism*. Sentimentalism as construed by American women in the nineteenth century, I would suggest, is a complex imaginative phenomenon comprised, yes, of feeling, but of feeling constellating around and valorizing a distinctive set of emotional priorities and a specific moral vision.[21] I think it is accurate to say that the sentimental imagination at its core manifests an irresistible impulse toward human connection; sentimentalism in its pure essence envisions—indeed, *desires*—the self-in-relation.[22] Seen in this light many of its characteristics, both its strengths and its weaknesses, become self-explanatory.[23]

In sentimental texts women, writers and readers, yearned for bonding, and it was affiliation on the planes of emotion, sympathy, nurturance, or like-minded moral or spiritual inclination that they desired. Violation, actual or threatened, of the affectional bond provides primary tension in the sentimental text and leads to bleak, dispirited, sometimes outraged representations of human loss as well as to idealized portrayals of human connection.[24] In this vision, the ultimate threat to human existence is not contamination of the self by social bonds—as it is in many of the classic men's texts of the era. Rather, the highest threat is the tragedy of human separation, represented by severed human ties: lost love, failed or disrupted family connections, distorted or uncollegial community, and the loss of the hope of reunion and/or reconciliation in the afterlife.[25] In this worldview the highest human imperative is a moral responsibility based either on Christian altruism or on common human vulnerability and need. As Alice Cary suggests in a statement that could almost stand as a sentimental manifesto, human community and care are central to the ethos. "Orphaned as we are," Cary's narrator addresses the reader in "The Sisters," "we have need to be kind to each other—ready, with loving and helping hands and encouraging words, for the darkness and the silence are hard by where no sweet care can do us any good."[26] Idealistic? Unrealistic? Perhaps. But Carol Gilligan's recent psychological investigations of the moral orientations of women would seem to suggest that such a vision, grounded in responsiveness to relationships, provides enduring and compelling motivation for women even today. Attention to the experience of women, Gilligan says, shows that "self is known in the experience of connection and defined . . . by interaction, the responsiveness of human engagement."[27]

The ethos of connection and "sweet care" affects women's sentimental writing in various ways, both thematic and stylistic. Tales of abandoned wives, of widows, of orphaned children, of separated families, of death-bed scenes, far from being, in their essence at least, reductive narrative clichés, become either evocative cultural metaphors for an omnipresent looming existential threat, the potential devastation of deeply experienced human connections, or depictions of all too common social tragedies based on the failure of society to care for the disconnected.[28] To the sentimental mind these images do not wallow in excessive emotionality; rather they partake of essential reality and *should* be treated with heightened feeling. An emphasis on accessible language, a clear prose style, and familiar narrative conventions and character types defines an aesthetic whose primary impulse is also generated by a prioritizing of connection, an impulse toward communication with as wide an audience as possible.

When seen in this light, as an imaginative mode generated by a dominant pattern of cultural perception, gender-related but not necessarily gender-specific, manifesting itself in narratives privileging affectional ties, characterized by plot conventions, character types, and language usage designed to address the primary vision of human connection in a dehumanized world, sentimentalism becomes a literary mode we can begin to address with some form of objectivity. Moving from an informed understanding of the sentimental mode, critics can then begin to address individual texts. Sentimental texts can be strong or weak; they can be radical or conservative; they can be personally empowering or restrictive; they can be embodied in powerful language or poorly written; they can adhere to the strictest limitations of stereotype and conventional narrative patterns, or they can elaborate the possibilities of convention in significant ways; they can be exploitive or sincere; they can be spurious or honest. We will have taken a giant step on the road to recovering our literary heritage when we can react to the word *sentimental* neither pejoratively nor defensively. An adequate comprehension of the sentimental impulse will reveal that like all human feeling it can be used for good or ill, can be transcendent or degraded.

The recovery of the sentimental will have significance not only for women's writing. The sentimental imaginative mode is not confined to a specific genre—for instance to those women's domestic novels that have generally been thus designated, and thus dismissed. Rather it is more useful to see it as a specific type of imaginative energy rather than as a literary form or as a body of conventions. I would suggest that a clear understanding of the nature of sentimentality will enable critics to locate its traces in romantic and realistic texts, to see it as permeating in unexpected and varied ways literature by both men and women, and to recognize its presence in those select texts that have survived as part of the literary canon as well as in unknown or obscure works. Certainly Harriet Jacobs's focus on family and community in *Incidents in the Life of a Slave Girl: Written by Herself* (1861) defines a powerful sentimental dynamic that places her slave narrative in a strategic relation to mainstream novels by white women.[29] In addition, however, I would suggest that the image of the family on the scaffold around which *The Scarlet Letter* (1850) spins its exquisite fantasy of human and divine estrangement and reconciliation is equally a profoundly sentimental vision and that the novel becomes more complex for our recognition of it as such. The reconstruction of the sentimental will perforce benefit the newly recovered women's literature. In addition, the classic literature of the American nineteenth century will not suffer from such a reenvisioning; rather its provenance will be far more clearly defined.

The absence of early women's realism from our anthologies and course syllabi is yet another articulate omission—one that clearly indicates the biases of evaluative criteria, and, in addition, reveals the exclusionary functions of our conventions of periodization.[30] For American women's realism has been victim not only of the critical bias toward the masculine romance but also of a concurrent simplifying tendency to define literary eras in terms of a unified imaginative vision. Regionalism and literary realism in America have traditionally been considered developments of the late century, after the wave of romanticism had run its course in the 1850s. However, the recent work of feminist literary historians reveals that literary realism existed alongside romanticism and was well in place in the sketches and tales of women as early as the 1830s.[31] From the start, female realists were concerned with the attempt to portray with verisimilitude the American landscape and the dynamics of American community. By mid-century Susan Warner, Harriet Beecher Stowe, and Alice Cary excelled at representing the commonplace rhythms of daily life in a specific place at a specific time: rural New England, the antebellum South, the developing frontier. Later regionalists such as Mark Twain, Sarah Orne Jewett, Mary E. Wilkins Freeman, and Willa Cather wrote very much out of the same tradition that these early realists brought to fruition.

Although a close look at any one of the typically "feminine" lost genres would allow a glimpse into the vitality and significance of what has been eliminated from our literary heritage, it is perhaps early women's realism that is the most incomprehensible exclusion. For sentimentality one must reconstruct a major cultural gender ideology in order to render its validity and complexity visible. With social satire and social activist literature, one could, if so inclined, speak of a body of discourse delimited by the specific concerns of its era. But in many ways early women's realism is manifestly congruent with the much admired late-century realist aesthetics of Howells and James. Indeed, through Howells's tenure as editor of the *Atlantic Monthly,* the realist manifestos of the late century are historically linked to the work of the women writers. Howells may well have been the father of American literary realism, but it had many mothers.

Caroline Kirkland's *A New Home—Who'll Follow?* (1839) is a text very important among early realist narratives. *A New Home* exists outside the strictest chronological delineation of the American Renaissance, but the very existence of this early work exemplifies the difficulty of defining periods precisely when dealing with something as unpredictable as human imagination. In *A New Home* the newly developing American literary realism found a major full-length realization. A literary pioneer as well as an actual settler of the American West, Kirkland presents herself as being at a loss to define the mode of her study. Lacking even a rubric under which she could categorize her caustic exploration of pioneer experience in frontier Michigan, Kirkland invents a genre, calling her text "a sort of 'Emigrant's Guide.' "[32] In this satiric representation of rudimentary democracy in action, Kirkland consciously deromanticizes the literary vision of the American frontier. This is not a frontier fiction replete with noble savages and a wilderness waiting to be heroically conquered. This wilderness is not so much being conquered as it is being contaminated and exploited by an unbridled and unscrupulous commercialism. What Kirkland presents us with is mundane pioneer experience, "an unimpeachable transcript of reality,"[33] featuring mudholes, inadequate living quarters, unscrupulous land speculators, vulgar neighbors, and class conflicts.

Like later, better-known local color texts, *A New Home* offers ordinary daily life, local dialect, and a vivid representation of the geographical, economic, and social texture of a unique region at a crucial era in its development; as Sandra Zagarell demonstrates, Kirkland delineates, in careful detail, the complex process of community formation.[34] Issues of class anxiety and a uniquely American vulgarity, of money, ethics, and American opportunism, of day-to-day individual survival within a less than congenial community, of the deterioration of the American democratic vision: much of the literary material developed by later realists, regionalists, and naturalists appears here in a self-reflexive and complex class-conscious idiom. In *A New Home* we find a groundbreaking text, one that initiates and defines a specifically American realist aesthetic.

Published in the early 1850s, Alice Cary's *Clovernook* tales also excel in their presentation of the regional peculiarities of American life. Cary portrays with gritty intensity and honesty the emotional impoverishment and ignorance of settlers on the Ohio frontier. The conventional realistic privileging of character over plot characterizes her work; "the affairs of other people interest me,"[35] she says as she renders a monochromatic, surprisingly modern vision of simple lives characterized by mundane aspirations, thwarted passion, casual cruelty, truncated emotions, and seemingly intolerable loss. In "Uncle William's," a meandering conversation between a group of ordinary people on a stagecoach yields evidence of madness, suicide, physical deformity, child abuse, wife abuse, and premarital sex, along with glimpses into the commercial and material preoccupations of the travelers.

A commitment to the representation of ordinary life fuels Cary's vision, and a canny disclaimer of traditional "literary" intent provides her with impeccable realist credentials. She represents herself as having "a brain so unfruitful of invention" that, were she to attempt "a flight in the realms of fancy," she would inevitably end up "making Puck or Titania discourse after the manner of our landlord at the Clovernook Hotel, or the young women whose histories I began to mark when we were girls together in the district school."[36] Yet her imagination is vivid in its regional specificity; "unfruitful" as her brain might be, Cary's local characters come to life with all the three-dimensionality of one's seatmate on a Greyhound bus trip through Middle America.

Kirkland and Cary, like their literary heirs Stowe, Jewett, and Freeman, capture in fiction the voices, local eccentricities, and community life of particular geographical areas, as well as unique phases of American social and economic experience. However, in their visions we find the cool objectivity of contemporary cultural analysis, untinged by the elegiac pastoralism of later New England regionalism. With the inclusion of these and other early realists in the story America tells itself about its literary past, we complicate and enrich our literary heritage. The congruence of these texts with the accepted tenets of literary realism suggests that their omission from consideration has little to do with their quality or with "inappropriate" subject matter. Rather, the gender of their authors, along with their inconvenient chronological placement "outside" the era of realism, has led to assumptions about quality and subject matter that have rendered the texts invisible.

A more precise and comprehensive account of women's writing in mid-century America will significantly alter the imaginative topography of the American literary landscape. Sentimentalism, while it should certainly not be used as a blanket term to designate all women's literature at mid-century, will perforce become visible as an authentic mode of expressing valid human experience. With its valorization of the affectional and the relational, sentimentalism, properly defined and rationally assessed, will call conventional genre classification, with its implicit correlative of evaluation, into account. The critically dominant individualistic, romantic text will be seen as existing not in some sphere of transcendent undefiled aesthetic integrity but in dialogue with a mode of representation that in a significant number of instances powerfully challenges basic tenets of a philosophy of individualism. In addition, traditional periodization conventions will be called into question by an accurate chronicling of the development of literary realism in America. No longer will we be able neatly to divide the century between an early- and mid-century romantic dominance and the late-century ascendancy of realism. In fact, a thorough familiarity with women's writing reveals that at least three dominant modes of imaginative preoccupation, the sentimental, the romantic, and the realistic, contended for expression in the literary mainstream, shadowed, as David Reynolds has shown, by their less respectable counterpart, popular sensationalism.[37] Far from being discrete and consecutive modes of imagining, these literary discourses coexisted, sometimes uneasily, sometimes quite comfortably, in a welter of texts, both popular and elite, whose permeable boundaries permitted much dialogue between contending literary intentions, themes, and languages.

Although in the past fifty years we have come a long way from Matthiessen's and Pattee's polarization of the American Renaissance into two irreconcilable literary camps, the assumptions and biases of that influential era are still institutionalized, permeating and shaping curricula, course syllabi, anthologies,[38] graduate program requirements. A reassessment of genre classifications, with their embedded evaluative connotations, and of periodization conventions should serve to encourage a salutary institutional restructuring. Including women once again in the story of our literary past reveals the contours of that past to be far more shifting and evasive than we knew. Complicating our understanding of the imaginative energies that have fueled American experience, this inclusion contributes to the recovery of a literature that was markedly diverse in its representation of American life.

NOTES

This paper was prepared with the support of research fellowships from The National Endowment for the Humanities and from Fordham University. Earlier versions were presented at Hamilton College and at the Modern Language Association Convention. I wish to thank Judith Fetterley and Sandra Zagarell for commenting on earlier drafts of this study and for helping to shape its development in significant ways.

1. F. O. Matthiessen, *American Renaissance: Art and Expression in the Age of Emerson and Whitman* (London: Oxford University Press, 1941), xxvi.

2. Fred Lewis Pattee, *The Feminine Fifties* (New York: D. Appleton-Century, 1940), 3–4. Although Pattee defines the era as "feminine," he includes certain men's texts in that category. Henry Wadsworth Longfellow's "Hiawatha" and *The Gunmaker of Moscow* by Sylvanus Cobb, for instance, each receive a full chapter treatment. To write for the populace, to elicit *feeling* from the masses, it would seem, is in Pattee's mind equated with femininity, no matter what the subject matter or the gender of the author. See note 3.

3. In "Mass Culture as Woman: Modernism's Other," Andreas Huyssen demonstrates that core attributes of modernism were generated by a gendered anxiety that equated the feminine with the popular and with ordinary life, and rejected all three (*After the Great Divide: Modernism, Mass Culture, Post Modernism* [Bloomington: Indiana University Press, 1986], 44–62).

4. Caroline Kirkland, *Forest Life* (1842; reprint, Upper Saddle River, N.J.: Literature House, 1970), 16, 19, 21–24.

5. Jane Tompkins, *Sensational Designs: The Cultural Work of American Fiction: 1790–1860* (New York: Oxford University Press, 1985), 126.

6. Nina Baym's groundbreaking essay, "Melodramas of Beset Manhood: How Theories of American Fiction Exclude Women Authors," *American Quarterly* 33, no. 2 (1981): 123–139, reveals the traditional critical construct of the American Renaissance to be essentially masculine, individualistic, and countercultural in its vision of the "confrontation of the American individual, the pure American self divorced from specific social circumstances, with the promise offered by the idea of America" (131). Yet, as Baym shows, as educated white, middle-class males the classic writers were indeed in the social mainstream, marginalized only slightly by their positions as writers in a commercial culture. Baym defines the ideological stance they adopted as "a consensus criticism of the consensus" (129).

7. In a recent essay Susan Harris argues that the complexity of popular nineteenth-century women's literature can best be seen by placing it in the context

of contemporaneous popular discourses, examining "the ways that it springs from, reacts against, or responds to the plots, themes, languages in the discursive arena that engendered it at the same time that it creates new possibilities for that arena by reshaping old words into new ones." In so doing we "establish the terms of the debate(s) in which the text participates, the positions it takes, and how these positions are embodied in its textual structure" (" 'But is it any *good?*': Evaluating Nineteenth-Century American Women's Fiction," *American Literature* 63 [March 1991]: 43–61; also reprinted in this volume).

8. The proliferation of historicism in literary studies, an approach to texts that identifies ways in which literature is inevitably, to a greater or lesser degree, a product both of the culture that produces it and the culture that evaluates it, has enabled us to look at our literature for qualities other than the "transcendence" and "universality" we have privileged for so long.

9. Given our current understanding of the problematics of interpretive constructs, it would be as naive to construct a totalizing theory of the feminine imagination as it would be to speak of an "American" character or "the New England mind." (See Brook Thomas, "The New Historicism and Other Old-fashioned Topics," in *The New Historicism*, ed. H. Aram Veeser [New York: Routledge, 1989], 198.) Yet as long as we avoid the distortions of essentialism, the investigation of significant tendencies and coherences in imaginative priorities has much to teach us. Thus, it is not my intention to suggest that women's writing is *confined* to the preoccupations I investigate here, merely that they are suggestive predominating characteristics.

Indeed, as several critics have noted, the gender discourse of mid-century women's texts is significantly mixed; conflict and tension can be seen in individual texts as well as within the body of work by and large. Amid the sincere Christian altruism of women's novels, for instance, can be found marked protofeminist insight (see note 22). However, the predominant tendencies in mid-century writing can be seen more clearly by contrasting women's texts from that era with the poetry and fiction of late-century writers. The 1870s saw the beginnings of a new and often quite divergent ethos in women's writing. Authors such as Kate Chopin, Elizabeth Stuart Phelps, Charlotte Perkins Gilman, Constance Fenimore Woolson, and others were to varying degrees more conscious of their feminism and more self-consciously artistic in their literary endeavors.

10. One might initially think that this delineation of the priorities of women's literature would exclude Emily Dickinson, the one woman writer from mid-century who has been most unquestioningly included in traditional constructs of the American literary canon. Yet a close examination of the entire range of her oeuvre—rather than simply those poems most anthologized and discussed— reveals a strong, if often frustrated, impetus toward affectional connections. For other of Dickinson's affinities to her more conventional female contemporaries, see my recent study, *Dickinson and the Strategies of Reticence: The Woman Writer in Nineteenth-Century America* (Bloomington: Indiana University Press, 1989).

11. The conventional critical attitude toward sentimental texts has been one of contempt and derision. Purveyors of this critical stance are too numerous to note,

but typical treatments can be found in Herbert Ross Brown's *The Sentimental Novel in America: 1789–1860* (Durham, N.C.: Duke University Press, 1940) and Alexander Cowie's "The Vogue of the Domestic Novel: 1850–1870," *South Atlantic Quarterly* 41 (1942): 416–424. Ann Douglas's *The Feminization of American Culture* (New York: Avon, 1977) is perhaps the most influential attack in recent years on the tenets of sentimentalism, and that study is now a decade and a half old. Current revaluative thinking on the nature of literary sentimentalism encompasses a wide range of very varied definitions, none of them incompatible with the understanding of the senti- mental imagination as being characterized by an impulse toward human sympathy and connection. Among useful texts in the field are the following: Mary Kelley, "The Sentimentalists: Promise and Betrayal in the Home," *Signs* 4, no. 3 (1979): 434–446; Karen Halttunen, *Confidence Men and Painted Women: A Study of Middle- Class Culture in America, 1830–1870* (New Haven: Yale University Press, 1982); Tomp- kins, *Sensational Designs;* Philip Fisher, *Hard Facts: Setting and Form in the American Novel* (New York: Oxford University Press, 1985); Amy Schrager Lang, "Slavery and Sentimentalism: The Strange Career of Augustine St. Clare," *Women's Studies* 12 (1986): 31–54; Fred Kaplan, *Sacred Tears: Sentimentality in Victorian Literature* (Prince- ton: Princeton University Press, 1987); Fred G. See, "Harriet Beecher Stowe and the Structure of Desire," chapter 2 in *Desire and the Sign* (Baton Rouge: Louisiana State University Press, 1987); Nancy Schnog, "Inside the Sentimental: The Psychological Work of *The Wide, Wide World*," *Genders* 4 (1989): 11–25; Claudia Tate, "Allegories of Black Female Desire; or Rereading Nineteenth-Century Sentimental Narratives of Black Female Authority," in Cheryl A. Wall, ed., *Changing Our Own Words: Essays on Criticism, Theory, and Writing by Black Women* (New Brunswick, N.J.: Rutgers University Press, 1989).

12. Tompkins, *Sensational Designs*, 123.

13. Useful recent studies addressing various individual aspects of the aesthetics of American sentimentalism are: Elaine Sargent Apthorp, "Sentiment, Naturalism, and the Female Regionalist," *Legacy* 7, no. 1 (Spring 1990): 3–21; Annie Finch, "The Sentimental Poetess in the World: Metaphor and Subjectivity in Lydia Sigourney's Nature Poetry," *Legacy* 5, no. 2 (Fall 1988): 3–18; and Susan Harris on the use of sentimental language in "But is it any *good?*"

14. Nina Baym has also noted the implicit pejorative component of the word as it has been used in conventional criticism: "The term 'sentimental' is often a term of judgment rather than of description, and the judgment it conveys is of course adverse" (*Woman's Fiction: A Guide to Novels by and about Women in America, 1820– 1870* [Ithaca: Cornell University Press, 1978], 24).

15. I wish to make it clear that not all women's writing from the early and mid- century is sentimental. Indeed, women's texts were often realistic, humorous, polemical, and even romantic. These various imaginative modes often exist, how- ever, in some dialogue with the predominating sentimental discourse. Further, it should be understood that it was not only women writers who were sentimental; certain male writers, such as T. S. Arthur and J. G. Holland, were unabashed sentimentalists, and other male writers—even those we define today as classic authors—occasionally dealt with subjects that could be defined as sentimental, employing sentimental conventions and language.

16. Judith Fetterley, ed., *Provisions: A Reader from 19th-Century American Women* (Bloomington: Indiana University Press, 1985), 25.

17. Susan Harris, in *19th-Century American Women's Novels: Interpretive Strategies* (New York: Cambridge University Press, 1990), 2–8, sees traditional twentieth-century criticism of women's texts as operating upon a set of assumptions that link it to "female irrationality and emotionalism" (2), and reveal in their analysis "a deep-seated revulsion from the feminine, for everything that points to 'excess' and the 'heart' in this literature is, by definition, within that realm" (5). This critical revulsion is not solely limited to issues of the feminine, however, but reveals itself to be an uneasiness about open emotion by and large. In his study of Dickens, Fred Kaplan finds an indication that the condemnation of sentimentality is "a frightened defense against its demands" (*Sacred Tears*, 41).

18. Baym, "Melodramas of Beset Manhood."

19. Fetterley, *Provisions*, 25.

20. Tompkins, *Sensational Designs*, 130.

21. Fred Kaplan in *Sacred Tears* defines the ethos of sentimentality as essentially moral in nature, motivated by a desire to share, and thus effect changes in, the wrongs of the world. Most Victorians, he says, "believed that the human community was one of shared moral feelings" (3) and that "sentimentality is an expression of the basic nature of human nature" (4). He links this to the "modern democratic ethos," a component of which is "the felt conviction that we are to a considerable extent responsible for individual and communal welfare" (4).

22. As critics have shown, many women's novels of the period focus on the struggle of a female character for self-determination and autonomy (Baym, *Woman's Fiction;* Harris, *19th-Century American Women's Novels*). This struggle may well take place in an environment where repressive external forces (social expectations, individual characters) attempt to force self-abnegation upon a protagonist. It must be noted, however, that in most cases this protofeminist process, even when pronounced, is part of a more complex gender dynamic, a particularly feminine struggle between the needs of the self and the need for the self-in-relation. In many texts the primary narrative tension is generated by an attempt to resolve in a satisfactory manner both the need for self-determination and the desire for relatedness. In *The Lamplighter* (1854) by Maria Cummins, for instance, Gertrude is caught between two sets of human obligations when she faces her benefactor's autocratic insistence that she do as he wishes because she owes him a great deal. She achieves autonomy by rejecting his ultimatum. This rejection is not for any selfish reason, however; rather, it enables Gertrude to choose a more pressing obligation—to care for a helpless friend. In so doing, she achieves an autonomy that is defined by individual choice within a community of care.

Responsiveness to the needs of others, of course, caused tension and conflict in the lives of women writers as well as in their texts. Louisa May Alcott, for instance, exhausted herself in her efforts to support her family by her literary efforts. Margaret Fuller, too, upon the death of her father renounced personal plans for travel and study and committed herself "to try to forget myself, and act for others' sakes" (*The Letters of Margaret Fuller*, ed. Robert N. Hudspeth [Ithaca: Cornell University Press, 1983–], 1:254).

23. These introductory notes on sentimentalism are preliminary to a more comprehensive study in which I will expand on the implications of my suggestions here. A fuller exploration of sentimentalism than I am prepared to give in this essay will examine the strengths and the weaknesses of sentimental literature as they are related to the generating imaginative dynamic. The strengths of sentimentalism are only now beginning to be examined, and much work remains to be done in terms of subject matter, conventions, language, aesthetics, and individual authorial treatment. Sentimentalism's weaknesses are notorious, and, significantly enough for a literary mode that has been considered so "trivial," they have been extraordinarily well documented. Any full and accurate investigation will find fascinating material in accounting for both the classic excesses of sentimentalism and the excessive diligence of its critics in pointing them out.

24. In her reading of *The Wide, Wide World* Nancy Schnog notes that for Susan Warner attachment and separation become "the unit[s] of experience around which women organize and posit meaning in their lives" (14). She says, "Warner locates the distinctive character of the feminine sphere in the value it places on the primacy of relation" (13).

25. See Joan Burbick, "'One Unbroken Company': Religion and Emily Dickinson," *The New England Quarterly* 53 (1980): 62–75, and Susan Juster, "'In a Different Voice': Male and Female Narratives of Religious Conversion in Post-Revolutionary America," *American Quarterly* 41, no. 1 (1989): 34–62, for insightful discussions of women's construction in affectional terms of the issues surrounding religious conversion. Jane Tompkins in *Sensational Designs* locates sentimentalism in the context of Christian narratives of redemption.

26. Alice Cary, "The Sisters," in *Clovernook Sketches and Other Stories*, ed. Judith Fetterley (New Brunswick, N.J.: Rutgers University Press, 1987), 64.

27. Carol Gilligan, "Remapping the Moral Domain: New Images of Self in Relationship," in *Mapping the Moral Domain: A Contribution of Women's Thinking to Psychological Theory and Education*, ed. Carol Gilligan, Janie Victoria Ward, and Jill McLean Taylor (Cambridge: Harvard University Press, 1988), 3–19 (7). One must, of course, be cautious about reading historical data through the lens of a theory based on current psychological research. In addition, Gilligan's conclusions are based primarily on data gathered from middle-class, white female experience, so one must be cautious about generalizing to other groups. Further, it must be stressed that Gilligan's research does not indicate that a motivational orientation grounded in relationship is *exclusively* a feminine characteristic. Rather, she concludes that such an orientation, while present to varying degrees in both sexes, is markedly more characteristic of women than of men (7). Yet, in spite of all these qualifications, the congruences between her conclusions and the imaginative priorities of sentimental texts are marked and should be noted.

28. The sentimental ethic lends itself to powerful expressions of outrage at social wrongs and serves as an effective imaginative instrument to encourage social change. Philip Fisher, in *Hard Facts*, demonstrates ways in which popular sentimentalism worked to mediate and transform images of the oppressed in the American consciousness. In a discussion of *Uncle Tom's Cabin* he investigates the issue of

slavery, and how Stowe's radical fiction worked to redefine the concept of slave, transforming black characters in the popular imagination from objects into human beings. "At its center is the experimental extension of normality, that is, of normal states of primary feeling to people from whom they have been previously withheld" (98). "The sentimental novel," he elaborates, "creates the extension of feeling on which the restitution of humanity is based by means of equations between the deep common feelings of the reader and the exotic but analogous situations of the characters" (118).

29. In *Reconstructing Womanhood: The Emergence of the Afro-American Woman Novelist* (New York: Oxford University Press, 1987), Hazel V. Carby cautions against seeing Jacobs's text in terms of norms for white female identity. According to Carby, Jacobs understands that "to be bound to the conventions of true womanhood was to be bound to a racist, ideological system" (50). This is an ideology that for a multitude of reasons—economic, legal, cultural—"could not take account of her experience" (49). Claudia Tate, on the other hand, identifies the use by nineteenth-century black women writers of the conventions of sentimental narratives as empowering. Through the use of sentimental narrative conventions, she says, black writers claim "the consummated rights of family" that had previously been denied blacks under slavery ("Allegories of Black Female Desire," 126). I would suggest that sentimental experience in its fundamental generative impulse of human connection and commitment does underlie Jacobs's recounting of her experience, and that this proclivity constitutes an experience not delimited by race. The sentimental impulse may well have spawned certain conventions that came to be associated with the texts of white middle-class "true womanhood," but in itself it is not exclusive to them.

30. Paul Lauter discusses the origins of conventional periodization and its distortion of literary history ("Race and Gender in the Shaping of the American Literary Canon: A Case Study from the Twenties," *Feminist Studies* 9, no. 3 [1983]: 435–463). He proposes new categories, such as Colonization/Decolonization and Urbanization, that would "bring into focus, rather than obscure, the experience and culture of people of color and of white women" (453).

31. For work on the early women realists see: Josephine Donovan, *New England Local Color Literature: A Woman's Tradition* (New York: Ungar, 1983); Annette Kolodny, *The Land Before Her: Fantasy and Experience of the American Frontiers, 1630–1860* (Chapel Hill: The University of North Carolina Press, 1984); Judith Fetterley, "Introduction" to *Provisions;* Elizabeth Ammons, "Introduction" to *How Celia Changed Her Mind and Selected Stories,* by Rose Terry Cooke (New Brunswick, N.J.: Rutgers University Press, 1986); Judith Fetterley, "Introduction" to *Clovernook Sketches and Other Stories,* by Alice Cary (New Brunswick, N.J.: Rutgers University Press, 1987); Sandra Zagarell, "Introduction" to *A New Home—Who'll Follow?,* by Caroline Kirkland (1839; reprint, New Brunswick, N.J.: Rutgers University Press, 1990); Judith Fetterley and Marjorie Pryse, eds., *American Women Regionalists: A Norton Anthology* (New York: Norton, 1992).

32. Caroline Kirkland, *A New Home—Who'll Follow?,* ed. Sandra A. Zagarell (1839; reprint, New Brunswick, N.J.: Rutgers University Press, 1990), 1. In her

"Introduction" Zagarell locates this text in the "emerging genre" of the village sketch, primarily a feminine literary mode (xxviii).

33. Kirkland, *A New Home,* 1.

34. Zagarell, "Introduction" to *A New Home,* xxviii ff.

35. Alice Cary, "Uncle William's" (1853), in Fetterley, *Provisions,* 235.

36. Ibid., 223.

37. David S. Reynolds, *Beneath the American Renaissance: The Subversive Imagination in the Age of Emerson and Melville* (New York: Knopf, 1988).

38. Judith Fetterley and Joan Schulz discuss at length the inclusion of women writers in anthologies of American literature ("A MELUS Dialogue: The Status of Women Authors in American Literature Anthologies," MELUS 9, no. 3 (Winter 1982). They find that in major anthologies from the early 1980s women authors were allotted from 7 to 14 percent of available space. Since then, however, the new *Heath Anthology of American Literature* (Lexington, Mass.: D. C. Heath, 1990) has made available a thoroughly reconstructed anthology including a representative collection of women's voices.

CARLA L. PETERSON

"Doers of the Word": Theorizing African-American Women Writers in the Antebellum North

THROUGHOUT THE NINETEENTH CENTURY, a number of black women traveled throughout the northeastern, mid-Atlantic, and midwestern states, insisting on their right to preach, lecture, and write on such topics as religious evangelicalism, abolitionism, moral reform, temperance, and women's rights. Adapting a verse from the Epistle of James to describe their self-appointed cultural mission, they referred to themselves as "doers of the word."[1] In invoking themselves as such, these cultural workers recognized the extent to which their efforts to "elevate the race" and achieve "racial uplift" lay not only in their engagement in specific political and social activities but also in their faith in the performative power of the word—both spoken and written. For these women—Jarena Lee, Maria Stewart, Nancy Prince, Sarah Parker Remond, Frances Ellen Watkins (Harper), Mary Ann Shadd (Cary), Harriet Jacobs and others—writing constituted a form of doing, of social action continuous with their political, social, and cultural work.

To analyze the writings of these northern black women, I have found it necessary both to historicize notions of literature and to broaden literary study into a larger field of cultural investigation. Rather than seek from a late-twentieth-century perspective to reify early African-American texts into a literary canon or tradition that would either parallel or be integrated within the dominant one(s), I have followed nineteenth-century African-American definitions of what constitutes a literary text. At the end of a chapter entitled "Afro-American Literature" in *The Work of the Afro-American Woman* (1894), Gertrude Mossell appended a list of publications that juxtaposes slave narratives, sociological texts, fiction, journalism, history, religious studies, poetry, spiritual autobiographies, and more.[2] This list includes—as does my own study—genres and texts that would be considered either "nonliterary" by modernist criteria, and thus more appropriate to the fields of history or sociology, or "minor" by historical standards, and thus unworthy of serious attention. Mossell's inclusions thus sharply underscore the political significance of modernist disciplinary/aesthetic exclusion: the erasure from scholarly investigation of minority texts considered insufficiently "important" or "beautiful" by dominant cultural standards. Further extending this reevaluation of the African-American literary text, I suggest that literary analysis can no longer merely focus on texts as pure objects but must examine how these were shaped both by a politics of publication (for example, access to mainstream publishing houses, self-publication, white abolitionist patronage) and by a politics of reception (for example, multiple audiences, audience constraints).

Working with such notions from an explicitly feminist perspective, this essay seeks to define and theorize the discourse of African-American women in the antebellum North as generated both from within their culture and as a response to the dominant discourses of racism and sexism. As such, it proposes a methodology rather than definitive analyses of particular literary texts. In the process, I remain aware that my historical reconstruction is grounded, in Donna Haraway's terms, in a "partial perspective" offering "situated knowledges."[3] My "partial perspective" is revealed from the outset in the series of questions that I ask about antebellum African-American women and their literary production: What empowered them to act, to speak out, and to write? From what particular site(s) did they write? How might one distinguish between their social activism and their literary representation of it?

From my "situated" location, I have been struck by the limitations of current theory and its vocabulary to analyze the cultural production of black women. If, indeed, "all the women are white, all the blacks are men, but some of us are brave," how can we conceptualize the brave, and with what terminology?[4] For the very word "brave" opens onto indefiniteness and multiplicity rather than neat categorization, and points toward an idea of "selfhood" that cannot be fully articulated. Accompanied by neither noun nor adjective that would specify race or gender, the very use of "brave" here forces us to recognize the extent to which sociological categories have reified notions of subjectivity and to rethink the ways in which they might be utilized, in the process dismantling binary modes of thought and throwing traditional systems of difference into crisis. Following Nancy Hewitt, we might instead think of the subject as a *compound* "composed of elements that are chemically bonded to each other, the composition of each being transformed so that the original components can no longer be separated from each other."[5]

I would further suggest that the "brave" in the antebellum North worked and wrote from positions of marginality, from social, psychological, and/or geographic sites that were peripheral to the dominant culture and, very often, to their own. This notion of marginality is, however, as problematic as that of the brave, for, if positions at the center tend to be fixed, such is not the case for locations on the periphery, which can move and slide along the circumference, so to speak. Indeed, the black women I study repeatedly shifted approaches, strategies, and venues as they sought to achieve their goals of racial uplift. Furthermore, we must be wary of constructing a fixed binary that opposes and hierarchizes center and margin, for such positionings are conceptualized, to return to Haraway's terms, only from "partial" and "situated" perspectives. Finally, we must be careful not to fetishize positions on the margins as "pure" spaces of "radical openness and possibility" but must recognize that "margins have been both sites of repression and sites of resistance."[6] Indeed, margins are often uncomfortable places within which to be located; as the lives of African-American women, past and present, exemplify, they can be sources of horrifying pain, generators of unspeakable terrors, particularly in their exploitation of the black female body.

How can we begin, then, to conceptualize African-American culture in the antebellum North? We need first of all to recognize the extent to which dominated peoples can never take *place* for granted and how, in fact, conditions of colonization, both internal and external, come to privilege the category of space equally to that of historical time.[7] In the colonizing process, geography becomes of central importance, and what Edward Said has asserted as paradigmatic for externally colonized peoples is equally pertinent to the history of African Americans:

[What] radically distinguishes the imagination of anti-imperialism . . . is the primacy of the geographical in it. Imperialism after all is an act of geographical violence through which virtually every space in the world is explored, charted, and finally brought under control. For the native, the history of his/her colonial servitude is inaugurated by the loss to an outsider of the local place, whose concrete geographical identity must thereafter be searched for and somehow restored . . . historically and abductively from the deprivations of the present.[8]

For nineteenth-century African Americans, this local space was double. It was, on the one hand, that place in Africa, before the Middle Passage, from which they or their forebears had been kidnapped, but to which they for the most part did not wish to return, except perhaps through imaginative speculation. On the other hand, it was also that place in America— South or North—which functioned as what Foucault has called a "disciplinary partitioning" in America's "carceral continuum," an enclosed panoptic space by means of which the dominant culture marked the exclusion of African Americans (and other racial/ethnic minorities) in order to keep them under constant surveillance, discipline them, and produce "docile bodies."9 But if, from the point of view of those in power, such a panoptic space was designed to subjugate and police the Other, from the point of view of this Other it constituted "home." In the North this home came to be those black communities segregated within the Jacksonian city. While constituting a separate and distinct social group within these cities, African Americans remained, however, a heterogeneous and shifting population, as did their experiences; such diversity undermines any essentialist notions of blackness that we might be tempted to construct.

Differences within these communities manifested themselves in a number of ways, but tended ultimately to sort themselves out along class lines. The elite, exemplified by Mary Ann Shadd and Frances Ellen Watkins among others, possessed a high degree of literacy and worshipped primarily in the black A.M.E., Episcopalian, and Presbyterian churches. Its male members found steady employment as small business owners and craftsmen or, less frequently, ministers and teachers. As James Horton has shown, the men of this elite aspired—often unrealistically—to incorporate the dominant culture's ideology of true womanhood into its social code and thereby privatize its women.10 In contrast, the black subaltern class, which Jarena Lee exemplifies, was composed primarily of unskilled laborers, its women employed chiefly as domestics and laundresses. Less literate, this group was rooted in oral and folk culture and formed the bedrock of Methodist and Baptist churches.

While such social stratification was real enough, African-American elite and subaltern classes taken together nonetheless formed a common cultural group, and, as Gary Nash has noted, "the lines that separated [their] cultural expressions . . . were never tightly drawn."11 In fact, these black urban communities represented what Stallybrass and White have called a "hybrid place" in which categories usually kept separate—high and low, native and foreign, polite and savage, sacred and profane—commingle and result in cultural forms perceived as grotesque by the dominant culture.12 In particular, religious and entertainment practices, which were themselves adaptations of Africanisms to North American urban life, tended to bring together elite and subaltern classes throughout much of the antebellum period.

If the principles of hybridity upon which these black urban communities were based were inexplicable to the dominant culture in their disruption of fixed hierarchies and binary oppositions, to their own members they were readily comprehensible as necessary strategies for survival, self-empowerment, and community-building. Blacks needed not only to resist the forces of white racism but also to adapt themselves to a growing capitalist economy in which wealth was increasingly concentrated in the hands of a small number of manufacturers who controlled the wage labor of an urban work force composed of native whites, European immigrants, and blacks. At the very bottom of this work force, black men and women strove to transform their marginal status into a source of strength, to achieve social and economic autonomy by circumventing capitalist structures and holding on to precapitalist forms of behavior in their occupations, family patterns, and community activities.

Within this northern black population, however, the elite did separate itself out to some degree in order to provide intellectual and political leadership to the community. Working, speaking, and writing out of a particular set of social institutions—the Press, the Church, the Convention movement, and the Masonic lodges—this elite constructed a program of "racial uplift." This program has often been viewed as an attempt by the elite to replicate the values of the hegemony and assimilate into white middle-class culture by means of improved education, acceptance of Euro-American standards of civilization, and adherence to the dominant culture's ethic of hard work, self-help, and moral purity. To critique these racial uplift efforts as bourgeois and conservative, however, is to misunderstand the dynamics of social change under conditions of internal colonization. First of all, the black elite recognized the need to preserve racial solidarity: "Identified with a people over whom weary ages of degradation have passed," wrote Watkins in 1857, "whatever concerns them, as a race, concerns me."[13] Second, if this elite's assimilationist ideology was on one level complicitous with the dominant culture, at the same time it sought to subvert this culture, critiquing its failure to uphold its stated ideals and asserting the African American's right to both political freedom and cultural distinctiveness. Indeed, W. E. B. DuBois was later to characterize such racial uplift work as a "determined effort at self-realization and self-development despite environing opinion," and to argue that these early leaders had in fact inaugurated a new period in African-American history in which "the assertion of the manhood rights of the Negro by himself was the main reliance."[14]

Such notions of cultural hybridity were already fully articulated in the writings of Maria Stewart. As early as 1831, she openly lamented the fall of "poor, despised Africa," once "the seat, if not the parent of science, . . . the resort of sages and legislators of other nations," praised the rise of American civilization, and urged its imitation by African Americans: "I see [the American people] thriving in arts, and sciences, and in polite literature. Their highest aim is to excel in political, moral, and religious improvement. . . . The Americans have practiced nothing but head-work these 200 years, and we have done their drudgery. And is it not high time for us to imitate their examples, and practice head-work too, and keep what we have got, and get what we can?" Yet at the same time her writings exude a strong revolutionary note, as she repeatedly invoked the Old Testament rhetoric of prophecy to chastise America for its oppression of blacks, envisaging its destruction at the hands of God and predicting the resurrection of the African race in accordance with Psalm 68: " 'Ethiopia shall again stretch forth her hands unto God.' "[15]

Literary production like that of Stewart may thus be seen as an important part of the self-empowerment and community-building strategies of the African-American elite, but it was also one that gave rise to complex problems of commodification. For if black leaders strove through writing to implement the stated objective of *Freedom's Journal,* "We wish to plead our own cause," they found such pleading vastly complicated by the dominant culture's market economy, which increasingly regulated the production and dissemination of literary texts. Through the very act of authorship black writers separated themselves from their community, constituting themselves into a separate class of writers and readers and thereby working to some extent against community cohesiveness. Furthermore, in adopting the dominant culture's language and in bowing to the inevitable constraining presence of a white audience, they implicated themselves to an even greater degree into the structures of the hegemony. Such an implication was most strongly felt in the writers' need to accommodate themselves to an indifferent or even unsympathetic audience and enter into an impersonal relationship of exchange whereby their books became a commodity and their dissemination a money transaction subject to the whims of an alienated readership and the vagaries of the marketplace.

Given this disruptive potential of writing, what kind of discourse could African-American writers invent for themselves in the antebellum period in order to reaffirm community and achieve racial uplift? One common eighteenth-century myth held that enslaved blacks were but "talking apes" whose ability to speak had become the very cause of their enslavement, in contrast to those left behind in the jungle who had "refrained from speaking in order to avoid being made slaves."[16] But antebellum

African-American discourse cannot be dismissed as a mere assimilationist aping of the dominant discourse that inevitably leads to enslavement to the values of the hegemony. On the contrary, I would argue that this discourse is in fact highly *productive,* as it is generated from within the African-American community and borrows the vocabulary and categories of the dominant discourse only to dislocate them from their privileged position of authority and adapt them to the "local place." African-American discourse constitutes, then, a particular form of Stallybrass and White's cultural hybridity, one that, as Homi Bhabha has suggested in another context, effectively deconstructs the dichotomy embedded in the assumption that colonial power manifests itself either in "the noisy command of colonialist authority or the silent repression of native traditions." I would contend that antebellum black discourse disrupts the dominant discourse and challenges its boundaries by inscribing both *presence* and *absence* in its texts. On the one hand, it introduces what Bhabha has called "denied knowledges" from the native culture into the dominant discourse so as to estrange the latter's basis of authority;[17] on the other hand, it may also configure a silence around the gaps that open up between the interfaces of the official language of the text and the cultural difference brought to it by native tradition.[18] Counteracting the text's tendency toward cultural complicity, such presences and absences work to subvert literary commodification and to meet the challenge of addressing multiple audiences. They constitute important cultural spaces and in fact function as sites of resistance.

Within the context of antebellum black discourse in general, how can we specify black women's culture and writing? We need first of all to locate the particular position(s) of black women within the "local place" constituted by northern urban communities—to examine the various spaces they inhabited, and to look at how they crossed different social and geographical boundaries and negotiated "private" and "public" spheres. In so doing, we must emphasize spatial plurality by remaining attentive to the many ways in which the variables of race, gender, class, and culture complicated the politics of location of antebellum black women. From such a perspective of heterogeneity, general paradigms break down; the private/public dichotomy must be adapted to specific historical circumstance. As we shall see, the discourse of these black women constitutes a form of hybridity in its simultaneous disruption of the dominant discourse *and* construction of particular knowledges of the "brave."

Historians of the dominant culture have typically located nineteenth-century women within the "private" sphere as opposed to the "public," which remained the province of men. More recently, however, scholars have insisted that this public/private dichotomy is far too general and simplistic, and needs to be reconceptualized. They point out, first of all, that the private sphere is everywhere infiltrated by the public. Women's duties as laborers in the household, as procreators, and as socializers of children are all carried out in the name of the public interest; they may more properly be termed "domestic" rather than "private."[19] Moreover, since free black males of this period were denied most civil and political rights, they could obviously not participate in activities in the national public sphere to the same extent as men from the dominant culture and class. Such a constraint helped minimize but not eradicate the domestic/public dichotomy in antebellum northern black communities.

Like women of the dominant culture, black women saw "domestic economy" as an empowering cultural model. As we have seen, however, the domestic sphere of black culture cannot be conceptualized in the same way as that of white society. Indeed, given the economic system that undergirded antebellum northern communities, as well as the demographic situation of black women—greater percentage than men, low fertility and/or birth rate—African-American familial life cannot be construed in the same terms as the white middle-class family. We cannot make assumptions about the primacy of the nuclear family nor of women as wives and mothers; rather, we need to think in terms of broader domestic networks, both kin and non-kin. In fact, many black women activists occupied "anomalous" positions as unmarried, widowed, and/or childless women. They were thus freed from many of the domestic obligations that burdened other women. But, ever aware of the importance of preserving the integrity of black family life and its domestic networks, these women sought to make of the family a site of cultural resistance. They constitute striking examples of how, to quote Mina Caulfield, "families, generally under the leadership of women, have fought back, defending subsistence production as it becomes more precarious, cementing family bonds and building new networks of mutual support as the old ones come under attack, consolidating and developing cultures of resistance—cultures which, like the role of women and family life itself, have been devalued under imperialist ideology."[20] Thus, Maria Stewart, Nancy Prince, and Frances Watkins insisted that black women dedicate themselves to proper household maintenance, child rearing, gardening, diet, and hygiene.

Furthermore, as we have seen, for black women as well as for black men the domestic sphere extended well beyond the family into the community itself, into what I call the "ethnic community sphere."[21] Black women joined together in female benevolent associations that coexisted alongside similar male organizations in order to take care of others in the community and, in particular, of each other. They involved themselves in a politics of domestic economy, which provided a solid base for cooperative community action. Maria Stewart, Nancy Prince, Frances Watkins, and Harriet Jacobs, for example, devoted themselves to moral reform activities, creating "asylums" to shelter destitute young women, organizing mutual aid societies to succor the needy, forming literary societies to improve the intellectual and moral quality of black women's lives, and participating in the free produce and temperance movements. Black men, who were themselves deeply engaged in moral reform work, welcomed these benevolent activities, which they saw as necessary to the success of racial uplift. This ethnic community sphere thus functioned as an intermediate sphere situated somewhere between the domestic/private and the public. It can be viewed as "public" in that it is located outside the "home" and remains preoccupied with the welfare of the general population, but it is also "domestic" in that it represents an extension of the values of "home" into the community. And it is "private" insofar as it is able to remain hidden, abstracted from the gaze of the dominant culture. For nineteenth-century African Americans, this sphere was vital to the preservation of both the bodily integrity and psychic security of families and individuals.

Finally, many of these black women also entered into the "national public sphere" as workers, principally as domestics and seamstresses; Jarena Lee, Maria Stewart, Nancy Prince, and Frances Watkins are examples of such women workers. In such roles they had little prestige but did gain economic independence as well as the geographical mobility and physical freedom that would enable them to participate in the public work of evangelicalism and abolitionism. Yet, most important, limits *were* placed on black women's activities beyond the community level, in what I call the "ethnic public sphere" of social institutions dominated by men of the black elite—the Church, the Press, the Masonic lodges, and the Convention movement, whose goals were to promote public civic debate on broad issues of racial uplift.[22] Thus, in the first several years of its existence women were denied membership in the American Moral Reform Society; moreover, women were neither allowed to attain leadership positions in the A.M.E. Church nor permitted to voice their opinions at the annual national conventions; finally, considerable opposition was mounted within the black community against Mary Ann Shadd's editorship of the *Provincial Freeman*. In thus restricting the role of black women in the articulation of racial uplift programs, black men of the elite strove, in what they believed were the best interests of the community, to contain heterogeneity, silence difference, and gender blackness as male.

How, then, could black women enter into the arena of public civic debate? I would contend that they were able to do so by "achieving" an additional "oppression," by consciously adopting a self-marginalization that became superimposed upon the already ascribed oppressions of race and gender and that paradoxically allowed empowerment. Typically, this marginalization took the form of religious evangelicalism, which led black women into those socially liminal spaces created by the Second Great Awakening, of public lecturing to "promiscuous assemblies" forbidden to contemporary white middle-class women, and/or of extensive travel also uncommon to their white counterparts at that time. In the process, these women entered into various hybrid spaces that freed them from the fixed social and economic hierarchies determined by capitalism. In one sense, these spaces functioned as a center, allowing the women freedom of self-expression as well as the power to effect social change. At the same time, however, these spaces remained marginal sites of oppression that separated the women from their "homes" and "native" communities, forcing an unfeminine exposure of the body and reminding them of their difference, their inferior and outsider status.

Indeed, black women in the antebellum period were conceptualized by the dominant culture chiefly in bodily terms in contrast to middle-class white women whose femininity, as defined by the cult of True Womanhood, cohered around notions of the self-effacing body. In descriptions in Frederick Law Olmsted's *Journey in the Seaboard Slave States* and Fanny Kemble's *Journal of a Residence on a Georgia Plantation,* for example, the black female body, always public, is perceived primarily as a laboring, working body, and hence is masculinized. Intimately linked to the physical labor of black women, however, was their reproductive labor, as well as the recognition that slave women often served to fulfill the sexual pleasure of their masters and to nurture the latters' children. Feminine functions were thus superimposed on masculine ones to create a complexly ambiguous portrait of the antebellum black woman. As a result, the public exposure of black women cultural workers on the margins could only be perceived by the dominant culture, and by a segment of the black male elite as well, as a form of social disorder that confirmed the black female body as grotesque.[23]

How, then, did black women conciliate these differing interpretations of the black female body as empowered *and* disordered? I would suggest that they turned to the literary representation of self-marginalization—to the writing of self, spirituality, and travel, the reprinting of public lectures, the creation of fictional worlds—in an attempt to order disorder, to negotiate public exposure, to decorporealize the self, and thereby legitimize their activities on behalf of racial uplift. Specific choice of genre—spiritual or secular autobiography, ethnography, fiction—further allowed these women writers to manipulate point of view: in autobiography the self seeks to represent the self, in ethnography the Other, and in fiction fictionalized versions of the self (and Other) from multiple outside perspectives.

Both historical and literary studies have subsequently buried and silenced these writings. In seeking to recover them, I present here a brief discussion of three texts, not to suggest yet another literary tradition or canon, but to offer symptomatic readings that address the problematics of discourse and literary representation raised earlier—the negotiation of literary commodification, the effort to establish narrative authority, the creation of hybrid discourses that endorse both denied knowledges and silences.

Jarena Lee constitutes an early example of a black female spiritualist who participated in the evangelical fervor of the Second Great Awakening. Historians such as Alice Rossi and Carroll Smith-Rosenberg have brilliantly described how the industrial advances of the early nineteenth century represented improvement in the lives of certain Americans but marked a distinct loss in social and economic stability for many women and for most blacks. They further argue that these marginalized groups then turned to evangelicalism as an outlet for their frustrations, participating in what Smith-Rosenberg has called the liminal spaces and experiences of the Second Great Awakening, in which the carnivalesque flourished.[24]

Lee's memoirs, *The Life and Religious Experience of Jarena Lee*, published in 1836, record her active participation in the evangelical movement. They portray an individual who, although but a "poor coloured female instrument," lived with the conviction that she had been singled out by God and empowered by Him to preach the Gospel in public.[25] To fulfill His Providential design, Lee found herself obliged to resist the patriarchal institutions of marriage, family, and Church that would have confined her to the domestic sphere, and enter the socially liminal spaces of the Second Great Awakening. In this space hierarchies of class, race, and gender are deconstructed, and the individual self loses its boundaries to merge with the other congregants and with the Godhead. This sphere is structured not according to a capitalist economy of exchange but rather following what Luce Irigaray has called an alternative economy of mysticism—a transgressive libidinal economy that exists outside the labor market and its symbolic linguistic order and is characterized by the nonrational, the sensual, the oral, the carnivalesque.[26]

Inhabiting such a space free of commodification, exchange, and profit systems, why would Lee choose to memorialize her religious experiences in writing? Quite clearly, she believed that by writing she could narrate the story of her call to grace to a wider audience and thereby gain more converts to the evangelical cause. I would argue, however, that Lee also turned to literary self-representation in an attempt to justify her public exposure, and that she viewed writing and publication as tools of legitimization that would permit her to forge an entrance into the dominant economy and, in particular, gain acceptance into the all-male hierarchy of the A.M.E. Church. In this sense, writing became for her a necessary supplement.

Lee's memoirs are written within the framework of the spiritual autobiography. Such writing constitutes an instance of Foucauldian counterdiscourse that has a double function here as it is designed to negotiate the interface between dominant and minority discourse on the one hand and the liminality of evangelical experience and the orthodoxy of the A.M.E. Church on the other. Lee's reliance on the conventions of the spiritual autobiography, a genre that has occupied a privileged place in the western literary canon from Saint Augustine on, suggests an implicit desire on her part to enter into the master's discourse and legitimize her writing. This very reliance, however, is also a form of counterdiscourse, for it asserts the African American's possession of a soul, validation by God, and subjection to His divine Providence. Furthermore, it authorizes the African-American narrator to interpret his or her own life through recourse to Providential design and typological analogy.

But Lee's memoirs are also a hybrid discourse informed by both silences and denied knowledges. Indeed, unlike the white abolitionist Lydia Maria Child, who did not hesitate to publicize the physical and vocal gestures of another black female evangelist, Julia Pell, "with a voice like a sailor at mast-head, and muscular action like Garrick in Mad Tom,"[27] Lee refused either to specularize herself in the bodily act of preaching or to record her sermons in writing. Body and speech are both silenced, but their aspirations to power enter into Lee's memoirs in the form of dreams, visions, and trances—of hell, Satan, Christ, suicidal desire, resurrection— that fuse Africanisms with Christian symbology. Acknowledging that these may well be perceived as "a fiction, the mere ravings of a disordered mind" (34), Lee sought to make sense of them through the interpretive act of narration. Thus, while writing allowed Lee to erase the "public" body, it also led her to silence the "private" voice of religious ecstasy in favor of a more "public" language that she hoped would be acceptable to institutionalized religion. That she did not accomplish her purpose and that her narrative remained a marginal hybrid discourse is signaled by the A.M.E. Church's refusal to finance its republication, insisting that it was "written in such a manner that it is impossible to decipher much of the meaning contained in it."[28]

A second form of self-marginalization adopted by antebellum black women was that of travel. In a letter to Mary Ann Shadd's *Provincial*

Freeman, published out of Canada West in the 1850s, a correspondent, John N. Still, conceptualized the stance of the "colored tourist" as a means of achieving the "common cause" of racial uplift: "I find that by a little observation and attention, that volumes of useful information relative to our people, their pursuits inclinations, circumstances, condition and progress, may be readily obtained. I shall endeavor to extend my observations, first to Society, in general; secondly, Churches, Schools, etc., and Business pursuits, in which colored people are now, or may engage in; and, thirdly, a brief notice of the principle Colored Men and Women in public and private life, under the following heading:—'Incidents, Interviews, and Observations.' By a Colored Tourist."[29]

To Shadd, such ethnographic analyses of one's own people could indeed serve to build self-reliant agricultural communities in Canada that the black emigrants could call "home." But they also pointed self-referentially back to Shadd's own complex position both as an insider living in a black township in Canada West and as an outsider, a journalist observing her own community. Moreover, the very concept of "tourist" could only problematize the notion of "home" for Shadd as well as for all African Americans in the 1850s. If Shadd were indeed on tour, where then was home? Can home ever be specified for the African transplanted to American soil? Is the African American not always already a "colored tourist"? In both her tourism and her journalism, Shadd sought to deconstruct the notion of home as a place of origin and a primary point of reference by constantly reaffirming her own geographic and social displacement. She further transformed her own marginalization into a source of both personal empowerment and community-building, recognizing that it was only from the Canadian provinces that she, the first African-American newspaperwoman, could challenge the racial-uplift strategies of prominent black male abolitionists at home and offer a viable alternative to the political leadership of Frederick Douglass.

Nancy Prince represents yet another kind of black woman traveler whose extensive journeys to such foreign lands as Russia and Jamaica both empowered and marginalized her, and for whom writing constituted a means of ordering the disorder, and privatizing the public exposure, of the black woman traveler. Her two travel narratives, *The West Indies* (1841) and *A Narrative of the Life and Travels of Mrs. Nancy Prince* (1850), written most probably for a double audience of black and white abolitionists, nicely illustrate the stance of the black female social explorer who authorizes herself to gaze at the Other, but must in turn, and despite all attempts at self-protection, become a commodity and subject herself to this Other's gaze.

Mary Pratt has outlined two basic models for eighteenth- and nineteenth-century male-authored European ethnographies and travel narratives. The first, Pratt suggests, combines a particularized account of
personal experience with a more generalized "objective" description of
the habits and customs of the people visited. In this model, great importance is attached to the scene of arrival, which establishes the traveler/
ethnographer's right to be there and to gaze upon the natives. If properly
presented, neither the validity of his personal point of view nor the
generalizations that derive from it are open to question, based as they are
on assumptions about the European male's cultural superiority and right
to gaze. In the second model, the gazing I/eye of the traveler is self-
effaced, hides behind the passive voice, thus depersonalizing the narrative. Nonetheless, the text exudes European self-consciousness as the *I*
invisibly takes over, denuding the landscape of its indigenous people and
refusing to record any moments of contact between self and natives.[30]

In her West Indies narrative, an account of her travels to Jamaica in the
1830s to assess the conditions of the local population after Emancipation,
Prince combined these dominant ethnographic models in interesting ways
to produce a hybrid text that inscribes both silences and denied knowledges within it. In the narrative, Prince initially appears to resort to deper-
sonalized ethnographic observation, as she steadily fixes her controlling
gaze outward, offering "objective" scientific descriptions of Jamaican geography and history, while shrouding her personal life and motivations in
privacy and refusing to allow herself to be gazed at. In fact, however, a
hidden critique of colonial history is already embedded within these pages
as Prince's account of the natural disasters repeatedly visited upon Jamaica
functions as a trope for the evils of slavery. As the narrative progresses,
Prince gradually transformed herself into a participant-observer who actively participates in the reconstruction of post-Emancipation Jamaica,
seeking in particular to establish "an assylum for the orphan and the outcast."[31] Such an ethnographic stance led her to turn her gaze on the Jamai-
cans and thereby move from a position of racial solidarity to one of
cultural difference as she portrays this native population as primitive Others in need of racial uplift.

Prince's ethnography is, then, one that is written backward, presenting
us first with its ethnographic conclusions and only belatedly introducing
us to the fieldworker herself. Indeed, it is only toward the end of the
pamphlet, once her ethnographic and authorial power has been fully established, that Prince narrates the scene of arrival and, in the last paragraph,
reveals herself willing to risk public self-exposure. Admitting that her
narrative strategy has been designed to maintain her privacy and shield her

bodily self from the reader's gaze—"my personal narrative I have placed last in this pamphlet, as of least consequence"—she finally relinquishes her stance of ethnographer gazing at the Other and allows the reader to see herself being gazed at, revealing for the first time her racial identity: "He [Mr. Horton, a white missionary] was much surprised to see me, and had much to say about my color, and showed much commiseration for my misfortune at being so black" (15).

The gradual shift toward fiction writing in the 1850s, exemplified here by Frances Watkins (Harper), represents yet another strategy through which antebellum African-American women writers attempted to negotiate public exposure of the body and acquire a socially legitimized public authority. [32] Watkins was a well-known lecturer who spoke to both promiscuous and racially integrated audiences on such issues as abolitionism, temperance, and racial uplift. In her oratory, Watkins sought, despite her gendered position, to locate her authority in what the contemporary rhetorician Hugh Blair termed the Eloquence of the Pulpit. Indeed, a review of an 1866 speech analogized her lecturing platform to the pulpit, commenting that "she *felt* that she had been ordained to this ministry—for the service of the pulpit is not the only ministry that God has appointed." [33] A popular form of oratory in its appeal to the masses, the Eloquence of the Pulpit is directed at the heart. But if it permits "warm and glowing expressions" and the display of "the most passionate figures of Speech," it must nonetheless preserve the gravity, simplicity, and dignity of expression required by its subject. [34] Watkins achieved such an oratorical style by relying on classical models of rhetoric, in particular the Ciceronian *style périodique*. While this classical style was slowly being superseded by the more modern *style coupé,* characterized by terseness, sententious brevity, and point, its very traditionalism made it highly useful to Watkins. [35] Familiar to many in her audience, it functioned as a marker of social status, suggesting the presence of a well-educated and cultured mind. As such, this style fulfilled an authenticating role similar to Frederick Douglass's use of classical rhetoric in his 1845 *Narrative;* it offered Watkins's audiences the necessary ethical proof that, in Blair's words, "the Preacher himself [is] a good man." [36]

Pulpit oratory remained, indeed, the province of good men, and in engaging in public speaking Watkins could not escape charges of unfeminine behavior. Seemingly internalizing conventional notions of femininity, she once mockingly referred to her role of public lecturer as that of "an old maid . . . going about the country meddling with the slaveholders' business, and interfering with their rights." [37] And even in the postbellum period, her public speaking prompted invidious comments about both her race and gender: "I don't know but that you would laugh if you were to hear some of the remarks which my lectures call forth," she wrote to a friend. " 'She is a man,' again 'She is not colored, she is painted.' "[38]

Fiction writing became, then, a discursive space through which Watkins could escape such probing questions about her race and gender yet still force her voice to be heard. In 1859 she published a short story, "The Two Offers," in the *Anglo-African Magazine* through which she sought to make fictional representation serve both personal and cultural goals. In the story Watkins strove to forge a narrative authority that would remain unquestioned by creating a third-person omniscient narrator who is nowhere explicitly identified. Furthermore, in resorting to the genre of sentimental fiction she was able to explore those seemingly private issues of romance and marriage that in fact have wider social implications, to analyze in particular the values of domesticity and their relationship to the public sphere. Thus, what initially appears to be a conventional courtship plot quickly becomes a cautionary temperance tale as drink destroys a family and thus rends the social fabric. Finally, in turning to fiction, Watkins hoped to deflect the public's gaze away from herself by inscribing the female body in fictional form. In fact, her story further disrupts the public's gaze as Watkins's narrator refuses to give the reader a detailed physical description of her two heroines. While she suggests their upper-class status, she refuses to ascribe a racial identity to them; it is the male body of the drunkard husband alone, upon which are written the ravages of alcoholism, that is exposed to the reader. And, in the course of the narrative, she successfully substitutes representations of the female body with those of language as she seeks to construct appropriate forms of discourse through which women can come to voice.

While "The Two Offers" ostensibly appears to be the story of a conventional sentimental heroine, Laura Lagrange, and her poor choice between two marriage offers, it is in fact a kind of hybrid text that gradually reveals a submerged plot, that of Laura's cousin, Janette Alston. Janette's story frames Laura's and seems at first to serve a purely functional purpose. It is Janette who initiates the opening expository conversation that enables the reader to learn about Laura's two offers; it is Janette's earlier unhappy romance that foreshadows Laura's later doomed marriage; and, finally, it is Janette's independence and self-reliance that underscore Laura's weakness. Yet "The Two Offers" is also about Janette, the "old maid" in whom "nature . . . put . . . a double portion of intellect."[39] For Janette is a writer who can authorize her own life in a way that Laura cannot. This point is tellingly made at the beginning of the story as Laura finds herself unable to make a choice between her two marriage offers and thus cannot finish writing her letters to her suitors. Laura's choice of husband occurs in fact outside the narrative frame and, once it is made, she is unable to make any further narrative choices; after her marriage she simply becomes a "weary watcher at the gates of death" (313). In contrast, Janette is able to make choices. If, at the beginning of the story the narrator informs us that the heartbroken Janette has chosen the vocation of poet, by the tale's end she has transcended the status of fictional character to enter into history and merge with both Watkins and the disembodied narrator.

In "The Two Offers" the reader is never explicitly informed of the narrator's identity; yet it is clear that her authority derives not only from her capacities as a fiction maker but from her firm grounding in, and understanding of, history. Indeed, in an important passage midway through the story, the narrator interrupts the flow of her narration to shift from fictional to social/historical discourse and contrast the woman of fiction, described as "a frail vine, clinging to her brother man for support, and dying when deprived of it" to the "true woman" of social history in whom "conscience should be enlightened, her faith in the true and right established, and scope given to her Heaven-endowed and God-given faculties" (291). Laura obviously conforms to the definition of the woman of fiction, who has chosen confinement in the private domestic sphere, lives entirely within the world of emotions, and "trie[s] to hide her agony from the public gaze" (312). To the narrator, she is not interesting, and thus must die, not only as a character but as a model for black women. Over her, the narrator chooses Janette, the true woman, whose life bears a close resemblance to Watkins's own. Thus, by the end of the story Janette, like Watkins, has chosen to devote the rest of her life to service in community and public spheres, in particular to the "unpopular cause" of abolitionism and to the development of "right culture" in women (313).

Yet the story does not only offer the reader a parallel between Janette's life and Watkins's own; it suggests as well a conflation between the narrator and Watkins herself. Indeed, in the passages presenting her ideas on womanhood as well as in her final discussion of Janette's choices, the narrator turns to Watkins's speeches to find models for her own narrative discourse; the Eloquence of the Pulpit is transferred to the printed page and made respectable for use by a woman writer. Thus, in the same *Anti-Slavery Bugle* article in which she had described herself as a meddling old maid, Watkins gave an account of a lecturing tour in which she exhorts her black audiences in much the same terms that the story's narrator does: "We need women whose hearts are the homes of a high and lofty enthusiasm, a noble devotion to the cause of emancipation, who are willing to lay time, talent, and money, on the altar of universal freedom."[40] Janette, then, merges not only with Watkins but with the narrator whose fictional self depends on Watkins's historical existence yet whose body remains shielded from the public's gaze. "The Two Offers" suggests, then, the degree to which history and fiction are interdependent and fiction functions as an important strategy for both the representation of self and of African-American history. Beyond that, it also indicates how Watkins, like Jarena Lee, Nancy Prince, and others, made use of literary representation to mediate between public and private spheres, between exposure and concealment of the black female body, in order to continue the crucial work of racial uplift.

NOTES

1. Olive Gilbert and Frances Titus, *Narrative of Sojourner Truth* (Boston: Published for the Author, 1875), 250.

2. N. F. Mossell, the *Work of the Afro-American Woman* (Philadelphia: George S. Ferguson, 1894), 64–66.

3. Donna Haraway, "Situated Knowledges: The Science Question in Feminism and the Privilege of Partial Perspective," *Feminist Studies* 14 (Fall 1988): 575.

4. The phrase derives, of course, from the title of the book edited by Gloria T. Hull, Patricia Bell Scott, and Barbara Smith (Westbury, N.Y.: Feminist Press, 1982).

5. Nancy A. Hewitt, "Compounding Differences," *Feminist Studies* 18 (Summer 1992): 318.

6. bell hooks, "Choosing the Margin as a Space of Radical Openness," in *Yearning: Race, Gender, and Cultural Politics* (Boston: South End Press, 1990), 151. See also William Andrews, *To Tell a Free Story* (Urbana: University of Illinois Press, 1986), 167–204, for a discussion of the "uses of marginality" by ex-slave narrators.

7. For other references to "internal colonization," see Robert Blauner, "Internal Colonialism and Ghetto Revolt," in *Black Society in the New World*, ed. Richard Frucht (New York: Random House, 1971), 365–381, and Gayatri Spivak, "Who Claims Alterity?" in *Remaking History*, ed. Barbara Kruger and Phil Mariani (Seattle: Bay Press, 1989), 274, 278.

8. Edward Said, "Yeats and Decolonization," in *Remaking History*, ed. Kruger and Mariani, 10–11, 13.

9. Michel Foucault, *Discipline and Punish*, trans. Alan Sheridan (New York: Vintage Books, 1979), 195–228.

10. See also James Oliver Horton, "Freedom's Yoke: Gender Conventions Among Antebellum Free Blacks," *Feminist Studies* 12 (Spring 1986): 69–72 especially.

11. Gary Nash, *Forging Freedom* (Cambridge: Harvard University Press, 1988), 222.

12. Peter Stallybrass and Allon White, *The Politics and Poetics of Transgression* (Ithaca, N.Y.: Cornell University Press, 1986), 27.

13. Frances Ellen Watkins, "The Colored People in America," in *Poems on Miscellaneous Subjects* (Philadelphia: Merrihew & Thompson, Printers, 1857), 53.

14. W. E. B. DuBois, *The Souls of Black Folk* (New York: New American Library, 1969), 84, 86.

15. Maria W. Stewart, *Meditations from the Pen of Mrs. Maria W. Stewart* (Washington, D.C., 1879), 68, 28, 32.

16. Hester Hastings, *Man and Beast in French Thought in the Eighteenth Century* (Baltimore: Johns Hopkins University Press, 1936), 111.

17. Homi K. Bhabha, "Signs Taken for Wonders: Questions of Ambivalence and Authority under a Tree Outside Delhi, May 1817," *Critical Inquiry* 12 (Autumn 1985): 154–156.

18. I paraphrase here the discussion of the function of silences in postcolonial texts in Bill Ashcroft, Gareth Griffiths, and Helen Tiffin, *The Empire Writes Back* (London: Routledge, 1989), 54–55.

19. For more extensive discussions of these points, see Linda K. Kerber, "Separate Spheres, Female Worlds, Woman's Place: The Rhetoric of Women's History," *Journal of American History* 75 (1988): 9–39; Joan Kelly, "The Social Relation of the Sexes," in *Women, History, and Theory* (Chicago: University of Chicago Press, 1984), 1–18.

20. Mina Davis Caulfield, "Imperialism, the Family, and Cultures of Resistance," *Socialist Revolution* 2 (1974): 74.

21. My use of the terms "ethnic community," "national public," and "ethnic public spheres" is an amplification of the vocabulary employed by Margaret S. Boone, "The Uses of Traditional Concepts in the Development of New Urban Roles," in *A World of Women*, ed. Erika Bourguignon (New York: Praeger, 1980), 235–269.

22. For other discussions of the social roles of black women in the antebellum period, see Horton, "Freedom's Yoke," and Julie Winch, *Philadelphia's Black Elite* (Philadelphia: Temple University Press, 1988), 121.

23. For a discussion of the female grotesque, see Mary Russo, "Female Grotesques: Carnival and Theory," in *Feminist Studies/Critical Studies*, ed. Teresa de Lauretis (Bloomington: Indiana University Press, 1986), 213–229.

24. *The Feminist Papers From Adams to de Beauvoir*, ed. Alice Rossi (New York: Columbia University Press, 1973), 241–274; Carroll Smith-Rosenberg, *Disorderly Conduct* (New York: Oxford University Press, 1985), 129–164.

25. Jarena Lee, *The Life and Religious Experience of Jarena Lee*, in *Sisters of the Spirit*, ed. William Andrews (Bloomington: Indiana University Press, 1986), 37.

26. Luce Irigaray, *Speculum of the Other Woman*, trans. Gillian C. Gill (Ithaca, N.Y.: Cornell University Press, 1985), 191–202.

27. Lydia Maria Child, *Letters From New York* (New York: C. S. Francis, 1845), 76.

28. Quoted in Andrews, Introduction to *Sisters of the Spirit*, 6.

29. *Provincial Freeman*, June 30, 1855.

30. Mary Pratt, "Scratches on the Face of the Country," *Critical Inquiry* 12 (Autumn 1985): 119–143.

31. Nancy Prince, *The West Indies* (Boston: Dow & Jackson, Printers, 1841), 15.

32. See also William Andrews, "The Novelization of Voice in Early African

American Narrative," *PMLA* 105 (January 1990): 23–24, and my article, "Capitalism, (Under)development, and the Production of the African-American Novel in the 1850s," *American Literary History,* forthcoming.

33. *Christian Recorder,* September 15, 1866.

34. Hugh Blair, *Lectures on Rhetoric and Belles Lettres* (London: W. Strahan, T. Cadell, 1783), 2:106.

35. For a fuller discussion of the shifts in oratorical styles in the antebellum period, see Lawrence Buell, *New England Literary Culture* (Cambridge: Cambridge University Press, 1986), 142–143.

36. Blair, *Lectures,* 106.

37. *Antislavery Bugle,* April 23, 1859.

38. Quoted in William Still, *The Underground Railroad* (Philadelphia: Porter and Coates, 1872), 772.

39. Frances Ellen Watkins, "The Two Offers," *Anglo-African Magazine* 1 (September 1859): 288–291 and (October 1859): 311–313.

40. *Antislavery Bugle,* April 23, 1859.

DEBORAH CARLIN

"What Methods Have Brought Blessing": Discourses of Reform in Philanthropic Literature

For although humane impulse be instinctive, as ancient as human society, although tenderness for the sufferer together with yearning pain over the sinner followed hard upon the loss of innocence, yet only Literature has preserved the story. She chronicles mistakes, warns of pitfalls, and notes what methods have brought blessing.

Mrs. Frances A. Goodale, The Literature of Philanthropy *(1893)*

IN 1887 JANE ADDAMS was in Europe, recovering from a breakdown she suffered after dropping out of the Women's Medical College in Philadelphia. In her 1910 memoir, *Twenty Years at Hull House,* she recorded a conversation she had during that European excursion with her mother, in which Mrs. Addams remonstrated her daughter that young women in general enjoyed so many more "opportunities" than had their mothers. Although Addams kept silent, her impassioned internal retort appears in her memoir, and soon gives way to an analysis of the conditions of young women in her station and class. "You do not know," Addams said to her mother,

"what life means when all the difficulties are removed! I am simply smothered and sickened with advantages. It is like eating a sweet dessert the first thing in the morning."

Addams wrote:

This, then, was the difficulty, this sweet dessert in the morning and the assumption that the sheltered, educated girl has nothing to do

203

with the bitter poverty and the social maladjustment which is all about her, and which, after all, cannot be concealed, for it breaks through poetry and literature in a burning tide which overwhelms her; it peers at her in the form of heavy-laden market women and underpaid street laborers, gibing her with a sense of her uselessness.[1]

Addams would, a short two years later, answer this pervasive "sense of uselessness" by opening the doors of Hull House and inaugurating one of the most famous settlements in the United States.

Elizabeth Stuart Phelps also paid tribute to the power of literature to awaken privileged Americans in 1910, one year before her death, when she acknowledged the impact that Rebecca Harding Davis's "Life in the Iron Mills" (1861) had made on her as an impressionable young author: "That story was a distinct crisis for one young writer at the point where the intellect and the moral nature meet. . . . One could never say again that one did not understand. The claims of toil and suffering upon ease had assumed new form."[2]

For a surprising number of both women readers and women writers after the Civil War then, the question of what to do, and what one *could* do when confronted by direst poverty, was a pressing one that required the attempt to articulate some answers. And of the approximately 250 novels about American economics published between 1870 and 1900,[3] a substantial number dramatize the conversion of their wealthy female protagonists from benighted "feminine" ignorance of the ways of the urban American world to an impassioned realization of their social obligation to the exploited working classes upon whom their fortunes have been built. But although different writers suggest various solutions to the economic injustices of late-nineteenth-century America—including the organization of labor, enlightened leadership by the wealthy, and improved environmental conditions for the poor—much of the literature written by women is, quite simply, a literature of philanthropy. It stresses good will, generosity, and monetary contributions as the agencies of social welfare, rather than advocating any specific social plan of improvement, restoration, radicalization, or transformation of existing economic apportionments as the foundation of more far-reaching reforms.

It is also a literature that has remained, essentially, noncanonical, since it does not adhere to the existing definitions of sentimental novels or of literary domesticity that have heretofore dominated the critical investigations of nineteenth-century women's literature.[4] Nor has it secured a place in the canon of American realism, despite its easy accommodation into the changing definitions of realism during the past thirty years, from what Amy Kaplan calls "a progressive force exposing social conditions to a conservative force complicit with capitalist relations."[5] Indeed, not only do women's philanthropic novels embody progressivism and conservatism simultaneously, but they also concern themselves fundamentally with what Kaplan identifies as one of the central issues in realism, the inescapable problem that "representing social change is inseparable from the problem of representing social classes."[6]

Defining precisely what social criticism is in this period remains both arbitrary and problematic, however, since much of the literature written about poverty after the Civil War is rooted in a middle-class perspective and is essentially spectatorial in nature. After the 1842 publication of *American Notes,* in which Charles Dickens described slum life in New York City's notorious Five Points district in luridly metaphoric detail, a series of books appeared that purported to "report" on conditions in the slums. Clearly indebted to Eugène Sue's serialized novel *Les Mystères de Paris,* which also appeared in 1842, works such as Ned Buntline's [E. Z. C. Judson] *The Mysteries and Miseries of New York* (1848), J. W. Buel's *Metropolitan Life Unveiled; or The Mysteries and Miseries of America's Great Cities* (1882), and Helen Campbell, Thomas W. Knox, and Thomas Byrnes's *Darkness and Daylight: or Lights and Shadows of New York Life* (1891) represented voyeuristic examinations of vice and crime that relied on sensationalism to keep their readers interested, despite the sometimes genuine impulse for reform that animated such an approach.[7] The line then, separating serious social investigation and simple sensationalism can be an obscure one. Jacob Riis's chronicle of New York tenement conditions, *How the Other Half Lives* (1890), is a case in point. Punctuated by halftone photographs taken by Riis himself, the book organizes itself as a walking tour of New York ghettos led by the photographer/journalist/reformer Riis, who guides the reader through neighborhoods composed as chapters—"Chinatown," "Jewtown," and "The Bend." Combining trenchant analysis of slum conditions with a marked inclination for ethnic stereotyping, *How the Other Half Lives* depends upon its ability to make the middle-class spectator see (quite literally, through the lens of Riis's camera), and its ability to shock the spectator into some kind of emotional and, presumably, moral response. In the same vein, Alvan Francis Sanborn's *Moody's Lodging House and Other Tenement Sketches* (1895) employs a narrator who, disguised as a vagrant, visits and reports on the terrible conditions in the cheap lodging houses of Boston.[8]

As Alan Trachtenberg has argued, the transformation of American cities after the Civil War into an environment determined by spectacular displays of difference was

the result of new forces of production and distribution pulling in a working class from the countryside, creating on one hand intensely crowded living quarters close to places of work, and on the other new places for the display of goods and for shopping. Divisions of space and of styles of life, between production and consumption, were the most visible marks of a new social order imposing itself on older sites. The process was plain and disclosed itself in the growing divisions between rich and poor that beset mid- and late-nineteenth-century urban society.[9]

Underlying every spectacle of social ill or of seemingly insurmountable social and economic difference is the moral imperative to *act* after one has *seen,* although how to act is not always immediately apparent. Basil March, in Howells's *A Hazard of New Fortunes* (1890), is an apt representative of both the moral discomfort and the moral uncertainty middle-class Americans faced in the city. Throughout much of the novel, March enjoys riding the Third Avenue elevated because he continually encounters "some interesting shape of shabby adversity."[10] As his experience in the city diversifies, however, he comes to both loathe and fear the "spectacle" around him, since he is unable to "release himself from a sense of complicity with it, no matter what whimsical, or alien, or critical, attitude he took" (265).

As Howells illustrates, the moral crisis for middle- and upper-class Americans of this period was their increasing sense of complicity in the economic inequality and social injustice of U.S. society, which they witnessed on a daily basis far more frequently than they had in the past. Indeed, if one lived in a factory town or in a major East Coast city, the yawning gulf of disparity between comfort and squalor, between wealth and poverty, between confidence and despair, was altogether unavoidable. But whereas Basil March, when confronted by the seething social cauldron of New York City, grows increasingly disoriented and, in fact, morally numb concerning the conditions surrounding him ("he was still uncertain just what the convictions were that he had been so staunch for" [384]), women philanthropists and writers suffered no such ambiguity. "Who," queried Lucia True Ames Mead—suffragist, writer, and reformer—"is to do this work" of redressing "this belated side of human progress?"

Chiefly those who have time; those whose energies are not mainly given to iron and coal and wood, to things that perish with the using; those who are fitted by inclination and opportunity to deal with human wills and tastes and affections. Women may not devise twenty-story structures or tunnel under East River. But they may abolish the brothel and saloon and transform the tenement house. They may plan no reform of the tariff or currency, but they may create a public sentiment which shall largely divert civic expenditure into different channels.[11]

Mead's argument, entitled "The Privileged Woman" and delivered to audiences of women in and around Boston, incorporates the rhetoric of leisure and privilege at the same time that it acknowledges the limitations of the female sphere in late-nineteenth-century America. Although women do not participate in the larger economic world of industry, or architecture, or finance, they nonetheless are uniquely suited "by inclination and opportunity" to address the social ills that an increasingly industrial society fostered. Indeed, Mead suggests, because women are, by nature, different from men, to them belongs "the work of spiritualizing the nation, of changing its mind," and they are "*more than any other citizens to be held accountable if that task is left undone.*"[12] Referring to Helen Campbell as the sole female writer in *Darkness and Daylight,* the Reverend Lyman Abbott declares rhetorically in that book's preface, "Who but a woman could describe to women the scenes of sin, sorrow, and suffering among this people that have presented themselves to her womanly eye and heart?"[13] By claiming that the powers of sensitivity, empathy, spirituality, and concern are uniquely feminine, middle-class women reformers not only managed to appropriate and articulate the only kind of power available to them at this time, but they also, as Jill Conway argues, discovered "a basis for criticizing an exploitive economic system in which women of their class played no active part."[14]

Yet as the literature of this period well illustrates, the very foundation upon which philanthropic fiction constructs its argument—that women are innately sensitive to the plight of the socially and economically dispossessed, and, more important, that they are endowed with the leisure to minister to the needs of the poor—is also its greatest limitation. Since "most Americans considered women's importance as the linchpin of domestic life undiminished,"[15] it was only within this domestic province that women writers and philanthropists believed they had something valuable to contribute. By insisting that reform or philanthropy properly fall within the boundaries of a female universe, these novels ultimately cannot enact serious reform because of their adherence to the conventions of "true womanhood." Transposing the domestic sphere into the public, these fictions necessarily ignore the broader economic causes of class disparity and instead concentrate on ameliorating the immediate effects of poverty within the living environment. In espousing the power of "true womanhood," these novels both overdetermine and radically circumscribe the nature and effect of the reforms they so fervently advocate. As Jill Conway notes in her historical study of the American women's reform movement, basing "one's social criticism upon the idea that feminine intuition could both diagnose and direct social change was to tie one's identity as a social critic to acquiescence in the traditional stereotype of women."[16] Rather than representing reform as a "real departure from women's traditional domesticity,"[17] these narratives conceive of women reformers within an essentially conservative ideology; the home, for American women in the late nineteenth century, *was* the world.[18]

This curious, paradoxical combination of female empowerment and traditionally conservative expression occurs throughout the literature of philanthropy, and dictates the kind of reform work available to women in the late nineteenth century. Perhaps the most important and influential venture female philanthropists undertook was that of "friendly visiting" in the slums and tenements. Newly established charitable organizations begun after the war encouraged women to engage in such excursions, and this activity was performed by "friendly volunteers" who called upon the poor, ascertained their needs, and endeavored to assist them. So widespread was such "friendly visiting" that "by 1892 women outnumbered men among the 4,000 volunteers enrolled in Charity Organization work in the United States."[19] Such access to tenements, slums, and factories has several noteworthy consequences in women's fiction of this period. Although women were unable or unwilling to tromp around back alleys like Jacob Riis, or to adopt the urban masquerade of Tom-a-Bedlam like Francis Sanborn, they too employed the power of the spectacle to frame their fictions formally and to shock their audience into an awareness of the disgraceful social conditions in their midst. The middle-aged female narrator of Margaret Sherwood's 1895 novel, *An Experiment in Altruism,* for instance, admits:

> A kind of morbid fascination drew me continually to the foreign quarters. I liked the picturesqueness of the crowded streets, where women in gay head-dresses chattered, holding their babies in their arms. I liked the alley-ways lined with old-clothes shops, and the corners where Russians, Italians, Germans, Jews congregated, talking, laughing, quarrelling. The quaint children in old-world garments interested me; and the aged, wrinkled faces of men and women roused often a feeling of remembrance, as if I had known them somewhere, in book or picture.[20]

The narrator's "morbid fascination" with the immigrant other typifies the voyeurism of sensationalist literature; similarly, the sense of artistic distance that separates her from the "picturesqueness" of the scene recalls the standard perspective of tenement tales. Sherwood carefully signals, however, the difference that this particular spectacle has made on her narrator's moral and social vision:

> Something at last became real to me: that was the misery of the poor. . . . I saw on the one side hunger, sin, ignorance, and they weighed down upon me like a nightmare. I became familiar with the crowded quarters of the city, where the population was nine hundred to the acre. I knew the inside of great shops where women worked and starved on two dollars a week. (21)

Exposing their sheltered heroines and, presumably, their equally sheltered readers to "how the other half lives" is an obligatory component of women's philanthropic fiction, and this awakening frequently originates in the friendly visit. Characters such as Perley Kelso in Elizabeth Stuart Phelps's *The Silent Partner* (1871) adopt the role of "friendly visitor," usually by accident at first and then consciously by choice as they begin to know individuals among the working classes. Perley, for example, ministers to the mill hands employed in her father's factory, in which she is also the "silent partner" of the novel's title. So too in Alice Wellington Rollins's *Uncle Tom's Tenement* (1888), a novel that explores the awakening of its heroine, Effie Sinclair, to the poverty around her. Throughout the narrative, Effie makes innumerable trips to the tenements in her well-equipped carriage, bringing flowers one time, and the promise of employment the next; she even considers the idea of devoting her life to tenement work, a notion she is persuaded by her family finally to abandon.

Indeed, one of the inevitable consequences of friendly visiting was a confusion about what kind of assistance women could render to the less fortunate. "The average matron," Lucia True Ames Mead admitted, "feels, when she is once awakened to a sense of civic duty, that the burden is greater than she can bear. She is bewildered by the growing complexity and immensity of the social and industrial problems."[21] A young woman like Effie Sinclair is equally perplexed by the different and more desperate society she has come to see and understand and, as a consequence, is "quite mixed up in her mind and her philosophy" about what she can do to contribute to social betterment.[22] Most often, the suggestions offered by philanthropic organizations and charities stressed the natural domestic talents women possessed that could be immediately employed to brighten, beautify, and magically transform the tenement into a home. Joseph Lee, the vice-president of the Massachusetts Civil League, for example, touts the transformation of middle-class women into Amazonian warriors of cleanliness when they begin work in the slums:

A woman has a feeling about dirt which men only pretend to have. The reaction which the sight of dirty streets produces in her, when once she has come to look upon the matter as being within her sphere, is something of which every head of a family has learned to stand in awe. She has, in such cases, a directness of method, a scorn for obstacles or excuses, an absence of any sense of humor as applying to the situation, that is very difficult to stand up against. She does not get over it as a man does, and she cares nothing for political affiliations or official proprieties.[23]

Lee's hyperbolic claims of female power are, perhaps not surprisingly, contained and expressed within the womanly "sphere"; consequently, much emphasis was placed on how middle-class women could transport their "civilizing" notions of domesticity into the unacculturated and, significantly, largely immigrant, slums. As a result, the "reforms" women were able and encouraged to enact were largely cosmetic, as in the "Flower Missions" Helen Campbell extols for the aesthetic and, literally, enlightening effect they have when distributed to the poor: "Not till one has seen how pale faces light, and their hands stretch eagerly for this bit of brightness and comfort, can there be much realization of what the Flower Mission really does and what it means to thousands of beneficiaries."[24] Emphasizing gentility above all else, this particular expression of women's philanthropy betrays a conservatism about where the proper responsibility for slum conditions lies; as one character in Rollins's *Uncle Tom's Tenement* exclaims, "I tell you, it is *not* the poverty that makes the home; it is the home that makes the poverty" (31–32). Attributing the living conditions of poverty to the impoverished themselves accomplished two things: it enabled both philanthropic and charitable organizations to ignore the underlying problem of class and capitalism, and it asserted optimistically that these conditions could and would be changed by the middle-class women volunteers who entered the tenements ready to instill the lesson that "taste and thrift are the essentials of a home whether in a compact city flat or on the windswept, sunlit hillside."[25]

Although such rhetoric, with its insistence that "taste and thrift" are possible in all economic circumstances, repressed the class differences between the inhabitants of the slums and their "friendly visitors," the ongoing drama of "social amelioration" remained the most widely discussed and fictionally rendered tenet of charity work. Modeled on their own literary and musical clubs designed to fill leisure time with cultural accomplishment, women philanthropists were encouraged to start clubs in the slums that would provide "the opportunity for social intermingling and consequent moral culture."[26] The primary function of such clubs was to inspire imitation: "The value of their ministry lies . . . in the fact that for one hour a day unkempt boys and girls are brought into contact with a young man or a young woman whom they admire, then learn to love, and so instinctively take as a pattern to be imitated."[27] Lucia True Ames Mead dramatically renders one account of how such imitation could result in what she depicts as a kind of social conversion:

> A certain young lady of Boston went every Saturday to a poor tenement-house and took home a little girl eight or nine years old, whose mother went out daily to earn her bread. The child, who had previously been left to play on the street, was learning vulgarity and becoming a little street waif. Her new friend, on reaching her home, gave the child a bath, dressed her in clean underwear, taught her to care for her person and to mend her clothing. She then sometimes took her to the kitchen to see a dessert prepared and then to the family luncheon, where gentle instruction in good table manners accompanied the accustomed dainties. After the meal, a walk, a story, or games, or music, filled a happy afternoon. This weekly visit to what seemed to the child a little earthly paradise made such a profound impression on her life. Better manners, better English and a new standard of living were carried back to the tenement-house. Sweet Miss Ethel became the child's patron saint and the inspirer of laudable ambition. It cost a patient, persistent sacrifice of one whole day every week, but it meant the lightening of a widow's burden, and the saving of a little soul.[28]

The effects of poverty in Mead's instructionary tale are alleviated by simple exposure to a different, and better, way of life. Vulgarity is washed away with a bath, street manners are redressed by clean underwear, and culture—dessert preparation, table manners, and better English—is literally "carried back to the tenement-house" by the reformed child. Implicit as well in Mead's account is a contradictory ethos regarding class that pervades most philanthropic literature. On the one hand, the domestic and religious values of the middle class were what philanthropists hoped to teach the poor, and such values unquestionably occupied an elevated position in the social hierarchy; they represented, as Mead asserts, a "laudable ambition" to which the poor should aspire. At the same time, however, that this kind of class distinction was introduced into the public debate about living conditions, philanthropic literature resolutely avoided or denied the economic origins of difference between the working poor and the privileged classes who ministered to them. If the poor could learn the manners and customs of the middle class, could they ever attain the leisure to practice them that only economic security could provide? This question was one that proponents of "social amelioration" necessarily ignored, since its answer would represent a far more radical, and, indeed, threatening program of social uplift than improved manners alone. As one cynical young woman in Sherwood's *An Experiment in Altruism* remarks when she overhears that her friends will start a literary club with weekly parties for the poor, "In short . . . we will elevate the masses by Swinburne and *frappee!*"[29] For many professional practitioners of charity, such a program was the only kind of "social intermingling" they allowed themselves to envision.

In one respect, the irresolvable class contradictions embodied within philanthropic fiction can be attributed to the variable "gospels" that inform their discourse about wealth and poverty, social responsibility and individual self-interest. Seemingly posited against Andrew Carnegie's *The Gospel of Wealth* (1900) is the "social gospel" of reform-minded upper and middle classes who, like Carnegie, were concerned primarily with the uses to which wealth was put, rather than with a rejection of capitalist economics altogether. Willing to adopt moderate reforms rather than endorsing a radical reorganization of social life and class hierarchy, proponents of the "social gospel," generally known as Christian socialists, adhered to the belief "that capitalism was not organically evil or unworkable, but rather a good economic system suffering from explosive yet easily removable unchristian practices."[30] Such an outlook necessarily eschewed analysis of the social system in favor of a concern with individual human agency and moral behavior. The Women's Christian Temperance Union (WCTU), for example, rigorously followed a philosophy that blamed not labor practices but the moral weakness of the individual laborer. Their solution was that "drunkenness breeds poverty; eliminate drunkenness and the economic problems of the working class will disappear. As late as 1886 [Frances] Willard stated that the central question of labor reform was not 'how to get higher wages,' but 'how to turn present wages to better account.' "[31] Christian socialists, consequently, sought to create and foster the social consciousness of both capital and labor by shaping individual ethical motives. It was not class distinctions themselves that were the problem, but rather class distinctions "based on superior economic power used for selfish ends" that formed the backdrop for the nation's social ills.[32] The national character of business and industry, Christian socialists firmly believed, if built upon a noble individual character and the practice of Christian ethics, would automatically eliminate the excesses, inequities, and evils of industrialism in favor of a kinder, more charitable system.

Much of the postbellum fiction written by women adopts this perspective of Christian socialism and represents reform through the discourse of American individualism, but with one salient difference. Unlike Andrew

Carnegie, female protagonists and characters in these novels do not captain the considerable wealth of their own industries; rather, they are its beneficiaries and, ultimately, its consumers as well, since they are allowed to spend money but not allowed to earn, invest, or control it in any way. Most accounts of the period acknowledge that this lack of capital is explicitly gendered, yet they insist that women still can contribute within their appointed economic role. Mead, for instance, argues that women possess considerable and far-reaching power through the enlightened exercise of their pocketbook when she exclaims that, "though women invent little machinery, they control the markets of the world. They create demand; they guide taste; they set standards."[33] In a more patronizing vein, Edward Thomas Devine, the aptly named General Secretary of the Charity Organization Society of the City of New York, assures women of their supreme importance as, yet again, the arbiters of power and influence in the domestic sphere:

> There are then two distinct ways in which we may increase prosperity. We may make goods more cheaply by improving our productive processes, or we may make better use of what we have produced, which will involve our making an even better selection among the things which we are able to buy. Speaking generally . . . the first is man's work, the second is woman's work. The mill, the factory, the railway, the mine and the farm are man's domain. But the home, where all the fruits of human toil are at last enjoyed, is woman's realm. The great opportunities for advance and improvement in the immediate future are in the field of wealth consumption or use, rather than in the rougher and better known field of work and industry.[34]

Protected and sheltered from the debasing world of business, women never participate in, and consequently are exonerated from, the nastier and morally ambivalent decisions about profits and public welfare. They are either daughters of wealthy capitalists, as in *The Silent Partner* and *Uncle Tom's Tenement,* or they inherit a vast fortune by some quirk of fate, as in Lucia True Ames Mead's *Memoirs of a Millionaire* (1889). Working within their circumscribed sphere, women can control only the expenditure of their own personal energies and wealth, not those of the factories or the mills to whose injustices and deplorable conditions they respond. Although the heroines *feel* acutely the difference in living conditions between themselves and the working classes, the narratives do not clearly focus their criticism on the economic disparity within society. Rather, they indict only those individuals from the privileged classes who ignore their responsibilities toward those less "fortunate," in the literal sense of this word as a consequence of fate or chance, rather than as the inevitable outcome of competitive capitalism. Or, with equal frequency, they pose the problem as one of individual moral conscience for the woman who benefits from an economic system in which she has no say.

Examples of both a valorized American individualism and of a conservative middle-class protectionism abound in this fiction. In Mead's *Memoirs of a Millionaire,* for instance, Mildred, the recently enriched heroine, declares her position as a Christian socialist early in the novel with the statement that she has gone over to the "New Theology," a creed that will guide her distribution of monies among various organizations and individuals.[35] In *Uncle Tom's Tenement,* Alice Rollins is explicit about the trickle-down theory of economic reform. As Mr. Dramrell, a wealthy manufacturer, declares to his employees, explaining why he feels profit sharing is unfair to the capitalist/businessman: "I believe the remedy lies at present in each individual working out his own salvation, and the solution of his dependents, in his own sphere. The remedy lies, not in rousing the poor, but in rousing the rich. Not in rousing the rich, either, to a sense of how they are oppressing the poor, but to a sense of how much more they might do for the poor" (328). Other texts represent American individualism through the heightened sensitivity of a feminine consciousness. In Margaret Deland's ironically titled collection of stories, *The Wisdom of Fools,* one tale concerns a woman who tries to puzzle her way through the moral maze of capitalism and complicity:

> Robert Blair's sister had no economic or ethical theories; she had only an anguished heart at the suffering in that dreary mill town, a dreadful bewilderment at its contrast with the untouched luxury of her brother's house. That she should find a child in one of the tenements dying at its mother's barren breast, while her own children fared sumptuously every day; that a miserable man should curse her because her brother was robbing him of work, and warmth, and decency, even, while she must bless that same brother for what he was giving her, was a dreadful puzzle. . . . She had no ambition to reform the world. She did not protest against the "unearned increment," nor did she have views as to "buying labor in the cheapest market." She did not know anything about such phrases. The only thing that concerned her was whether she, living on her brother's money, had any part or lot in the suffering about her?[36]

Ultimately, "Robert Blair's sister," whose dependence extends even to her own name, chooses to impoverish herself and her children because she cannot reconcile her ease with the suffering of others. Although the text regards her individual solution as ineffectual, and even needlessly sacrificial, it nonetheless orients its criticism of capital solely through her uninformed, impractical, and yet unwaveringly Christian sense of personal responsibility. And in those rare instances when women actually do control capital, as does Mead's heroine, the expression of her newfound influence is conveyed in a rhetoric of religious purpose and fervor: "After the real meaning of the thing dawned upon me . . . I began to comprehend that I, whose golden dreams had been quietly put aside forever, was now actually to realize those dreams, to exchange prose for poetry, and insignificance and uselessness for such tremendous power such as I had always longed for" (46). Although certainly philanthropic in effect, one aspect of charitable expenditure is that money becomes a dramatic catalyst for deliverance from powerlessness and from uselessness, and, to some degree, from the restrictions of being unmarried and female in a society dictated by both masculine and industrial needs and demands.

No writer illustrates this paradox between the reform impulse and the restrictions of gender better than Elizabeth Stuart Phelps. In her 1896 autobiography, *Chapters from a Life,* Phelps articulated her deeply held belief that "the province of the artist is to portray life as it is; and life *is* moral responsibility. . . . so far as one is able to command attention at all, one's first duty in the effort to become a literary artist is to portray the most important, not altogether the least important, features of the world he lives in."[37] The "features" of life portrayed in Phelps's novels are often concerned with the struggle of women to assert themselves and their desires (artistic, moral, religious, philosophical) in a society that ignores, belittles, or refuses their claims of personal agency and social power. Phelps's 1871 novel, *The Silent Partner,* which dramatizes the articulation of social injustices at the same time that it demonstrates the containment of female activity within the social sphere, is a text cited in examinations of women's reform literature, and one that dramatizes clearly the limitations of this genre.[38] Phelps's novel of one year earlier, however, *Hedged In* (1870), is equally revealing about the moral imperative that guides women's behavior and attitudes toward the less fortunate, and the pervasive sense of fatalism that informs the narrative's suspicion about whether Christian charity and social change make any difference whatsoever.

In startling clarity, *Hedged In* advocates the doctrines of Christian socialism at the same time that it renders their social ineffectuality. The novel's plot traces the unfortunate beginning and eventual salvation of Nixy Trent, a young woman reared in the roughest of slums (Thicket Street), who becomes pregnant, abandons her child to an orphange, and is finally given a home by Margaret Purcell and her daughter, Christina. There Nixy, who retakes her Christian name, Eunice ("good victory"), grows happy and healthy under the shelter of Margaret and Christina's love and confidence and is successfully employed as the schoolteacher in her community. For a full three-quarters of its narrative, *Hedged In* seems to agree with Eunice's assessment that environment determines character and that, consequently, real reform is possible: "I seem to think as I shouldn't have been like as I am, ma'am, if I'd had chances instead."[39] Yet when an old friend from the tenement appears to inquire innocently about her baby, Eunice decides that she must, in adherence to her Christian beliefs, own the child and acknowledge her shame. Her decision raises a furor in the town; the school committee tries to discharge her, and her neighbors treat her as if she is diseased. And though Margaret and Christina stand by her and eventually win over the prejudice of the town, Eunice declines rapidly and is unable to escape the feeling that "society had hedged her in on every side" (210). Both she and her child are dead by the novel's end.

The paradox of *Hedged In* is that it dramatizes the reform and the salvation of an individual woman while it simultaneously seems to doubt what power Christian principles have in a nominally Christian world. And implicit within this paradox is the text's nagging doubt that one can ever escape her origins, that the difference of class is ultimately immutable. Like much philanthropic fiction, *Hedged In* begins with a middle-class female spectator revealing the horrors of the slum to the reader. The novel's narrator, Jane Briggs, enters Thicket Street in the opening chapter, entitled "As It Is," and is overcome by its filth, despair, and raging poverty. She flees, staggering "back through the filth into pure air and sunshine" (6). The second chapter, "As It Was," returns to Thicket Street to introduce the story of Nixy Trent and the birth of her illegitimate son. Yet what is startling about such an opening is its confirmation that nothing has changed between the "then" and the "now" of Thicket Street. As its name suggests, once one has fallen into Thicket Street, it is impossible to find a way out.

Nixy herself realizes that the aspirations she entertains for a better life will be foreclosed inevitably by the barrier of class: "All the 'chances' closed with spring-locks when *she* drew near. The hand of every man was against her. All the world held up its dainty skirts. All the world had hedged her in" (85). Despite Nixy's adoption by the Purcells and her transformation into Eunice, she never escapes the past she has left behind; it reappears not only in the guise of her child but also in the person of the child's father, whose "grimy" clothes and face contrast sharply with the "whiteness" (265) that now colors Eunice's face and hands. Even Christina, who seems to be the incarnation of Christian charity and love, is referred to in the novel as "une femme blanche," a term that signifies not only her purity and innocence but also her privilege of class: "She looked across her child into Christina's confident young eyes, and thought, with exceeding bitterness, how far beyond, forever beyond, *her* reach was that whiteness which could 'afford' to put both shining hands into the ditch and draw them forth unstained" (213–214). Although one premise of the novel is that Christianity forgives Nixy as a fallen woman and promises her rebirth as Eunice, the narrative internalizes the oppositional assertion that one can never escape one's origins or one's past. Despite Eunice's belief that God "has agreed to 'remember sins and inequities no more forever,' " she is plagued throughout the novel by the question, "shall *we—can* we—forget?" (250). Ultimately, the only promise held out to Eunice is, ironically, what she herself offers her former friend Moll, the opportunity "to die like a decent woman" (276). Eunice is persuaded to change from her accustomed robe of black into a white dress on Christina's wedding day. The dress suggests both Eunice's salvation and her elevation from one class to another; like Christina, she too is worthy to adopt the dress of "une femme blanche." Yet this moment of Christian and class apotheosis also signals her death; reflecting the fate that awaits her, Eunice's white dress causes her to be "drenched . . . in the redness" of the setting sun (290). Although she plans to return to Thicket Street and take up tenement work as part of her Christian mission, she dies inexplicably five pages later "at the foot of the great wooden cross" (295) she has installed in her bedroom. Eunice has indeed been "saved," in both Christian and environmental terms, yet the novel cannot conceive of any place for her in society. It seems to argue that Christian charity can enable one to transcend environment and class, but it also insists that origin is inescapable and, in Eunice's case, that it will haunt one forever, making the promise of a new life nothing more than an unreachable goal.

The Silent Partner also unconsciously betrays the limits of Christian socialism with regard to class difference, although as Phelps indicates in a note preceding the text, her intention is to examine capitalist practices through the lens of Christian ethics: "Had Christian ingenuity been generally synonymous with the conduct of manufacturing corporations, I should have found no occasion for the writing of this book." Perley Kelso, the silent partner of the Hayle and Kelso mills owing to the premature death of her father, awakens to the disparity of class between capitalist and worker, rich and poor, as she begins a series of "friendly visits" to the mill tenements. Guided by Sip Garth, an honest if occasionally abrasive mill hand, Perley, who is ignorant—she believes that mill work could not be "a better or healthier occupation. You get so much exercise and air"— has her ignorance stripped away by the reality of what she witnesses: rotting tenements, sick children, lack of sanitation, long work hours, and little food.[40] Phelps, cataloguing these conditions for both Perley and the reader, notes the "official" source of some of her information (111), and is skeptical of too sanguine or laudatory accounts of factory life such as those written about the "Lorenzo factory-girls" (234–235), possibly an allusion to some of the articles that appeared in the *Lowell Offering*.⁴¹ When Perley is finally awakened to the conditions around her, her description to Sip is characterized by a conflict between class and consciousness.

> "You do not understand," she cried, "you people who work and suffer, how it is with us! We are born in a dream, I tell you! . . . We are not cruel, we are only asleep. Sip Garth, when we have clear eyes and a kind heart, and perhaps a clear head, and are waked up, for instance, without much warning, it is *nature* to spring upon our wealth, to hate our wealth, to feel that we have no right to our wealth. . . . I never knew until to-night what it was like to be poor. It wasn't that I didn't care, as you said. I didn't *know*. I thought it was a respectable thing, a comfortable thing; a thing that couldn't be helped. (127–128)

Perley's realization that poverty *can* be alleviated, however, is drastically curtailed by her lack of power over the actual conditions in the mills. Refused an active partnership because of her gender, Perley resorts to the only kind of improvements she is able to make. She makes a practice of attending church with the factory hands, and, in a gesture of egalitarianism and democratic sensibilities, she institutes evening socials in her home, to which she invites both mill workers and her society peers. Although this evening of "social intermingling" does more to unravel the prejudices of the rich than it does to elevate the poor, Perley does pay to have a Bierstadt painting transported from her Boston home for the aesthetic education of the hands, and she introduces classical music (Beethoven) to them. Ultimately, in juxtaposing these two different classes, the novel suggests that money is less of a determinant than one might suspect: "They [the mill hands] did not, after all, leave a very different impression upon the superficial spectator from that of any thirty people whom Fly Silver might collect at a *musicale*" (226).

Despite the possibility of class sympathy endorsed by the novel, *The Silent Partner*, like *Hedged In*, cannot effectively bridge what it calls "the fixed gulf of an irreparable lot" (21), or the immutable difference of environment and class determined by economic conditions.⁴² Sip, for example, explains to Perley that moral conduct alone is insufficient to lift people out of their environment when she asserts that "you may be ever so clean, but you don't *feel* clean if you're born in the black" (201). Although Sip is encouraged by Perley to try a variety of other jobs, she returns in the end to the mill, insisting that her inability to escape is an inherited, generational trait: "It's in the blood" (288). This quality of fatalism also determines the decisions each woman makes regarding marriage. Perley chooses not to marry first Maverick Hayle and then Stephen Garrick because she realizes that marriage would require her to become a silent partner for life: "If I married you, sir, I should invest in life, and you would conduct it" (262). Sip, conversely, does want to marry, but decides that she cannot because "I'll never bring a child into the world to work in the mills. . . . I've heard tell of slaves before the war that wouldn't be fathers and mothers of children to be slaves like them. That's the way I feel, and that's the way I mean to feel" (287–288). Perley too is equally circumscribed by her own beliefs, including her insistence that she is "only a feeler . . . not a reformer" (241). Consequently, although her rigorous adherence to principles of Christian socialism seems radical in its demands upon the wealthy, it confines its charges to the stirrings of individual conscience and agency alone: "*The law of Christ spreads out its claims very far beyond the circle of mere pity or natural kindness, and in absolute and peremptory terms demands for the use of the poor . . . the whole residue of talent, wealth, time, that may remain after primary claims have been satisfied*" (242).

Yet what constitutes a "primary claim" is also at issue in this novel, and nowhere is it expressed more ambivalently than in the competing claims of capital and labor. Early in the novel, Perley receives a lecture from Mr. Hayle senior, who argues that "the state of the market is an inexorable fact . . . before which employer and *employé* . . . have little liberty of choice" (67–68). Perley feels that this explanation is false but, curiously, is unable to articulate what her opposing philosophy might be: "There is *something* about the relations of rich and poor, of master and man, with which the state of the market has nothing whatever to do. There is *something*,—a claim, a duty, a puzzle, it is all too new to me to know what to call it,—but I am convinced that there is *something* at which a man cannot lie and twirl his moustache forever" (141).

Perley's failure to signify this "*something*" represents nothing less than the ultimate failure of Christian ethics in this novel, for this significant instance of speechlessness stands in direct opposition to the speech Perley makes to the striking mill hands late in the novel. Chastising them for their lack of trust in Garrick, she convinces them that their wages are being reduced because of the genuine financial problems plaguing the mill. Although she is perfectly sincere in her belief, the text answers her explanation by reducing the problem into the "*something*" that Perley ultimately does not apprehend because it lies wholly beyond her experience, that "*something*" being the reality and the injustice of labor's subordination to capital: "It doesn't mean a dollar's worth less of horses and carriages, and grand parties to the Company, such a trouble as this don't seem to. And it means as *we* go without our breakfast so's the children sha'n't be hungry; and it means as when our shoes are wore out, we know no more than a baby in its cradle where the next pair is to come from. That's what reduction o' wages means to *us*" (252).[43] This bald statement of class conflict cannot, in the end, be reconciled with either Perley's Christian socialism or Sip's conversion to an itinerant preacher, insisting that "rich and poor, big or little, there's no way under heaven for us to get out of our twist, but Christ's way" (299). Such a complacent acceptance seems especially troubling in the outspoken and often angry Sip. By resorting to a discourse of Christian patience and passivity in its conclusion, *The Silent Partner*, perhaps unwittingly, endorses *laissez-faire* capitalism as its "primary claim," to which the revisionary spirit of Christian ethics, and indeed, feminine sensitivity, runs a distant second.

Ultimately, although the often explicitly stated purpose of these novels is to institute reforms, the contradictory discourses of exposure and containment, and of activity and passivity, create, at best, an ambivalent articulation of how conditions in industrial America can be made more equitable. Indeed, though Benham, the journalist in Rollins's *Uncle Tom's Tenement*, asserts confidentially that "I've faith enough in human nature to believe that if people only *knew*, only believed, only could *see* the facts, they would bestir themselves" (46), such a coherent social response to obvious inequities never occurs in these novels. Jill Conway speculates that the tendency of women's philanthropic fiction to represent social problems and to offer solutions within the framework of traditional domesticity "indicates the controlling power of the stereotype of female temperament which continued unaltered from the 1870s to the 1930s . . . for the stereotype of the female personality was an essentially conservative one although women reformers coupled it with social innovation and occasionally with trenchant social criticism."[44] Like Sip Garth in *The Silent Partner*, women's fiction of this period speaks from its position of marginality and disempowerment to recognize and critique social disparity within the gilded age as "plating over" (30), challenging, therefore, the acceptance of immutable economic differences in a democratic society. And it marks a watershed in the tradition of women's literature, exploring strategies of behavior, accountability, awakening, and empowerment in *both* a personal and a political sense, arguing that women's sensitivities and priorities have a significant role to play in the national scene. Yet also like the converted Sip Garth at the end of *The Silent Partner*, these novels ultimately endorse Christian passivity and patience as a way of weathering social injustice; the rhetoric of reform they adopt stresses individual agency and conscience rather than any substantial changes within the capitalist economic system. And in this regard, women's philanthropic fiction of the late nineteenth century finds itself enclosed within its own room of privilege, gazing beyond its windows at the social spectacle outside, much like the narrator at the end of Rebecca Harding Davis's "Life in the Iron Mills" (1861). Surrounded by possessions signifying leisure and ease—"A half-moulded child's head; Aphrodite; a bough of forest-leaves; music; work; homely fragments, in which lie the secrets of all eternal truth and beauty"—Davis's narrator ponders the unanswerable questions of "desperate need" and human suffering raised by the novel's tale of Welsh iron-workers.[45] Yet her novel provides no answers; instead, it turns its gaze toward the East, countering the suffering embodied in its narrative with the solace that there, "God has set the promise of the Dawn" (65).

NOTES

The opening quotation is from Frances A. Goodale, ed., *The Literature of Philanthropy* (New York: Harper & Brothers, 1893), 1.

1. Jane Addams, *Twenty Years at Hull House* (1910; reprint, New York, New American Library, 1960), 65.

2. Elizabeth Stuart Phelps, "Stories That Stay," *Century Magazine* 59 (November 1910): 120.

3. Walter F. Taylor, *The Economic Novel in America* (Chapel Hill: University of North Carolina Press, 1942), 59.

4. Nina Baym, in *Woman's Fiction, A Guide to Novels by and about Women in America, 1820–1870* (Ithaca: Cornell University Press, 1978), identifies a basic "overplot" that determines her analysis of women's fiction during this period: "In essence, it is the story of a young girl who is deprived of the supports she had rightly or wrongly depended on to sustain her throughout life and is faced with the necessity of winning her own way in the world . . . which is in the most primitive terms the story of the foundation and assertion of a feminine ego" (11, 12). Mary Kelley, in *Private Woman, Public Stage: Literary Domesticity in Nineteenth-Century America* (London: Oxford University Press, 1984), focuses instead on "the existence of positive and substantive elements in the domestic experience and thus in women's experience" (ix). Both approaches emphasize the psychologically internal and the architecturally interior as a response to the negative valuations of women's experience and, consequently, women's literature in most canonical formulations.

5. Amy Kaplan, *The Social Construction of American Realism* (Chicago: University of Chicago Press, 1988), 6. Readers interested in the historical debate about realism's relation to the canon of American literature, as well as in the current arguments over what exactly is its relation to the urban, industrial, and capitalist society it represents, will find useful Kaplan's excellent overview (1–14).

6. Ibid., 10.

7. See David Reynolds, *Beneath the American Renaissance* (New York: Alfred A. Knopf, 1988), on antebellum instances of "lurid urban-exposé novels" (54–91), and Janis P. Stout, *Sodoms in Eden: The City in American Fiction Before 1860* (Westport, Conn.: Greenwood Press, 1976), on urban stereotypes in popular fiction (21–43). Despite the sensationalistic bent of her report in *Darkness and Daylight*, Helen Campbell remains one of the more committed and successful reformers of her

time. After the publication in 1882 of *The Problem of the Poor,* in which she de-scribed the work of a city mission on the New York waterfront, the *New York Tribune* commissioned her to begin a study about working women in Manhattan's needle trades and department stores. These weekly exposés, begun in 1886, were collected the following year in her well-regarded study, *Prisoners of Poverty.* Using her firsthand knowledge of the conditions of life for working and poor women in New York, Campbell also produced two novels during this period, *Miss Herndon's Income* (1885) and *Miss Melinda's Opportunity* (1886), both texts in which their heroines awaken to the moral uses to which their quite considerable capital ought to be, and is, put.

8. Closely related, in subject if not in intent, to reform-minded literature and journalism are tenement tales, which approach urban life as interesting snippets of local color. Popularized by men like H. C. Bunner, the editor of *Puck,* and Columbia University literature professor Brander Matthews, these sketches self-consciously employ an Anglo-American "slummer" who visits the Lower East Side in search of interesting material. Matthews's *Vignettes of Manhattan* (1894), for instance, is narrated by Rupert de Ruyter, a Knickerbocker writer who strolls down Mulberry Bend to view humanity in all its human and comic manifesta-tions. Frequently romanticized, often idealized, such portraits of the immigrant other seem to reverse the claims of sensational journalism, representing sanitized and ultimately safe versions of the hapless poor, who live their lives with as much dignity, pretension, and comedy as any human being can muster. David Fine, in *The City, the Immigrant, and American Fiction, 1880–1920* (Metuchen, N.J.: Scare-crow Press, 1977), provides an excellent catalog of tenement tales (37–52).

9. Alan Trachtenberg, "Experiments in Another Country: Stephen Crane's City Sketches," in *American Realism,* ed. Eric J. Sundquist (Baltimore: Johns Hop-kins University Press, 1982), 138.

10. William Dean Howells, *A Hazard of New Fortunes* (1890; reprint, New York: New American Library, 1965), 159. All further references to this work will appear in the text.

11. Lucia True Ames Mead, *To Whom Much Is Given* (New York: T. Y. Crowell & Company, 1899), 28.

12. Ibid., 29–30.

13. Helen Campbell, Colonel Thomas W. Knox, and Inspector Thomas Byrnes, *Darkness and Daylight; Or, Lights and Shadows of New York Life* (Hartford, Conn.: A. D. Worthington and Company, 1892), vii. It is interesting to note that while Abbott's preface advertises gendered differences in the three accounts of New York City, the accounts are virtually indistinguishable. Although interspersed in Camp-bell's section are some tales of mission and charity work, essentially her account of "Life and Scenes in Dens of Infamy and Crime" is no less sensationalistic and certainly no more sympathetic than Byrnes's "Low Lodging-Houses of New York—Places That Foster Crime and Harbor Criminals." In fact, Campbell in-dulges in some surprisingly unsympathetic and even hostile pronouncements about the immigrant poor who struggle for survival in the tenements: "The brutal Ameri-can is of the rarest. It is because New York is less an American city than almost any other in the United States that the need for the 'Society for the Prevention of Cruelty

to Children' was so sore. As the foreign element increased, and every form of ignorance with it, drunkenness as well as *natural* brutality worked together" (170, emphasis added). Ignoring the relation between poverty, despair, drunkenness, rage, and frustration, Campbell instead makes synonymous "foreign," "ignorance," and "natural brutality."

14. Jill Conway, "Women Reformers and American Culture," *Journal of Social History* 5 (Winter 1971/72): 167.

15. Barbara Bardes and Suzanne Gossett, *Declarations of Independence: Women and Political Power in Nineteenth-Century American Fiction* (New Brunswick, N.J.: Rutgers University Press, 1990), 106. For an excellent analysis of women's reform fiction that arrives at conclusions somewhat different from my own, see their chapter on "Capitalism, Sex, and Sisterhood," 100–129.

16. Conway, "Women Reformers," 167.

17. Ibid., 166.

18. See both Carroll Smith-Rosenberg's *Disorderly Conduct: Visions of Gender in Victorian America* (New York: Alfred A. Knopf, 1985) and Mari Jo Buhle's *Women and American Socialism, 1870–1920* (Urbana: University of Illinois Press, 1983) for related discussions of women's roles during this period.

19. Robert H. Bremner, *From the Depths: The Discovery of Poverty in the United States* (New York: New York University Press, 1956), 52.

20. Margaret Sherwood, *An Experiment in Altruism* (New York: MacMillan and Company, 1895), 22. All further references to this work will appear in the text.

21. Mead, *To Whom*, 44.

22. Alice Wellington Rollins, *Uncle Tom's Tenement* (Boston: The William E. Smythe Company, 1888), 58. All further references to this work will appear in the text.

23. Joseph Lee, *Constructive and Preventive Philanthropy* (New York: The MacMillan Company, 1913), 89.

24. Campbell, Knox, and Byrnes, *Darkness and Daylight*, 311.

25. Edward Thomas Devine, *The Practice of Charity: Individual, Associated and Organized* (New York: Lentilhon & Company, 1901), 70.

26. Lyman Abbott, Preface, *Darkness and Daylight*, 52.

27. Ibid., 50.

28. Mead, *To Whom*, 33.

29. Sherwood, *Experiment*, 73.

30. Arthur Mann, *Yankee Reformers in the Urban Age* (Cambridge, Mass.: Belknap Press, 1954), 77–78. Richard Hofstadter, in *The Age of Reform* (New York: Vintage Books, 1955), points out that, as a rule, "successful resistance to reform demands required a partial incorporation of the reform program" (132). Christian socialism perhaps inadvertently aided capitalist resistance, for as Robert Bremner notes, "While public aid to the poor was neglected, or even regarded with downright hostility, private charity flourished. Those who favored ending public relief outside almshouses and infirmaries argued that private benevolence was adequate to succor the needy who were not so completely dependent as to require institutional care" (*From the Depths*, 50).

31. Quoted in Ruth Bordin, *Woman and Temperance: The Quest for Power and*

Liberty, 1873–1900 (Philadelphia: Temple University Press, 1981; reprint, New Brunswick N.J.,: Rutgers University Press, 1990), 104. By 1889, however, Bordin records that Willard had adopted a far more radical position: "Willard advocated that fundamental reform of the economic system begin with relief for the unemployed, the five-and-a-half-day week, free technical education, free school lunches, and gradual nationalization or municipal ownership of the railroads, the telegraph,· public utilities, and factories" (108).

32. Claude Reherd Flory, *Economic Criticism in American Fiction 1792–1900* (Philadelphia: University of Pennsylvania, 1936), 13.

33. Mead, *To Whom*, 28.

34. Devine, *The Practice of Charity*, 69.

35. Mead, *To Whom*, 24.

36. Margaret Deland, "The House of Rimmon" in *The Wisdom of Fools* (Boston: Houghton, Mifflin and Company, 1897), 95–97. Deland, like Howells, was a native midwesterner who became part of the established Boston literary circle. Her best-known novel, *John Ward, Preacher* (1888), addresses both religious debate and marital incompatibility. She wrote realistic literature well into the twentieth century and in 1926 was elected to the National Institute of Arts and Letters. In 1941, at the age of eighty-four, she published her autobiography, *Golden Yesterdays.*

37. Elizabeth Stuart Phelps, *Chapters from a Life* (Boston: Houghton, Mifflin and Company, 1896), 263, 265. For monographs on the life and work of Phelps, see Lori Dunn Kelly, *The Life and Works of Elizabeth Stuart Phelps, Victorian Feminist Writer* (Troy, N.Y.: Whitston, 1983), and Carol Farley Kessler, *Elizabeth Stuart Phelps* (Boston: Twayne, 1982).

38. Bardes and Gossett, in *Declarations of Independence,* for example, analyze *The Silent Partner* (110–111, 117–121) in conjunction with Howell's *A Woman's Reason* (1882), Beverley Ellison Warner's *Troubled Waters* (1885), and Mary E. Wilkins Freeman's *The Portion of Labor* (1901).

39. Phelps, *Hedged In* (Boston: Fields, Osgood, 1870). All further references to this work will appear in the text.

40. Elizabeth Stuart Phelps, *The Silent Partner, A Novel and The Tenth of January, A Short Story* (Old Westbury, N.Y.: The Feminist Press, 1983), 51. All further references to this work will appear in the text.

41. Philip S. Foner, in *The Factory Girls* (Urbana: University of Illinois Press, 1977), notes that, ironically, what engendered Harriet Farley's impassioned 1840 essay in defense and praise of factory work was an attack by Orestes A. Brownson (in the *Boston Quarterly Review*) on the chastity of female mill operatives. See Foner, 31–37, for Farley's essay and Sarah G. Bagley's more militant reply.

42. Recent feminist analyses have focused on "the community of women" in the novel and have suggested that class differences are overcome by the recognition of gender solidarity. See especially "Work and the Bridging of Social Class: Elizabeth Stuart Phelps, *The Silent Partner* (1871)," in *Unlikely Heroines: Nineteenth-Century American Women Writers and the Woman Question,* ed. Ann R. Shapiro (New York: Greenwood Press, 1987), 37–51, and Judith Fetterley, " 'Checkmate': Elizabeth Stuart Phelps's *The Silent Partner*," *Legacy* 3 (Fall 1986): 17–29.

43. See Fay M. Blake, *The Strike in the American Novel* (Metuchen, N.J.: The Scarecrow Press, 1972), for an overview of labor conflict representation. Blake's work contains an especially useful annotated bibliography of noncanonical strike fiction, 207–275.

44. Conway, "Women Reformers," 166.

45. Rebecca Harding Davis, *Life in the Iron Mills and Other Stories,* ed. Tillie Olsen (Old Westbury, N.Y.: The Feminist Press, 1985), 65.

Breaking the Sentence: Local-Color Literature and Subjugated Knowledges

LIKE MANY OF THE PROTAGONISTS in nineteenth-century women's local-color literature, Miss Lucinda, in Rose Terry Cooke's 1861 story of that title, is an eccentric middle-aged spinster who lives happily in a separate, marginal rural world. Her main companions are her animals, and her main occupation is tending them, her house, and her garden. The story is set "in a State in these Disuniting States," evincing the regional-versus-federal dialectic central to local-color literature.[1]

Cooke's treatment of Lucinda's story is satirical, suggesting that her principal audience was a federal or national one, that of an urbane Bostonian, and indeed the story was first published in the *Atlantic Monthly*. Cooke claims, however, in an opening apology that her sympathies are with commonplace rural people like Lucinda. "I have the same quick sympathy for Biddy's sorrows with Patrick [i.e., with Irish immigrants] that I have for the Empress of France. . . . So forgive me . . . patient reader, if I offer you no tragedy in high life, no sentimental history of fashion and wealth, but only a little story about a woman who could not be a heroine" (151). Yet Cooke's satirical attitude indicates a distancing from her subject, suggesting that she is viewing her from the perspective of an outsider, one who sees herself as wiser and more knowledgeable, and Lucinda as ignorant and quaint. A modern critical reader may, however, wish to resurrect the ethos of Lucinda, counterposing it against the disciplinary knowledge endorsed by the author that would colonize Lucinda and her world in a process of normalization.

One may label this a "genealogical" hermeneutic, following French theorist Michel Foucault. In the first of his lectures in *Power/Knowledge*, Foucault advocates searching for "*subjugated knowledges.*"[2] "[I]t is through the re-appearance of . . . these local popular knowledges, these disqualified knowledges, that criticism performs its work" (82). The knowledge Foucault has in mind is "a particular, local, regional knowledge, a differential knowledge incapable of unanimity" (82); it is a "minor" knowledge (85). The critic's job, he suggests, is to "emancipate historical knowledges from [their] subjection" within "the hierarchical order of power associated with science" and to render these silenced knowledges "capable of opposition and of struggle against the coercion of a theoretical, unitary, formal and scientific discourse" (85). The location of "resistant practices," alternatives to "totalizing" disciplines, is thus a vital task for the modern political critic.[3]

In employing a genealogical approach to Cooke's story the critic discovers that like many characters in local-color literature, Lucinda evinces a marginal, local, alternative knowledge that is cast in opposition to unifying translocal disciplines. However, she is forced to renounce this knowledge and to conform to imposed norms. The disciplinary process is effected by a French dancing master, Monsieur Jean Leclerc, whose name, "the clerk," suggests the bureaucratic functionary whose chief historical mission has been to impose rationalizing disciplines upon the populace. Leclerc enters Lucinda's world when he helps her recapture a pig who had gotten loose.

Lucinda's relationship with her animals, Leclerc feels, is too undisciplined, a view the author shares. Indeed, her animals lived in her house on equal terms with her: "Her cat had its own chair . . . her dog, a rug and basket," and her blind crow had a "special nest of flannel and cotton" (156). Lucinda does not believe in imposing a hierarchical disciplinary grid upon her creatures. She feels "that animals have feelings . . . and are of 'like passions'" with people and that they have souls (162–163). The author believes that Lucinda's undisciplinary practice is out of line (162–164).

Once Leclerc is installed in Lucinda's house (he had injured himself during the pig chase and she is nursing him back to health), he begins disciplining her animals. He commences by "subduing" her German spaniel, Fun; the narrator cites (apparently nonironically) a legitimizing proverb: "'Women and spaniels,' the world knows, 'like kicking'" (168). Leclerc then takes on Lucinda's other dog, Toby. "[A] few well-timed slaps, administered with vigor, cured Toby of his worst tricks: though every blow made Miss Lucinda wince, and almost shook her good opinion of Monsieur Leclerc" (169). Leclerc also disposes of her pet pig when he becomes too unmanageable.

The taming process is applied not only to the animals but also to Lucinda herself. A crucial episode in the story concerns Lucinda's dancing lessons. Dancing here represents an alien discipline to which the rural woman tries awkwardly to conform. The other students laugh at the odd outfits she wears to the lessons, signifying her nonconformity; her "peculiar" practice of the steps is a further sign of her deviance (176). During the days in which she is learning to dance her animals are neglected.

The denouement of the story is that Lucinda and Leclerc marry, and the final note is one of ridicule against Lucinda for her "sentimental" views of animals. In particular, Lucinda's willful ignorance of the fate of her pig, whom Leclerc had had slaughtered and sold as ham, is rightly seen as morally corrupt, but the author herself does not allow Lucinda to develop an alternative solution to the pig's rambunctiousness, which she might have done had she not been under the influence of Leclerc and his exchange-value ethic. In short, the story is about the erosion and elision of Lucinda's relationship/use-value ethic and its replacement through the imposition of an alien discipline, metonymically represented by the dancing; it is about the colonization of Lucinda and her world.[4]

Lucinda's subdual reflects the fact that homogenizing institutions were gaining hegemony in the nineteenth-century Western world. Leclerc's French origin unintentionally highlights the fact that the normalizing disciplines that were encroaching upon rural eccentricity by mid-century were rooted in Cartesian Enlightenment rationalism. Much of Foucault's work has been devoted to describing the process of this encroachment.

In *Discipline and Punish* he identifies the prison as the model disciplinary grid to which other modern institutions such as hospitals and asylums conform. In the first volume of his *History of Sexuality,* Foucault focuses upon the emergence of pseudoscientific disciplines such as sexology, which "entomologized" sexual lifestyles into species and subspecies of deviance, thus ideologically colonizing people's life-world.[5]

All these developments are part of what Husserl called the "mathematization" of the world effected by the imposition of the Cartesian/Newtonian paradigm, that material reality operates as a machine. Decades before Foucault, Marxist Frankfurt School theorists Max Horkheimer and Theodor Adorno saw the rationalizing process as a form of dominance. Transforming the world of nature "into mere objectivity," the Cartesian paradigm effects "the extirpation of animism."[6] Its practices, as seen in the scientific method, are dictatorial and manipulative (9). It requires the "subdual of difference, particularities" (22). In the impartiality of scientific knowledge, "that which is powerless has wholly lost any means of expression" (23).

Horkheimer and Adorno see the confrontation between the witch,

Circe, and Odysseus in Homer's epic allegorically as a representation of this process. Circe turns Odysseus's men into pigs; the pig was a sacred animal to Demeter, which connects Circe to this ancient cult (71). "Miss Lucinda" may be seen as a reversal of this ancient story; it is not the Greek goddess who is triumphant in this story with her "insurrectionary" holistic knowledges but rather the representative of modern mathematizing, unitary discourse, the French dancing master.

The literature of the nineteenth-century New England local-color school, which was dominated by women, records in one of its principal subtexts the clash between dominant, colonizing, mathematizing disciplines and the rural, eccentric culture Foucault saw as having counterhegemonic potential. Scores of stories concern marginal communities peopled by deviant, often witchlike women who live in predisciplinary peace with their animals in a green-world environment. At times the authors were sympathetic to the characters whose lives were being erased by the encroaching disciplines. At other times the authors seem to ally themselves with the forces of "progress," as Cooke does in "Miss Lucinda," joining in the colonization of their characters.

Mikhail Bakhtin notes that through much of Western history there has been a kind of linguistic dialectic between centrifugal and centripetal forces: the former tending toward a unitary "Cartesian," "official" language; the latter toward diffused regional dialects and vernaculars (heteroglossia).[7] Throughout the Middle Ages until the early modern period Latin was the dominant official language. Vernaculars were unofficial, oral languages, used in rural and domestic environments. Latin was employed in official institutions, such as the Church and the university. Women were, of course, barred from this official discourse.

As the modern states began to take shape, casting a unitary identity upon their territory, the imposition of a standard, "official" vernacular upon all regions became imperative. This process may be seen as a colonization, another instance of the imposition of a centralized unitary grid upon regional eccentricity, identified by Foucault. In his study of the process in France, Pierre Bourdieu sees the repression of dialect by "official languages" as a form of "symbolic violence," reflecting a kind of class struggle.[8] "[T]he most striking" feature of the forced adoption of official language "is the silence to which those dispossessed of the official language are condemned . . . lacking the means of legitimate expression, they do not speak but are spoken to."[9]

I would argue that there appears to be a correlation between the eclipse of use-value production (with its personalist, eccentric character) by production for exchange and industrial production (with its unified, quantitative character) and the repression of regional eccentricity in language—dialect—by an official, standardized linguistic economy.[10] Indeed, Elsa Nettels notes that a common metaphor in nineteenth-century thinking about language treated it as "verbal currency." Words were seen as being "coined and put in circulation. . . . Speakers careless of the standard keep 'counterfeit coin in circulation' but in time 'usage may stamp it current' and make it 'legal tender.'"[11]

The imposition of official standard English versus the use of dialect was a hotly discussed issue in the United States in the nineteenth century. William Dean Howells, for example, the subject of Nettels's study, encouraged the use of dialect in literature (and thereby helped foster the local-color school), although he evinced ambivalence toward it in his own writing.

After the Civil War the power and authority of the regions were increasingly replaced by the national government, a process that encouraged the acceptance of a national linguistic standard. Regionalist writers were, like Howells and Sarah Orne Jewett, torn between affirming the authority of the region and acceding to the federalizing imperative. In his study of Jewett, *"A White Heron" and the Question of Minor Literature,* Louis A. Renza concludes that Jewett is essentially a federalist writer.

Renza develops his case through theory elaborated by French critics Gilles Deleuze and Felix Guattari in their study of Kafka. Although their theory of "minor" literature has some apparent applications to Jewett— indeed to all women writers—the fact that for them "minor" equates with "modernist" suggests the limitations inherent in this approach, since many of the writers they deal with—Beckett, Joyce, Kafka—have been accorded major critical status. What is attractive in Deleuze and Guattari's theory is their idea of "deterritorialization." One of the hallmarks of minor literature, according to them, is that it is written in a "deterritorialized language."[12] To write from such a position means "to find one's own point of underdevelopment, one's own *patois* [dialect], one's own third world" (33). Their theories seem particularly relevant to the writings of the women local colorists whose works are still considered minor and who arguably wrote from a deterritorialized position within the patriarchal state.

Renza recognizes the applicability of these ideas to Jewett. A story like "A White Heron" (1886) can be seen as representing "'points of nonculture and underdevelopment, the zones of a linguistic third world' intent on sabotaging the major language of American patriarchal culture."[13] The story concerns a confrontation between an urban ornithologist, a representative of the scientific disciplines identified by Foucault, and a preliterate rural girl, over the location of a white heron, which the man wishes to kill and stuff for his collection. In the end the girl refuses to reveal the bird's whereabouts, thus remaining loyal to her woodland sanctuary and refusing to capitulate to the demands of science. "No, she must keep silence!"[14]

Renza recognizes the exclamation point as the moment when "Jewett herself inscribes her regionalist-ideological resistance" to federalist culture; it is "a positive act of regionalist resistance" (54). Thus, Renza argues, one can see the story as "an ideological allegory" of "rejection of the postbellum federalist world" (48). "The *Gemeinschaft* of Jewett's . . . writing . . . replaces [Parrington's] main currents with 'Maine' currents or narratives concerning 'country by-ways' or other local topoi" (47). Renza, however, who practices deconstructive criticism, proceeds to deconstruct this intepretation, arguing finally (a point he does not deconstruct) that Jewett ultimately has a "nonironic federalist perspective" (56). Using Jewett's 1893 preface to *Deephaven,* in which she claims she was motivated by a desire to make "the people of [the] state . . . acquainted with one another," Renza maintains, "Jewett's writing virtually surrenders to American Union demands that regionalist subcultures underwrite its *e pluribus unum* ethos" (62).[15]

Renza, like others who have recognized what he calls the "regionalist/union binary" (47) in the writing of Jewett and other local colorists, ignores, neglects, or does not see the feminist subtext in that "binary." It was not simply a matter of identifying with their region against homogenizing, federalizing tendencies; it was also and perhaps principally a matter of defending their own life-world against the encroachments of modern normalizing disciplines that would relegate it to the status of deviant.

Two less-well-known works by Jewett are key to this interpretation: her novel *A Country Doctor* (1884) and a story, "An Autumn Holiday" (1880). The novel, which concerns the then unorthodox project of a young girl to become a doctor, is centrally concerned with deviance. As I have proposed elsewhere, it is not just the deviant notion of a woman having a professional career that is at issue, but also the question of deviance from gender norms.[16] By the time the novel was published the theories of the sexologists, especially those of Richard von Krafft-Ebing in the *Psychopathia Sexualis,* were well known. The latter work is a series of "case studies" of people who were "tainted with antipathic sexual instinct."[17] Oliver Wendell Holmes's parody of the term *antipathy* in his 1885 novel *A Mortal Antipathy* suggests the extent to which Krafft-Ebing's theories had been popularized.

Jewett's novel appears to be, on one level, a repudiation of the Krafft-Ebing notion of deviance, sexology being a signal instance of the Foucauldian normalizing discipline. The main character, Nan Prince, has the earmarks of what Krafft-Ebing called a "viragint," a species of woman who adopted a "mannish" style and was attracted to other women. Although

Nan does have a crush on a female classmate (which Jewett sees as normal), she was not "the sort of girl who tried to be mannish."[18] Nevertheless, like Krafft-Ebing's "female urning" (another species of female deviant), Nan is a tomboy: she "may chiefly be found in the haunt of boys. She is their rival in play. . . . Love for art finds a substitute in the pursuits of the sciences" (*Psychopathia*, 399). Similarly, Nan (who, as noted, becomes a physician). displays a "lack of skill and liking for female occupations" (*Psychopathia*, 419) and has a "bold and tomboyish style" (*Psychopathia*, 420). In one of the central episodes of the novel, Nan quickly responds in a crisis and sets a man's dislocated shoulder while her suitor stands helplessly by, feeling "weak and womanish, and somehow [wishing] it had been he who could play the doctor" (266). In this novel Jewett was resisting the normalizing discipline of sexology, affirming instead the right of women to follow their own "deviant" bent.

An even more powerful rejection of normalization occurs in Jewett's "An Autumn Holiday." This story concerns Daniel Gunn, a retired militia captain, who "got sun-struck" and comes to believe he is his dead sister Patience.[19] He begins wearing her clothes, adopting her feminine manners, and participating in traditionally female activities, such as the sewing bees of the Female Missionary Society. In short, he is a transvestite, although Jewett does not use this or any other derogatory term to classify him.

Rather than ship their old neighbor off to an asylum, however, the villagers decide to accommodate him. One woman even makes him a dress in his size because his sister's clothes are a tight fit. Rather than force him, therefore, into a prefabricated form, the form is adjusted to him—unlike Miss Lucinda, who is forced to conform.

The story was originally entitled "Miss Daniel Gunn," but somewhere in the federalizing, normalizing editorial process it got changed to the more respectable "Autumn Holiday." Yet Jewett's central point in this story is to endorse acceptance of deviance. Despite their bemusement, the townspeople are compassionate toward Daniel and do not stigmatize him as "other." This story, I contend, reflects a local resistance to normalizing disciplines of the type identified by Foucault.

The oppositional culture found in the literature of the New England local-color school, which originated with Harriet Beecher Stowe in the 1830s, is rooted therefore in a resistance to disciplinary knowledges and practices that annulled or colonized women's life-worlds.[20] It is upon this subjugated knowledge—a paradigm case of the local, deviant culture Foucault saw as insurrectionary—that I choose to focus the rest of this article. It goes without saying, therefore, that I believe the term *local color*, despite its connotations of "minor" and "inferior" (or perhaps because of them), is a more insurrectionary one than the tamer, more acceptable, *regionalist*.

Local-color literature is known for its emphasis upon regional particularities and eccentricities, upon local differences in setting, clothing, manners, and dialect. What has not been understood heretofore was that the women writers' willingness to use dialect and slang was itself an insurrectionary, heretical gesture. Ann Douglas notes it was a violation of the ideological "cult of true womanhood," because "ladies were known by their correct speech." As Stowe and the other local-color writers knew, "The vernacular and the wit it inspired were officially off limits to American women."[21] Stowe, however, said she had an "unsanctified liking for slang."[22]

The first (in historical terms) disciplinary practice to which the women local colorists evinced unambiguous resistance was Calvinism. While its origins as a theology antedate the emergence of Foucauldian disciplines, by the early to mid-nineteenth century Calvinism had reified into a set of social practices, a disciplinary order of the Foucauldian type, which forced upon women an ideology of subservient conformity, a life of intellectual and emotional stasis, and often physical deprivation. Stowe's story "The Deacon's Dilemma" (1860) adumbrates the theme of the oppressed wife under the sway of a tyrannical husband who imposes a Calvinist ideological grid upon her. She is forbidden to have a flower garden, for example, because it is not useful. Too "meek" to protest, she remains nevertheless inwardly resentful. "The poor woman had a kind of chronic heartsickness . . . but she never knew exactly what it was she wanted."[23] The husband's dictum, therefore, elides the woman's desire, for personal expression, for community, for deviant or "local" color—all of which the garden represents.

Stowe's two great local-color novels, *The Minister's Wooing* (1859) and *Oldtown Folks* (1869), focus centrally on the women's culture of resistance to Calvinism. In *Oldtown Folks* Stowe clearly sees Calvinism as a tyrannical unifying disciplinary order against which she affirms the undisciplined behavior of Sam Lawson and the disorderly and subversively diverse heterogeneity of Grandmother Badger's household. Stowe notes that the Calvinist position is that disciplinary order must be imposed lest the "depravity of matter" get out of hand. In the "universe . . . everything was tending to slackness, shiftlessness, unthrift"; to counter this entropy, Calvinists believed one must rigorously "keep things in their places."[24]

Stowe's resistance to this thesis is embodied in the comic character Sam Lawson, the indolent, undisciplined "village do-nothing" (30). Lawson's dilatory attempt to repair a clock metonymically reflects a clash between the modern clock-dominated sense of time, which Stowe connects with Calvinist discipline, and the predisciplinary ethos of Sam's rural mentality. The narrator recounts the incident:

> I shall never forget the wrath and dismay . . . he roused . . . by the leisurely way in which, after having taken our own venerable kitchen clock to pieces and strewn the fragments all over the kitchen, he would roost over it in endless incubation, telling stories, entering into long-winded theological discussions, smoking pipes, and giving histories of all the other clocks in Oldtown, with occasional memoirs of those in Needmore, the North Parish, and Podunk. (32)

His attitude toward the clock is animistic: "clocks can't be druv. . . . They's jest got to be humored" (32). Sam explains further, when he is urged to hurry up and stick to his task, that he "can't be druv" either (33). Sam, therefore, exemplifies an antidisciplinary, resistant posture. Significantly, he is not governed by linear instrumental rationality but by an associative meandering narrative style that does not excise the details it encounters, considering them irrelevant or unimportant, but embraces them in a holistic, inclusive vision—a style affirmed in other local-color works.[25] And, like many local-color characters, Sam has a special connection with animals; indeed he articulates what would today be called an animal rights position: "I can't bear to see no kind o' critter in torment. . . . Fish has their rights as well as any on us" (31). He thus blurs the boundaries between the species, resisting the hierarchical discipline of the "great chain of being" in favor of a nonimperialistic, nonhierarchical vision, similar to that practiced by Lucinda before the arrival of Monsieur Leclerc.

The centrum of Stowe's culture of resistance is Grandmother Badger's kitchen. There a full range of characters—blacks, American Indians, whites, from all classes and ages and both genders, as well as animals—mingle and communicate in relatively nondiscriminatory, nonjudgmental fashion. No discourse is privileged: "So passed an evening in my grandmother's kitchen,—where religion, theology, politics, the gossip of the day, and the legends of the supernatural all conspired to weave a fabric of thought quaint and various" (76).[26]

Modern disciplines and professions are unknown in Oldtown. Each person is accomplished in a variety of tasks and conversant in a range of "unofficial" knowledges. Nervy Randall, for example, one of the most engaging characters, is a spinster who knows how to navigate a ship, teaches Latin, raises bees, makes butter. She is also a knowledgeable herbalist. She exemplifies Marx's celebrated vision of unalienated labor articulated in *The German Ideology* where one can "hunt in the morning, fish in the afternoon, rear cattle in the evening, criticize after dinner, just as [one has] a mind, without ever becoming hunter, fisherman, cowherd, or critic."[27] None of these tasks has congealed into a profession or discipline and none has priority over another. In the preindustrial, predisciplinary world of Oldtown, people operate more at random, not in accordance with a professional "career" imperative; nor are they allocated to special institutional spaces. The community is heterogeneous. A striking sign of this noncompartmentalized space is the acceptance of dogs in church.

Resistance to Calvinism as an alien discipline is also a major theme of Rose Terry Cooke's. In most of her works that discipline is imposed on wives by husbands. Several Cooke stories depict oppressive husbands who deprive their wives of even the most meager physical and emotional sustenance. The most dramatic of these are "Freedom Wheeler's Controversy with Providence" (1877) and "Mrs. Flint's Married Experience" (1880). An early story, "Uncle Josh" (1857), resembles Stowe's "Deacon's Dilemma" in portraying a woman dying of physical and emotional deprivation because all variety, all pleasure, all recreation has been pressed out of her life.

One of Cooke's most powerful critiques of the Calvinist discipline of the body comes in her story "Too Late" (1875). Hannah Blair is a pathetic example of a woman who has been repressed into a near catatonic emotional state. Her mother's house signifies the inner erasure of these women's lives. It "was kept in a state of spotless purity. . . . Flies never intruded there; spiders still less." It is "speckless" and without decoration. Similarly, in her domestic rituals "no flour was spilled . . . no milk ever slopped from an overfull pail; no shoe ever brought in mud."[28] In short, it is a place of impeccable order.

Brought up in such an atmosphere Hannah spends much of her time relentlessly preparing her trousseau with "diligent sternness." Yet underneath, "her delight [in her fiancé] was full even to oppression, when she sat by herself and sewed like an automaton" (220). Hannah learns, however, that her betrothed had committed some unspecified indiscretion and cancels the wedding, refusing to see him. Later she contracts a loveless marriage with another and runs a rigorously disciplined household. Only on her deathbed does she reveal what an agonizing psychological struggle it had been to impose upon herself the discipline she believed was required by her religion to reject her suitor. After hearing her decision, he had called up to her window. She recounts, "I was wrung to my heart's core. . . . I was upon the floor, with my arms wound about the bedrail and my teeth shut like a vice, lest I should listen to the voice of nature. . . . I thought flesh would fail in the end; but it did not. I conquered then and after" (232). The image of a body being tortured through the

imposition of a discipline could not be more graphic; it is a painful figura-
tion of the conquering or colonizing of the local body by a translocal
ideological discipline—in this case, Calvinism.

Mary E. Wilkins Freeman, one of the later local colorists, continued
Cooke's critique of Calvinism; in her treatment, its religious roots are
buried in the past, so that it seems to be a mindless internalized discipline
perpetuated as a social practice for no apparent reason. In her 1899 introduction to *Pembroke*, for example, Freeman says that she saw this propen-
sity as pathological, citing as an example the story of "a man who objected
to the painting of the kitchen floor, and who quarreled furiously with his
wife concerning the same. When she persisted . . . and the floor was
painted, he refused to cross it to his dying day, and always, to his great
inconvenience . . . walked around it."[29] Many of her characters seem similarly trapped in the mechanism of meaningless disciplines. "An Honest
Soul" (1884), for example, records the frustrating experience of Martha
Patch, an elderly spinster who supports herself as a seamstress. After
completing two quilts, which takes two weeks, Martha notices that she
has switched the material and thus has to redo her work. Upon completing this laborious task, however, she realizes she had it right the first time,
and thus has to redo the quilts a third time. Meanwhile, she is physically
exhausted and starving. The oppressive sense of compulsion in this story
is so strong that one almost senses the presence of a demonic power
controlling Martha's life, clamping her within its mechanism.

Joanna, a character in Jewett's *Country of the Pointed Firs* (1896), similarly imposes a self-flagellatory discipline upon herself. This woman exiles
herself to a solitary, austere, marginal life on an island in punishment for
having committed the "unpardonable sin" of blaspheming God in the
wake of a suitor's betrayal. Although the other members of the community are accepting and compassionate toward Joanna and respectful of her
decision, they clearly see her behavior as purposelessly destructive. Almira
Todd, the main character, an herbalist-healer, considers Calvinism
the major source of Joanna's plight. In commenting upon Joanna's funeral
on the island, Mrs. Todd notes, "She'd got most o' the wild sparrows as
tame as could be, livin' out there so long among 'em, and one flew up and
lit on the coffin an' began to sing while [the minister] was speakin'. He
was put out by it, an' acted as if he didn't know whether to stop or go on.
I may have been prejudiced, but I wa'n't the only one thought the poor
little bird done the best of the two."[30]

Like *Oldtown Folks*, *The Country of the Pointed Firs* and many Jewett
stories may be read as affirming an alternative to the colonizing disciplinary grids of modern industrial culture. Like Stowe's novel and the other
local-color works, it appears to have been conceived dialectically as a

negative criticism of the homogenizing, federalizing tendencies of the modern world. Several characters here as in other Jewett works lament the loss of eccentricity. Mrs. Fosdick, a visitor, exclaims, "What a lot o' queer folks there used to be about here. . . . Everybody's just like everybody else, now" (60). Mrs. Todd agrees: "In these days the young folks is all copy-cats" (60). The title character in "Miss Debby's Neighbors" (1883), a tailoress, complains that business has fallen off now that people are buying "cheap, ready-made clothes." "She always insisted . . . that the railroads were making everybody look and act of a piece, and that young folks were more alike than people of her own day."[31] In another story, a local herbalist, Mrs. Goodsoe, also blames mass transportation and communication systems: "['T] was never my idee that we was meant to know what's goin' on all over the world to once. . . . [I]n old times . . . they stood in their lot an' place, and were n't all just alike, either, same as pine-spills."[32]

Mrs. Goodsoe specifically attacks modern medicine and its disregard of herbal remedies. Modern doctors, she says, are "bilin' over with book-larnin' [but] . . . truly ignorant of what to do for the sick. . . . Book-fools I call 'em" (57). Rather, people's health was best ensured through the use of local herbs: "[F]olks was meant to be doctored with the stuff that grew right about 'em; 't was sufficient and so ordered" (59).

But even Mrs. Goodsoe feels her knowledge of herbal traditions is weak compared with her mother's, and the narrator—as in *The Country of the Pointed Firs,* a younger, "outsider" woman—is less hostile to modern "progress" than she. It is this mediation of the outsider perspective, the intrusion of urban mathematizing disciplines—modern medicine in this case—that leads Renza to characterize Jewett as a federalist writer. Yet Jewett, unlike Cooke in "Miss Lucinda," manifests a genuine ambivalence: the local customs remain as a strong countervalence to the forces of disciplinary "progress."

Mrs. Goodsoe's insistence that the herbs be locally grown points to a central tenet of the community ethos celebrated in *The Country of the Pointed Firs* and other local-color works. In this preindustrial, predisciplinary environment, time is not measured by the clock, goods are not appreciated for their abstract exchange value, and people are not uprooted and homogenized through mass media stereotypes. Rather, they remain rooted in their own eccentric (de)territory; their produce comes from their own familiar environment—Mrs. Todd grows her own herbs and/or gathers them from local habitats. She ministers to people as individuals with histories and not in accordance with abstract symptoms and diagnoses.

Mrs. Todd's comments about the sparrow on Joanna's coffin suggests the nature of religion envisaged in *The Country of the Pointed Firs.* Unlike Calvinism, with its abstract alien systems, Jewett proposes a kind of panpsychism, a religion in which the transcendent is embodied in the everyday. Rather than a religion of monotheistic mastery, what we see in *Pointed Firs* is rather a kind of heterogeneous polytheism. The gods are local, unhypostasized presences.

Unlike Jewett, Mary E. Wilkins Freeman focuses less on the alternative community and more on the resisting practices of women whose life-worlds are being threatened by the intrusion and imposition of alien disciplinary forces. Several concern critiques of asylums. "Sister Liddy" (1891) is set in an "almshouse" where the poor—young and old—and the insane are kept. One of the inmates, Polly Moss, a sadly deformed woman, tells stories about her fictitious well-to-do sister. Her fantasies constitute a kind of "anticipatory illumination," an imagined alternative to her own be-nighted, confined existence.³³ "A Mistaken Charity" (1891) concerns the escape of two sisters, one deaf and the other blind, from an asylum, back to their own home, the details of which are then lovingly embraced. In the asylum they had been forced to wear uniforms, which include caps that the sisters despise. "[N]othing could transform these two unpolished old women into two nice old ladies. They did not take kindly to white lace caps and delicate neckerchiefs."³⁴ When they leave, they place the caps defiantly on bedposts, thus repudiating the imposition of sameness. Two other Freeman stories—"Bouncing Bet" (1900) and "The Elm Tree" (1903)—concern rejections of asylum life.

In several Freeman stories the lives of women who are living peacefully with their animals or children are violated by the intrusion of an alien authority who destroys their world. Often the authority figure resembles the modern social worker-bureaucrat who has the power to intervene in people's private life-worlds. In "Brakes and White Vi'lets" (1887) a girl's father claims custody from her grandmother, using a medical theory that the grandmother's home is too damp and will bring about consumption. He thus removes the child; the grandmother has the choice of moving to an alien environment with the girl or remaining in her beloved home. She finally decides to move, requesting wistfully that "a root of white vi'lets an' some brakes" be dug up, "so I kin take 'em with me" (117)—a pathetic attempt to keep her local roots with her even while acceding to their destruction.³⁵

"A Gatherer of Simples" (1884) similarly concerns a rural "yarb woman," an herbalist, who informally adopts a child only to have its urban grandmother claim custody so it can be raised properly. The child runs back to her adoptive mother, however, and the grandmother dies, so the story ends happily. "Old Woman Magoun" (1905) is a tragic version of a similar plot. Here again it is a grandmother who is raising a granddaugh-ter; in this case it is the father who claims custody when the child is entering puberty. He thinks the grandmother is raising her too narrowly; she thinks he intends to sell the child into prostitution. To save her, the grandmother allows her to eat the poisonous berries of the deadly night-shade, which kill her. Thus, the old woman is willing to use her local knowledge of herbs perversely, to save the child from being inscribed in the circulatory system of patriarchal power/knowledge, which entails the exchange of women.

In "A Poetess" (1891), another poignant Freeman story, the alien discipline that destroys the title character's life-world is that of aesthetic criteria. Betsey Dole, another impoverished spinster, lives happily in her green-world bower, which is "all a gay spangle with sweet-peas and red-flowering beans, and flanked with feathery asparagus."[36] Betsey's calling is writing poetry, particularly verse for local consumption, occasional mourning poetry, which she writes to console neighbors who are grieving. Her reward comes not from having her work praised by distinguished critics or published in famous journals—and thus being stamped in the currency of academic literary discourse—but rather in the emotional comfort it brings her friends. Unfortunately, however, she learns that a local clerical authority, a minister, has branded her work as sentimentalist trash. Accepting his verdict, she burns all her work and soon dies. The silence and erasure imposed upon this woman by a translocal discipline could not be more graphic.

In *A Room of One's Own* Virginia Woolf says women writers must "break the sentence" if they are to express their own subjugated knowledges.[37] Woolf means that women must break with past rhetorical traditions, but one may interpret her phrase more broadly as implying that women must resist the disciplinary sentences imposed upon them that obscure their truths.

In this study I have suggested that women writers of the local-color school dealt centrally with the colonization of local traditions and life-worlds by translocal homogenizing disciplines. Miss Lucinda's awkward execution of alien dance steps suggests the coerced conformity such colonization entailed. In certain of Sarah Orne Jewett's works it becomes apparent that sexology was one of the central normalizing disciplines that threatened to erase women's anomalous lifestyles in the late nineteenth century. In works by Stowe, Cooke, and Freeman the disciplinary practices of Calvinism are resisted; Stowe's character Sam Lawson in *Oldtown Folks* comes to exemplify local eccentricitry and nonconformity.

In American history the process of cultural colonization was evinced principally in the federalizing imperative that gained hegemony in the post–Civil War period, which encouraged the dominance of Cartesian mathematizing, normalizing disciplines such as sexology over women's "deviant" life-worlds. Earlier a comparable disciplinary role was played by the ideology of Calvinism.

Although the local-color writers were unambiguous in their resistance to Calvinism, they were less clear about the claims of federalism and modern science. Nevertheless, in their works may be found the voice of resistance to the disciplinary sentences imposed upon rural eccentricity and deviant life-worlds in the nineteenth century.

In my view it is imperative that these subjugated, resistant voices be resurrected so as to generate alternative literary and political history. Necessarily, such a process engenders political questions such as why these knowledges were subjugated in the first place, and why the authors sometimes capitulated to that colonization, as in "Miss Lucinda." The principal purpose of our critical endeavor, however, must be to reveal the existence of these counterhegemonic tendencies and thus to provide ourselves with elided knowledges that can enrich our own struggle against cultural imperialism. In this sense the rewriting of literary history to include the perceptions disclosed in this study is a political task.

NOTES

1. Rose Terry Cooke, "Miss Lucinda," in *"How Celia Changed Her Mind" and Selected Stories,* ed. Elizabeth Ammons (New Brunswick, N.J.: Rutgers University Press, 1986), 152. Further references are cited in the text. For a discussion of the local-color tradition see Josephine Donovan, *New England Local Color Literature: A Women's Tradition* (1983; reprint, New York: Continuum, 1988).

2. Michel Foucault, *Power/Knowledge: Selected Interviews and Other Writings, 1972–1977,* ed. Colin Gordon (New York: Pantheon, 1980), 81. Further references are cited in the text.

3. Herbert L. Dreyfus and Paul Rabinow, *Michel Foucault: Beyond Structuralism and Hermeneutics* (Chicago: University of Chicago Press, 1982), 202.

4. The terms *use-value* and *exchange-value production* are Marxist. The former involves creation of goods for immediate use, where the material produced usually retains a more personal, emotionally charged, or qualitative character, and where production relations are generally more personal. Under exchange-value production, which entails the circulation of emotionally neutralized goods, relationships are based upon abstract quantification. See Karl Marx, *Capital,* in *Karl Marx: Selected Writings,* ed. David McLellan (New York: Oxford University Press, 1977), 422–423.

5. Michel Foucault, *Discipline and Punish: The Birth of the Prison,* trans. Alan Sheridan (New York: Pantheon, 1977), and *Histoire de la sexualité,* vol. 1, *La Volonté de savoir* (Paris: Gallimard, 1976).

The term *colonization of the life-world* is from Jürgen Habermas. See especially his *Theory of Communicative Action,* vol. 2, *Lifeworld and System: A Critique of Functionalist Reason* (Boston: Beacon, 1987), 355–357 and 391–396.

6. Theodor W. Adorno and Max Horkheimer, *Dialectic of Enlightenment,* trans. John Cumming (1944; reprint, New York: Continuum, 1988), 5. Further references are cited in the text.

7. M. M. Bakhtin, *The Dialogic Imagination: Four Essays,* ed. Michael Holquist, trans. Caryl Emerson (Austin: University of Texas Press, 1981), 271.

8. Pierre Bourdieu, *Ce que parler veut dire: l'économie des échanges linguistiques* (Paris: Fayard, 1982), 36, 137. Bourdieu also develops correlatives between linguistic and market exchange (59ff.)

9. John B. Thompson, *Studies in the Theory of Ideology* (Berkeley: University of California Press, 1984), 46

10. In general, Marxists have correlated the ascendancy of the mathematizing paradigm with the rise of mercantile capitalism and exchange-value production. See especially Alfred Sohn-Rethel, *Intellectual and Manual Labour: A Critique of Epistemology,* trans. Martin Sohn-Rethel (1978; reprint, Atlantic Highlands, N.J.: Humanities Press, 1983).

11. Elsa Nettels, *Language, Race, and Social Class in Howells's America* (Lexington: University Press of Kentucky, 1988), 19.

12. Gilles Deleuze and Felix Guattari, *Kafka: Pour une littérature mineure* (Paris: Editions de Minuit, 1975), 30. Further references are cited in the text.

13. Louis A. Renza, *"A White Heron" and the Question of Minor Literature* (Madison: University of Wisconsin Press, 1984), 35. Further references are cited in the text.

14. Sarah Orne Jewett, "A White Heron" (1886), in *The Country of the Pointed Firs and Other Stories* (Garden City, N.Y.: Doubleday Anchor, 1956), 170.

15. Sarah Orne Jewett, *Deephaven and Other Stories,* ed. Richard Cary (New Haven, Conn.: College and University Press, 1966), 32.

16. Josephine Donovan, *After the Fall: the Demeter-Persephone Myth in Wharton, Cather, and Glasgow* (University Park: Pennsylvania State University Press, 1989), 37–41.

17. Richard von Krafft-Ebing, *Psychopathia Sexualis, with Especial Reference to the Antipathic Sexual Instinct,* trans. F. J. Rebman (New York: Medical Art Agency, 1906), 285. Further references are cited in the text.

18. Sarah Orne Jewett, *A Country Doctor* (Boston: Houghton, Mifflin, 1884), 160. Further references are cited in the text.

19. Sarah Orne Jewett, "An Autumn Holiday," in *Country By-Ways* (Boston: Houghton, Mifflin, 1881), 153.

20. While not technically in the local-color tradition, Stowe's great novel *Uncle Tom's Cabin* may also be seen in terms of the regional/federal (normalizing) dialectic, if "regional" is seen as the women's sphere, which resisted practices sanctioned in the federal public sphere. It is well known that Stowe was motivated to write her novel because of the passage of the federal Fugitive Slave Law in 1850. That law imposed upon all citizens the requirement of returning fugitive slaves to their owners. Stowe counseled civil disobedience to this law in her novel, in the name of a women's-sphere ethic of caring. In other words, Stowe proposed resistance to the imposition of a legal "discipline" that would annul a marginal women's ethic

and culture. Many of the white women in the novel form a culture of resistance, helping blacks to escape from slavery, in opposition to the federal law.

21. Ann Douglas, Introduction to *Uncle Tom's Cabin* (New York: Penguin, 1981), 15.

22. Ibid., 16; see also Nettels, *Language, Race,* 34.

23. Harriet Beecher Stowe, "The Deacon's Dilemma," *Independent* 12 (November 22, 1860): 1.

24. Harriet Beecher Stowe, *Oldtown Folks* (1869; reprint, Boston: Houghton, Mifflin, 1894), 94. Further references are cited in the text.

25. A characteristic format used in the local-color story is a meandering, undisciplined, gossipy narration. In "Miss Debby's Neighbors" the complaint is made about this style that the narrator's method "of going around Robin Hood's barn between the beginning of her story and its end can hardly be followed at all" (Sarah Orne Jewett, "Miss Debby's Neighbors," in *The Mate of the Daylight and Friends Ashore* [Boston: Houghton Mifflin, 1884], 191.)

Rather than the linear, progressive plot of instrumental rationality, these stories progress in a seemingly undirected manner. "An Autumn Holiday" is fairly typical. It opens with a young woman, a Jewett persona, wandering through the fields, stopping here and there, to describe the setting in some detail. Eventually she discovers an isolated rural home where two sisters are spinning. The women begin reminiscing; one story associatively sparks another. Out of this gossipy oral history finally emerges the central tale, the story of Daniel Gunn. "The Courting of Sister Wisby" (1887) similarly concerns two women gathering herbs for the first several pages, until gradually the older herbalist reminisces about "Sister Wisby," and thus the central tale emerges. Numerous other stories use this (un)convention.

26. Grandmother Badger is herself a Calvinist and is classist, but Stowe's egalitarian vision is unambiguous as an ideal, however compromised it may have been in practice.

27. Karl Marx, *The German Ideology,* in *Karl Marx: Selected Writings,* ed. McLellan, 169.

28. Rose Terry Cooke, "Too Late," in "*How Celia,*" ed. Ammons, 215. Further references are cited in the text.

29. As cited in Perry Westbrook, *Mary Wilkins Freeman* (New York: Twayne, 1967), 94.

30. Jewett, *Country of the Pointed Firs,* 72. Further references are cited in the text.

31. Jewett, "Miss Debby's Neighbors," in *Mate,* 191.

32. Sarah Orne Jewett, "The Courting of Sister Wisby," in *The King of Folly Island and Other People* (Boston: Houghton, Mifflin, 1888), 59. Further references are cited in the text.

33. The term *anticipatory illumination* (*Vor-Schein*) was coined by Marxist critic Ernst Bloch. See *The Utopian Function of Art and Literature,* ed. and trans., Jack Zipes (Cambridge, Mass.: MIT Press, 1988).

34. Mary E. Wilkins [Freeman], "A Mistaken Charity," in *A Humble Romance and Other Stories* (1887; reprint, New York: Garrett Press, 1969), 244.

35. Mary E. Wilkins [Freeman], "Brakes and White Vi'lets," in *A Humble Romance,* 117.

36. Mary E. Wilkins [Freeman], "A Poetess," in *A New England Nun and Other Stories* (New York: Harper, 1891), 140.

37. Virginia Woolf, *A Room of One's Own* (1929; reprint, New York: Harcourt, Brace, 1957), 85.

DIANE LICHTENSTEIN

The Tradition of American Jewish Women Writers

THE NOVELS, STORIES, POEMS, ESSAYS, plays, letters, memoirs, and diaries that American Jewish women produced during the nineteenth century form a unique literary tradition.[1] My goal in describing this tradition is to provide a more accurate and fully developed context within which to read a particular group of texts. These works, all of which fit into previously established categories, including American literature, Jewish literature, Jewish-American literature, and women's literature, deserve to be read in relation to other works by American Jewish women writers who were raising similar questions about their roles and identities. To read these texts in relation to one another refines and enriches our understanding not only of the specific body of writing, but also of what we label American literature.

In identifying this hitherto unacknowledged tradition, I proceed not by constructing a meritocracy of texts, but by adopting a principle of inclusivity. Such inclusivity is necessary to insure that readers understand Jewish women as whole and legitimate subjects rather than as inconsequential, or strange, objects/outsiders/others (and therefore not worthy of a place in the "real" canon).[2] In adopting this critical principle of inclusivity, I must ask the question, What criteria define the tradition? As I use the term, a tradition does not depend on an "intraliterary dimension"—"writings receiv[ing] and exploit[ing] the presence of earlier writings," as Richard Brodhead explains.[3] Instead, I suggest that a group of texts produced by writers who share a distinctive sociohistorical position coalesce into a tradition.

American Jewish women writers have often been undervalued or ig-

nored because their work has not been read in the context of that sociohistorical position (specific experiences, values, interests, and needs of
authors as well as audiences). This essay begins to reconstruct that context. It also initiates the process of bringing together works that have been
widely scattered, and thereby provides us with keener understanding of
specific texts by reading them next to one another. When we locate American Jewish women writers and their texts in relation both to one another
and to their context, we find ourselves newly able to recognize in their
work a tradition.[4]

In order to gain the fullest possible understanding of the Jewish
women's writing, we must "relax our standards and expectations of genre
itself."[5] That is, we must concern ourselves less with the rhetorical definitions of genres and more with the interrelationships among specific texts.
Two assumptions underlie this stance. The first is that any piece of writing
by an American Jewish woman may be relevant; this allows a large body
of specific textual evidence to "speak" and thereby shape our critical conclusions, a process that is, ideally, more honest than using predetermined,
and possibly irrelevant, critical criteria to predetermine what evidence we
"find." The second assumption, based on the fact that the tradition of
American Jewish women's writing includes texts in a variety of genres,
suggests that the common thematic ground among those texts transcends
conventional generic boundaries.

Because many of these texts do not fit neatly into "high literary"
genres, they seem to be "marginal"—on the outside of "real" American
literature. Ironically, however, the "literature by and about those who
seem to be on the edges of American culture can perhaps best represent
what happens within that culture," as Mary Dearborn suggests in *Pocahontas's Daughters: Gender and Ethnicity in American Culture.*[6] "Marginal" writers, according to this analysis, develop a special vision of the dominant
culture because of their distinctive vantage point on the periphery. Emma
Lazarus, for one, offers us such a view; she longed to be part of the
American literary world, as she perceived it, but she learned that as a
woman and as a Jew she would not achieve the status of a Longfellow or a
Bryant. The essays and poems written toward the end of her life reveal
not only an awareness of her position but also the dynamics of the mid-
and late-nineteenth-century American literary scene.

For the American Jewish woman writer, marginality often manifested
itself in an awareness of the need for dual citizenship. Specifically, this
awareness took the form of double national loyalties, holidays, and
even sets of friends. According to Werner Sollors, this "acute sense of
doubleness" is common to ethnic writers.[7] Also common is a heightened
awareness of audience; that is, these writers "begin to function as translators

of ethnicity to ignorant, and sometimes hostile, outsiders and, at the same time, as mediators between 'America' and greenhorns."[8] Dearborn adds, "Audience . . . is the ethnic text's professed reason for being."[9] For Jewish women this awareness of audience meant using their roles as educators both to assure other Jews that, despite the pain of anti-Semitic words or acts, being a Jew was noble and vital, and to improve the status of Jews among non-Jews.

The texts within the nineteenth-century American Jewish women's literary tradition were written by individuals who lived in every region of the United States, from New York and Philadelphia to Charleston, Savannah, Cincinnati, Chicago, and San Francisco. Although Rebecca Franks and Miriam Gratz, among others, wrote some letters and occasional poems in the eighteenth century, I designate the chronological beginning of the tradition as 1815, when Rachel Mordecai Lazarus of Wilmington, North Carolina, began her twenty-three-year correspondence with the British novelist Maria Edgeworth.

Lazarus and the other women whose work constitutes the tradition were, for the most part, Sephardic Jews (descendants of Spanish and Portuguese Jews) or German Jews.[10] This is because the Jewish population in America consisted primarily of Sephardic and German Jews until the 1880s, and because the now more popularized and recognizable Eastern European Jewish women did not begin writing in English in significant numbers until the turn of the century. I see this ability to write English— and, more specifically, American English—as a significant criterion in establishing a tradition of *American* Jewish women writers. Equally important is the writer's consciousness of her Jewish identity. These two criteria help define the tradition of nineteenth-century American Jewish women as those writers who perceived themselves as Americans and Jews, and who, as a result of this perception, sought ways to reconcile the sometimes conflicting demands of their dual citizenships.

In her work on the black women's literary tradition, Barbara Smith argues that "thematically, stylistically, aesthetically, and conceptually Black women writers manifest common approaches to the act of creating literature as a direct result of the specific political, social, and economic experience they have been obliged to share."[11] Like black women, the nineteenth-century American Jewish women writers who constitute the tradition I am describing "manifest common approaches" because of the experience they were obliged to share. These experiences—living up to expectations of ideal American and Jewish womanhood, and living as Jews in America—in turn helped shape the tradition's three defining themes: womanhood (American and Jewish); national identity (American and Jewish); and American Jewish womanhood. The third theme, which follows from and at least in part depends on the first and second themes, developed most noticeably in the later years of the nineteenth century, when American Jewish women were gaining the confidence to identify themselves as a unique and valuable group.

Womanhood

The nineteenth-century American Jewish woman understood that two nations asked for her loyalty and that her loyalty to each would be measured by how well she adhered to the mythic ideals of womanhood. The ideal of middle-class American Jewish culture was the Mother in Israel. As the term came to be used in the nineteenth century, it described the model "Jewess," the wife, mother, or daughter who dedicated herself to the well-being of her family, and through the family, the Jewish nation. She was the Old Testament Deborah (the original Mother in Israel—Judges 5:7) transposed into the modern world; religiously committed and capable, she could conquer any task if it were for the benefit of parents, children, husband, synagogue, or Jewish community. This Mother in Israel bore striking resemblance to the middle-class Christian True Woman whose primary role was that of "guardian of religion and spokeswoman for morality" and whose "sphere was the hearth and the nursery."[12] The similarities between these womanly ideals was not a coincidence; the Jewish woman in America "was affected by all the social and economic currents that determined the status of the gentile American woman, for the German Jewish community in America, while retaining its Judaism, with seeming ease assimilated the mores, attitudes, and ideological patterns of the rising American middle class of which it was a part."[13]

The True Woman was not a static icon; like all cultural ideals, she was subject to a myriad of economic, political, and religious forces. By the end of the century, these forces had produced the "new woman" who was capable of earning her own living and leading an independent life.[14] For the American Jewish woman, the changes were exciting as well as frightening: as correct "feminine" American behavior became more problematic, so, too, did demonstrating one's American identity through acting the part of the proper American woman. At the same time, proving one's loyalty to Judaism still required a primary commitment to the home; despite the dramatic changes in white, middle-class America, American Jews continued to equate traditional family life with the preservation of Judaism.

In order to make concrete the ways in which the theme of womanhood permeates the texts of American Jewish women, I will discuss two writers, one from the middle of the century—Rebekah Gumpert Hyneman—

and one from the end of the century—Josephine Lazarus. Although each had a unique vision of what it meant to be a woman, many of the tensions that emerge from both their works were also felt by other writers in the tradition.

To defuse these tensions, Hyneman (1812–1875) created a synthesis of American and Jewish gender roles in both her life and writing; through this synthesis she attempted to demonstrate that she was both a committed Jew and a loyal American. The daughter of a Jewish father and a Christian mother, Hyneman chose very deliberately to live her life as a Jew, marrying a Jewish man and living according to Orthodox standards. As a middle-class American Jewish woman, she followed the directives for both a True Woman and a Mother in Israel; she devoted herself to her sons and to the memory of her husband after he disappeared on a business journey.

The introduction to her volume of poetry, *The Leper and Other Poems* (1853), expresses Hyneman's nervousness about her poetry: "In presenting my unassuming little volume to the public, I feel more than the usual share of timidity attendant upon such ventures, for I come before them unknown and unnamed." She went on to explain that she expected her coreligionists to overlook faults in the poems, but "to those whose path is not as mine, and who may not be disposed to judge with equal leniency, I have no excuse to offer, but screen myself behind the shield of insignificanc[e]."[15] Conscious of the propriety of an "unknown and unnamed" woman presuming to publish a collection of poetry, Hyneman framed her creativity in the convention of a female apology, and thus attempted to deny responsibility for that work. And her reference to her two audiences, one Jewish and the other non-Jewish, speaks provocatively not only to the need she felt to be read, and accepted, by her two nations, but her belief that as a Jewish woman she would find greater support among Jews than Christians.

Reflecting the Jewish and American (Christian) tensions in her life, a number of poems from *Leper,* and a short story, reveal the methods by which Hyneman combined Christian and Jewish womanly ideals in her writing. "Female Scriptural Characters," for example, transforms heroic Biblical figures into nineteenth-century American women. (This series of poems first appeared in *The Occident and American Jewish Advocate* between 1846 and 1850 and then was included in *Leper.*) Even as she sang the praises of Sarah, Rebekah, Leah, Rachel, Miriam, Ruth, Naomi, Esther, Jochebed, Deborah, Huldah, Judith, and Hannah, Hyneman reduced these women's valorous deeds to acts of feminine propriety, as we see in her description of Judith:

She leaves that scene of blood behind,
　And speeds through many a lonely dell;

. . . .

How fearfully her woman's soul
Had mocked at Nature's soft control—
　How well her mission sped!
Oh! not by woman's gentle hand
　Should blood be shed or victory won;
Yet, for her God, her love, her land,
　What hath not woman done?

Hyneman extols Judith's courage but assures us that her actions grow out of love for country and God. She is not hardened to battle or murder but, rather, masters her feelings of repugnance in order to serve her people. Hyneman uses the contrast between the woman's "gentle hand" and the blood of the battle to heighten the incongruity of the scene. Neither the True Woman, nor even the Mother in Israel, has a regular place on the battlefield; the proper woman's war is against immorality, nonobservance of religious laws, and family members' illnesses.

The poem "Woman's Rights" (*Leper*) makes this last point explicit. Despite the provocative title, the poem tells us not that a woman has the right to vote or to work, but rather that she has the "right" "to soothe the couch of pain" as well as to make man's home an earthly paradise and "to teach the infant mind." Woman, Hyneman tells her audience,

. . . is a flower that blossoms best, unseen,
　Sheltered within the precincts of her home;
There, should no dark'ning storm-cloud intervene,
　There, the loud-strife of worldings never come.
Let her not scorn to act a *woman's* part,
　Nor strive to cope with manhood in its might,
But lay this maxim closely to her heart—
　That that which God ordains is surely right.

This poem reinforces the imagery of "Judith"; in effect it explains that the biblical heroes acted not as surrogate men, but as True Women who fought to protect their nation and the extended family of the Jewish people. As ideal women, they exercised their "right" to serve others. Even more than "Female Scriptural Characters," "Woman's Rights" depended on the rhetorical structures of the True Woman. Through these it seems to have accommodated a Christian audience, demonstrating that Hyneman's characters had learned the cultural codes of middle-class America and therefore could be held up as public proof that a Jewish woman was as true a True Woman (and therefore as American) as a Christian.

Hyneman also accommodated a Jewish audience, particularly in "The Lost Diamond" (published in *The Occident and American Jewish Advocate* in 1862).[16] The story's loosely related episodes exaggerate the virtues of the Malchoirs' Jewish family life and emphasize the roles of Jewish women within that inviolable family. No Malchoir ever strays from Judaism or the family; it would be impossible to deny one without destroying the other. Daughter/sister Esther understands that she cannot relinquish her faith even for her family's economic well-being (she is offered such an opportunity through a rich Christian woman's proposal that requires Esther's conversion to Christianity), and daughter/sister Anna knows in her heart and mind that she cannot marry a non-Jewish man (fortunately, this man, Dr. Lascelle, confesses late in the story that he is actually Jewish). Hyneman's story emphasizes the pride, family cohesiveness, honesty, and unswerving devotion of Jews; it also reminds its readers that Jewish women in particular understand the intricate interdependence of family and Judaism.

Unlike Hyneman, who remained safely sheltered in the conventions of American Jewish womanhood, Josephine Lazarus (1846–1910) attempted to expand the parameters of women's roles. Lazarus, sister of Emma, was the daughter of respected and financially secure Jewish parents who provided homes in New York City and Newport, Rhode Island, as well as private educations, for their six daughters and one son. Writing at the end of the century, Lazarus sought help from other women who had discovered passageways through the maze of both non-Jewish and Jewish gender expectations. Although the role models proved disappointing as often as they proved helpful, the process of writing about other women seems to have provided a method for Lazarus to explore and even solidify her own attitudes. In one of her biographical sketches of a non-Jewish American woman, Margaret Fuller, for example, Lazarus seems to have been searching for answers to the puzzles of her own secular conflicts. When she said of Fuller, "Opposing forces were constantly at war within her—the intellect and the emotions, the large, unasking sympathies, and the close, hungry human affections," Lazarus could have been describing herself.[17]

According to Lazarus, Fuller's conflict was between the intellect and the home, a place where she could rest. Presumably she found her home, literally and metaphorically, in her marriage to Giovanni Angelo Ossoli and in motherhood, "the clue to all life's mazes," the event that refreshed her whole being.[18] Despite this seeming resolution, Fuller's "complex nature" needed some large, unifying principle that could coordinate all the facts of life, and bring them into harmony and accord; in other words, some deep spiritual conviction. . . . Lacking this, her ideals were always human, her kingdom was of the earth, and she never gained that full mastery and knowledge of the earth which alone can make us free— free of self and the limitations of sense.[19]

In criticizing Fuller for being human and earthbound, Lazarus sounded as if she were also realizing her own lack of transcendent freedom. Disappointed in Fuller and possibly in herself, she repeatedly returned to images of flightlessness and limitation.

In her sketch of Madame Dreyfus, Lazarus seems to have needed to articulate an idealized image of Judaism and womanhood in order to convince herself and her readers that her unique identity *was* valuable. *Madame Dreyfus. An Appreciation* (1899) focuses less on the woman as a unique individual and more on the type of perfect womanhood she represented. Lazarus described Dreyfus, wife of the French army Captain Alfred Dreyfus (falsely accused of treason in 1894 and finally pardoned in 1900), as an "immortal" star, an "ideal of true womanhood" whose "innate and inherent" characteristic might very well be "the simple capacity of loving, truly and unselfishly—with that forgetfulness of self in whomsoever, in whatsoever she truly loves, whereby she truly finds herself."[20]

The extended essay on Dreyfus is interesting not only for its statements about women but also because Dreyfus was Jewish. Although Lazarus did not dwell on this shared identity, she concluded her "appreciation" by discussing anti-Semitism as well as Alfred Dreyfus's Jewishness. But she then quickly proclaimed that Madame Dreyfus would be remembered not because she was Jewish but because she was a "starry soul, who takes her place among the Immortals, among those 'not born to die.' "[21] A Jewish woman, Lazarus seems to have been suggesting, could fulfill all of the requirements of proper womanhood, and even stand as a perfect model of that ideal. Encoding her own need for acceptance through the veil of Dreyfus's image, Lazarus sought that coveted space where she could be both woman and Jew.

Lazarus, writing at the end of the century, had to contend with ideals of womanhood that were in flux. These changing ideals help explain how she could describe woman as a self-sacrificing creature (Madame Dreyfus) but also declare,

Woman is entering to-day into a new consciousness, a new knowledge and experience of herself and of the world; restless, impatient to throw off old restraint and allegiance, in order that she may test and prove her own powers and freedom . . . that she may more fully know and find herself—her own, her real, her whole self, not in another, but in herself.[22]

Although the ideal American woman of the 1890s was no longer the ministering angel of Hyneman's "Woman's Rights," the middle-class "clubwoman" still operated as the center of the domestic sphere. As the texts I have quoted from reveal, ideals of womanhood were so integral to American and Jewish ideology that even a progressive thinker such as Lazarus could not completely imagine her way beyond them. Speaking as representatives of the American Jewish women's tradition, both Hyneman and Lazarus remind us that gender expectations constitute one of the primary components of the sociohistorical context within which American Jewish women wrote.

Nationalities

For nineteenth-century American Jews, identifying one's nationality raised complex questions regarding loyalty. Could one be an American and a Jew at the same time? Could or should one always be equally loyal to both? Was America the new Israel, the promised land? Hovering around many of these questions was a feeling of unease—an "anxiety of displacement"; that is, the women within the tradition experienced a sense of exile even on their American "native ground." Constantly reminded that they were not Anglo-Saxon Protestants, although they were white, they experienced a feeling of displacement because they were "other" as Jews (and as women). In most cases, the anxiety compelled them to work diligently to establish for themselves and their families a secure place in America; this anxiety and its consequences were inseparable from the deeply felt belief that the Jewish woman was responsible for the Jewish family and through that family the Jewish nation.

The texts of three writers, whose lives and work span most of the nineteenth century, form the base for the discussion of the theme of nationalities. These three women—Rachel Mordecai Lazarus, Emma Lazarus, and Emma Wolf—projected individual interpretations of how to be American and Jewish simultaneously, yet their general concerns about national identity link them to each other as well as to many additional writers in the tradition.

The letters that Rachel Mordecai Lazarus (1788–1838) sent to Maria Edgeworth between 1815 and 1838 reveal the "anxiety of displacement" hovering below the surface calm of pride and gratitude. The correspondence actually began when Lazarus, then a teacher in her father's school, wrote to suggest that Edgeworth had depicted the character Mordecai in her novel *The Absentee* (1812) as a negatively stereotypical Jew. Although Lazarus did not know Edgeworth, she trusted that her letter would find a sympathetic listener rather than a resentful or hostile one, and she felt confident enough in her Jewish identity to challenge Edgeworth's caricature.

As part of her verbal challenge to Edgeworth, Lazarus explained that "in this happy country [the United States], where religious distinctions are scarcely known, where character and talents are all sufficient to attain advancement, we find the Jews to form a respectable part of the community."[23] Having lived in Warrenton and Wilmington, North Carolina, she and her friends of "persuasions different from her own" learned to look "upon the variations of the other as things of course—differences which take place in every society."[24] Thirteen years later, in 1828, Lazarus again noted the "spirit of unity and benevolence among [the townspeople of Wilmington] as ought to exist between virtuous members of the same community, and tho' many feel and even express regret at the difference of religious sentiment which exists between us, it proves no barrier to mutual kind offices and sincere regard."[25] Perhaps in antebellum North Carolina Jews were as welcome as Lazarus suggests. Her religious difference *was* noted, however, if not openly condemned; indeed, the "regret" the other Wilmington inhabitants expressed might have emanated from anti-Semitic feelings that Lazarus did not want to confront. Bent on preserving an image of the unified and benevolent American town whose citizens lived together harmoniously, she created with her words a world that fully accepted her as Jew.

Emma Lazarus (1849–1887), writing in the middle of the century, also used her words to affirm her national identities. Even more than Rachel Mordecai Lazarus, however, Emma Lazarus had the luxury of defining herself through her literary identity rather than through conventional female American and Jewish roles: because she was born into a family with economic and social privileges, she never had to work, marry for financial security, or take on responsibility for family members. In addition, she received an excellent education under private tutors, studying Greek and Latin, among other subjects. Perhaps it was her education, as well as the literal and emotional support provided by her father, which provided her with the confidence to step onto the "public stage" of authorship with very little of the conflict that many other mid-nineteenth-century women writers, American and Jewish, experienced.[26] In fact, even at sixteen, when her first volume of poetry was published with her father's help and money, she knew with surprising sureness that she wanted and deserved the role of American author. It was through this role, as well as that of Jewish author, that she affirmed her two national identities.

The near-simultaneous appearances of her essay "American Literature" and her volume of poetry *Songs of a Semite* remind us that Lazarus sought to create a strong, integrative voice that would establish her as a serious American, as well as a Jewish, writer. In "American Literature" Lazarus set out to defend American literature against George Edward Woodberry's claim in the May issue of the *Forthrightly Review* that America had no tradition, and that America's poets had left no mark. Against this attack Lazarus argued that Emerson had given rise to an American "school of thought and habit of life" and that writers such as Hawthorne, Whitman, Lowell, Holmes, and Stowe had been trained in this school.[27] Lazarus concluded that "the literary history of the past fifty years contrasts favorably with that of the past fifty years in England—the only period with which it can, with any show of justice, be compared."[28] The defensive tone of the essay suggests that Lazarus felt compelled to prove the viability and worth of American literary figures, as well as of American values and experiences, in order to justify her own identity as an American author.

In *Songs of a Semite,* she openly celebrated her Jewish identity.[29] In "The Banner of the Jew," for example, Lazarus called upon "Israel" to "Wake" and "Recall to-day/The glorious Maccabean rage." She exhorted contemporary Jews to act in the spirit of their ancestors:

> Oh for Jerusalem's trumpet now
>   To blow a blast of shattering power,
> To wake the sleepers high and low,
>   And rouse them to the urgent hour!
> No hand for vengeance—but to save,
> A million naked swords should wave.
>
> Oh deem not dead that martial fire,
>   Say not the mystic flame is spent!
> With Moses' law and David's lyre,
>   Your ancient strength remains unbent.
> Let but an Ezra rise anew,
>   To lift the *Banner of the Jew!*[30]

Proud, even defiant, Lazarus was no longer one of the "sleepers." Feeling the urgency of her identity as a Jew, she had begun to use her pen as a "naked sword," prepared for battle against complacent Jews and anti-Semitic non-Jews. Reconfirmed in her commitment to Judaism by the early 1880s, Lazarus proudly turned to Jewish subjects in her writing.

Lazarus's American and/or Jewish identities served as the focus of many of her most compelling works. And even when these identities were not a central theme, the interdependence between the two formed a crucial context in which Lazarus constructed her creative voice. That is, she would not have been as effective on behalf of Jews if she had not believed deeply in America's freedoms, and she could not have been as moving a writer if she had not discovered how important her Jewish identity was. Her best-known poem, "The New Colossus," illustrates the interdependence of her identities.

> Not like the brazen giant of Greek fame,
> With conquering limbs astride from land to land;
> Here at our sea-washed, sunset gates shall stand
> A mighty woman with a torch, whose flame
> Is the imprisoned lightning, and her name
> Mother of Exiles. From her beacon-hand
> Glows world-wide welcome; her mild eyes command
> The air-bridged harbor that twin cities frame.
> "Keep, ancient lands, your storied pomp!" cries she
> With silent lips. "Give me your tired, your poor,
> Your huddled masses yearning to breathe free,
> The wretched refuse of your teeming shore.
> Send these, the homeless, tempest-tost to me,
> I lift my lamp beside the golden door!"[31]

Through Lazarus's imagination, the Statue of Liberty has come to articulate symbolically the ideals that America collectively believes about itself. Although Lazarus did not invent the image of a young nation free from the prejudices and restrictions of "ancient lands," her poem has helped solidify the beliefs that in America Jews and other "huddled masses" will find a solution to the anxiety of displacement and that the "wretched refuse," the "homeless" outsider, will metamorphize into an American citizen, an insider who brings new vitality to her/his adopted nation.

Emma Wolf (1865–1932) also experienced anxiety about her place in America, but she expressed her feelings as well as her resolutions through concrete answers to difficult questions about assimilation rather than through poetic metaphors. Her 1892 novel, *Other Things Being Equal,* specifically addressed the concerns of those Jews to whom Judaism had become a pale religion at best and a liability to one's social and business standing at worst. In a revealing early scene, for example, Jennie Lewis, cousin of the main character, Ruth Levice, asks, "What does possess your parents to mix so much with Christians?" Ruth replies, "Fellow-feeling, I suppose. We all dance and talk alike; and as we do not hold services at receptions, wherein lies the difference?" Jennie retorts that "There *is* a difference" which Christians never let Jews forget.[32] Later in the novel, Jennie poses another difficult question: Why do you use the expression Day of Atonement rather than Yom Kippur? "Because 'Atonement' is English and means something to me," Ruth responds.[33] English, not Hebrew or even German, was the language of assimilated Jews.

Questions such as Jennie's were not abstract meditations for many American Jews of the late nineteenth century. Indeed, a large number of these Jews resembled the Levices in socializing with non-Jews, observing few Jewish holidays, and identifying more with American society than with an ancient Hebrew race. And like the Levices, Americanized Jews were pondering the complicated matter of intermarriage. Wolf forced the issue by having Ruth Levice fall in love with a Christian, Dr. Herbert Kemp. The resolution: Jews and Christians could marry provided each respected the other's identity. Although Wolf did not advocate the denial of one's Judaism, even when one married a non-Jew, she refused to ignore the social problems experienced by Jews or the reality of Jews who were not comfortable with that identity.

Unlike Rebekah Hyneman's "The Lost Diamond," which resolved its conflict of a Jewish woman loving a non-Jewish man by simply removing the obstacle in the fairy-tale conclusion where Anna Malchoir's love object, Dr. Lascelle, reveals himself to be Jewish, *Other Things Being Equal* offered no easy solution. Wolf made it clear that her doctor is most certainly Christian, and that he will not convert to Judaism; the two lovers will have to learn to live with their differences. But she also made it clear that a Jew does not lose his or her Judaism by marrying out of the faith. The characters in Wolf's novel are Jews whose names are anglicized and whose habits are middle-class American. Many of them struggle to resolve their feelings about being Jewish in a predominantly Christian America. Like her characters, and like many of the writers whose work makes up the Jewish women's tradition, Wolf sought answers to questions about the significance of an American Jewish national identity. Ironically, the affirmation of that identity served to alleviate the "anxiety of displacement" by providing the much needed sense of inclusion in a native place.

American Jewish Womanhood

As my discussion of the themes of womanhood and nationalities suggests, American Jewish women writers often explored the meaning of their composite identities in segments. Toward the end of the nineteenth century, however, a growing number of these women sought ways to confirm, rather than simplify, the complexity of their identities as well as to declare allegiance not only to Americans, Jews, or women but to themselves, as American Jewish women. This late-century celebration, which was both cause and effect of the increasing self-confidence of American Jewish women, took a variety of concrete forms, including the convening of a Jewish Women's Congress and the publication of the *American Jewess,* a magazine for Jewish women edited by a Jewish woman.

Between September 4 and September 7, 1893, ninety-three American Jewish women from over twenty-nine cities joined ranks to discuss the privileges as well as liabilities of being American Jewish women. Organized by Hannah Greenebaum Solomon, the Jewish Women's Congress convened under the auspices of the Chicago Columbian Exposition's Parliament of Religions. Most of the participants were upper-middle-class women who had been involved in club and charitable work; they used the Congress and their expertise to establish the National Council of Jewish Women, still in existence today.

Without exception, the women who spoke at the Congress expressed pride in being Jews and Jewish women. Eva L. Stern's praise for Judaism's treatment of women epitomizes the common sentiment:

Who in the whole history of the world was the first to elevate woman? to teach delicacy to woman? to command honor of woman, and to insist upon her rights . . . ? Moses, who has purged and cleansed the morals of the world. . . . He purified thoughts about woman, and created for her a place in life, next in dignity to man.[34]

Although Stern was sincere, we, with one hundred years of hindsight to help us, can see the irony of idealizing the "delicacy," "honor," "purged and cleansed morals," and "purity" that Judaism used to "elevate" but also to contain women. We can also appreciate the ambiguity of the concluding clause's "next": alongside, or behind?

Woman's familial responsibilities were not the only concern of the delegates; as Jews who had achieved relative acceptance within American communities, the women attending the Congress also felt loyal to their American nation. Yet even as they voiced appreciation to America, many delegates recognized the precarious position they filled. In what must have been a sobering moment, Esther Witkowsky stated,

There was no land of promise for the persecuted Jew of the 16th century; we have found one here in America; the Holy City may not lie within its boundaries, but the route thither certainly does. 'Next year in Jerusalem' prays the orthodox Jew; let us hope that *here,* in the future, he may forget this prayer, believing that he has found what he has sought.[35]

To Witkowsky and other women at the Congress, America was the land of opportunity and "promise"—the future Jerusalem of the West, which had not yet fulfilled its promise to Jews or to other minorities. At the same time that Witkowsky felt gratitude for the historical anomaly of America's relative tolerance of her people, she also recognized that being a Jew made her vulnerable.

Although many of the speeches sound conservative to us a hundred years after they were delivered, the fact is that the assembled women felt strongly that they were participating in a great progressive movement. The delegates' decision to use full names rather than "Mrs. Henry XYZ," in addition to the very existence of the Congress, indicate a movement away from traditional roles. As to why it had taken Jewish women longer to participate in "women's rights" activities, Sadie American explained that the Jewish woman

> needed to make no movement for herself . . . [or] for others, but has been content through her influence to impel [the] man to move. Because her work has been done largely in the home, because the man has been the medium of communication, the Jewish woman has been a little slower to feel the heart-beats of her time than have other women.[36]

Despite the changes implied by American's last sentences, the organizers of the Congress "chose to place their conference in the ranks of the religious rather than women's assemblies," a decision that suggests that they "identified themselves first as Jews and only second as females."[37]

The rhetoric of the speeches delivered at the Congress was occasionally sentimental, and often conventionally dramatic. One speaker echoed another, particularly in rearticulating the myths of womanhood and the Jewish woman's role in the family and Judaism. The women believed in these myths and in their Jewish identities at the same time that they wanted to explore the new options becoming available to all American women. Underneath the pious and emotional phrasings of the women's speeches was great energy; feeling their potential as American Jewish women speaking to other American Jewish women, the delegates were ready to confront a challenging world.

The same energy is apparent in *The American Jewess* (1895–1899). "Devoted to Social, Religious and Literary Subjects," it was the only Jewish magazine devoted to the interests of women, the only illustrated Jewish monthly, and the only Jewish publication sold at newsstands.[38] The magazine printed fiction, poetry, and essays, as well as reporting on the activities of the National Council of Jewish Women. Like other middle-class women's magazines of the period, the *American Jewess* directed women's choice of activities, in and out of the home. Unlike other magazines, however, this Jewish publication also directed its readers to cultivate an American Jewish identity in themselves and their families. Rosa Sonneschein, herself an "American Jewess" of Chicago, founded and edited the magazine. The daughter of a prominent Hungarian rabbi, Sonneschein had lived as a socialite in both Prague and St. Louis. Then, after thirty years of marriage, she was divorced by her husband in 1892. Presumably because she received no alimony, she launched *American Jewess* as a personal business venture.

In 1898, Sonneschein wrote an editorial, "The American Jewess," in which she explained that the Jewish family had taken on an American character; children, for example, regarded parents as dear, good friends, but not as authorities. And while the Jewish woman was still the ruler of the household, she was by no means only a "homebody." Most important, she

> loves her country intensely. Her patriotism is innate and imperishable, and for her country she would sacrifice her gold and her jewels. . . . Rachel, the mother in Israel, need not weep for her American daughters. Although a new era has dawned with changed condition, and although she takes part in the joys and sorrows of the nation and is eager to reach the new and the beautiful, she nevertheless remains Jewish in spirit, in feeling, in faith and in conviction.[39]

Like Josephine Lazarus, Sonneschein recognized the changes occurring in women's lives. Unlike Lazarus, however, she sought a way to reconcile the conflicting demands placed on the American *Jewish* woman. That such a goal was difficult to achieve is indisputable; even the exuberant prose in this passage could not completely conceal the doubt that the need for repeated pledges of allegiance reveals.

Although it boldly proclaimed that the American Jewish woman had a unique identity, *The American Jewess* could not attract and hold enough readers to make it a viable publication. Perhaps Sonneschein was correct when, in her "Valedictory," she accused American Jews of being "ashamed to have their neighbors and the letter carriers know that they are interested in Jewish matters."[40] Or perhaps there simply were not enough middle-class Jews to read and support yet another domestically centered magazine. Despite its limited success, *The American Jewess* serves as an emblem of the American Jewish woman's unique identity, and the fact that it appeared at the very end of the century reminds us that American Jewish women were facing the new century with ever-increasing confidence in themselves.

The American Jewess, along with the other texts I have discussed, suggests that nineteenth-century American Jewish women valued free expression and learned to use it in their personal struggles to be female citizens of both the American democracy and the ancient Jewish nation. For these women, writing was neither a hobby nor a lucrative occupation but, more, often, a means for reconciling the demands of womanhood and their two nations. Ironically, writing was not the smoothest path they might have chosen, roughened as it was by notions of female inferiority and stereotypes of uncouth Jews. Yet despite many obstacles, a number of women did use their writing to explore and validate the "themes" of womanhood, nationalities, and American Jewish womanhood. In so doing, they contributed to what we may now begin to recognize as a unique and valuable literary tradition.

NOTES

I would like to thank Steven Diamond, Carolyn Lichtenstein, Virginia Powell, and Lisa Haines Wright for their insightful reading of drafts of this essay.

1. I develop my definition of tradition more fully, and I provide more examples from the tradition, in *Writing Their Worlds: The Tradition of Nineteenth-Century American Jewish Women Writers* (Bloomington: Indiana University Press, 1992).

2. I am indebted to Henry Louis Gates, Jr., for the insight regarding "subjectivity" and literary traditions. See, for example, Gates's "Whose Canon Is It Anyway?," *New York Times Book Review,* February 26, 1989, 1, 44–45.

3. Richard Brodhead, *The School of Hawthorne* (New York: Oxford University Press, 1986), 13.

4. Although she doesn't specify her criteria for selection, Joyce Antler has included in her twentieth-century "tradition of American Jewish women's writing" those writers whose "imaginative and complex shapings of American Jewish experience, and especially, of the experience of Jewish women" compel our attention. See her introduction to *America and I: Short Stories by American Jewish Women Writers* (Boston: Beacon, 1990), 18–19.

5. Mary V. Dearborn, *Pocahontas's Daughters: Gender and Ethnicity in American Culture* (New York: Oxford University Press, 1986), 15.

6. Ibid., 4.

7. Werner Sollors, *Beyond Ethnicity: Consent and Descent in American Culture* (New York: Oxford University Press, 1986), 249.

8. Ibid., 250.

9. Dearborn, *Pocahontas's Daughters,* 40.

10. Throughout the remainder of this essay, I present the Sephardic and German Jewish women as culturally equivalent; I do this not because I think that the two groups' differences are nonexistent or insignificant, but because in the context of

class, ideals of womanhood, and conflicts between America and Judaism, the Sephardic and German Jewish women represented themselves in ways that were more similar than different.

11. Barbara Smith, "Toward a Black Feminist Criticism," in *All the Women Are White, All the Blacks Are Men, But Some of Us Are Brave,* ed. Gloria T. Hull, Patricia Bell Scott, and Barbara Smith (Old Westbury, N.Y.: Feminist Press, 1982), 164.

12. Carroll Smith-Rosenberg, "The Hysterical Woman: Sex Roles and Role Conflict in Nineteenth-Century America," *Social Research,* 39 (1972): 655–656.

13. Charlotte Baum, Paula Hyman, and Sonya Michel, *The Jewish Woman in America* (New York: New American Library, 1975), 53.

14. Lynn D. Gordon, in the "The Gibson Girl Goes to College: Popular Culture and Women's Higher Education in the Progressive Era, 1890–1920," *American Quarterly* 39 (1987): 211–230, and Carroll Smith-Rosenberg, in the "The New Woman as Androgyne: Social Disorder and Gender Crises, 1870–1936," in *Disorderly Conduct: Visions of Gender in Victorian America* (New York: Oxford University Press, 1985), 245–296, provide valuable information regarding the attitudes toward the new woman, particularly in her role as college student.

15. Rebekah Gumpert Hyneman, *The Leper and Other Poems* (Philadelphia: A. Hart, 1853), iii.

16. Rebekah Gumpert Hyneman, "The Lost Diamond," *The Occident and American Jewish Advocate* 19 (March 1862): 551–555; 20 (April–July, 1862): 10–15, 71–75, 117–123, 163–171.

17. Josephine Lazarus, "Margaret Fuller," *The Century* 45 (1893): 932.

18. Ibid., 930.

19. Ibid., 932.

20. Josephine Lazarus, *Madame Dreyfus. An Appreciation* (New York: Brentano's, 1899), 8, 13, 49.

21. Ibid., 54.

22. Ibid., 9–10.

23. Letter from Rachel Mordecai Lazarus to Maria Edgeworth, August 7, 1815, in *The Education of the Heart: The Correspondence of Rachel Mordecai Lazarus and Maria Edgeworth,* ed. Edgar E. MacDonald (Chapel Hill: University of North Carolina Press, 1977), 6.

24. R. M. Lazarus to Edgeworth, *Education,* 6.

25. R. M. Lazarus to Edgeworth, *Education,* 163.

26. For a full discussion of the anxiety the "private woman" felt about stepping onto the "public stage" of authorship, see Mary Kelley, *Private Woman, Public Stage: Literary Domesticity in Nineteenth-Century America* (New York: Oxford University Press, 1984).

27. Emma Lazarus, "American Literature," *The Critic* O.S. 1, no. 12 (1881): 164.

28. Ibid., 164.

29. Emma Lazarus, *Songs of a Semite: The Dance to Death and Other Poems* (New York: American Hebrew, 1882).

30. Emma Lazarus, "Banner of the Jew," stanzas 4, 5, *Songs of a Semite.*

31. Emma Lazarus, "The New Colossus," *Poems of Emma Lazarus* (Boston: Houghton, Mifflin, 1888), 1: 202–203.

32. Emma Wolf, *Other Things Being Equal* (Chicago: A. C. McClurg, 1892), 10.

33. Ibid., 129.

34. Eva L. Stern, "Charity as Taught by the Mosaic Law," in *Papers of the Jewish Women's Congress* (Philadelphia: Jewish Publication Society of America, 1894), 142.

35. Esther Witkowsky, "Discussion of Pauline H. Rosenberg's 'Influence of the Discovery of America on the Jews," in *Papers of the Jewish Women's Congress,* 76.

36. Sadie American, "Organization," in *Papers of the Jewish Women's Congress,* 243–244.

37. Deborah Grand Golomb, "The 1893 Congress of Jewish Women: Evolution or Revolution in American Jewish Women's History?," *American Jewish History* 70 (1980): 66.

38. *American Jewess* 1 (September 1895): 314.

39. Rosa Sonneschein, "The American Jewess," *American Jewess* 6 (February 1898): 209.

40. Rosa Sonneschein, "Valedictory," *American Jewess* 8 (August 1899): 3.

❧ SUSAN K. HARRIS ❧

"But is it any good?":
Evaluating Nineteenth-Century
American Women's Fiction

THE REVIVAL OF INTEREST in nineteenth-century American women's literature is less than fifteen years old.[1] Since Nina Baym published *Woman's Fiction* in 1978, it has become academically respectable to acknowledge interest in works like Susan Warner's *The Wide, Wide World* or Fanny Fern's *Ruth Hall,* and they are slowly becoming features of the academic terrain. Mary Kelley's *Private Woman, Public Stage,*[2] Alfred Habegger's *Gender, Fantasy, and Realism,*[3] Jane Tompkins's *Sensational Designs,*[4] the articles in *Legacy: A Journal of Nineteenth-Century American Women's Writing,* and articles in *Signs, American Quarterly, ESQ,* and others are all signposts to the new territories. But with the notable exception of Tompkins, few scholars have ventured to construct appropriate evaluative criteria. Rather, there appears to be an unspoken agreement not to submit nineteenth-century American women's novels to extended analytical evaluation, largely, I think, because the evaluative modes most of us were taught devalue this literature a priori.

I propose that we initiate an ongoing dialogue that will enable us to talk fruitfully about pre-twentieth-century American women's literature in terms of "good" and "bad," that we begin creating methodologies that will ramify the implications of Tompkins's *Sensational Designs.* One avenue is to learn how to describe noncanonical American women's literature in terms of *process*—that is, to see it within the shifting currents of nineteenth-century American ideologies. Acknowledging that imaginative literature is both reactive and creative, we can examine the ways that it springs from, reacts against, or responds to the plots, themes, languages in the discursive arena that engendered it at the same time that it creates new possibilities for that arena by reshaping old words into new ones. For Richard Rorty, this happens through the creation of new metaphors that evolve over time into new ideas; "truth," he claims, is neither "out there" nor "in here"; rather it is compounded of a set of linguistic contingencies. What we know, believe, is dependent on our ability to speak it, and our ability to speak it depends on the slow historical conjunction of ideas, images, and metaphors that evolve into the languages available to us. [5] For Hans Robert Jauss, literary works continuously interact with their readers to create, over time, new moral and aesthetic perceptions: "The relationship between literature and reader can actualize itself in the sensorial realm as an incitement to aesthetic perception as well as in the ethical realm as a summons to moral reflections."[6]

If we accept these fluid accounts of the relationship between language, consciousness, and social change as the bases for reshaping our ways of perceiving what imaginative literature is, what it does, and how it "works," we will have a tool that will help us create criteria for evaluating noncanonical literatures of the past and, equally important, for acknowledging our own motives for doing so and the implications of our own critical acts. Our first step is to acknowledge the ideological basis of our endeavor. What teleological shape the literature we are examining has is imposed on it by us, retrospectively; it is not inherent in the material itself. We are doing so, first, because we see ourselves positively, if not as end points then at least as significant markers; second, because we are drawn to nineteenth-century women's texts despite their apparently antithetical values and want to find some way of talking about them; and, third, because we are searching for antecedents to ourselves and the future we envision that we have not found in canonical texts and canonical ways of reading them.

I am not suggesting that we read these texts ahistorically. Rather, historical contextualization is a vital aspect of what I am calling process analysis. I *am* suggesting, however, that we clarify our own motives. Acknowledging why we are doing what we do will enable us, once we have understood the books' relationships with their own time, to reach back and see how they contribute to ours. If we look at them as both reactive and creative rather than asking them to self-consciously embody "timeless truths," we can understand their aesthetic, moral, and political values, both for their contemporaries and for us. While traditional criticism tends to examine literary works either historically, rhetorically, or ideologically, the method I am calling process analysis investigates all three axes in its contemplation of any given work. Consequently, although specific analytical tasks may look the same as they have always looked (pursuing metaphors, for instance), the final mosaic produced by process analysis looks very different because it has shifted the hermeneutic and evaluative projects into a far more complex socio-temporal scheme. And unlike traditional Anglo-American criticism, process analysis foregrounds the relationship of the literary-critical task to the critic's stance in her own time.

In order to show, within the scope of an essay, how this can work, I am going to focus on sentimental novels written by American women primarily between 1840 and 1870. We have begun to create a literary history for nineteenth-century American women's novels, a "remapping" of hitherto unknown terrain.[7] Within this history, enough research has been conducted among the novels that used to be classed as "literary sentimentality" to enable us to make some generalizations about the group, and this in turn should help us formulate critical questions about individual texts. For instance, critics have long noted—mostly with distaste—that the large majority of nineteenth-century American women's novels have "happy endings" in which their heroines marry and give up any idea of autonomy.[8] Recent critics, however, have pointed out that a closer view shows that the novels also question that inscription, even when their structures submit to it.[9] Despite following a fairly consistent pattern culminating in the protagonist's marriage to a dominating man, most sentimental novels also challenge the idea of female subordination, either through their plots, their narrators' addresses to the reader, or their patterns of rhetoric. In other words, their themes and structures tend to work at cross-purposes. Once dismissed as confused, such texts are now described as dialogic. This is not simply a cynical relabeling for young jargonists. Rather, it is evidence of a critical paradigm shift that gives us much more access to the novels than we ever had before. Attuned, on the one hand, to shifts in structural approaches to fiction, and, on the other, to reader-response criticism, we are now able to recognize that the dialogic patterning inherent in the novels' structures facilitates readers' participation in the novels' ideological debates. In other words, attention to structure is central to contextual placement. Prior to evaluating any given nineteenth-century sentimental novel, then, it is important to establish the terms of the debate(s) in which the text participates, the positions it takes, and how these positions are embodied in its textual structure.

There are many ways of going about situating a text within a historical debate. As groundwork for evaluating sentimental novels by American women, however, it seems especially important to investigate the impact of public ideologies on market strategies because these directly influence the novels' structures. Nineteenth-century America was characterized by strident—although often contradictory—*public* pronouncements about what constituted the nature of the two sexes (any others were not mentioned). I stress public because it is clear that, privately, there was considerable agonizing over the subject, just as there was over the subject of different races and their intrinsic "natures" and "characteristics." The differences between what reviewers saw happening in the texts and what we see happening when we factor in the existence of more than one linguistic construct of gender is a fascinating illustration of ideologically based reading strategies. By and large, reviewers and publicists subscribed to an essentialist definition of female nature, while the texts attempt to persuade women that they can re-create themselves. Given the nature of the public discourse and the power it had in the marketplace, writers aiming for a popular audience had to observe, at least superficially, essentialist rules for inscribing female protagonists and for their narrators' attitudes toward their heroines' adventures.

The conflict between public and textual definitions of female possibilities may well be the primary cause of the tensions between structure and theme that the novels display. One of the areas opened up by the study of noncanonical literature has been the examination of "the marketplace" as a condition of production. (Perhaps no surer proof exists of the influence of the New Critics than the fact that this is a "discovery.") By "conditions of production" I mean less the biographical circumstances of the individual author—which is Mary Kelley's focus in *Private Woman, Public Stage*—than the demands of the booksellers, reviewers, and buyers for whom the book is intended and that women authors could not—at least if they wanted to publish—ignore. With Kelley's study, Ann Douglas's *The Feminization of American Culture*,[10] Baym's *Novels, Readers, and Reviewers*,[11] and Cathy N. Davidson's *Revolution and the Word*[12] give us information about the values held by eighteenth and nineteenth-century arbiters of literary taste. For instance, Baym speculates:

> Apart from the question whether novelists were or were not radical in the particularities of their social, sexual, or personal world views . . . lies the possibility that the form of the novel assumes discontent as the psychological ground from which it springs. The essence of plot . . . is that something is wrong; there is a disturbance that needs correcting. Because women and youths mostly read novels, it was thought, their discontents in particular would be ministered to and hence exacerbated. The conviction of many contemporary students of popular culture that popular forms sedate discontent was not held by this earlier group of critics. If, as many feminist critics have argued, the "better novel" appears regularly to be instinct with misogyny, this

may not be an accident. Novels putting women in their place may well have been selected by reviewers as better than—more true to nature than—novels that legitimated their discontents. [13]

Of course what this meant for authors was that any challenges to the public definition of "women's place" had to be covert if they wanted to sell. The contradictions between structure and theme provide one way of doing that: the emotional and cognitive discrepancies aroused by the texts permit readers alternative modes of processing them. One mode, written to conform to "public" values, privileges female subordination through structural closure; the other, appealing to "private" values, privileges female independence through structural open-endedness. Processing these novels, then, depends on the reader's choice of interpretive modes. Challenges to the public definition of women's place are embedded in texts' structures and accessible only to readers who are predisposed to grasp them.

Evidence suggests that nineteenth-century readers were quite capable of reading texts in more than one mode. One of the most illuminating examples that I have discovered of this multileveled reading process was recorded in 1848 by the author Lydia Maria Child in a letter to a close friend:

> I had read Jane Eyre before you had the kindness to send a copy. I was perfectly carried away with it. I sat up all night long to finish it. I do not at all agree with the critics who pronounce Rochester unloveable. *I* could have loved him with my whole heart. His very imperfections brought him more within the range of warm human sympathies. *Ought* Jane to have left him at that dreadful crisis? She was all alone in the world, and could do no harm to mother, sister, child, or friend, by taking her freedom. The tyrannical law, which bound him to a mad and wicked wife, seems such a mere figment! I wanted much, however, to make *one* change in the story. I liked Rochester all the better for the impetuous feeling and passion which carried him away; but I wanted conscience to come in and check him, like a fiery horse reined in at full gallop. At the *last* moment, when they were ready to go to church to be married, I wish he had thrown himself on her generosity. I wish he had said, "Jane, I *cannot* deceive you!" and so told her the painful story he afterward revealed. There might have been the same struggle, and the same result; and it would have saved the nobleness of Rochester's love for Jane, which has only this one blot of deception. I am glad the book represents Jane as refusing to trust him; for in the present disorderly state of the world, it would not be well for public morality to represent it otherwise. But my

private opinion is, that a real living Jane Eyre, placed in similar circumstances, would have obeyed an *inward* law, higher and better than
outward conventional scruples.[14]

Here Child demonstrates both awareness and approval of social constraints—the sense that public morality was fragmenting and that literature's function was to teach readers moral conduct—and applauds the
text's resulting definition of female nature (Jane flees from the horror of
bigamy because in order to be a heroine she has to be instinctively virtuous). At the same time, however, Child reveals her private reading, which
recognizes that a character as independent as Jane would have pursued her
own desires rather than complying with social fictions. The sexual and
social tensions inherent in the text itself stimulate the modes in which it
will be processed. In Child's "public" reading, social mandates are foremost. In her "private" reading, autonomy and sexual desire are privileged
over social mandates. The possibilities for autonomy inherent in each
"reading" of female nature are embodied in the radically different episodes
of the novel. Child processes both, in full consciousness of what she is
doing.

Child's enthusiastic response to *Jane Eyre* was typical; Charlotte Brontë
was one of the most powerful direct influences on American women
writers, and their novels reflect the energy with which she inscribed Victorian conflicts about gender and autonomy. Moreover, in the American
texts the energy produced fuels new possibilities for female self-creation.
The contradictory structures of sentimental American texts highlight
rather than obscure these possibilities. If a heroine creates an autonomous
self and succeeds in impressing it on her society and her reader for six
hundred pages, she has left convincing evidence that it can be done. The
fact that she gives it all up upon marriage in the last twenty-five pages
should have less of an impact on readers—especially readers themselves
entertaining dreams of autonomy—than the fact that she succeeded. (Or
less long-term impact. My personal theory is that the renunciation of
autonomy in the face of the marriage proposal has its strongest impact
when these books are first read—probably because it involves sex[15]—but
that over time readers tend to remember protagonists' extended quests for
autonomy rather than their sudden, and fairly formulaic, renunciations.)
The standardized conclusions may even have annoyed nineteenth-century
readers as much as they do twentieth, thus undermining their "message."

Moreover, the "middles" of sentimental novels—the long narratives of
the heroine's self-creation and social success—may well explain why such
very different texts emerged later in the century. There is a fairly sharp
ideological dissimilarity between the apparently conservative sentimental

women's novels of the 1840s–1860s and the fairly radical ones of the 1870s–1890s. Examining the earlier novels as process enables us to see that rather than springing forth unheralded, the later novels evolve from the quests for autonomy explored in their predecessors and articulated so frequently that, despite their failures, the "traces" they left came to be "real." For Herman Melville, referring to his own work, such traces were accessible to the "eagle-eyed reader," who grasped truths "covertly, and by snatches." Melville contrasts this perceptive reader to the "superficial skimmer of pages,"[16] the same reader whose reading behavior Augusta Evans Wilson (author of *St. Elmo*) castigates as the "hasty, careless, novelistic glance."[17] Both writers acknowledge the subversive capacities of written texts, the fact that some, at least, were deliberately written to pass muster with a careless or conservative readership and to appeal to discerning readers. In regard to mid-century women's novels, perceptive readers would recognize that these texts argued against essentialist definitions of the feminine. In Jauss's terms, these early texts articulate new possibilities for female aspiration and behavior that are later realized both in subsequent fiction and in the social and political realms.[18]

To understand thoroughly what the readers as well as the reviewers saw in these texts we would have to do an exhaustive reader-response search, a project I have attempted and found exceedingly difficult, largely because, then as now, few ordinary readers recorded their responses to books they read. Those who did seemed to share our predilection for dividing their reading into high and low cultures; they recorded responses to "serious" literature (biographies, essays, sermons) far more often than for "light" novels. But this division is also part of the social construction of literary values,[19] an aspect of the linguistic revolution with which we are concerned. What may be more important than diary and letter records of actual reading is the fact that the same writers also indicated in other contexts a variety of concerns that the novels address. For example, many expressed a wish to improve their educations—their classical, not their domestic, educations—to learn Greek, Latin, and the higher mathematics. As Gerald Graff has recently reminded us, these were the cornerstones of the most esteemed educational apparatus, enabling those who mastered them to enter the ministry and law.[20] Despite the disaster most classical educations may have been in fact, in theory men so educated had mastered society's highest wisdom. Women's desire to achieve similar educational levels suggests that they, too, sought wisdom—in a culture that publicly and medically denied women the ability to think beyond their ovaries.

When, then, a woman protagonist in a novel masters abstruse languages, philosophy, world history, and mythology (as does the heroine of *St. Elmo*), she presents a model of female achievement for readers already predisposed to valorize educated women. What Wilson presents is a quest for autonomy and power that succeeds before she forces it to fail; not only does the protagonist become a scholar, she also becomes famous, powerful, and fully conscious of her own imperatives, a heroine who cries out that "I love my work! Ah, I want to live long enough to finish something grand and noble . . . something that will follow me across and beyond the dark, silent valley . . . something that will echo in eternity!"[21] By the time she gives it up to marry her overbearing minister-lover, the text has proved that women can become very powerful intellectuals.

In terms of its plot, *St. Elmo* manages to juggle sexual attraction, intellectual zeal, and public success, all before it surrenders to the requirement that it end by merging its heroine with the male figure who embodies everything she had sought for herself. In terms of its structure, it creates a heroine whose relationship with her self and her public mirrors the relationship Wilson implies exists between *her* text and its readers. Seen within the process framework I am proposing, *St. Elmo* is an excellent novel because it not only textually embodies the heroine's quest but also self-consciously places that quest within the cultural struggle over gender possibilities and then critiques its own project.

In preparing to reevaluate these novels, then, one set of questions we can ask is functional and historical: what needs did they serve for their intended audience? Did they, as imaginative literature, somehow present the "spiritual truth" of women's aspirations as essays and other more forthright genres could not? Did they give hope to readers, let them know that there were other questing souls out there? (In Elizabeth Stuart Phelps's *The Story of Avis*, Avis discovers her life's goal to be an artist while reading *Aurora Leigh*.) What effect does the text's structure have on its theme or themes? What kinds of cognitive or emotional discrepancies exist, and how might contemporary readers have responded to them? What is the power of fascination the texts hold? Is it the same power that holds us (those of us who read them) today? If so, can we describe it? Is it sexual?—moral?—aesthetic?—affective?

Because we have admitted that our endeavor is ideological, we can evaluate the novels in terms of their contribution to the expansion of women's possibilities (i.e., politically), as well as for the degree of power with which they present their subjects. For the novels to be published and favorably reviewed, they had to conform to the strictures articulated above; for them to achieve their "subversive" objects, they had to find a form that would embody these dual, and often contradictory, ideas. There are a number of ways this can be done: as in *St. Elmo*, the plot can outweigh the narrator's interpretive gestures or the dense "flowery" rhetoric can hide heretical phrases and clauses; as in *Ruth Hall*, the narrator can play more than one role (in which case the text risks being labeled "confused"). However this task is accomplished, there must be a point on which the antithetical impulses balance. Another set of evaluative criteria, then, lies in determining how well the texts strike the balance between socially and textually created ideological imperatives.

Creating a methodology for evaluating textual structures and assessing readers' access to subversive propositions is one side of the task. The other is to create one for evaluating the language(s) that constitute the texts' building blocks. Process analysis lets us see how the discursive modes of nineteenth-century texts both reflect and engage their society's ideological diversity. In a culture shifting from the conception of truth residing "out there," in the objective world, or "in here," in the subjective world, to a conception of truth as linguistically determined (i.e., contingent, in Rorty's use of the term[22]), women were latecomers. The novels that have been labeled "sentimental" embody women's entry into the fray. These display the battle of languages with particular intensity because they focus on the ways that language creates gender and the possibilities for autonomous selfhood. One of the objections often raised about these novels is that their protagonists do not have strongly defined, individual characters—that they are not female American Adams, creating a New Woman for a New World. Here, as Baym did in "Melodramas of Beset Manhood,"[23] we can approach women's texts by looking at criteria used to evaluate American male texts, criteria that tend to thematize the struggle between an autonomous self associated, in some way, with timeless truth, and a corrupt, temporal society (Huck's struggle with his conscience). In these canonical male texts, the traditional critical story informs us, heroes flee from social coercion (mostly defined as female). One of their strategies is to get rid of the women, to exist, as critics from Leslie Fiedler on have suggested, in an essentially and happily single-sexed universe. These are American Romances; their models are Christian texts, and their premise is that truth and selfhood are "real," that they reside within the individual and can and should be discovered. Canonical American male novels value the individual over his society.

In contemporary women's texts, on the other hand, the basic thematic is less self against society than self against self; that is, the women's internal conflicts represent conflicting definitions of womanhood. The characters battle themselves far more often, and with greater intensity, than they engage an openly corrupt society. One of the selves is most usefully seen as Nietzschean, willing itself into power and existence (which is what differentiates it from Huck, whose integral self is discoverable by readers, but not willed into being by the character); the other is the self that is socially determined. Both selves are presented metaphorically: in Richard Rorty's terms, these texts embody a battle for definition that pits two linguistically contingent worldviews against one another. Neither the self struggling to come into being nor the one (usually spoken by the narrator) socially determined has any intrinsically objective reality; rather, the validity of each rests on the reader's capacity for processing it. If the male texts are quintessentially Christian/Romantic quests, demonstrating the value of the True Soul against a corrupting society, the female ones are self-consciously contingent: they concern protagonists willing themselves into existence in an effort to *create* their own society. Never going so far into fantasy as to assume the possibility—or desirability—of living without other people, the women's novels anticipate the *real* problem of the twentieth century: how to nurture and protect a self that has only just become aware of its own possibility and that is trying to work out the parameters of its obligations to others.

Meanwhile, *other* voices continue to insist that women are Platonic essences, that the individual is only a historical accident, and that what really matters is her conformity to the eternal feminine. The clashing of these antithetical constructs provides the aesthetic and moral energy of the texts; moreover, the slow swells, the burgeoning of figures recording protagonists' struggles to create themselves, constitute the linguistic "traces" that enable us, in retrospect, to track the evolution of what would eventually become the figure of the New Woman. When Hagar Churchill, of E.D.E.N. Southworth's *The Deserted Wife,* insists that "*I* have a will! and tastes, and habits, and propensities! and loves and hates! yes, and conscience! that all go to make up the sum total of a separate individuality—a distinct life! for which *I alone* am accountable, and *only* to God!"[24] and then proceeds to create a successful life for herself and her children without male help, she has inscribed a dynamic predecessor to later novels that celebrate independent women. Similarly, Elizabeth Drew Stoddard's *The Morgesons* foregrounds the word "possession" in reference to its iconoclastic protagonist; the figure shifts from its demonic to its self-creating (as in "self-possession") associations as the heroine increasingly understands her own powers. With our consideration of how well the text juggles its thematic and structural obligations, then, we can determine how effectively it embodies the discursive battles that engender it.

This involves a more thorough investigation into the nature of sentimental language and its values than most twentieth-century academic readers have cared to conduct. In fact, sentimental language is probably the aspect of pre-twentieth-century American women's literature that modern readers resist most. It is often difficult to process because it is so baroque, and it often seems vacantly redundant. But these are precisely the aspects of it that can and should be directly engaged. Certainly one function of sentimental language was to create a sacred space dedicated to women, analogous to the private sphere in which they moved. As Jane Tompkins demonstrates, sentimental language is intertextually related to religious language, both functionally and aesthetically.[25] Religious language functions as part of a ritual intended to draw participants' attention away from their temporal lives and make them focus on their spiritual relationship to the divine. Auditors are encouraged to conceive of their experiences metaphorically, placing them in a universal context, to reenvision themselves as part of a set of universal patterns. Similarly, sentimental language functions ritualistically, having set patterns of imagery and rhythm that strive to reenvision women, to continually project them in terms of universal patterns. Ultimately, what is created is a Platonic image of the feminine that is intensely intertextual. Shot through with allusions to nature, the Bible, classical mythologies, and medieval literature, sentimental language is constantly referring to texts beyond the boundaries of that in which it appears. Sometimes these *are* empty, mindless. Often, they project an image of ideal womanhood whose implications for the individual are painfully repressive. Just as often, however, they serve to place the female protagonists within a world/historical context of female endeavor and, obliquely, female oppression. In fact, the intertextual portions of the individual novels, taken out of the contexts of the works and brought into conjunction with each other, create a dialogue of their own about the nature and status of women that is simultaneously historicized and universalized. It is the locus of the ideological battle about women.

Our devaluation of the language with which this battle has been conducted has prevented us from recognizing it. Once we do so, we also can evaluate its occurrence in individual texts. How effectively does it engage the issues? What is the author's position? How astutely does she analyze her subject? What are the energy exchanges between the way she inscribes women in general and the way she describes her heroine? What, exactly, does her figurative language *do*?

Any analysis and/or evaluation of sentimental discourse must determine how deliberately its figures are employed. The prevailing critical assumption has been that in these novels the baroque metaphors are all rather mindlessly borrowed. Borrowed they are, but very self-consciously; they are used to serve a variety of functions, and, over time, they are revitalized, feminized into figures pregnant with possibility. At least one writer uses them offensively: to attack as well as to explore definitions of female nature. In *Ruth Hall* Fanny Fern alternates between sentimental and acerbic language, all in the interest of defending women's right to be economically independent. The girl whom we meet on her bridal eve meditating on her future and wondering "would love flee affrighted from [her] bent form, and silver locks, and faltering footsteps"[26] finds that love has nothing to do with survival; after her husband's death Ruth painfully learns that the patriarchal society that valorizes clinging, dependent women will also shut its doors if they ask for cash. Before the book ends Ruth has not only become a successful writer, she has also learned to hold her maternal ("sentimental") affections in abeyance while she negotiates long-term publishing contracts. This time meditating not on love but on her choice between immediate money, available by selling her copyright, or a percentage, which would delay her reunion with one child and incur continued privation for the other, Ruth muses that the copyright money is "a temptation; but supposing her book should prove a hit? and bring double, treble, fourfold that sum, to go into her publisher's pockets instead of hers? how provoking!" and she decides, "No, I will not sell my copyright; I will rather deny myself a while longer, and accept the percentage" (RH, 153). Juxtaposed to the figurative language with which Ruth was introduced, this sharp language of commerce challenges the original inscription's premise that true women have to depend on love for survival.

Another way sentimental language is used to change consciousness is as a political tool, as when Frances Harper, in *Iola Leroy*, images her black, enslaved heroine as a fair damsel imprisoned in a dark castle: the narrator refers to "the beautiful but intractable girl who was held in durance vile" and images her rescue as being "taken as a trembling dove from the gory vulture's nest and given a place of security."[27] Here, the language is directed to those who identify with the values of the white community; its figures strenuously attempt to make readers accept Iola as a white ("dove") heroine because that is the only way these readers will identify with her as a "real" woman/human. In other words, the language itself acknowledges white Americans' inability to empathize with black Americans. Harper's language here has a double function: first to project her black protagonist within the parameters of white sympathy, i.e., as white, then to lift her female protagonist to heroic status as a damsel from the heroic ages. Only after having captured the white-oriented reader's sympathy through this idealized image does the text then project its other heroine, the heroine's heroine, Lucille Delany: a physically black woman who Iola claims "is my ideal woman. She is grand, brave, intellectual, and religious" (*IL*, 242). In other words, the fair damsel the text valorizes has her own agenda; she does not speak in white figures herself, and she looks to black women for role models. Thus the intertextually "white" or "European" references serve both to obscure and to point toward the text's alternative values. Seen retrospectively, the trace record left by Iola's own values makes the novel a precursor to twentieth-century black American women's texts that self-consciously valorize dark-skinned black women.

The oneiric nature of sentimental language also merits examination, for it often signals the existence of a radically feminist shadow text. Stowe's *The Minister's Wooing,* for instance, constantly places its protagonist, Mary Scudder, within a cosmic dream, associating her with shells, nests, and the ocean. With repeated references to the Virgin Mary, with Mary Scudder's friendship with an unhappily married woman named Virginie who insists that her private self, the self capable of happiness, is unmarried; and with the example of independent "spinsters" who arrange life to suit themselves, these references create a countertext within the novel that argues against marriage—the story's plot—and for a state of empowering "virginity." As with the medieval allusiveness of Harper's figures, the oneirism of Stowe's portrayal serves at once to obscure—it can be read as part of Stowe's portrayal of Mary's adolescent sensibility—and to highlight this countertheme. If dreams express our repressed desires, texts that dream (as opposed to texts that feature dreams) have to be evaluated for the contexts, and contents, of their dreams.

Structure and language, then, are the dual focuses of process analysis. Each demands three levels of study: the first, contextual, places the text within its own time; the second, rhetorical, examines narrator/narratee contracts and the ways in which the text may play with cultural significances; the third, retrospective, searches for traces of changing consciousness, building blocks for an ideologically self-conscious literary history. Together, they offer a paradigm that produces evaluative as well as investigative questions.

Some of these questions have arisen in the course of this essay. While continued dialogue will change it, a tentative list might look something like this:

1. What is the author's degree of consciousness about her protagonist's status in a patriarchal society; that is, where does the novel stand in the sociopolitical spectrum of its time? How does the author demonstrate her political stance? What thematic, narrative, and aesthetic choices does she make in order to exhibit its position within her sociopolitical world? Books I would rank high on this list would include Stoddard's *The Morgesons,* Warner's *The Wide, Wide World,* Stowe's *The Pearl of Orr's Island,* and Southworth's *The Deserted Wife.*

2. What modes (thematic, narrative, linguistic) does the author employ to balance the story of her protagonist's self-creation with the socially and/or generically dictated need to deny female selfhood and originality?

3. How does the text embody the *linguistic* debate; that is, what discoursive worldviews are brought into conjunction or confrontation? Though I have only addressed sentimental language in this essay, there are' many other modes operating in the texts themselves. Two often discussed in earlier critical works are "realism"—i.e., representational discourse—and the vernacular. With sentimentality, these are probably the most relevant discoursive modes in nineteenth-century sentimental novels by American women. But many other modes operate as well. A fruitful way to approach these might be through a methodology constructed from Mikhail Bakhtin's concept of heteroglossia, which gives us a "poetics" for discussing the fictional representation of multiple discoursive modes and the worldviews they express.[28] For example, even the most genteel women's texts often feature vernacular and/or working-class characters whose voices implicitly (and occasionally explicitly) counter the dominant, essentialist definitions of female nature held by the middle-class protagonists, the narrators, and, often, the authors.

4. What functions do the characters serve and what means has the individual author used to "mark" her characters for her readers? It has always struck me that Susan Warner chose an extraordinarily resonant name for the feisty, independent aunt against whom the sanctimonious heroine of *The Wide, Wide World* struggles. Fortune Emerson, who tries to teach her reluctant charge that only self-reliance will bring self-respect, stands alone in the novel as a fully realized, financially and emotionally independent woman. Disliked by the protagonist, and cast within the frame of the wicked stepmother by the author, she nonetheless exists as an example of the rugged, rural American woman. Readers seeking to read Ralph Waldo Emerson into female possibility can see in Aunt Fortune Emerson one way for women to achieve success in the American landscape.

5. What stylistic devices does the author choose and how skillfully and appropriately does she employ them to embody the issues with which she is concerned? For example, if she employs classical allusions, how does she use them to illustrate her own, or her characters', positions in the ideological debate in which she is engaged? For instance, Susanna Rowson's *Charlotte Temple* (1794) plays with the semantics of the word "content" as she evokes a classical image of female virtue whose "name is *Content*."[29] This text valorizes passive heroines, but its implication that con*tent*ed women lack *content* is a position that later sentimental novels will vigorously refute.

6. What were the marketing conditions under which the novel was produced (including serialization) and how well does the author juggle the marketing demands and her artistic and thematic requirements?

7. What is the intertextual *gestalt* of the novel? From what other texts

does it take its premises? How does it transform these premises to fit its own peculiar needs? How appropriate is its "rereading" or its "misprisioning" of the earlier texts? (Louisa May Alcott's *Work: A Story of Experience* is framed by *Pilgrim's Progress.* Yet its Celestial City is temporal, and its holy community distinctly female.)

8. What later ideological or political debate does it anticipate? Reading retrospectively, what textual trace-markers can we detect that could have helped change the shape of later women's novels? How useful is this text as a precursor of that debate? (Does Fortune Emerson become Alexandra Bergson? Does Lucille Delany become Dessa Rose?)

This is of course only a sketchy overview of some of the ways nineteenth-century American women's novels work and some of the questions we can ask about them. As we continue to study them and the culture that produced them, we will be continuously finding new areas to explore. Meanwhile, it is time for us to begin assessing the territories already discovered.

NOTES

"But is it any *good?*" was first published in *American Literature* 63, no. 1 (March 1991): 43–61.

1. Prior to World War II, American women's literature had a recognized place in literary history, as works by Herbert Ross Brown (*The Sentimental Novel in America, 1789–1860* [Durham, N.C.: Duke University Press, 1940]), and Fred Lewis Pattee demonstrate. Pattee's *The First Century of American Literature, 1770–1870* (1935; reprint, New York: Cooper Square, 1966) is generally measured and fair. Not until his *The Feminine Fifties* (New York: Appleton-Century, 1940) did he set the tone for the intensely misogynist evaluations, and finally silence, that followed. With the exception of Helen Waite Papashvily's *All the Happy Endings: A Study of the Domestic Novel in America, the Women Who Wrote It, the Women Who Read It, in the Nineteenth Century* (New York: Harper, 1956) and parts of Henry Nash Smith's *Virgin Land: The American West as Symbol and Myth* (Cambridge, Mass.: Harvard University Press 1950), little work focusing specifically on nineteenth-century women writers was produced before the "revival" of the 1970s.

2. Mary Kelley, *Private Woman, Public Stage: Literary Domesticity in Nineteenth-Century America* (New York: Oxford University Press, 1984).

3. Alfred Habegger, *Gender, Fantasy, and Realism in American Literature* (New York: Columbia University Press, 1982).

4. Jane Tomklins, *Sensational Designs: The Cultural Work of American Fiction, 1790–1860* (New York: Oxford University Press, 1985).

5. Richard Rorty, "The Contingency of Selfhood," in Rorty, *Contingency, Irony, and Solidarity* (Cambridge and New York: Cambridge University Press, 1989), 27–28.

6. Hans Robert Jauss, "Literary History as Challenge," in Jauss, *Toward an Aesthetic of Reception* (Minneapolis: University of Minnesota Press, 1982), 41.

7. See Annette Kolodny's "A Map for Rereading: Gender and the Interpretation of Literary Texts," *New Literary History* 11 (1980): 451–468; reprinted in Elaine Showalter, ed., *The New Feminist Criticism: Essays on Women, Literature Theory* (New York: Pantheon Books, 1985), 46–62.

8. Papashvily, *All The Happy Endings*.

9. A good example of this is Joanne Dobson's "The Hidden Hand: Subversion of Cultural Ideology in Three Mid-Nineteenth-Century Women's Novels," *American Quarterly* 38 (Summer 1986): 223–242.

10. Ann Douglas, *The Feminization of American Culture* (New York: Avon Books, 1977).

11. Nina Baym, *Novels, Readers, and Reviewers: Responses to Fiction in Antebellum America* (Ithaca: Cornell University Press, 1984).

12. Cathy N. Davidson, *Revolution and The Word: The Rise of the Novel in America* (New York: Oxford University Press, 1986).

13. Baym, *Novels, Readers, and Reviewers*, 172.

14. Milton Meltzer and Patricia G. Hollands, eds., *Lydia Maria Child: Selected Letters, 1817–1880* (Amherst: University of Massachusetts Press, 1982), 238–239.

15. Habegger's *Gender, Fantasy, and Realism*, especially pages 15–20, probably has the best analysis to date of the sexual appeal of nineteenth-century American women's novels.

16. Quoted by Steven Mailloux in *Rhetorical Power* (Ithaca: Cornell University Press, 1989), 36–37. I am grateful to Professor Mailloux for furnishing me with advance pages of this text and reminding me of Melville's remarks.

17. Augusta Evans Wilson, *St. Elmo* (Chicago: M. A. Donohue & Company, n.d.), 439.

18. "The horizon of expectations of literature distinguishes itself before the horizon of expectations of historical lived praxis in that it not only preserves actual experiences, but also anticipates unrealized possibility, broadens the limited space of social behavior for new desires, claims, and goals, and thereby opens paths of future experience" (Jauss, *Toward an Aesthetic of Reception*, 41).

19. See Baym, *Novels, Readers, and Reviewers*, for an analysis of the Victorian creation of taste and its impact on mid-century American literature.

20. Gerald Graff, *Professing Literature: An Institutional History* (Chicago: University of Chicago Press, 1987), esp. ch. 1.

21. Wilson, *St. Elmo*, 371.

22. "[O]nly sentences can be true, and . . . human beings make truths by making languages in which to phrase sentences" (Rorty, "The Contingency of Language," in *Contingency, Irony, and Solidarity*, 9).

23. Nina Baym, "Melodramas of Beset Manhood: How Theories of American Fiction Exclude Women Authors," *American Literature* 33 (Summer 1981): 123–139; reprinted in Showalter, *The New Feminist Criticism*, 63–80.

24. E.D.E.N. Southworth, *The Deserted Wife* (Philadelphia: T. B. Peterson, 1855), 229.

25. Tompkins, "Sentimental Power: *Uncle Tom's Cabin* and the Politics of Literary History," in *Sensational Designs*, 122–146.

26. Fanny Fern, *Ruth Hall and Other Writings,* ed. Joyce W. Warren (New Brunswick, N.J.: Rutgers University Press, 1986), 13. Subsequent references to this text are cited parenthetically as RH. In her Introduction to the novel, Warren discusses both the theme of economic independence and the stylistic dualities of Fern's writing.

27. Frances E. W. Harper, *Iola Leroy* (1893; reprint, Boston: Beacon Press, 1987), 38. Subsequent references to this text are cited parenthetically as IL.

28. M. M. Bakhtin, *The Dialogic Imagination,* trans. Caryl Emerson and Michael Holquist (Austin: University of Texas Press, 1981). The most pertinent essay is the last, "Discourse in the Novel." A preliminary model for such an analysis is David R. Sewell's *Mark Twain's Languages: Discourse, Dialogue, and Linguistic Variety* (Berkeley: University of California Press, 1987).

29. Susanna Rowson, *Charlotte Temple,* ed. Cathy N. Davidson (New York: Oxford University Press, 1986), 34.

❦ PAUL LAUTER ❦

Teaching Nineteenth-Century Women Writers

DURING THE LAST TWENTY YEARS the opportunities and challenges to teach nineteenth-century American women writers have widened almost beyond the comprehension of those trained in previous decades. When I was in graduate school in the 1950s at Indiana and Yale, we read Emily Dickinson. Period. Today, that would be considered a scandal. The changes have been great, and good; virtually every historical generalization about the development of nineteenth-century American culture has come to be questioned, as have, increasingly, the hierarchies of value that have undergirded the received canon. And critical terms long used to dismiss women's works as "sentimental" or of merely "regional" interest have begun to undergo newly positive transformations.[1] Yet these changes have not always been easily accommodated in classrooms. In this essay I address a number of what I perceive as significant issues in nineteenth-century American women's writing, especially as these are focused by teaching practice. I separate these issues into what I have called the problem of texts, the problem of history, the problem of context, the problem of subject, the problem of form, the problem of difference, and the problem of standards. As will be plain, the names are occasionally arbitrary and the categories somewhat overlap; taken together, these "problems" suggest that seriously including women writers in what has been called "American literature" entails not simply a small change here or there but more fundamental alterations of intellectual categories and institutional arrangements,[2] as well as of teaching practice. In any case, these categories may provide frameworks useful not only for those of us who were expected to know no more than Dickinson, but for those expecting to teach no less than Frances Ellen Watkins Harper and Lydia Maria Child.

Teaching does not take place in an institutional vacuum. On the contrary, the reconstruction of teaching practice has depended heavily upon certain basic material changes, most particularly in the texts available for us. As recently as the 1980s, a comprehensive course on nineteenth-century American women writers could only be taught by copious use of the copying machine. If you wanted your students to know anything of Harper or Child—or even anything *about* them—you had no choice. That is, beyond the brief anthology selections of seventeen writers (including Harper) one finds in Gilbert and Gubar's *Literature by Women*,[3] the nine (spread over two volumes) in the *Norton Anthology of American Literature*,[4] or the twelve in the 1987 *Harper American Literature*,[5] few texts were readily available.

The only piece of Child's writing then in print was an excerpt from *Hobomok* (1824) in Lucy Freibert and Barbara White's useful volume, *Hidden Hands*.[6] Apart from that book, only Judith Fetterley's pioneering 1985 collection, *Provisions: A Reader from 19th-Century American Women*,[7] had resurrected such women, and others like Caroline Kirkland, Fanny Fern and Alice Cary, from oblivion. Now, however, full works by writers like Child are available, together with books by E.D.E.N. Southworth, Rose Terry Cooke, Catharine Maria Sedgwick, and others, as part of Rutgers University Press's excellent American Women Writers Series.[8] Jane Tompkins has edited a reissue of what was America's first real best-seller, Susan Warner's *The Wide, Wide World* (1850).[9] Additionally, Oxford University Press has issued the remarkable Schomburg collection of the writings of nineteenth-century black women, including the work of Anna Julia Cooper, Pauline Hopkins, and Mrs. N. F. Mossell, among others. Many of these white and black women are also included in the new *Heath Anthology of American Literature* (1990),[10] the final product of the Reconstructing American Literature project.

As for Harper, 1987 was a good year. After making the 1986 edition of *Granger's Index to Poetry* and the *Cambridge Handbook to American Literature*, she was prominently represented in Mary Helen Washington's important collection, *Invented Lives*.[11] As part of another new series reprinting fiction by black women, Beacon Press has recently reissued her 1892 novel, *Iola Leroy*, with a fine introduction by Hazel Carby.[12] Her collected poems constitute one of the Schomburg volumes, and Carby's new book, *Reconstructing Womanhood*,[13] devotes a full chapter to Harper as well as two to Pauline Hopkins. She has even twice made the pages of the *New York Times Book Review*, in Henry Louis Gates's review essay on the Washington book and the tradition of black women's writing and in a Sunday *Times* review of the Schomburg series.

Now one might reasonably ask why I invoke Southworth and Harper, Child and Cary when we have accessible lots of the work of the "main" nineteenth-century American women writers—Fuller, Stowe, Dickinson, Jewett, Freeman, Chopin, Gilman. Is this not an inversion of those older forms of pedantry that insisted upon studying John Pendleton Kennedy's *Swallow Barn,* and authors like Johnson Jones Hooper, Jones Very, and Frederick Goddard Tuckerman? Those last three are, in fact, included in one or more of the American literature anthologies, unlike Southworth, Harper, Child, or Cary. But the point isn't to match every Johnson Jones Hooper with an E.D.E.N. Southworth or every excerpt from Cooper with one from Child. The problem is that we are only at the beginning of the process of reevaluating literary works of the past in the light provided by today's feminist and minority criticism. Those of us who have grown up in the United States are all products of its capitalist economic and social relations, even if we call ourselves socialists. Thus we are likely in practice to share with our unabashedly entrepreneurial sisters and brothers much of America's individualistic, competitive, materialistic culture—however much we might theoretically deplore these. So, too, as literary people we have been acculturated by the work of those we have been taught are significant: Hawthorne and Melville, Emerson and James. We become what Judith Fetterley has called "resistant readers" to presumptively "classic" texts only through a slow process that involves decentering them from our structures of valuation. In practice, I think, that process necessarily involves reading many alternative texts and talking about them with others—what one best does in the classroom. That we cannot do without the texts. Indeed, we need more than the usual single story by Stowe or Jewett or Freeman offered by most anthologies. We need to sift a richness of possibility in order that we may cook up a new American canon— which our students or grandstudents may in their turn set on the shelf.

When the academic wing of feminism first generated a publishing component in the early 1970s, we searched for works whose literary qualities were substantially similar to those of the dominantly male and white texts that had formed our tastes. Thus we published and promoted works like Gilman's "The Yellow Wallpaper" and Davis's "Life in the Iron Mills," both now enshrined in American literature anthologies. Writers like Harper and Child seemed "propagandistic" or "sentimental." Furthermore, we assumed that even a text like Elizabeth Stuart Phelps's *The Story of Avis,* whose politics continue to be relevant, was unlikely to be used in classes and thus was economically not feasible to publish—much less *Hobomok* or *Ruth Hall.* That presses like Rutgers, Oxford, and Beacon are now successfully distributing works by Child, Harper, Fern, and Southworth tells something of the broadening of the base of a revisionist study of American literature.

It also marks a step in the process I was describing. It says that the decentering and reconstructing of what we call "American literature" has been carried forward to new ground. Critics and historians like Elizabeth Ammons, Nina Baym, Hazel Carby, Barbara Christian, Joanne Dobson, Josephine Donovan, Judith Fetterley, Annette Kolodny, Marjorie Pryse, Jane Tompkins, Mary Helen Washington, and Sandra Zagarell, among others, [14] have provided purchases in the rugged terrain of literary history from which we can get fresh looks at its peaks and valleys . . . and, it may be, come to revise our views of what we thought were its more prominent features. But again, criticism without text is an exercise in abstraction. For it is not merely literary concepts and historical configurations that are undergoing reconstruction; it is our *consciousness,* that set of internal assumptions and outlooks that forms what we see, or even what we look at. The experience of fictions, the encounter with writers of another time, are part of what shape consciousness, as Frederick Douglass points out in an important section of his *Narrative.*[15] Consciousness, to speak crudely, shapes standards of value, the bases on which we determine texts to be sufficiently significant to include in curricula and reading lists. Thus, in a certain paradoxical way, the very availability of texts helps, by shaping consciousness, to determine their availability. But that is only one problem.

Equally important is the need to revise historical understanding in two distinct ways, our next problems. We have largely been taught to think in terms of unitary—or at least of what are called "mainstream"—traditions in American literature: *THE American Tradition in Literature,* as one anthology is titled [emphasis added]. But, in fact, American culture is deeply heterogeneous. The history of fiction constructed around the canonical writers—Poe, Hawthorne, Melville, James, Twain, Hemingway, Faulkner, and Fitzgerald—is altogether a different history from that which emerges from a study of key white women or black writers of fiction. At the beginnings of the feminist reconstruction of the canon, it was argued that novelists like Chopin or Wharton succeeded in creating formally complex works of timeless excellence—that is, succeeded in precisely the terms critics had used to valorize canonical male writers. The women's exclusion from the canon was thus demonstrably an exercise in prejudice, which, we optimistically assumed, would be corrected as it was perceived. But simply placing women into a dominantly male tradition is clearly a first, and inadequate, step—however much it remains our primary mode. In time, therefore, critics began to construct a separate history of women's (as well as of black) narratives, focusing on writers like

Stowe, Harper, Jewett, Freeman, Hopkins, Cather, Glasgow, and Hurston, as well as on Chopin and Wharton. That history continues to emerge as, for example, the origins of realism get pushed earlier and earlier into the nineteenth century, to women writers like Caroline Kirkland, Alice Cary, and Susan Warner. Kirkland, in turn, leads us to the English village sketches of Mary Russell Mitford. Nor are these earlier women interesting only as the inadequate predecessors of Crane and Howells; indeed, pairing them with such later male realists offers a very useful pedagogical technique for perceiving the overlapping and distinctive features of each.

The first issue I want to raise here, however, is not that of the derivation of literary styles but the question of how literary texts are perceived as encoding and transmitting powerful ideas, how they are *historical agents*. For example, in introducing Thoreau, one anthology says in a manner characteristic of writing about him that in 1849, three years after refusing to pay his poll tax, "he formalized his theory of social action in the essay 'Civil Disobedience,' the origin of the modern concept of pacific resistance as the final instrument of minority opinion, which found its spectacular demonstration in the lives of Mahatma Gandhi and Martin Luther King."[16] Ten years before Thoreau spent his night in the Concord lockup, Angelina Grimké, in her "Appeal to the Christian Women of the South" (1836), wrote in the cadences of a biblical prophet:

> Can you not, my friends, understand the signs of the times; do you not see the sword of retributive justice hanging over the South, or are you still slumbering at your posts?—Are there no Shíphrahs, no Puahs among you who will dare in Christian firmness and Christian meekness, to refuse to obey the *wicked laws* which require *women to enslave, to degrade and to brutalize woman?* . . . Is there no Esther among you who will plead for the poor devoted slave? . . . Listen, too, to her magnanimous reply to this powerful appeal; "I *will* go in unto the king, which is *not* according to law, and if I perish, I perish."[17]

In fact, of course, the idea of nonviolent resistance, indeed of nonviolent positive action, was a commonplace of evangelical Christianity during the early nineteenth century, especially among abolitionists like the Grimkés and William Lloyd Garrison. No one would deny that Thoreau gave powerful expression to the idea, or that in certain important respects he helped secularize the mode of prophetic testimony, although perhaps in his time the example of not paying a small tax was less persuasive than the nonviolent conduct of the members of the Ladies' Anti-Slavery Society when they were attacked in 1835 by a mob of "gentlemen of property and standing" in Boston.[18]

My objective here is in no sense to debunk Thoreau. But I do think it important to help students (and ourselves) see through two commonplace canards of intellectual history. One concerns the notion that "great ideas" (for example, civil disobedience) spring, like Athena, from the foreheads of great, and generally male, geniuses ("*his* theory of social action"). The other fallacy is that such ideas are transmitted, as it were, from mountaintop to mountaintop, like smoke signals: Thoreau to Gandhi to King. In fact, as this instance suggests, ideas frequently develop in a complex interaction between the practice of many, often nameless, individuals caught up in the power of a cause—abolition, the rights of workers or of women—and the formalizing power of what the nineteenth century called a "Poet." The Poet names—no small power—what she and others had learned to do. Those of us devoted to cultural study tend, it seems, to assimilate to naming all the power of this process, but that is to falsify reality as well as to aggrandize the work of commentator and critic—as if texts alone determined history and academic theorists in New Haven were the engines of change.

An equivalent pedagogical problem is posed by tracing the idea of "civil disobedience" from Thoreau only through men of great public standing, like Gandhi and King. Nonviolent direct action is, in fact, a primary weapon of the weak and dispossessed, and therefore of women, as is brilliantly demonstrated by Mary E. Wilkins Freeman in her story "A Church Mouse." In this story, the heroine, Hetty, an elderly woman alone in the world, is driven from her dwelling by its sale following the death of the woman with whom she has lived. By standing in the way of the main church deacon as he rakes hay, "clogging" his farming with her "full weight," however slight, she manages to obtain the keys to the meetinghouse, and, despite the opposition of the minister and deacons, even to set up her quilt and cookstove in order to live there. As Freeman says, "When one is hard pressed, one, however simple, gets wisdom as to vantage-points. Hetty comprehended hers perfectly. She was the propounder of a problem; as long as it was unguessed, she was sure of her foothold as propounder." Ultimately, Hetty's passive resistance—she locks the church door against the deacons when they attempt to move her out—mobilizes the support of the women of the community, who speak up on her behalf and against the men's attempts to remove her by violence. Thus she is enabled to stay in what has become her "home." It is a small triumph, but perhaps closer to the political experience of most of our students—especially nowadays—than the wonderful but remote demonstrations of soul-power of Gandhi and King—or even the dominating assertiveness of Thoreau himself.

A different historical problem is the need for *contexts* not often available to us, given the compartmentalized organization of the American academy. Take, for example, Frances Ellen Watkins Harper's poem "Aunt Chloe's Politics," published in her 1872 book, *Sketches of Southern Life*.

AUNT CHLOE'S POLITICS

Of course, I don't know very much
  About these politics,
But I think that some who run 'em,
  Do mighty ugly tricks.

I've seen 'em honey-fugle round,
  And talk so awful sweet,
That you'd think them full of kindness,
  As an egg is full of meat.

Now I don't believe in looking
  Honest people in the face,
And saying when you're doing wrong,
  That "I haven't sold my race."

When we want to school our children,
  If the money isn't there,
Whether black or white have took it,
  The loss we all must share.

And this buying up each other
  Is something worse than mean,
Though I thinks a heap of voting,
  I go for voting clean.

At one level, a poem like this may be taken to explain the existence of American Studies as a discipline. For it comes to full life when one illuminates it with the insights of both literary and historical analysis. Harper is remarkably successful in suggesting the speech patterns, syntax, and vocabulary of an unschooled southern black woman without, on the whole, presenting her in dialect. This is clearly a conscious and I would say political choice, for in *Iola Leroy* Harper does portray a number of dialect-speaking characters. Here, however, she wishes to draw a shrewd and upright woman of the people who is not, like Stowe's Aunt Chloe, distanced from her audience, white or middle-class black, by the "color," so to say, of her language. Like most Americans, this Aunt Chloe uses some slang—like "honey-fugle round," to cajole or wheedle, and "a heap"; some nonstandard grammar—"have took it"; and the mock ignorance of the savvy—"I don't know very much/About these politics." Harper carefully establishes in the third line—"But I think that some who run 'em"— Aunt Chloe's control of standard, informal English before, in the next to last line—"Though I thinks a heap of voting"—she presents her using a specifically southern black locution.

Aunt Chloe's language is, I believe, designed to legitimate her keen political commentary for an audience unused to the idea of women, much less *black* women, voting. In these five stanzas she touches on many of the most sensitive political issues of the Reconstruction period, especially in the South: for example, whether public funds should be appropriated for the education of children, white or black; and the conduct of some black male politicians who used race loyalty to excuse corruption. She also touches on the general level of political morality at a time that saw the exposure of Boss Tweed in 1871 and the Crédit Mobilier scandal in 1872.

All of this is, I think, implicitly an argument for Aunt Chloe's right to vote, which emerges only in the last line. This was not, if we will recall, a distant and unlikely possibility in 1872. After all, women had gone to the polls in Wyoming and Utah in 1870 and 1871, and neither the territories nor the Republic had tottered. It was in 1872, after women had previously attempted to vote in ten states and in the District of Columbia, that Susan B. Anthony tried to cast her ballot in the presidential election. Although Harper, like Frederick Douglass, had broken with Anthony and Elizabeth Cady Stanton over the issue of the Fifteenth Amendment, like them she worked to support a federal women's suffrage amendment, first introduced into the Congress in 1868 and given considerable visibility by Victoria Woodhull's congressional testimony in January of 1871. The fundamental point Harper here articulates both in and through Aunt Chloe is consistent with what she presented in her 1894 address to the World's Congress of Representative Women on "Woman's Political Future." There she said:

> Political life in our country has plowed in muddy channels, and needs the infusion of clearer and cleaner waters. I am not sure that women are naturally so much better than men that they will clear the stream by virtue of their womanhood; it is not through sex but through character that the best influence of women upon the life of the nation must be exerted.
>
> I do not believe in unrestricted and universal suffrage for either men or women. I believe in moral and educational tests. I do not

believe that the most ignorant and brutal man is better prepared to add value to the strength and durability of the government than the most cultured, upright, and intelligent woman.

Two decades before, Harper had presented such strength of character in the persona of Aunt Chloe. The only point in the 1894 speech implicitly absent from "Aunt Chloe's Politics" is Harper's insistence that "the hands of lynchers are too red with blood to determine the political character of the government for even four short years." It has taken eighty years and more to fulfill this objective.

The problem, of course, is that few English majors, not to speak of American literature specialists in graduate school, really learn much about American history. Even the minimal details on which I touched above will not be found in any basic American history text and are found in relatively few introductory courses, and that mite is essential to reading "Aunt Chloe." Ordinarily, this line of reasoning leads to a defense of American Studies, but that is not my point. My contention here is that writing by marginalized groups—women or "minorities"—is for a number of reasons more directly implicated in the immediate problems of historical change.[19] Then any arrangement that systematically separates the texts from the historical contexts in which they are embedded arrests our capacity to read them. The point is *not* that, say, black texts need to be read as social documents rather than as formal structures of language; nor that "majority" texts "transcend" their historical moments and therefore have no politics. All literary works perform functions within their times, although the functions, and thus the politics, of texts that emerge from a dominant culture may be more deeply buried under what have become widely shared assumptions. To miss the politically stabilizing force of Shakespeare's histories and tragedies, for example, is to miss precisely what allowed his wide popularity. The presumed transcendence of such works, like their canonical status, measures the social power of the values they promoted.

If one pursues this line of argument, one is inevitably drawn to the contention that academic structures in America maintain what turns out in practice to be a racist and sexist division of knowledge. Thus the problem of context involves considerably more than providing "background" that marginally extends the reading of a text. Rather, it raises the fundamental problem of how the organization of knowledge (and study) promotes particular social and political interests. These issues cannot, it seems to me, remain submerged in a classroom dealing seriously with women's writing. To ignore them implicitly accepts the argument of formalist critics that the political functions of a poem like "Aunt Chloe's Politics" are, at best, secondary concerns, that the proper study of literary texts is their abstract form, and that works that insist upon their contexts are inevitably of lesser value than those that supposedly "transcend it." Rather than calling into question the value of Harper's work, I would want to question the legitimacy of academic structures that have left it in an intellectual limbo.

Further, focusing on women's texts, especially those of women of color, reassembles what students often do "know" about history. For example, I have often taught Sui-Sin Far's (Edith Eaton) story "In the Land of the Free" as an archetype of the immigrant tale. It is, after all, about the clash between Old and New World cultures, about the exploitation of new immigrants, about a contest for the loyalty of the new generation between Old World parents and New World authorities. But it also dramatizes the differing stakes in these conflicts of immigrant women and men—and, critically for Anglo students in particular—the common yet distinctive experiences of Chinese in America. The very commonalities and differences of the story seem to help make available to students significant elements of their own histories.

What is at stake in the historical bases of a poem like "Aunt Chloe's Politics" is the question of what one considers important. Harper offers another painful case in point. Apart from the two 1986 books I mentioned before, she does not appear in any of the usual guides to American literature: not the 1962 *Reader's Encyclopedia of American Literature,* the still-standard 1968 *American Authors, 1600–1900,* nor even the 1983 *Oxford Companion to American Literature.* All three, I should say, contain entries for Edward (Ted) Harrigan, author of *The Mulligan Guard Chowder,* among other plays, and two of them for Henry Harland, author of *The Cardinal's Snuff Box.* Frances Harper does not appear in *Webster's American Biographies* (1974), nor even in Webster's 1980 *Biographical Dictionary,* which does include George McLean Harper, who was professor of literature at Princeton in the early part of this century and author of *The Legend of the Holy Grail* and *Literary Appreciations,* and Robert Francis Harper, who was an Assyriologist at Yale and at the University of Chicago, where his brother was president. Nor had she made the *Encyclopedia Britannica,* at least into 1984, although that work includes entries for Robert Almer Harper, who did research on the cytology of reproduction among fungi, and on Jesse Harper, who coached football at Notre Dame both before and after Knute Rockne.

Our historian colleagues offer no more encouraging record. There is no entry for Frances Harper in the 1982 *Encyclopedia of American History,* edited by Richard B. Morris, and perhaps ironically published by Harper and Row (whose American literature anthology ignores Harper). The history encyclopedia does contain entries for Fletcher Harper, the originator of *Harper's Bazaar,* an important women's magazine; Robert Goodloe Harper, who named the country of Liberia; and William Harper, who, responding to *Uncle Tom's Cabin* in 1852, published a collection of essays called *The Pro-Slavery Argument.* Indeed, I've found no reference to Frances Harper in any of the standard history texts, not even in James MacGregor Burns's 1985 *The Workshop of Democracy,* which advertises itself as chronicling "America from the Emancipation Proclamation to the eve of the New Deal."

We are engaged here, I think, not with the particular problem of Harper's significance as a literary or historical figure—she was after all, the most widely read black woman writer of the nineteenth century—than with the issue of *what* is significant and how it gets to be so in the academic world. It is what I like to call the problem of subject matter: what we consider important—the Notre Dame football coach, for example, or racist responses to *Uncle Tom's Cabin*—depends on who "we" are—on one's "subject position," in current critical terminology—and the assumptions about gender and race to which we have been trained. One way of bringing this problem of subject into focus is to choose in teaching passages and themes that bring differences into relief.

For example, we might begin with the theme stated in the title of the second chapter of *Walden:* "Where I Lived and What I Lived For." The problem of a place to live is central to many nineteenth-century women's texts, including "A Church Mouse." We find it in works as diverse as Kirkland's *A New Home—Who'll Follow?,* Warner's *The Wide, Wide World,* a number of Child's *Letters from New York,* Harriet Jacobs's (Linda Brent) *Incidents in the Life of a Slave Girl,* Jewett's story "A New Year's Visit." The home provides the central locus of values in *Uncle Tom's Cabin,* especially as it is incarnated in the Quaker settlement; indeed, for Stowe, the breaking up of home and family is the primary symbol for the sinfulness of slavery. Likewise, the restoration of family provides Stowe with her primary symbols of order. Further, being deprived of, and searching to establish, a stable home is a central subject in what Baym calls "woman's fiction."

The issue in these books may be clarified by contrasting them with how Thoreau addressed the question of where and how he lived. The opening of that chapter, often skipped for the better-known passages about his house, living deliberately, simplifying, and fishing in the stream of time, establishes a context in which power over one's world is assumed rather than achieved through struggle:

> At a certain season of our life we are accustomed to consider every
> spot as the possible site of a house. I have thus surveyed the country

on every side within a dozen miles of where I live. In imagination I have bought all the farms in succession, for all were to be bought, and I knew their price. I walked over each farmer's premises, tasted his wild apples, discoursed on husbandry with him, took his farm at his price, at any price, mortgaging it to him in my mind; even put a higher price on it,—took everything but a deed of it,—took his word for his deed, for I dearly love to talk,—cultivated it, and him too to some extent, I trust, and withdrew when I had enjoyed it long enough, leaving him to carry it on. . . . Wherever I sat, there I might live, and the landscape radiated from me accordingly. What is a house but a *sedes,* a seat?—better if a country seat. . . . Well, there I might live, I said; and there I did live, for an hour, a summer and a winter life; saw how I could let the years run off, buffet the winter through, and see the spring come in.

How wonderful this passage is; yet how absurd it would sound in the mouths of Hetty the "Church Mouse," or of Linda Brent, hiding from her slavemaster for seven years in the attic of her grandmother's house; of Stowe's Eliza or even George Harris, or of Ellen Montgomery, the heroine of *The Wide, Wide World.* Or, perhaps, in the minds of our students. What Thoreau confidently takes for granted is precisely, for the characters I've mentioned, the problem. Heard, as it were, from their ears, this passage perfectly demonstrates the assumptions as well as the rhetoric of privilege.

Thoreau's initial move here is contained in the universalizing "our" and "we," which at once attempt to incorporate the reader into his experience and effectively demand that "we" share in its qualities. What are these? Leisure and mobility: "I have thus surveyed the country." A degree of financial resource: "In imagination I have bought." Privileged information: "I knew their price." An almost mythic egocentrisism: "The landscape radiated from me." And a relationship to farm and farmer partly presented in the metaphors of male dominative sexuality, which "takes," "enjoys," and "withdraws." All of this constructs an assumption of power over environment—"I could let the years run off"—likewise projected by the verbs: "surveyed," "bought," "knew," "buffet." And it establishes the terms upon which we may visit Thoreau in his personal castle.[20]

We might contrast this passage with what Caroline Kirkland writes about her connection to the establishment of the village of Montacute on the banks of the Turnip in the Michigan frontier:

When my husband purchased two hundred acres of wild land on the banks of this to-be-celebrated stream, and drew with a piece of chalk on the bar-room table at Danforth's the plan of a village, I little thought I was destined to make myself famous by handing down to posterity a faithful record of the advancing fortunes of that favored spot.

"The madness of the people" in those days of golden dreams took more commonly the form of city-building; but there were a few who contented themselves with planning villages, on the banks of streams which certainly could never be expected to bear navies, but which might yet be turned to account in the more homely way of grinding or sawing—operations which must necessarily be performed somewhere for the well-being of those very cities. It is of one of these humble attempts that it is my lot to speak, and I make my confession at the outset, warning any fashionable reader who may have taken up my book, that I intend to be "decidedly low."

In contrast to the position of power from which Thoreau surveys the countryside, Kirkland's is a view from below: a village, not a city; the commonplaces of grinding and sawing, not the "golden dreams" of city building; a "decidedly low" chronicle, not a fashionable tale. If her husband's aspirations are modest indeed—"chalk" on a "bar-room table," a village on the Turnip—hers are even more so, as the mock heroics and the alliteration of "f" toward the end of the first paragraph suggest. Kirkland's self-deprecating irony anticipates her reader's derision at the trivia of frontier life, but it also effectively grounds her freedom as observer and chronicler in a realistic appraisal of the situation into which she has been placed by her husband's purchase. Her problem is to construct a home and a book from the "meagre materials" handed to her—materials "valuable only for [their] truth"—and from the ill-assorted cultural furnishings she has brought from the East. Simplifying her household by, for example, turning a "tall cup-board" into a corn-crib, is not a matter of choice but of making the most of the little one has—which is also her stance as a writer.[21]

In certain respects, of course, the focus of women writers on a home reflects ideas about women's "sphere," the notion that a woman's creativity could be expressed, and her moral authority developed, through her organization of home and family as the alternative to the corrupt world of business. But writers did not need to share the ideology developed by Catharine Beecher and Harriet Beecher Stowe to focus on this subject. The problem of a place to live, of establishing and maintaining a home, arose realistically from the repeated experience of being displaced because, as in Kirkland, a man decided to pull up stakes and move West or, as in Fanny Fern's *Ruth Hall*, he suffered business reversals or died, leaving wife and children without resources, or abandoning slaves to be sold off. In real life, such problems confronted Sara Willis Parton (Fanny Fern),

Warner, Southworth, and Louisa May Alcott; it was because husbands died or were financially unstable, or because fathers were improvident, that they took up writing. Making a place to live in the woods or the city is thus not so much a metaphor for the construction of an autonomous self but a straightforward matter of day-to-day survival.

Further, the problem of home and family is deeply connected in many of the writings, as in many of the lives, of nineteenth-century women with the problem of creativity. Mid-century ideology fixed women's primary duty as maintaining home and family. To discharge that duty, women like Warner and Southworth, and in a sense Stowe, had to earn sufficient money as authors; their work as writers was, first, a means for insuring family stability. In her story, "Psyche's Art," Louisa May Alcott presents a heroine who achieves artistic substance only by first devoting herself to family duty. But later, in a work like Elizabeth Stuart Phelps's *The Story of Avis,* and of course in Chopin's *The Awakening* and Mary Austin's *A Woman of Genius,* art or a version of self-creation is posed against the tenacious and draining obligations of home and family—as had in fact originally been the case for a writer like Stowe. I am not suggesting that this complex of themes fails to appear in the work of men, but seldom, if ever, is it so central. It is, of course, only as we take a woman artist seriously that books that focus on that subject become important to us. Once again, we can observe the intersecting force of consciousness significantly shaped by the material reality of available texts.

Just as the writing of women coheres around distinguishing themes, so may it emphasize certain genres and use them somewhat differently; here we encounter the problem of form. Judith Fetterley has pointed out, in explaining the structure of *A New Home—Who'll Follow?* (1839), that Kirkland tried to solve what was at once an artistic and a social problem by posing her narrative as an adaptation of a series of letters. Writing for publication was an activity still viewed in many quarters as inappropriate to women, precisely because it was public. Letter writing, however, sustained the quality of private communication, often between women. In a sense, the letter form offered the possibility of being at once public and private. That may explain the popularity of the form with many women writers of the antebellum period. Sarah Grimké's major work was *Letters on the Equality of the Sexes* (1838); among Lydia Maria Child's most successful books were the two series of *Letters From New York;* and Jane Swisshelm again adopted the form in her *Letters to Country Girls* (1853). One might argue that the letter form of Margaret Fuller's late dispatches to the New York *Tribune* allowed her a peculiarly successful balance of personal and political observation.

But perhaps the most fascinating adaptation of the letter form to the needs of a kind of publication was made by Emily Dickinson. We are all familiar with Dickinson's characterization of her poems:

> This is my letter to the World
> That never wrote to Me—

A number of Dickinson's letters *are* poems; others, although not written in verse formally, can still be scanned.[22] But perhaps more to the point: it is within the context of letters that Dickinson undertook her major form of "publication," that is, making her work known to a "public." In her characteristic way, to be sure, Dickinson redefined that "public" as the largely individual recipients of the letters. But it remains the case that by far the largest number of her poems to find readers during her lifetime— fully a third of them, in fact—did so within the context provided by letters.

Thus, when we speak of the importance of the "discontinuous" forms—letters, journals, diaries—to the canon of women's writing, we need, I think, to be aware of how these served a number of compatible functions. They are, of course, modes of private expression of self. They also can be forms of publication for a selected audience. And, as I have suggested, they can be generic means for bridging private and public worlds. Since students are more likely to have written in these forms than in any others, they provide, as well, an important point of entry into the often unnecessarily distanced world of the creative artist. One can generate assignments in which students use the conventions of their own letter writing to accomplish certain of a writer's goals; or, in reverse, apply the conventions of a writer's "letters" to their own purposes.

Form can also be shaped by a writer's sense of her or his marginality. Consider four books published within approximately a quarter century of one another: Jewett's *The Country of the Pointed Firs* (1896), Charles Chesnutt's *The Conjure Woman* (1899), Sherwood Anderson's *Winesburg, Ohio* (1919), and Ernest Hemingway's *In Our Time* (1924). In structure, they consist of apparently separable stories, but all are in fact unified narratives. In Jewett and Chesnutt, the stories themselves are told by rural, sometime magical, dialect speakers, primarily Mrs. Todd and Uncle Julius. However, their tales are set in frame plots and are narrated to readers by intermediaries, an urban woman and a northern white man, respectively. In Anderson and Hemingway, the framing narrative voices have atrophied, although traces remain. It seems to me that Jewett and Chesnutt must provide their audience with surrogates to interpret, guide, suggest responses, precisely because of the appreciable distance between, on the one side, the world of matriarchs—the country of the pointed firs—and the slave world of violence and conjure, and, on the other side, the increasingly urbanized culture of the turn-of-the-century buyer of books. By contrast, Anderson and Hemingway, like Thoreau, can assume a certain identity among themselves, their white, male heroes, and a substantial segment of their readership. Further, the central theme of Jewett and Chesnutt concerns success and failure in establishing a community of feeling among people in their tales, in their frame plots, and between authors and readers as well. This process depends upon the narrative structure; indeed that structure of incorporation provides a paradigm for the process of establishing community. Anderson and Hemingway, on the other hand, write versions of male *bildungsroman*, largely defined in American bourgeois culture as *isolated* experiences within society or nature. Narrative form thus embodies and tries to implement social and compositional objectives.

This discussion seems to me to suggest how far afield was the common wisdom about Jewett, to the effect "that her principal artistic skills are in style and characterization rather than in plot."[23] Elizabeth Ammons has suggested that in a book like *The Country of the Pointed Firs* Jewett's organizing principles are simply different from the "hierarchical mode" of conventional narrative and are designed rather in a "webbed, net-worked" design that may be identified with female patterns of development and socialization.[24] Ammons's suggestive argument about the form of Jewett's narrative can be extended into other of her works, like "The Foreigner." What these observations about Jewett suggest is that in examining the formal qualities of nineteenth-century white women and black writers we will often have to set aside assumptions about structural norms and ask, rather, why a story or a volume assumes its particular design. That question has led us to reconstruct *The Country of the Pointed Firs* and, in some respects, *The Conjure Woman* not as defective precursors of the modernist classics of Anderson and Hemingway, but as distinctive classics in their own modes.

These comments about *difference* lead directly to my sixth problem. A pedagogical strategy of pairing works seems to me the most useful way of getting at difference. For example, in courses at San Jose State University and at Trinity College I have linked Hawthorne's *House of the Seven Gables* and Stowe's *The Minister's Wooing;* Twain's *Pudd'nhead Wilson* and Chesnutt's *The Marrow of Tradition;* Jewett's *Country of the Pointed Firs* and Anderson's *Winesburg, Ohio;* Hemingway's *A Farewell to Arms* and Hurston's *Their Eyes Were Watching God;* F. Scott Fitzgerald's *The Great Gatsby* and Meridel LeSueur's *The Girl;* T. S. Eliot's *The Wasteland* and Langston Hughes's *Montage of a Dream Deferred;* Nella Larsen's *Passing* and William

Faulkner's *Light in August*. I have taken up together Emerson and Fuller,
Child or Jacobs and Thoreau, Poe and Alice Cary, and considered pairing
Dreiser's *Sister Carrie* and Mary Austin's *A Woman of Genius,* Henry Ad-
ams and W.E.B. DuBois, Jean Toomer's *Cane* and Gertrude Stein's *Three
Lives,* just to mention what might be a few sugestive examples. Similarly,
I have placed together suggestive theoretical texts by Eliot, Genevieve
Taggard, and Amy Lowell. Many of us know how effective such pairings
can be, simply at the level of generating classroom response.

But something more fundamental is at stake. Placing the Hawthorne
and Stowe works side by side allows us to see how radically similar their
literary origins were, how they work with closely related assumptions,
materials, and sentiments. Both frame examinations of the significance of
America's Puritan heritage within conventional romance plots. In these,
the wise purity of an American princess redeems the straying, never evil,
although unconventional boy. Neither Phoebe nor Mary possesses sufficient power to win over the evil geniuses—Judge Pyncheon and Burr—
who cross their paths. But each combines the intense practicality and
naturally inspired values necessary to establishing domestic tranquility,
marriage, home, for themselves and those around them. In this respect
they are much like the heroines of other women's novels of the 1850s.

The very "relatedness" of these books in these and many other ways
forces our students to reexamine what it was, and is, that has defined
Hawthorne as a "classic" and Stowe as, at best, an imposing figure in the
popular tradition. In fact, their differences as well as their similarities raise
this issue, for they offer very distinct centers of value, narrative strategies,
and understandings about the force of history. In a certain sense, history
does not exist for Hawthorne, as for many of his Romantic contemporaries; it simply reflects, generation by generation, the repeated operation of
Pyncheon greed and Maule's curse, inheritances of domination and blood.
His interest lies in the impact of such persisting forces on the aesthetic
temperament, embodied in Clifford. Thus Hawthorne's characters can
emerge from the closed circle of essentially repeated events only by the
unconvincing *dei ex machina* that kill off Judge Pyncheon and his son, hitch
Phoebe and Holgrave, and thus permit the happy ending commanded by
sentimental tradition. The often-noted awkwardness of Hawthorne's plot
derives from his failure to find credible measures within its domestic
conventions to overcome Maule's curse.

For Stowe, the legacy of Puritanism is more complex than repeated
instances of "sin and sorrow": rather, it invested everyday life with
millenial significance, and therefore the diurnal activities of her people with
ultimate power. Thus, the "faculty" Mary derives from her mother's up-
bringing and the moral urgencies she inherits from her abolitionist father

provide a basis for order beyond the creation even of the best of Puritan divines, like the Reverend Mr. Hopkins. Hopkins sustains the moral intensity of Puritan forebears like Jonathan Edwards, especially in his condemnation of the sin of slaveholding, but he is also blinkered by his devotion to a heartless metaphysical system. That system fails to embrace the real-life needs for love and comfort of ordinary people facing the contingencies not of a mysterious curse, but of the common lot of separation, loss, and failure. The historical issue for Stowe, which bears directly upon the conduct of life in mid-nineteenth-century America, is how to sustain the moral seriousness and fervor of Puritanism without its terrorizing theology. The marriage that celebrates the ending of her book presents her symbolic solution to this problem as well as satisfying the period's conventions.

Hawthorne's work is a sustained, I would suggest an enclosed, meditation upon aestheticism outside history (which may be part of its attraction for aesthetically minded literary critics). Stowe's is, I think, an effort to translate the values of a previous era into actions comprehensible to a contemporary audience. One might say that Hawthorne's aim is to create a "timeless" fable, a transcendent allegory whose particular details are illustrative rather than defining. Stowe's book lives and breathes much more particularly in mid-nineteenth-century America—a fact that recollects the problem of context I examined above.

But these differences also raise the question of value: is Hawthorne's a "better" book for evading (transcending) the particular moment of its birth? Obviously, the answer to that question depends on what we mean by "better." If we accept the definitions of literary excellence constructed in significant measure from the canonical works and used to perpetuate their status, we will inevitably place most of the fiction by nineteenth-century white women and black writers at a discount, at best elegiac local colorists, at worst, domestic sentimentalists. Indeed, we will not see what these writers are attempting to accomplish, much less how well or poorly they do what Jane Tompkins calls their "cultural work."

Alfred Habegger illustrates this problem in his otherwise excellent book, *Gender, Fantasy and Realism in American Literature.* Habegger contends that Elizabeth Stuart Phelps's *The Story of Avis* is not a "classic," but "an important document for nineteenth-century literary and social history." *Avis,* he says, was "too feminine. That is to say, it was written for women, in defense of women's interests and in support of women's myths and values, and was therefore a highly partisan book. . . . It was not an exploration of the bitter antagonism between men and women [as, Habegger suggests, we find in Howells and James]; it was itself bitterly antagonistic."[25] I think it is true that *Avis* is partisan; the issue is whether the nonpartisan appearance of canonical writers is an "objective" fact or an artifact of the status critics attribute to them. The obvious case is, of course, Henry James's *The Bostonians*. As Habegger points out, those who attempted to canonize *The Bostonians* as one of James's supreme achievements, notably Philip Rahv and Lionel Trilling, really re-created it as an argument for their own politics, which had begun to feature a retreat from social activism. Pairing *The Bostonians* and *Avis*, or perhaps Twain's *Pudd'n-head Wilson* and Chesnutt's *The Marrow of Tradition*, suggests that in dealing with highly charged social issues writers from marginalized groups may *appear* partisan whereas those from the dominant culture can take on the coloration (white?) of "objectivity" or "universality."

But a more interesting case emerges by setting *The Portrait of a Lady*, generally accepted as one of James's best, with *Avis*. For here one encounters not the issue of attributed status and politics (as with *The Bostonians*) but the problem of a novel's *function* in the cultures in which it is read. One might well accept Habegger's account of *Portrait* as an enormously rich literary exploration of American masculinity and still dispute the value— to whom? for what?—of *Avis*. The question here is why people read novels, today or a hundred years ago. The extension of a work into the world indeed compromises its objectivity, makes it party to a cause, an incitement, a weapon, or "proof." We are accustomed to view such partiality as necessarily a defect, but that judgment depends upon how we define the "cultural work" fiction is designed to perform. After all, "objectivity" and detachment are hardly independent standards; on the contrary, they are generally banners in the human parade carried by those wishing to translate worldly power into cultural terms. The self-containment of a literary work generally extolled by critics in our culture then appears as no unassailable virtue, but as one problematic for classroom analysis.

Pairing works like those of Stowe and Hawthorne, James and Phelps, Chesnutt or Harper and Twain allows us and our students to clarify alternative assumptions about literary value rather than assuming the absolute validity of canonical literary standards. This is perhaps the most central problem of all, for so much of nineteenth-century women's writing has long been set at a discount; indeed the whole corpus has been construed in such trivializing ways—even in pointing to Dickinson as the notable exception—that no course of serious study can avoid the most thoroughgoing reexamination of settled standards. That is at once, I think, a directive for and an argument in favor of teaching nineteenth-century American women writers. The debate over "cultural literacy," multiculturalism, and the supposed foreclosing of American intellect is at heart a debate over standards of value. My own experience suggests that few enterprises bring these issues more sharply into focus than turning our attention, and that of our students, to writers like Child, Harper, Jacobs, Kirkland, Fern, and Phelps—as well as to Fuller, Stowe, Dickinson, Davis, Jewett, and Freeman. Their concerns, their ideas, their styles, the lives and cultures their work encodes place today's debates into the American history of which they form only the latest paragraphs.

NOTES

Parts of this paper, on Frances Harper, appeared in different form in *Legacy* 5 (Spring 1988): 27–34. Parts of it were first presented on a panel at the National Council of Teachers of English convention, Philadelphia, 1985. In something close to this form it was first published in my *Canons and Contexts* (New York: Oxford University Press, 1991). I wish to express particular appreciation to Joanne Dobson and Sandra Zagarell for their comments and suggestions about this article.

1. See, for example, the essay by Joanne Dobson in this volume and Marjorie Pryse, "'Distilling Essences: Regionalism and 'Women's Culture,'" paper presented at the American Literature Association, June 1991, Washington, D.C.

2. Which may help to explain the rather hysterical tone of some of the attacks on multiculturalism by certain academics who for too long have been wedded both to older paradigms of literary study and to older hierarchies of cultural practitioners.

3. Sandra M. Gilbert and Susan Gubar, *The Norton Anthology of Literature by Women* (New York: W. W. Norton, 1985).

4. Nina Baym et al., *The Norton Anthology of American Literature*, 2 vols., 2d ed. (New York: W. W. Norton, 1985).

5. Donald McQuade et al., *The Harper American Literature*, 2 vols. (New York: Harper and Row, 1987).

6. Lucy Freibert and Barbara White, eds., *Hidden Hands: An Anthology of American Women Writers, 1790–1870* (New Brunswick, N.J.: Rutgers University Press, 1985), 68–83.

7. Judith Fetterley, *Provisions: A Reader From 19th-Century American Women* (Bloomington: Indiana University Press, 1985).

8. Lydia Maria Child, *Hobomok and Other Writings on Indians*, ed. Carolyn L. Karcher (1986); Rose Terry Cooke, *"How Celia Changed Her Mind" and Other Stories*, ed. Elizabeth Ammons (1986); Fanny Fern, *Ruth Hall and Other Writings*, ed. Joyce W. Warren (1986); Louisa May Alcott, *Alternative Alcott*, ed. Elaine Showalter (1987); Alice Cary, *Clovernook Sketches and Other Stories*, ed. Judith Fetterley (1987); Harriet Beecher Stowe, *Oldtown Folks*, ed. Dorothy Berkson (1987); Catharine Maria Sedgwick, *Hope Leslie*, ed. Mary Kelley (1987); Caroline Kirkland, *A New Home—Who'll Follow?* (1988), ed. Sandra Zagarell; E.D.E.N. Southworth, *The Hidden Hand*, ed. Joanne Dobson (1988); Harriet Prescott Spofford, *Selected Stories*, ed. Alfred Bendixen (1988); Constance Fenimore Woolson, *Women Artists and Exiles: Stories*, ed. Joan Weimer (1988). The series also includes Mary Austin, *Stories from the Country of Lost Borders*, ed. Marjorie Pryse (1987); and Nella Larsen, *Quicksand and Passing*, ed. Deborah E. McDowell (1986). Rutgers also publishes Elizabeth Stuart Phelps's *The Story of Avis*, ed. Carol Kessler (1985).

9. Susan Warner, *The Wide, Wide World,* ed. Jane Tompkins (New York: Feminist Press, 1987).

10. Paul Lauter, et al., *The Heath Anthology of American Literature,* 2 vols. (Lexington, Mass.: D.C. Heath, 1990).

11. Mary Helen Washington, ed., *Invented Lives: Narratives of Black Women 1860–1960* (Garden City, N.Y.: Doubleday Anchor Books, 1987). Earlier articles about Harper are listed in Ann Allen Shockley, *Afro-American Women Writers 1746–1933: An Anthology and Critical Guide* (Boston: G. K. Hall, 1988). In addition, Harper's story "The Two Offers" was earlier reprinted with critical comment in *Old Maids,* ed. Susan Koppelman (Boston: Pandora Press, 1984).

12. Other twentieth-century authors included in this series are Gayle Jones, Ann Petry, Coleen Polite, Octavia Butler, Alice Childress, and Marita Bonner.

13. Hazel V. Carby, *Reconstructing Womanhood* (New York: Oxford University Press, 1987).

14. I am thinking, in addition to works previously cited, of, for example, Elizabeth Ammons, *Conflicting Stories: American Women Writers at the Turn Into the Twentieth Century* (New York: Oxford University Press, 1991) and "Crossing the Color Line: White Feminist Criticism and Black Women Writers," *Reading Black, Reading Feminist,* ed. Henry Louis Gates (London: Methuen, 1988); Nina Baym, *Woman's Fiction: A Guide to Novels by and about Women in America, 1820–1870* (Ithaca: Cornell University Press, 1978); Barbara Christian, *Black Women Novelists: The Development of a Tradition, 1892–1986* (Westport, Conn.: Greenwood, 1980), and *Black Feminist Criticism* (New York: Pergamon Press, 1985); Josephine Donovan, *New England Local Color Literature: A Woman's Tradition* (New York: Frederick Ungar, 1983); Annette Kolodny, *The Land Before Her: Fantasy and Experience of the American Frontiers, 1630–1860* (Chapel Hill: University of North Carolina Press, 1984); Jane Tompkins, *Sensational Designs: The Cultural Work of American Fiction, 1790–1860* (New York: Oxford University Press, 1985).

15. "The reading of these documents enabled me to utter my thoughts, and to meet the arguments brought forward to sustain slavery. . . . As I read and contemplated the subject, behold! that very discontentment which Master Hugh had predicted would follow my learning to read had already come, to torment and sting my soul to unutterable anguish. As I writhed under it, I would at times feel that learning to read had been a curse rather than a blessing. It had given me a view of my wretched condition, without the remedy. It opened my eyes to the horrible pit, but to no ladder upon which to get out" (*Narrative of the Life of Frederick Douglass* [New York: New American Library, 1968], 55). Douglass's is also a particularly striking account of the limits of consciousness, absent the possibility of action.

16. Sculley Bradley et al., *The American Tradition in Literature* (New York: Random House, 1981), 1:1444.

17. Angelina Grimké, "Appeal to the Christian Women of the South," *The Anti-Slavery Examiner* 1, no. 2 (September 1836): 25.

In 1893, writing about his twenty-fifth birthday, W.E.B. DuBois considers the relationship of his self-development to the needs of his people:

The general proposition of working for the world's good becomes too soon sickly and sentimental. I therefore take the world that the Unknown lay in my hands & work for the rise of the Negro people, taking for granted that their best development means the best development of the world. . . .

These are my plans: to make a name in science, to make a name in literature and thus to raise my race. . . .

I wonder what will be the outcome? Who knows?

I will go in unto the King—which is not according to the law & if I perish—*I perish.*

—(ms. in DuBois papers)

18. See Grimké, "Appeal," 23–24.

19. I develop this line of argument in "The Literatures of America—A Comparative Discipline," *Canons and Contexts* (New York: Oxford University Press, 1991), 57–61.

20. As in Emerson, a house becomes a metaphor for the self. Emerson wrote to Margaret Fuller that he would "open all my doors to your sunshine and morning air." But, Fuller later responded, her friend "keeps his study windows shut." Quoted by Joyce W. Warren, "The Gender of American Individualism," Warren, *The American Narcissus: Individualism and Women in Nineteenth-Century American Fiction* (New Brunswick, N.J.: Rutgers University Press, 1984), 77–78, from *Letters of Ralph Waldo Emerson,* ed. Ralph L. Rusk (New York: Columbia University Press, 1939), 2:337.

21. One might pursue an analogous set of contrasts between Thoreau and Lydia Maria Child's lament for the lost garden of Jane Plato in her account of a city fire (*Letters from New York* 16 [August 7, 1842]).

22. A number of these details were pointed out to me by Ellen Louise Hart of the University of California, Santa Cruz, and Katie King of the University of Maryland; this passage owes a great deal to conversations with them.

23. Gwen L. Nagel and James Nagel, "Introduction," *Sarah Orne Jewett: A Reference Guide* (Boston: G. K. Hall, 1978), ix.

24. Elizabeth Ammons, "Going in Circles: The Female Geography of Jewett's *Country of the Pointed Firs,*" *Studies in the Literary Imagination* 16 (Fall 1983): esp. 85, 89.

25. Alfred Habegger, *Gender, Fantasy and Realism in American Literature* (New York: Columbia University Press, 1982), 46.

❖ CONTRIBUTORS ❖

NINA BAYM is a professor of English and Jubilee Professor of Liberal Arts and Sciences at the University of Illinois at Urbana-Champaign. She is the author of numerous books, essays, and reviews on Americanist and feminist topics, including *The Shape of Hawthorne's Career* (1976), *Woman's Fiction: A Guide to Novels by and about Women in America, 1820–1870* (1978), *Novels, Readers, and Reviewers: Responses to Fiction in Antebellum America* (1984), *Feminism and American Literary History: Essays* (Rutgers University Press, 1992). She serves on the editorial boards of several scholarly journals and has chaired the Nineteenth-Century Literature Division of the MLA as well as the American Literature Section of the MLA.

DEBORAH CARLIN is an assistant professor at the University of Massachusetts, Amherst, where she specializes in late-nineteenth- and early-twentieth-century American literature and culture. She has published essays on Cather and Wharton, and her book, *Cather, Canon and the Politics of Reading* is forthcoming from the University of Massachusetts Press. She is currently at work on a collection of essays on sexuality and spectacle in American women's culture between 1920 and 1945.

JOANNE DOBSON is an assistant professor of English at Fordham University. She is a founding editor of *Legacy: A Journal of American Women Writers* and a general editor of the Rutgers University Press American Women Writers series. She is the author of *Dickinson and the Strategies of Reticence: The Woman Writer in Nineteenth-Century America* (1989), and the editor of the reprint edition of E.D.E.N. Southworth's *The Hidden Hand*. Currently she is working on a study of women writers during the American Renaissance.

JOSEPHINE DONOVAN is a professor of English at the University of Maine. She is the author of *Sarah Orne Jewett; New England Local Color Literature: A Women's Tradition; Feminist Theory: The Intellectual Traditions of American Literature; After the Fall: The Demeter-Persephone Myth in Wharton, Cather, and Glasgow; Uncle Tom's Cabin: Evil, Affliction, and Redemptive Love;* and other works.

JUDITH FETTERLEY is a professor of English and Women's Studies and Director of Graduate Studies for the Department of English at the State University of New York at Albany. She is the author of *The Resisting Reader: A Feminist Approach to American Fiction* (1978) and editor of *Provisions: A Reader from 19th-Century American Women* (1985), as well as the author of numerous articles on a variety of nineteenth- and twentieth-century American writers. With Joanne Dobson and Elaine Showalter, she founded the Rutgers University Press American Women Writers series. For this series, she edited a volume of the short fiction of Alice Cary. She is the coeditor, with Marjorie Pryse, of *American Women Regionalists, 1850–1910: A Norton Anthology,* and with Marjorie Pryse she is working on a critical study of the writers included in the anthology.

FRANCES SMITH FOSTER is a professor of American Literature at the University of California, San Diego. She is author of *Witnessing Slavery: The Development of the Ante-Bellum Slave Narrative* (1979), *A Brighter Coming Day: A Frances Ellen Watkins Harper Reader* (1990), and *Written by Herself: Literary Productions of African American Women, 1746–1892* (forthcoming).

SUSAN K. HARRIS is a professor of English at Pennsylvania State University, where she teaches American literature. She is the author of *Mark Twain's Escape from Time: A Study of Patterns and Images* (1982) and *Nineteenth-Century American Women's Novels: Interpretive Strategies* (1990), as well as articles in *American Literature, Studies in the Novel, Style,* and other journals.

KARLA F. C. HOLLOWAY's teaching and research focus on the intersections between linguistics, literary theory, and cultural studies. She has published essays in these areas, and is the author of three books, including *Moorings and Metaphors: Figures of Culture and Gender in Black Women's Literature* (1992). Her current work-in-progress is a book-length study, *Codes of Conduct: Ethics and Ethnicity in Literature.*

PAUL LAUTER is Allan K. and Gwendolyn Miles Smith Professor of Literature at Trinity College. He is general editor of the groundbreaking *Heath Anthology of American Literature*. His own most recent book is *Canons and Contexts* (1991), and he recently completed a study of proletarianism and American fiction. He is at work on a study of the origins of the American literary canon in the 1920s and 1930s and is directing a project to create a new multicultural and gender-fair high school literature curriculum.

DIANE LICHTENSTEIN is an associate professor of English and cochair of Women's Studies at Beloit College. In addition to several essays, including one focused on Emma Lazarus for *Tulsa Studies in Women's Literature*, and another on Fannie Hurst for *Studies in American Jewish Literature*, she has written a book-length study of nineteenth-century American Jewish women writers published by Indiana University Press.

CARLA L. PETERSON is an associate professor of English and Comparative Literature at the University of Maryland, College Park. She is the author of *The Determined Reader: Gender and Culture in the Novel from Napoleon to Victoria* (1986), coauthor with Shelley Fisher-Fishkin of " 'We Hold These Truths to be Self Evident': The Rhetoric of Frederick Douglass's Journalism," *Critical Essays on Frederick Douglass*, ed. Eric Sundquist (1990), and author of forthcoming essays on the nineteenth-century African-American novel. She is currently working on a book, *"Doers of the Word": African-American Women Writers in the North (1830–1879)*.

CAROL J. SINGLEY teaches American literature, feminist theory, and American studies at The American University, Washington, D.C., She has published articles on romance, the gothic, and female initiation, and is the author of *Edith Wharton and Longing*. She is coeditor with Susan Elizabeth Sweeney of a collection of essays, *Anxious Power: Reading, Writing, and Ambivalence in Narrative by Women*, forthcoming from SUNY Press. She is past president of the Edith Wharton Society and current Women's Caucus Representative on the Executive Council of the Northeast Modern Language Association.

JANE TOMPKINS teaches in the English Department at Duke University. She has written books and articles on American literature and culture—*Sensational Designs* (1985) and *West of Everything* (1992)—and is currently writing a book on teaching called *A Life in School*.

JOYCE W. WARREN teaches in the English Department at Queens College, CUNY. She is the author of *The American Narcissus: Individualism and Women in Nineteenth-Century American Fiction* (1984) and *Fanny Fern: An Independent Woman* (1992). She edited *Ruth Hall and Other Writings* by Fanny Fern (1986) and has published articles and reviews in various periodicals and collections, including *Legacy, American Literature, Women's Studies, Annals of Scholarship,* and *Nineteenth-Century Prose.* She is a member of the American Literature Section of the Modern Language Association and a consulting editor for *Legacy.*

SANDRA A. ZAGARELL, associate professor of English at Oberlin College, is editor of *A New Home—Who'll Follow?,* by Caroline Kirkland, and (with Lawrence Buell) of *The Morgesons and Other Writings, Published and Unpublished,* by Elizabeth Stoddard. She has published essays on nineteenth-century British and American literature and is at work on a study of fictional representations of community in nineteenth-century American literature.

❧ INDEX ❧

SMCL

3 5151 00114 2041

DATE DUE

MAR 1 7 1999	
JAN 3 1 2002	

DEMCO, INC. 38-2971